T0207364

Lecture Notes of the Institute for Computer Sciences, Social Informatics and Telecommunications Engineering 482

The LNICST series publishes ICST's conferences, symposia and workshops.
LNICST reports state-of-the-art results in areas related to the scope of the Institute.
The type of material published includes

- Proceedings (published in time for the respective event)
- Other edited monographs (such as project reports or invited volumes)

LNICST topics span the following areas:

- General Computer Science
- E-Economy
- E-Medicine
- Knowledge Management
- Multimedia
- Operations, Management and Policy
- Social Informatics
- Systems

Esa Hyytiä · Veeraruna Kavitha

Editors

Performance Evaluation Methodologies and Tools

15th EAI International Conference, VALUETOOLS 2022
Virtual Event, November 2022
Proceedings

 Springer

Editors
Esa Hyytiä ⓘ
University of Iceland
Reykjavik, Iceland

Veeraruna Kavitha ⓘ
Indian Institute of Technology Bombay
Mumbai, India

ISSN 1867-8211 ISSN 1867-822X (electronic)
Lecture Notes of the Institute for Computer Sciences, Social Informatics
and Telecommunications Engineering
ISBN 978-3-031-31233-5 ISBN 978-3-031-31234-2 (eBook)
https://doi.org/10.1007/978-3-031-31234-2

This Springer imprint is published by the registered company Springer Nature Switzerland AG
The registered company address is: Gewerbestrasse 11, 6330 Cham, Switzerland

Preface

We are delighted to introduce the proceedings of the 15th edition of the European Alliance for Innovation (EAI) International Conference on Performance Evaluation Methodologies and Tools (VALUETOOLS 2022). The conference was scheduled to take place in Ghent, Belgium, but due to the uncertainty about possible travel restrictions caused by the COVID-19 pandemic, VALUETOOLS 2022 was organized as a fully online conference, November 16–18, 2022. This conference brought together researchers, developers and practitioners from around the world and from different communities including computer science, networks and telecommunications, operations research, optimization, control theory, and manufacturing. The focus of VALUETOOLS 2022 was on methodologies and practices in modeling, performance evaluation, and optimization of complex systems.

The technical program of VALUETOOLS 2022 consisted of 18 full papers in oral presentation sessions. The papers were presented in six sessions: Session 1 – Game Theory, Session 2 – Queueing Models, Session 3 – Applications, Session 4 – Retrial Queues, Session 5 – Performance Analysis, and Session 6 – Networking and Distributed Computing. In addition to the regular presentations, the conference program included two keynote talks given by leading experts in the field. The first-day keynote talk was given by Samuli Aalto from Aalto University, Finland, with the title *"Gittins and Whittle Index Approaches to Queueing Problems"*. The second-day keynote was given by Nelly Litvak from University of Twente, Netherlands, with the title *"Red Light – Green Light Solution for Large Markov Chains"*. The keynote speakers were introduced by Dieter Fiems and Mor Harchol-Balter, respectively.

We like to thank everyone involved in the organization of VALUETOOLS 2022. To begin with, it was a great pleasure to work with such an excellent Organizing Committee team, led by Dieter Fiems and Mor Harchol-Balter; we are thankful for their hard work in organizing and supporting the conference. We are also very grateful to the Technical Program Committee, who completed the peer-review process for technical papers in a timely manner despite the unusually strict time constraints, and thereby helped us to put together a high-quality technical program. We are also grateful to the Conference Manager, Mikita Yelnitski, EAI in general, for their support, as well as to all the authors who submitted their papers to the VALUETOOLS 2022 conference.

The VALUETOOLS conference, initiated in 2006, aims at promoting research on performance evaluation methodologies and tools for various engineering or social complex systems. We strongly believe that the VALUETOOLS conference provides a good forum for all researchers, developers, and practitioners to discuss all science and technology aspects that are relevant to performance evaluation, analysis, and optimization of complex systems. We also expect that the future conferences will be as successful and stimulating as VALUETOOLS 2022, as indicated by the contributions presented in this volume.

November 2022   Veeraruna Kavitha
                                                        Esa Hyytiä

Organization

Steering Committee

Imrich Chlamtac   University of Trento, Italy

Organizing Committee

General Chair

Dieter Fiems   Ghent University, Belgium

General Co-chair

Mor Harchol-Balter   Carnegie Mellon University, USA

TPC Chair and Co-chairs

Esa Hyttiä   University of Iceland, Iceland
Rudesindo Nunez-Queija   University of Amsterdam, The Netherlands
Veeraruna Kavitha   Indian Institute of Technology Bombay, India

Sponsorship and Exhibit Chair

Dieter Claeys   Ghent University, Belgium

Local Chair

Joris Walraevens   Ghent University, Belgium

Workshops Chair

Koen De Turck   Ghent University, Belgium

Publicity and Social Media Chair

Sarah Dendievel   ICHEC Brussels Management School, Belgium

Publications Chair

Stella Kapodistria   TU Eindhoven, The Netherlands

Web Chair

Arnaud Devos   Ghent University, Belgium

Technical Program Committee

Jaya Krishnan Nair	IIT Bombay, India
Rachid El-Azouzi	Avignon Université, France
Konstantin Avrachenkov	Inria, Sophia Antipolis, France
Richard Combes	CentraleSupélec, France
Quanyan Zhu	New York University, USA
Doug Down	McMaster University, Canada
Kristen Gardner	Amherst College, USA
Sherwin Doroudi	University of Minnesota, USA
Vikas Vikram Singh	Indian Institute of Technology Delhi, India
Parimal Parag	IISc Bangalore, India
Rhonda Righter	UC Berkeley, USA
Marko Boon	TU Eindhoven, The Netherlands
Giuliano Casala	Imperial College, UK
Ioannis Dimitriou	University of Ioannina, Greece
Jean-Michel Fourneau	University of Versailles, France
Reinhard German	Friedrich Alexander University, Germany
Manu Kumar Gupta	IIT Roorkee, India
Yezekael Hayel	University of Avignon, France
Qi-Ming He	Waterloo University, Canada
Nandyala Hemachandra	IIT Bombay, India
Krishna Jagannathan	IIT Madras, India
Catalina M. Llado	University of the Balearic Islands, Spain
Lasse Leskela	Aalto University, Finland
William Knottenbelt	Imperial College, UK
Jose Merseguer	University of Zaragoza, Spain
Samir Perlaza	Inria Sophia-Antipolis, France
Tuan Phung Duc	Tsukuba University, Japan

Balakrishna Prabhu   CNRS-LAAS, France
Alexandre Reiffers-Masson   IMT Atlantique, France
Bruno Tuffin   Inria Rennes, France
Sabine Wittevrongel   Ghent University, Belgium
Li Xia   Sun Yat-sen University, China
Quanyan Zhu   NYU, USA
Alessandro Zocca   Free University, The Netherlands
Nigel Thomas   Newcastle University, UK

Contents

Game Theory

Strategic Customer Behaviors in Observable Multi-server Batch Service Queueing Systems with Shared Fee and Server Maintenance Cost

Ayane Nakamura[1]([⊠]) and Tuan Phung-Duc[2]

[1] Graduate School of Science and Technology, University of Tsukuba, Tsukuba, Japan
s2230122@u.tsukuba.jp
[2] Institute of Systems and Information Engineering, University of Tsukuba, Tsukuba, Japan
tuan@sk.tsukuba.ac.jp

Abstract. We consider an observable multi-server batch service queueing model where a shared server admission fee and maintenance cost for the monopolist are considered. Specifically, customers observe the number of full batches and waiting customers for an uncompleted batch, and then afterward decide to join or balk depending on their utility function. We analyze strategic customer behavior and find the equilibrium strategy. We also show numerical results for social welfare and monopolist's revenue in various settings depending on fee, batch size, and number of servers. Based on our results, we discuss the existence of optimal fee, batch size, and number of servers.

Keywords: Queuing · Strategic customers · Batch service · Shared fee · Server cost · Social welfare · Ride-sharing

1 Introduction

There has been a recent rise in share services. The most common example is public transportation. However, shared mobility services, such as ridesharing [1] have recently received attention with the spread of electronic cars and automatic vehicles. On ride-sharing platforms, customers with the same departure and arrival points form a group and travel together. A key feature of this system is that a customer's behavior is influenced by others, and vice versa. For instance, if there is less demand for ridesharing, a customer might abandon it as the waiting time for matching with other customers may be long.

In the field of queueing theory, many studies on the analysis of batch service queueing models with single, multi, and infinite servers (see e.g., [10, 13, 15]) have been conducted over the past half-century. Although these studies have derived the joint steady-state probabilities on the number of busy servers and batches,

© ICST Institute for Computer Sciences, Social Informatics and Telecommunications Engineering 2023
Published by Springer Nature Switzerland AG 2023. All Rights Reserved
E. Hyytiä and V. Kavitha (Eds.): VALUETOOLS 2022, LNICST 482, pp. 3–13, 2023.
https://doi.org/10.1007/978-3-031-31234-2_1

most prior research has not considered customers' strategic behavior depending on system states. One useful approach to analyze such customer behaviors is the economic analysis of queueing models from a game-theoretic perspective with customer choice following [14].

However, there are few studies dealing with batch service (i.e., group service) queueing systems with customer strategic behavior. Some research on clearing systems considering customer strategic behavior has been conducted (see e.g., [7–9,12]). The strategic behavior of customers in queueing systems with catastrophes has also been studied [2,3]. In a recent study, the routing decisions of strategic passengers in a transportation station were analyzed [11]. In addition, M/M/1 queues with batch services [4–6] have been studied for unobservable, observable, and partially observable cases.

As an extension of this research on single server batch service systems, we consider an observable $M/M/n$ queueing model with strategic customers assuming that a monopolist imposes an admission fee. Moreover, we analyze the model considering the cost of maintaining servers for the monopolist. In the context of a ride-sharing system, multiple servers in this model correspond to the vehicles on the platform. Considering such shared-mobility systems, the scenario where a monopolist (i.e., operator) prepares many vehicles is more believable. The server maintenance cost corresponds to the vehicles' gasoline and parking costs. Here, determining the optimal number of servers from the perspective of both monopolist and society, given the trade-off between customer income and server maintenance costs, is significant. We can assume that customers decide to use ridesharing depending on the expected waiting time. In addition, we assume that server service time corresponds to the time from when the car leaves the station to when it returns.

Studies on the queueing analysis of strategic customers in multi-server systems are few even though they have many practical applications. For example, studies on strategic joining in a $M/M/K$ queue with asynchronous and synchronous multiple vacations and $M/M/c$/Setup queue were recently conducted [16,17]. However, to the best of our knowledge, there is no research related to multi-server batch service queueing systems with strategic customers. As our model includes elements of batch service and multi-servers, we believe the analysis of this comprehensive model will be meaningful not only from a practical perspective but also theoretical.

The rest of this study is organized as follows. In Sect. 2, we describe the model setting and find the equilibrium strategy for customers. Using this, we show numerical results in Sect. 3 and discuss the optimal fee, batch size, and number of servers. Finally, Sect. 4 presents the conclusion and directions for future research.

2   Modelling

We consider a multi-server (n server) queueing model with batch service. We assume that the batch size is K and fee of service per batch is p, i.e., the fee for a customer is p/K. We also assume that the service time follows an exponential distribution with parameter μ. Customers arrive at the system according to a Poisson process with parameter λ and decide whether to join or balk the system after observing the state of the system. Specifically, we assume that a customer's threshold strategy is specified by a sequence $\mathbf{q} = (q_{0,0}, q_{0,1}, q_{0,2}, \dots)$, where $q_{m,j} \in \{0,1\}, m = 0,1,2,\dots, j = 0,1,\dots,K-1$ when an arriving customer finds m full batches and j customers for an uncompleted batch. The total number of customers in the system thus becomes $mK + j$.

Suppose that a tagged customer follows strategy $\mathbf{q'} = (q'_{0,0}, q'_{0,1}, q'_{0,2}, \dots)$ while the population of other customers follows $\mathbf{q} = (q_{0,0}, q_{0,1}, q_{0,2}, \dots)$. If the tagged customer sees the state (m, j) upon his arrival to the system, his utility is expressed as follows:

$$U(\mathbf{q'}, \mathbf{q}; (m,j)) = R - \frac{p}{K} - C_W \times S(m,j),$$

where R, C_W, and $S(m,j)$ denote the reward of receiving a service, waiting cost per unit time, and expected waiting time when he observes the state (m, j). Here, $R > p/K$ must always hold to avoid the obvious case where no one joins the queue. Thus, we can proceed with the analysis of multi-server model following a similar method as in the single server model of [4].

Lemma 1. *There exists a unique equilibrium strategy $(q^e_{m,j}; m \geq 0, 0 \leq j \leq K-1)$ as*

$$q^e_{m,j} = \begin{cases} 1 \text{ if } m \leq m^e_j, \\ 0 \text{ if } m > m^e_j, \end{cases}$$

where $m^e_0 \leq m^e_1 \leq \cdots \leq m^e_{K-1}$.

Proof. The proof method mainly follows [4]. First, we focus on the case where an arriving customer observes $(m, K-1)$. Once he joins the system, his batch is completed. In this case, his waiting time becomes 0 if $m < n$, and the sum of $(m - n + 1)$ exponential service times with parameter $n\mu$ if $m \geq n$. Therefore, the following equilibrium threshold holds:

$$q^e_{m,K-1} = \begin{cases} 1 \text{ if } m \leq m^e_{K-1}, \\ 0 \text{ if } m > m^e_{K-1}, \end{cases}$$

where $m^e_{K-1} = \left\lfloor \frac{n\mu(R-p/K)}{C_W} + n - 1 \right\rfloor$. This strategy is dominant. Since his batch is completed once he joins the system, his decision will not be affected by other customers.

Next, we consider the case where an arriving customer sees the state $(m, K-2)$. As discussed in [4], we have $q^e_{m,K-2} = 0$ if $q^e_{m,K-1} = 0$. Additionally, $S(m, K-2)$ is an increasing function of m that tends to ∞ as $m \rightarrow \infty$, which means there exists a unique m^e_{K-2} such that $S(m^e_{K-2}, K-2) \leq (R - p/K)/C_W < S(m^e_{K-2} + 1, K-2)$. Thus, the following holds:

$$q^e_{m,K-2} = \begin{cases} 1 \text{ if } m \leq m^e_{K-2}, \\ 0 \text{ if } m > m^e_{K-2}, \end{cases}$$

Thus, $m_{K-2}^e \leqq m_{K-1}^e$ as $q_{m,K-2}^e = 0$ if $q_{m,K-1}^e = 0$ as described earlier. Repeating this process for $j = K - 3, K - 4, \ldots$, we easily obtain this lemma. □

Next, we prepare the following lemma for $S(m, j)$ to derive m_j^e.

Lemma 2. *The expected waiting time for a tagged customer who observes state* (m, j) *is*

$$
S(m,j) = \begin{cases}
\dfrac{K-j-1}{\lambda} & \text{if } m < n, \\[2mm]
\dfrac{m-n+1}{n\mu} + \sum_{i=0}^{K-j-1} \left(\dfrac{K-j-i-1}{\lambda}\right) \dbinom{m-n+i}{i} \\[2mm]
\qquad \times \left(\dfrac{\lambda}{\lambda+n\mu}\right)^i \left(\dfrac{n\mu}{\lambda+n\mu}\right)^{m-n+1} & \text{if } m \geqq n.
\end{cases}
$$

Proof. The proof method mainly follows [4]. Given the case $j = K - 1$, the waiting time becomes 0 if at least one server is available, i.e., $m < n$, since a tagged customer is the last customer for completing a batch. If there is no available server, i.e., $m \geq n$, a tagged customer must wait until $m - n + 1$ batches are served. Given the case $j \neq K - 1$. If $m < n$, a tagged customer must wait until his batch is completed, i.e., $K - j - 1$ customers must arrive. Otherwise, if $m \geq n$, the expected waiting time can be expressed using the maximum value of two random variables as follows:

$$
S(m,j) = \mathrm{E}[\max(Y_{m-n+1}, Z_{K-j-1})], \qquad \text{if } j \neq K-1, m \geq n,
$$

where Y_{m-n+1} and Z_{K-j-1} denote Erlang-$(m - n + 1)$ and Erlang-$(K - j - 1)$ random variables with rates $n\mu$ and λ, respectively. The former corresponds to the total service time until a server becomes available and the latter to the waiting time until his batch is completed. A waiting time of a tagged customer equals the maximum value of these two times.

Let $N(Y_{m-n+1})$ denote the number of newly arrived customers during time Y_{m-n+1}. We can thus obtain the following transformation:

$$
\mathrm{E}[\max(Y_{m-n+1}, Z_{K-j-1})] = \mathrm{E}[Y_{m-n+1}] + \mathrm{E}[\max(0, Z_{K-j-1} - Y_{m-n+1})]
$$

$$
= \frac{m-n+1}{n\mu} + \sum_{i=0}^{\infty} \mathrm{P}(N(Y_{m-n+1}) = i) \times
$$

$$
\mathrm{E}[\max(0, Z_{K-j-1} - Y_{m-n+1}) \mid N(Y_{m-n+1}) = i]
$$

$$
= \frac{m-n+1}{n\mu} + \sum_{i=0}^{K-j-1} \mathrm{P}(N(Y_{m-n+1}) = i) \times
$$

$$
\frac{K-j-i-1}{\lambda}.
$$

Here, we obtain

$$
\mathrm{P}(N(Y_{m-n+1}) = i) = \int_0^\infty e^{-\lambda x} \frac{(\lambda x)^i}{i!} \frac{(n\mu)^{m-n+1}}{(m-n)!} x^{m-n} e^{-\mu n x} dx
$$

$$
= \binom{m-n+i}{i} \left(\frac{\lambda}{\lambda+n\mu}\right)^i \left(\frac{n\mu}{\lambda+n\mu}\right)^{m-n+1}.
$$

This concludes the proof. □

Therefore, we can immediately obtain the following theorem.

Theorem 1. *The thresholds m_j^e $(0 \leq j \leq K-1)$ of Lemma 1 are*

$$m_{K-1}^e = \left\lfloor \frac{n\mu(R - p/K)}{C_W} + n - 1 \right\rfloor,$$

$$m_j^e = \max \left\{ m; 0 \leq m \leq m_{j+1}^e \text{ and } S(m,j) \leq \frac{R - \frac{p}{K}}{C_W} \right\}, \qquad 0 \leq j \leq K-2.$$

We can thus obtain the steady state probability of the system $\pi_{j,m}$ numerically under the state space $S = \{(j,m); j \in \{0,1,\ldots,K\}, m \in \{0,1,\ldots,m_j^e + 1\}\}$. In addition, we obtain the blocking probability P_b, expected number of busy servers $E[S_b]$, expected number of idle servers $E[S_i]$, and expected number of waiting customers $E[L]$, respectively, as follows (note that we use Little's law for $E[S_b]$, and also PASTA for P_b):

$$P_b = \sum_{j=0}^{K-1} \pi_{j,m_j^e+1},$$

$$E[S_b] = \frac{\lambda(1 - P_b)}{\mu K},$$

$$E[S_i] = n - \frac{\lambda(1 - P_b)}{\mu K},$$

$$E[L] = \sum_{(j,m)\in S} \{\max(0, m - n)K + j\}\pi_{j,m}.$$

Furthermore, we consider server maintenance cost such as energy or parking costs in a ride-sharing platform. Let C_b and C_i denote the maintenance costs of a server when it is busy and idle, respectively. Here, we simply assume that $C_b > C_i$. We can derive the expected server maintenance cost $E[M]$ as follows:

$$E[M] = C_b E[S_b] + C_i E[S_i]$$
$$= (C_b - C_i)\frac{\lambda(1 - P_b)}{\mu K} + C_i n.$$

Using these performance measures, we obtain social welfare represented by SW as

$$SW = \lambda\left(R - \frac{p}{K}\right)(1 - P_b) - C_W E[L] + \lambda(1 - P_b)\frac{p}{K}$$
$$= \lambda R(1 - P_b) - C_W \sum_{(j,m)\in S} \{\max(0, m - n)K + j\}\pi_{j,m}.$$

Then, the monopolist's revenue MR is calculated by

$$MR = \lambda(1 - P_b)\frac{p}{K} - \mathrm{E}[M]$$
$$= \left(p - \frac{C_b - C_i}{\mu}\right)\frac{\lambda(1 - P_b)}{K} - C_i n.$$

3   Numerical Examples

This section shows numerical results for social welfare SW and monopolist's revenue MR. We show the results of those measures for various admission fee p, batch size K, and number of servers n. We discuss the optimal values of those parameters using our numerical results.

3.1   Fee (p)

There are optimal p such that they maximize both SW and MR. This result means that if a monopolist chooses the optimal p, this is also approximately social optimal. One reason considered is that the common function P_b in SW and MR has a large impact on the plummeting point of p. Additionally, customers never join the system when p increases beyond a certain level, resulting in a sharp decrease in both measures.

3.2   Batch Size (K)

Fig 2 shows the results for batch size K under the parameter setting $\mu = 30$, $n = 3$, $p = 20$, $C_W = 100$, $R = 30$, $C_b = 300$, and $C_i = 50$. For SW, there exists an optimal K unless λ is small, i.e., there is some customer demand for the system. As K increases, more customers can use the system by sharing resources (i.e., low fee). Therefore, people tend to obtain a reward R, increasing social welfare. However, if K becomes large, the customer waiting time and blocking probability customers will be large, reducing SW. Previous research on batch service M/M/1 queues without admission fees [4] showed that equilibrium social welfare tendency decreases as batch size increases. In this study, the effect of the sharing economy for SW will be clear considering shared fees (p/K).

On the other hand, MR decreases as K increases for any λ under the same parameter setting. This is probably due to the fee setting. We simply assume that one batch service is for p regardless of batch size; thus, fee per customer becomes p/K. By this assumption, customer fee decreases inversely as batch size increases. Although we consider server cost, this effect is large. In Sect. 4, we discuss how a more realistic and elaborate fee setting in future work may improve this tendency.

3.3 Number of Servers (n)

Finally, we show numerical examples for n. We assume that the parameter setting as $\mu = 30$, $K = 3$, $p = 50$, $C_W = 100$, $R = 30$, $C_b = 10$, and $C_i = 5$. In both graphs, there exist optimal n for large values of λ. These results show the trade-off between the increase in joining customers and server maintenance cost for n. Observing the graph in more detail, the optimal n in terms of social welfare is the same or larger than that of monopolist's revenue. Naturally, the monopolist hesitates to introduce additional servers from the perspective of server maintenance cost. However, from the social view, it seems better to introduce more additional servers to receive more customers and to reduce the waiting time and the blocking probability.

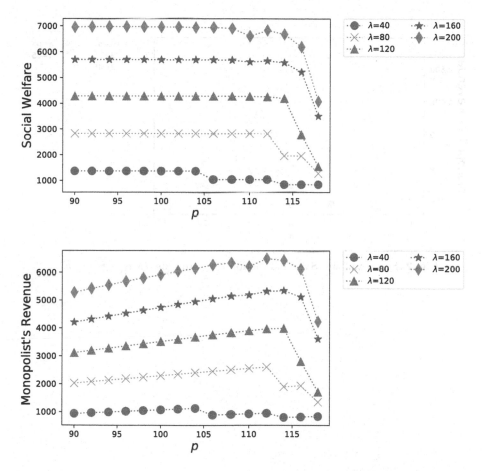

Fig. 1. Social welfare (SW) and monopolist's revenue (MR) against p.

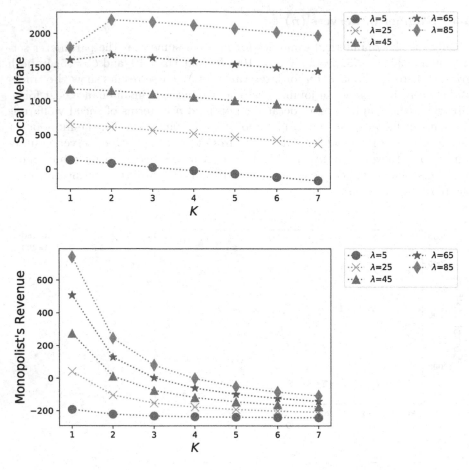

Fig. 2. Social welfare (SW) and monopolist's revenue (MR) against K.

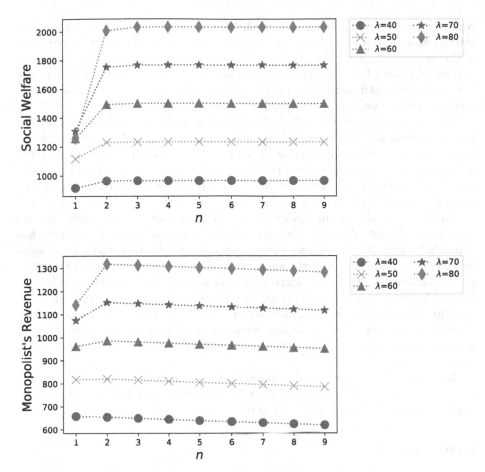

Fig. 3. Social welfare (SW) and monopolist's revenue (MR) against n.

4   Conclusion

In this study, we studied the observable batch service $M/M/n$ queueing system mainly for ridesharing applications, considering shared customer admission fee and server maintenance cost. Using analysis and numerical experiments, we have shown various tendencies of social welfare and monopolist's revenue against fees, batch sizes, and numbers of servers. For fees and number of servers, there exist some optimal points that maximize the two measures for relatively large customer arrival rates. For batch size, we have observed the optimal value to maximize social welfare. However, the monopolist's revenue decreases as batch size increases under the admission fee setting in this study.

An interesting topic for future research would be to investigate better ways to share fees such that the monopolist's revenue and social welfare increase. Although our equal distribution assumption is simple, it may be possible to consider a distribution method in which the longer the waiting time, the lower the fee. Moreover, a fee of K customers should not equal p. From the perspective of the monopolist, it may be more natural that a customer pays a fixed basic fee and an additional fee depending on batch size K. Finding a beneficial fee policy that improves both social welfare and monopolist's revenue in batch service systems will be challenging and significant future work.

We must also consider the effect of introducing multi-servers to society. In this study, we assumed that social welfare (SW) does not depend on server maintenance cost, since we assume that society's constituents receive the cost from the monopolist. However, excessive servers may negatively impact the environment and traffic congestion in the context of transportation systems. Deriving the optimal number of servers considering these elements is thus highly meaningful.

Furthermore, the extensions to unobservable or partially observable queues are also significant. Recently, the concept of Mobility as a Service (MaaS) has expanded widely [18]. In this framework, an operator (in this study, a monopolist) manages various transportation services and the recommended transportation modes for customers considering fee and waiting time through a web platform. Therefore, the observability of customers will be more flexible than the old transportation system such as buses or trains that depart according to fixed timetables and fees. The comparison among various policies, i.e., unobservable, partially observable, and observable is necessary for building an effective platform.

In this study, we have made simple assumptions using various parameters (e.g., K, C_W, C_b and C_i). However, it is essential to estimate realistic values using real data. This will be the focus of our next study.

References

1. Agatz, N., Erera, A., Savelsbergh, M., Wang, X.: Optimization for dynamic ridesharing: a review. Eur. J. Oper. Res. **223**(2), 295–303 (2012)
2. Boudali, O., Economou, A.: Optimal and equilibrium balking strategies in the single server markovian queue with catastrophes. Eur. J. Oper. Res. **218**(3), 708–715 (2012)
3. Boudali, O., Economou, A.: The effect of catastrophes on the strategic customer behavior in queueing systems. Naval Res. Logistics (NRL) **60**(7), 571–587 (2013)
4. Bountali, O., Economou, A.: Equilibrium joining strategies in batch service queueing systems. Eur. J. Oper. Res. **260**(3), 1142–1151 (2017)
5. Bountali, O., Economou, A.: Equilibrium threshold joining strategies in partially observable batch service queueing systems. Ann. Oper. Res. **277**(2), 231–253 (2019)
6. Bountali, O., Economou, A.: Strategic customer behavior in a two-stage batch processing system. Queueing Syst. **93**(1), 3–29 (2019)
7. Canbolat, P.G.: Bounded rationality in clearing service systems. Eur. J. Oper. Res. **282**(2), 614–626 (2020)
8. Czerny, A.I., Guo, P., Hassin, R.: Hide or advertise: the carrier's choice of waiting time information strategies. SSRN 3282276 (2018)
9. Economou, A., Manou, A.: Equilibrium balking strategies for a clearing queueing system in alternating environment. Ann. Oper. Res. **208**(1), 489–514 (2013)

10. Ghare, P.: Multichannel queuing system with bulk service. Oper. Res. **16**(1), 189–192 (1968)
11. Logothetis, D., Economou, A.: Routing of strategic passengers in a transportation station. In: Ballarini, P., Castel, H., Dimitriou, I., Iacono, M., Phung-Duc, T., Walraevens, J. (eds.) EPEW/ASMTA -2021. LNCS, vol. 13104, pp. 308–324. Springer, Cham (2021). https://doi.org/10.1007/978-3-030-91825-5_19
12. Manou, A., Economou, A., Karaesmen, F.: Strategic customers in a transportation station: when is it optimal to wait? Oper. Res. **62**(4), 910–925 (2014)
13. Nakamura, A., Phung-Duc, T.: Stationary analysis of infinite server queue with batch service. In: Ballarini, P., Castel, H., Dimitriou, I., Iacono, M., Phung-Duc, T., Walraevens, J. (eds.) EPEW/ASMTA -2021. LNCS, vol. 13104, pp. 411–424. Springer, Cham (2021). https://doi.org/10.1007/978-3-030-91825-5_25
14. Naor, P.: The regulation of queue size by levying tolls. Econometrica J. Econometric Soc. **37**, 15–24 (1969)
15. Neuts, M.F.: A general class of bulk queues with poisson input. Ann. Math. Stat. **38**(3), 759–770 (1967)
16. Nguyen, H.Q., Phung-Duc, T.: M/m/c/setup queues: conditional mean waiting times and a loop algorithm to derive customer equilibrium threshold strategy. In: Gilly, K., Thomas, N. (eds.) Computer Performance Engineering. LNCS, vol. 13659, pp. 68–99. Springer, Cham (2022). https://doi.org/10.1007/978-3-031-25049-1_6
17. Wang, J., Zhang, Y., Zhang, Z.G.: Strategic joining in an M/M/K queue with asynchronous and synchronous multiple vacations. J. Oper. Res. Soc. **72**(1), 161–179 (2021)
18. Wong, Y.Z., Hensher, D.A., Mulley, C.: Mobility as a service (MaaS): charting a future context. Transp. Res. Part A: Policy Pract. **131**, 5–19 (2020)

Learning a Correlated Equilibrium with Perturbed Regret Minimization

Omar Boufous[1(✉)], Rachid El-Azouzi[2], Mikaël Touati[1], Eitan Altman[2,3], and Mustapha Bouhtou[1]

[1] Orange, Châtillon, France
{omar.boufous,mikael.touati,mustapha.bouhtou}@orange.com
[2] LIA, University of Avignon, Avignon, France
rachid.elazouzi@univ-avignon.fr
[3] INRIA, Sophia Antipolis, Sophia Antipolis, France
eitan.altman@inria.fr

Abstract. In this paper, we consider the problem of learning a correlated equilibrium of a finite non-cooperative game and show a new learning rule, called Correlated Perturbed Regret Minimization (CPRM) for this purpose. CPRM combines regret minimization to approach the set of correlated equilibria and a simple device recommending to the players actions drawn from the empirical distribution in order to further stabilize the dynamic. Numerical experiments support the hypothesis of the pointwise convergence of the empirical distribution over action profiles to an approximate correlated equilibrium with all players following the devices' suggestions. Additional simulation results suggest that an adaptive version of CPRM can handle changes in the game such as departures or arrivals of players.

Keywords: Game theory · Correlated equilibrium · Learning

1 Introduction

Since their introduction [1,2] as a solution concept for non-cooperative games, correlated equilibria have gradually emerged as an appealing generalization of Nash equilibria. Correlated equilibria build upon the idea of correlated strategies, allowing for a non-independent randomization over actions by the players. More formally, a correlated equilibrium is an equilibrium of a game extended with an information structure defined by a probability space and a collection of player-specific events. Some of these structures known as "canonical" [3] lead to an interpretation in terms of a mediator [4] drawing an action profile according to a probability distribution and privately suggesting to each player her component. After receiving this recommendation, the player chooses her action. It was shown in [2] that the canonical structures are sufficient to generate all correlated equilibrium distributions.

© ICST Institute for Computer Sciences, Social Informatics and Telecommunications Engineering 2023
Published by Springer Nature Switzerland AG 2023. All Rights Reserved
E. Hyytiä and V. Kavitha (Eds.): VALUETOOLS 2022, LNICST 482, pp. 14–32, 2023.
https://doi.org/10.1007/978-3-031-31234-2_2

We consider the problem of learning a correlated equilibrium of a non-cooperative game with simple learning procedures and limited knowledge about the game (*e.g.* fictitious play, trial and error, regret-matching) [5]. Particularly, several adaptive heuristics imply the (almost sure) convergence of the empirical distribution over action profiles to the set of correlated equilibria [5–8] under relatively mild assumptions (*e.g.* every player may only know her utility function and the history of play). However, under these assumptions no learning rule implies a convergence to a correlated equilibrium distribution.

The main objective of this paper is to address the latter issue by introducing a new learning rule called Correlated Perturbed Regret Minimization (CPRM). In CPRM, players adaptively alternate between playing a regret minimization strategy to reduce the distance between the empirical distribution over action profiles and the set of correlated equilibrium distributions and following the suggestions of a device sampling from this distribution. In the long-run, the empirical distribution is expected to stabilize close to a correlated equilibrium with players following the device's suggestions.

1.1   Related Work

The majority of the literature on learning in games [9,10] studies the problem of learning pure and mixed Nash equilibria [11–16] with some contributions focusing on the convergence to equilibria satisfying properties such as Pareto efficiency [17,18] or welfare maximization [19,20].

The problem of learning correlated equilibria has received less attention in spite of a growing interest in the topic and the importance of the solution concept. In [6], Hart *et al.* propose a regret minimization strategy (using Blackwell's approachability [21]) and an adaptive heuristic called regret-matching. They show convergence of the empirical probability distribution over action profiles to the set of correlated equilibria. Similar guarantees are offered by calibration [8,22] but none of these procedures are known to guarantee the pointwise convergence of the trajectories to equilibrium points. In [23], Greenwald *et al.* present correlated-Q, a multi-agent reinforcement learning algorithm with an equilibrium selection feature in which a linear program is solved at each iteration to compute the polytope of correlated equilibria. Every player must know the game (utilities and sets of actions). In [24], Borowski *et al.* propose an uncoupled learning rule in which players rely on a public signal and select actions according to a perturbed process such that in the long-run, the joint strategy is a correlated equilibrium. The convergence is guaranteed if the public signal satisfies a certain condition which requires knowledge about the set of correlated equilibria. See [5,6,8,25] for other works on learning coarse correlated equilibria. Recent contributions [26,27] consider learning correlated equilibria of games in extensive form.

Finally, from an application perspective, correlated equilibria are relevant in engineering [28,29]. Particularly, [30] shows an algorithm using a correlation signal to synchronize the players' decisions so that they play a correlated equilibrium. However, the proposed approach seems to be limited to the considered system.

1.2 Outline

In Sect. 2, we define the model and provide the necessary preliminaries such as the relationship between correlated equilibria and regrets. In Sect. 3, we present the learning rule. In Sect. 4, we evaluate and discuss numerical performances of our solution. Section 5 concludes and shows possible directions of research and improvements.

2 Preliminaries

2.1 Notations

Vectors and tuples are denoted by small bold letters, matrices and random variables are denoted by capital letters. For $M \in \mathbb{R}^{m \times n}$, $M(i,j)$ denotes the entry in row i and column j and $||M|| = \max_{i,j} |M(i,j)|$. The ith component of x is denoted x_i and $x \geq y$ iff $x_i \geq y_i$ for every i. We use calligraphic capital letters for sets, $|\mathcal{S}|$ is the cardinality of the set $\mathcal{S}$ and $\Delta(\mathcal{S})$ is the simplex on $\mathcal{S}$ interpreted as the set of probability distributions on $\mathcal{S}$. The indicator function of an event A is denoted $\mathbb{1}_A$. We denote by $d(x,y)$ the Euclidean distance between x and y.

2.2 Model

Let $G = (\mathcal{N}, (\mathcal{A}_i)_{i \in \mathcal{N}}, (u_i)_{i \in \mathcal{N}})$ be an n-player finite non-cooperative game with set of players $\mathcal{N}$. The set of actions of player i is $\mathcal{A}_i = \{1, \ldots, l_i\}$ and the set of action profiles is $\mathcal{A} = \prod_{j \in \mathcal{N}} \mathcal{A}_j$. Player i's utility function is $u_i : \mathcal{A} \to \mathbb{R}$ such that her utility for the action profile $a \in \mathcal{A}$ is $u_i(a) = u(a_i, a_{-i})$. By extension, player i's expected utility for a probability distribution $q \in \Delta(\mathcal{A})$ is given by $u_i(q) = \sum_{a \in \mathcal{A}} q(a) u_i(a)$. In particular, her utility for the mixed strategy profile $(p_1, \ldots, p_n) \in \prod_{j \in \mathcal{N}} \Delta(\mathcal{A}_i)$ is $u_i(p_i, p_{-i}) = \sum_{a \in \mathcal{A}} \prod_{j \in \mathcal{N}} p_i(a_i) u_i(a_i, a_{-i})$.

Assume that G is played repeatedly at discrete times $t = 1, 2, \ldots$. A history of play until time t, denoted h^t, is a tuple of action profiles $h^t = (a^1, \ldots, a^t) \in \prod_{\tau=1}^{t} \mathcal{A}$ where a^τ is the action profile played at time τ.

Furthermore, assume that every player i knows her utility function u_i but not necessarily the utility function of other players and that at any time $t + 1$ every player knows the history of play h^t.

2.3 Correlated Equilibria

In this paper, we consider the concept of correlated equilibrium characterized by a probability distribution over action profiles, commonly interpreted as a distribution of play instructions, such that for each player, a recommended action is a best-response to the other players' actions assuming they follow their recommendations.

Definition 1 (Correlated β-equilibrium, [5]). *A probability distribution $q \in \Delta(\mathcal{A})$ is a correlated β-equilibrium if*

$$\forall i \in \mathcal{N}, \forall j \in \mathcal{A}_i, \forall k \in \mathcal{A}_i \quad \sum_{a \in \mathcal{A}: a_i = j} q(a)[u_i(k, a_{-i}) - u_i(a)] \leq \beta. \tag{1}$$

If $\beta = 0$, we have the usual definition of a correlated equilibrium [2].

As an example, consider the traffic intersection game involving two drivers arriving at an intersection. Each driver can either cross the intersection (action "*Go*") or wait (action "*Wait*"). When both drivers cross simultaneously, a collision occurs and both incur a utility of -1. Otherwise, the driver crossing gets $+1$ while the one waiting has 0. Utilities are shown in Table 1. There are two pure strategy Nash equilibria $(Wait, Go)$ with utilities $(0, 1)$, $(Go, Wait)$ with utilities $(1, 0)$ and a mixed Nash equilibrium $((1/2, 1/2), (1/2, 1/2))$ with utilities $(0, 0)$. Thus, the pure Nash equilibria result in unfair utility vectors and the mixed equilibrium is fair but inefficient. Correlated equilibria can help solving this problem by stabilizing more fair and efficient utility vectors. As an example, the probability distribution such that $\mathbb{P}(Go, Wait) = \mathbb{P}(Wait, Go) = 1/2$, $\mathbb{P}(Go, Go) = \mathbb{P}(Wait, Wait) = 0$ is a correlated equilibrium with utilities $(1/2, 1/2)$.

Table 1. Traffic intersection game.

	Wait	Go
Wait	(0, 0)	(0, 1)
Go	(1, 0)	(−1, −1)

2.4   Regret Minimization and Correlated Equilibria

Let $h^t = (a^1, \ldots, a^t)$ be the history of play until time t with empirical distribution of play q^t such that,

$$\forall a \in \mathcal{A}, \quad q^t(a) = \frac{1}{t} \sum_{\tau=1}^{t} \mathbb{1}_{a^\tau = a} \tag{2}$$

Following [6], define $D_i^t(j, k)$ the average utility difference for player i until time t when playing action k instead of j,

$$D_i^t(j, k) = \frac{1}{t} \sum_{\tau \leq t: a_i^\tau = j} \left[u_i\left(k, a_{-i}^\tau\right) - u_i\left(j, a_{-i}^\tau\right) \right] \tag{3a}$$

$$= \sum_{a \in \mathcal{A}: a_i = j} q^t(a) \left[u_i(k, a_{-i}) - u_i(a) \right] \tag{3b}$$

and regret $R_i^t(j, k) = \max\{0, D_i^t(j, k)\}$ which is the average gain of utility player i could have obtained if he had played k instead of j at previous iterations.

Remark 1. For any $\beta \geq 0$, we have $R_i^t(j,k) \leq \beta$ if and only if $D_i^t(j,k) \leq \beta$. Hence, from the definition of $D_i^t(j,k)$ in Eq. (3b) we have, $R_i^t(j,k) \leq \beta$ if and only if the empirical distribution $\boldsymbol{q}^t$ is a correlated β-equilibrium.

As proved in [6], Proposition 1 below shows that regrets converging to zero is necessary and sufficient for the sequence of empirical distributions to converge to the set of correlated equilibria.

Proposition 1. *Let* $(\boldsymbol{a}^t)_{t=1,2,\ldots}$ *be a sequence of plays* (i.e. $\boldsymbol{a}^t \in \mathcal{A}$ *for all* t) *and let* $\beta \geq 0$. *Then:* $\limsup_{t\to\infty} R_i^t(j,k) \leq \beta$ *for every* $i \in \mathcal{N}$ *and every* $j,k \in \mathcal{A}_i$ *with* $j \neq k$, *if and only if the sequence of empirical distributions* q^t *converges to the set of correlated β-equilibria.*

Furthermore, in [6] Hart *et al.* use Blackwell's approachability result to show that if at every iteration $t+1$ player i chooses an action drawn from the mixed strategy $\boldsymbol{\xi}_i^t$ satisfying,

$$\forall j \in \mathcal{A}_i, \sum_{k \in \mathcal{A}_i} \boldsymbol{\xi}_i^t(k) R_i^t(k,j) = \boldsymbol{\xi}_i^t(j) \sum_{k \in \mathcal{A}_i} R_i^t(j,k) \tag{4}$$

then $\{R_i^t\}_t$ approaches the negative orthant $\mathbb{R}_-^{|\mathcal{A}_i| \times |\mathcal{A}_i|}$,

$$\lim_{t\to\infty} d\left(R_i^t, \mathbb{R}_-^{|\mathcal{A}_i| \times |\mathcal{A}_i|}\right) \to 0 \text{ a.s} \tag{5}$$

Thus, if all players implement such strategy, the sequence of empirical distributions converges a.s. to the set of correlated β-equilibria.

In the next section, we propose a perturbed variant of this strategy, in which players synchronize probabilistically as they approach the set of correlated equilibria to stabilize the sequence of empirical distributions $\{\boldsymbol{q}^t\}_t$.

3   Learning Rule

Assume the history of play $\boldsymbol{h}^t$ with empirical distribution $\boldsymbol{q}^t$. In CPRM (Correlated Perturbed Regret Minimization), each player implements a mood-dependent strategy [12] such that in one mood, she uses a regret minimization strategy (to decrease her regrets and contribute in decreasing the distance to the set of correlated equilibria) and in the other she plays her component of an action profile sampled from $\boldsymbol{q}^t$ by a device.

3.1   Device

Assume a device drawing at time $t+1$ an action profile from the empirical distribution $\boldsymbol{q}^t$ and recommending to each player her component. Thus, if $\boldsymbol{b}^{t+1}$ is drawn, player i receives recommendation b_i^{t+1}. This device must know $\boldsymbol{q}^t$ at $t+1$ (not necessarily storing the history of play $\boldsymbol{h}^t$), must be able to transmit her component to every player but typically cannot access any other information about the game such as utility functions (thus being "unable to compute" a correlated equilibrium of G).

3.2 Players' Strategies

At time $t+1$, player i's mood m_i^{t+1} can be synchronous (denoted syn) or asynchronous (denoted $asyn$). If $m_i^{t+1} = syn$, then i plays b_i^{t+1} (sent by the device, see Sect. 3.1), else $m_i^{t+1} = asyn$ and player i chooses an action using the probability distribution ξ_i^t satisfying Eq. (4).

3.3 Players' Moods Dynamic

Given m_i^t and q^t, player i's mood evolves according to the following transition probabilities

$$\mathbb{P}(m_i^{t+1}|m_i^t, q^t) = \begin{cases} \varepsilon^{C_0 + ||D_i^t||} & \text{if } m_i^{t+1} = syn \text{ and } m_i^t = asyn \\ 1 - \varepsilon^{C_0 + ||D_i^t||} & \text{if } m_i^{t+1} = asyn \text{ and } m_i^t = asyn \\ \varepsilon^\gamma & \text{if } m_i^{t+1} = asyn \text{ and } m_i^t = syn \\ 1 - \varepsilon^\gamma & \text{if } m_i^{t+1} = syn, m_i^t = syn \text{ and } ||D_i^t|| \leq \beta \\ 1 - \varepsilon^\gamma & \text{if } m_i^{t+1} = asyn, m_i^t = syn \text{ and } ||D_i^t|| > \beta \end{cases} \tag{6}$$

where D_i^t is induced by q^t as defined in Eq. (3b) and the scalar parameter $\varepsilon > 0$ is called perturbation or noise of the process [31]. We show below a graphical representation of the moods dynamic at time t.

– If $m_i^t = asyn$ then player i moves to mood syn with probability $\varepsilon^{C_0 + ||D_i^t||}$,

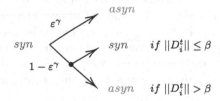

– If $m_i^t = syn$ then with probability ε^γ player i "experiments" and switches to $asyn$ to play the regret minimization procedure. Otherwise, with probability $1 - \varepsilon^\gamma$, if her maximum regret is lower than β she stays in mood syn and keeps on following the device's recommendation, else she changes to mood $asyn$ to play the regret minimization procedure.

The parameter $C_0 > 0$ is introduced to control the sensitivity of the process to regrets such that the transitions probabilities from $asyn$ to syn tend to zero as ε tends to zero. The constant γ is a parameter controlling the experimentation rate. Finally, β is a parameter defining the maximum "acceptable" value of regret for players to stay syn (relaxing in some sense the negative orthant condition of the Blackwell's regret minimization strategy). This parameter controls the approximation factor of the approximate correlated equilibria (see Sect. 2.3) that are expected to be stabilized by CPRM.

It can be shown that CPRM induces a perturbed non-homogeneous Markov process on a countable state space. We conjecture that if this process admits an asymptotic stationary distribution and the parameters are such that $\gamma > n2^{n-1}(C_0 + \beta)$, then the set of states with all-synchronous players and regrets below β is the only stochastically stable set of states [31]. The latter implies that in the long-run the players follow the suggestions of the device. Moreover, we expect the sequence $\{q^t\}_t$ to converge, implying that in the long-run the device draws action profiles from a correlated β-equilibrium distribution. A detailed analysis of this process is beyond the scope of the paper.

We report in Appendix A an implementable version of CPRM algorithm as a pseudo-code.

3.4   Adaptive CPRM

The previous model and learning rule assume that the same stage game G is played at every iteration. However, in many applications such as networks and communication systems [32], the set of players or utilities may change in time. This issue has not yet been thoroughly investigated in the literature. For instance, [33] assumes that every player may leave the game with a certain probability but is immediately replaced by a new player such that the total number of players is constant. In this section, we assume that the number of players may change in time and propose an adaptive version of CPRM, assuming that at any iteration, every player and the device (see Sect. 3.1) know the set of players in the game and the sets of action profiles.

In the following, we define an adjustment process preventing the learning phase from being re-initialized for the new stage game. First, the empirical distribution in the new stage game is updated in accordance with past plays. Second, every player plays following CPRM but using the updated empirical distribution. Third, following the latter first play in the new game, the empirical distribution is updated using a slightly modified update rule including an inertia parameter.

Let $\mathcal{N}^t$ be the set of players at time t and $\mathcal{A}^t$ be the corresponding set of action profiles. Assume that a new player l arrives at time $T \in]t, t+1[$ such that $\mathcal{N}^{t+1} = \mathcal{N}^t \cup \{l\}$ and $\mathcal{A}^{t+1} = \prod_{i \in \mathcal{N}^{t+1}} \mathcal{A}_i$. Let a_l be an arbitrary action in $\mathcal{A}_l$. To keep on relying on the properties of the empirical distribution induced by the learning rule until t, we define a new "empirical" probability distribution $\tilde{q}^t$ in $\Delta(\mathcal{A}^{t+1})$ to be used by the players at $t+1$ such that, for any profile $a \in \mathcal{A}$ and any action j in $\mathcal{A}_l$,

$$\tilde{q}^t(a, j) = \begin{cases} q^t(a) & \text{if } j = a_l \\ 0 & \text{else} \end{cases} \tag{7}$$

where (a, j) is the strategy profile in $\mathcal{A}^{t+1}$ such that the players in $\mathcal{N}^t$ play a and l plays j.

Assume that player l leaves at time $T \in]t, t+1[$. Then, at time $t+1$ we have $\mathcal{N}^{t+1} = \mathcal{N}^t \backslash \{l\}$, $\mathcal{A}^{t+1} = \prod_{i \in \mathcal{N}^{t+1}} \mathcal{A}_i$ and the empirical distribution must be updated to be in $\Delta(\mathcal{A}^{t+1})$. We consider the following update rule,

$$\forall a \in \mathcal{A}^{t+1}, \tilde{q}^t(a) = \sum_{y \in \mathcal{A}_j} q^t(a, y) \tag{8}$$

Assume that the following arrival or departure occurs at $T' > t+1$, then for any integer k such that $t+1 \leq t+k \leq T'$ the empirical distribution is updated at $t+k$ such that,

$$\tilde{q}^{t+k}(a) = \frac{t+k-1-\tau(t)}{t+k-\tau(t)} \tilde{q}^{t+k-1}(a) + \frac{1}{t+k-\tau(t)} \mathbb{1}_{\{a^{t+k-1}=a\}} \tag{9}$$

where $0 \leq \tau(t) \leq t$ is an inertia parameter at t controlling the responsiveness of the empirical distribution and learning to changes in the game. If $k = 1$ and $\tau(t) = t$, then $\tilde{q}^{t+1}$ equals the empirical distribution induced by a history of length one $h = (a)$. In other words, history is (in some sense) re-initialized and the players enter a new learning period. If $\tau(t)$ is negligible w.r.t. t, then the dynamic of the empirical probability distribution is not influenced by the inertia parameter. The constant $\tau(t)$ can therefore be interpreted as the inertia of the learning with respect to changes, making it more or less responsive to arrival and departures of players in the game being played. Other steps of CPRM are left unchanged. A detailed discussion of the inertia parameter is beyond the scope of this paper.

4   Numerical Results

In this section, we evaluate the performances of CPRM and its adaptive version. First, we consider a simple two-player matrix game to compare our solution to a well-known adaptive heuristic called regret-matching and to the no-regret learning procedure based on Blackwell's approachability both described in [6]. Then, we consider arrivals and departures of players in the game to observe how the adaptive version of CPRM performs. Finally, we conclude with a congestion game with larger sets of actions and player-specific cost functions [34]. For all experiments, the parameters in Table 2 were used.

4.1   Matrix Games

Constant Stage Game. We first consider the problem of learning a correlated equilibrium for the 3×2 matrix game shown in Table 3 admitting two mixed Nash equilibria $((1/12, 0, 11/12), (5/6, 1/6))$ and $((3/14, 11/14, 0), (5/6, 1/6))$ with respective utilities $(13/3, 73/12)$ and $(13/3, 82/7)$.

Table 2. Simulation Parameters.

	Value	Signification
β	0.05	Approximation factor
ε	0.01	Perturbation rate
γ	5	Experimentation rate
T	5×10^5	Number of iterations
C_0	1	Offset constant
τ	100	Inertia parameter

Table 3. Utility matrix of the two-player game.

	D	E
A	(2, 29)	(16, 7)
B	(4, 7)	(6, 13)
C	(4, 4)	(6, 6)

We consider the evolution in time ($0 \leq t \leq T$) of the empirical probability distribution $\{q^t\}_t$, maximal regrets $\{(\|R_i^t\|)_{i \in \mathcal{N}}\}_t$ and players' moods $\{(m_i^t)_{i \in \mathcal{N}}\}_t$.

Figures 1a to 2c show the evolution in time of maximal regrets and the empirical distribution over action profiles induced by regret-matching, Blackwell's procedure for regret minimization and CPRM. In Fig. 1, we observe that regrets decrease below the threshold $\beta = 0.05$ for each learning procedure. For regret-matching, this occurs around 2×10^6 rounds, hence the larger simulation horizon compared to the two other algorithms. This empirically supports the convergence of the three algorithms to the set of β-correlated equilibria (shown in [6] for the Blackwell's procedure and regret-matching). However, if both players apply Blackwell's regret minimization or regret-matching procedures, the regret trajectories do not stabilize implying that the empirical distribution over action profiles does not converge pointwise.

Figure 1c shows that the regrets induced by CPRM stabilize below the target threshold (even if not converging to zero), which confirms that the empirical distribution approaches the set of correlated equilibrium distributions and may converge. Furthermore, Fig. 2c shows very stable trajectories for the probabilities of each action profile, thus supporting the hypothesis of convergence. This is not the case for the trajectories induced by the regret-matching procedure on Fig. 2a or Blackwell's regret minimization strategy on Fig. 2b which do not stabilize on the graphs and at even larger timescales (not shown).

Figure 3 shows the evolution in time of the pairs $u(q^t) = (u_1(q^t), u_2(q^t))$ where $u_i(q^t)$ is the expected utility $u_i(q^t) = \sum_{a \in \mathcal{A}} q^t(a) u_i(a)$ for player i. For the sake of clarity of the figure, the plot displays one point every hundred points in the sample path, *i.e.* $(u(q^1), u(q^{101}), ...)$. The gray area represents the feasible pairs of utilities in the game with all possible probability distributions over action profiles. Figure 3a shows that starting from the initial action profile (A, D) with utilities $(2, 29)$, the trajectory stabilizes at a point in the vicinity of

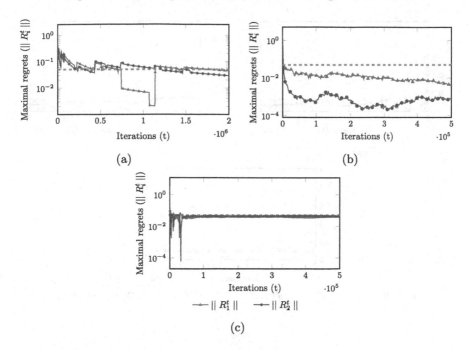

(a)   (b)

(c)

Fig. 1. Evolution of players regrets for the three algorithms: a) Regret-matching b) Blackwell-based regret minimization and c) CPRM algorithm.

the convex hull of the two mixed Nash equilibria. Figure 3b shows the trajectory approaching a correlated β-equilibrium at a smaller scale.

Figure 4 shows the evolution in time of the players' moods as a scatter-plot. In the first 4×10^4 iterations, the two players are mostly asynchronous, thus implementing a regret minimization strategy. Beyond 4×10^4, both players are synchronous, thus playing the action profile suggested by the device and drawn from q^t. In this regime, asynchronous realizations (not visible on the graph for the given simulation horizon) typically come from the fact that players "explore" regardless of their regrets due to the perturbation ε^{γ} in the dynamic.

Fraction of Time Spent in a Correlated β-Equilibrium. In this section, we consider the impact of the perturbation on the long-run behaviour of CPRM for the previous two-player game. Let $q^*(\varepsilon)$ be the correlated β-equilibrium experimentally reached with perturbation ε (last distribution in Figure 2c). In Fig. 5, we show the fraction of time the players are synchronous (thus following the suggestions of the device) and the empirical probability distribution is within a η-neighborhood (taking $\eta = 0.01$) to $q^*(\varepsilon)$. The complementary proportion of time, either corresponds to a distribution at a distance greater than η from $q^*(\varepsilon)$ or to the case where at least one player explores as a consequence of the perturbation.

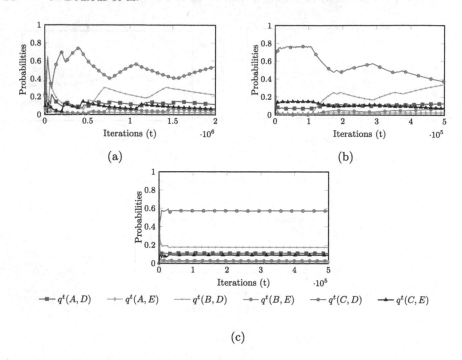

(a)   (b)

(c)

Fig. 2. Evolution of the empirical distribution over action profiles for the three algorithms: a) Regret-matching b) Blackwell's regret minimization and c) CPRM algorithm.

Figure 5 is an experimental evidence of the existence of a long-run regime such that both players follow the suggestions drawn from the correlated β-equilibrium $q^*(\varepsilon)$. Furthermore, the plot shows that the smaller the perturbation ε the greater the proportion of time spent in the vicinity of an approximate correlated equilibrium. This is consistent with the type of convergence expected from the perturbed Markov process and the conjecture stating that in the low perturbations regime, with probability close to 1, players are synchronous and the empirical distribution converges to an approximate correlated equilibrium.

Arrivals and Departures of Players. Previously, we have assumed that the same stage game is played at every iteration. In this section, we consider the numerical performances of the adaptive version of CPRM (see Sect. 3.4) and observe how the previous convergence results may be impacted as new players join or leave the game and utility functions change.

Assume that players start playing the game in Table 3 expanding into a three player game before evolving later on into a two-player game and eventually reverting back to the same three-player case afterwards as shown in Table 4. In the three-player game, the first two players keep their original sets of actions while the third player chooses the matrix (X or Y). The first new player joins the game at $T_1 = 509583$ and leaves at $T_2 = 1019541$ while the second arrives

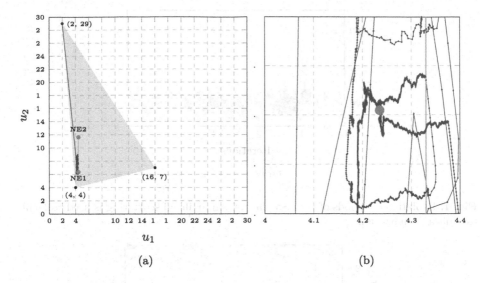

(a)   (b)

Fig. 3. (a) Trajectory (in blue) of the expected utilities starting from the initial action profile (A, D). Utilities at mixed Nash equilibria ($NE1$ and $NE2$) are shown in red. (b) Zoom-in showing the trajectory approaching a correlated β-equilibrium (red point) close to convex hull of Nash equilibria (in green). (Color figure online)

at $T_3 = 1529892$. Figure 6a shows the evolution in time of the maximal regrets of the players while Fig. 6b shows the evolution of probabilities for each profile. The arrival and departure of a player perturbs other players' regrets (red and blue curves correspond to the initial two players). It appears in Fig. 6a that for each game, the regrets are stabilized below the threshold β (dashed line) on the corresponding time interval. It can also be observed in Fig. 6b that for each game, the probability distribution over action profiles seems to converge on the corresponding time interval. These results show that CPRM may also be used in environments with arrivals and departures as long as each game is played for sufficiently long.

4.2   Congestion Game

As a final example of numerical experiment, we consider the problem of learning a correlated equilibrium in a congestion game [35] (a class of games particularly relevant w.r.t. network applications and resource allocation problems) with player-specific cost functions and larger action sets (the considered example has 108 action profiles) to test how relevant CPRM may be in this setting and its scalability with regards to the number of actions and action profiles. In a congestion game with player-specific cost functions, each player selects a feasible subset of resources and incurs a total cost defined as the sum of the costs of the chosen resources which depend on the player, each resource and the number of players using it.

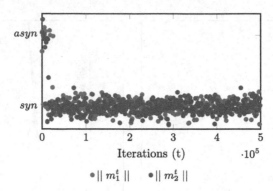

Fig. 4. Evolution of moods of the two players. An artificial scattering is used to facilitate data visualization.

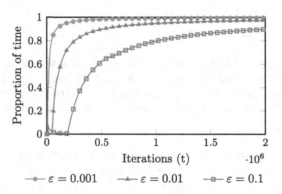

Fig. 5. Evolution in time of the proportion of time spent in the η-neighbourhood of the correlated β-equilibrium $\boldsymbol{q}^*(\varepsilon)$ for $\eta = 0.01$.

We consider the case where the resources are edges in a network and each player selects a subset of edges defining a path connecting a player-specific (*source, destination*) pair of nodes. Formally, this game is defined by the following collection of objects,

– a network $\mathcal{G} = (\mathcal{V}, \mathcal{E})$ with vertices and edges,
– a finite set $\mathcal{N} = \{1, \ldots n\}$ of n players,
– for every player i, a source-destination pair $(s_i, t_i) \in \mathcal{V} \times \mathcal{V}$,
– for every player i, an action set $\mathcal{A}_i$ defined as the set of paths connecting source node s_i with target t_i,
– for every player i and every edge $e \in \mathcal{E}$, a non-decreasing delay function $d_i^e : \mathbb{N} \to \mathbb{R}$.

Table 4. Sequence of stage games considered in the dynamic case. The stage game does not necessarily evolve at every iteration.

	D	E
A	(2, 29)	(16, 7)
B	(4, 7)	(6, 13)
C	(4, 4)	(6, 6)

↓

	D	E
A	(2, 29, 2)	(16, 7, 8)
B	(4, 7, 2)	(6, 13, 0)
C	(4, 4, 1)	(6, 6, 5)

X

	D	E
A	(9, 4, 0)	(4, 1, 4)
B	(8, 0, 1)	(6, 7, 2)
C	(11, 9, 3)	(2, 0, 4)

Y

↓

	D	E
A	(2, 29)	(16, 7)
B	(4, 7)	(6, 13)
C	(4, 4)	(6, 6)

↓

	D	E
A	(2, 29, 2)	(16, 7, 8)
B	(4, 7, 2)	(6, 13, 0)
C	(4, 4, 1)	(6, 6, 5)

X

	D	E
A	(9, 4, 0)	(4, 1, 4)
B	(8, 0, 1)	(6, 7, 2)
C	(11, 9, 3)	(2, 0, 4)

Y

Let $f_e : \prod_{i \in \mathcal{N}} \mathcal{A}_i \rightarrow \{0, \dots, n\}$ be the congestion function of edge e such that $f_e(\boldsymbol{a}) = |\{i \in \mathcal{N} : e \in a_i\}|$, *i.e.* the number of players using edge e. Given a strategy profile $\boldsymbol{a} \in \mathcal{A}$, player i has cost $c_i(\boldsymbol{a}) = \sum_{e \in a_i} d_i^e(f_e(\boldsymbol{a}))$.

Particularly, we consider the 4-player game with graph and pairs defined in Fig. 7, cost functions $d_i^e(x) = x$ for all $i \neq 2$, $d_i^e(x) = x^2$ for $i = 2$ and action sets,

- $\mathcal{A}_1 = \{''BCDEF'', ''BDEF'', ''BADEF''\}$
- $\mathcal{A}_2 = \{''BCDE'', ''BDE'', ''BADE''\}$
- $\mathcal{A}_3 = \{''DCB'', ''DEFAB'', ''DECB''\}$
- $\mathcal{A}_4 = \{''FDE'', ''FADE'', ''FABCDE'', ''FABDE''\}$

As before, we first have an interest in a constant stage game and then allow for the stage game to change because of arrival and departure of players.

Figure 8b shows the evolution with time of the empirical distribution q^t. Since we cannot show the 108 curves (one per action profile), we plot only the curves of the five action profiles with highest probabilities in the long-term. As in the previous example of the two-player matrix game, the curves support the conjectured convergence of the empirical distribution. This is to be put into perspective with the evolution of regrets shown in Fig. 8a, indicating that this long-run distribution is indeed a correlated β-equilibrium distribution. Then, in the long-run, the players follow a correlated equilibrium distribution of this game.

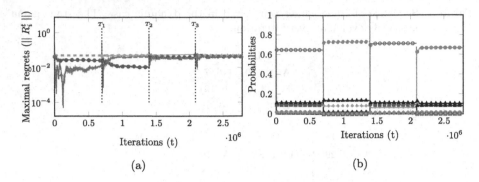

(a)   (b)

Fig. 6. Evolution of regrets (a) and the empirical distribution over action profiles (b) with arrival and departure of players (at times indicated with vertical dotted lines). The approximate equilibrium threshold β is marked with horizontal dashed line on the left figure.

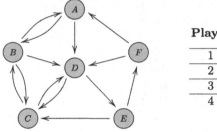

Player	Source node	Destination node
1	B	F
2	B	E
3	D	B
4	F	E

Fig. 7. Network graph of the game (left) and source-destination nodes of each player (right).

To conclude, we assume that some players join or leave the congestion game. As commonly considered in network applications, we assume stochastic departures and arrivals following a Poisson process with rate $\lambda = 1/27236$. We show the results for a realization of this process such that a fifth player with pair (B, D) arrives at $T_1 = 54377$ and players 3, 5 and 4 leave at respectively $T_2 = 81434$, $T_3 = 108702$ and $T_4 = 135882$ as shown in Fig. 9. As expected, in the interval $0 \leq t \leq T_1$, the regret curves are similar to the case without arrivals and departures of Fig. 8a as the game being played in the considered time frame is the same.

It can be observed from Fig. 10 that in the third, fourth and last phase, the correlated β-equilibrium played is an approximate pure Nash equilibrium as only one profile is played with a probability close to 1. In all cases, regrets in Fig. 9 remain below the approximation threshold β.

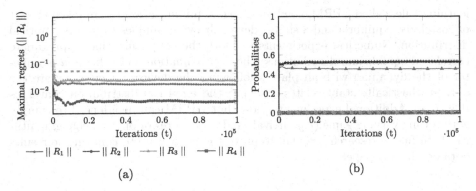

(a)   (b)

Fig. 8. (a) Evolution of the maximum regret for each player (curves of players 3 and 4 are not plotted because of low regrets and the logarithmic scale). (b) Evolution of the empirical distribution over the (five main) action profiles.

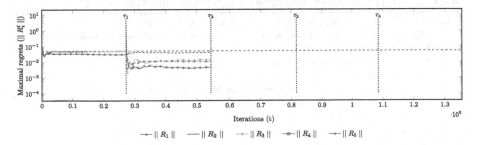

Fig. 9. Evolution of regrets with arrival and departure of players (at times indicated with vertical dotted lines). The approximate equilibrium threshold corresponds to the horizontal dashed line. Regrets with very small values are not displayed.

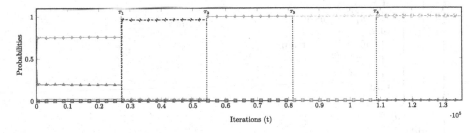

Fig. 10. Evolution of the empirical probability distribution. Only the five highest probabilities of action profiles are shown.

5   Conclusion

In this paper, we considered the problem of learning a correlated equilibrium in finite non-cooperative games with a particular focus on the open problem of convergence of the empirical probability distribution (over action profiles) induced by a learning rule to a correlated equilibrium distribution. We proposed a new learning rule, called CPRM, combining regret minimization to approach the set of correlated equilibria and a simple device drawing samples from the empirical distribution. Numerical experiments support the conjecture that approximate correlated equilibrium distributions (the approximation factor being a parameter of the dynamic) with all players following the devices' suggestions are the only stochastically stable states and that the empirical distribution converges pointwise. Additional experiments show that CPRM can be adapted to comply with a time-varying game (*e.g.* arrivals and departures of players, changing utilities). In future research, we plan to prove the conjecture to confirm the results obtained in this paper.

A   Appendix: Numerical Implementation of CPRM

Algorithm 1: Correlated Perturbed Regret Minimization (CPRM)

Let $G = (\mathcal{N}, (\mathcal{A}_i)_{i \in \mathcal{N}}, (u_i)_{i \in \mathcal{N}})$, $\varepsilon > 0$, $\beta > 0$, $C_0 > 0$, $\gamma \geq n2^{n-1}(\beta + C_0)$
Initialize moods $(m_i^1)_{i \in \mathcal{N}}$, history $h^1 = (a^1)$, empirical distribution q^1 and $(D_i^1)_{i \in \mathcal{N}}$
for *t=1, 2,...* **do**

    Draw an action profile $b^{t+1} = (b_1, ..., b_n)$ from q^t

    for $i \in \mathcal{N}$ **do**

        /* Play according to player i's mood & update mood   */

        Draw uniformly in $[0,1]$: $var \leftarrow Uniform(0,1)$

        if $m_i^t = asyn$ **then**

            if $\varepsilon^{||D_i^t||} > var$ **then**

                | $m_i^{t+1} \leftarrow syn$

            end

            Play a realization c_i of the mixed strategy in Eq. (4)

            $a_i^{t+1} \leftarrow c_i$

        else

            if $\varepsilon^\gamma > var$ **then**

                | $m_i^{t+1} \leftarrow asyn$

            else

                if $||D_i^t|| > \beta$ **then**

                    | $m_i^{t+1} \leftarrow asyn$

                end

            end

            $a_i^{t+1} \leftarrow b_i$

        end

    end

    /* Update the empirical distribution   */

    $q^{t+1}(a) \leftarrow \frac{t}{t+1} q^t(a) + \frac{1}{t+1} \mathbb{1}_{\{a^{t+1}=a\}}, \forall a \in \mathcal{A}$

    /* Update the vector of the average utility differences   */

    $\forall i \in \mathcal{N}, \forall j \in \mathcal{A}_i, \forall k \in \mathcal{A}_i, D_i^{t+1}(j,k) \leftarrow \sum_{\substack{a \in \mathcal{A} \\ a_i = j}} q^{t+1}[u_i(k, a_{-i}) - u_i(a_i, a_{-i})]$

end

References

1. Aumann, R.J.: Subjectivity and correlation in randomized strategies. J. Math. Econ. **1**(1), 67–96 (1974)
2. Aumann, R.J.: Correlated equilibrium as an expression of bayesian rationality. Econometrica: J. Econometric Soc. **55**, 1–18 (1987)
3. Forges, F.: Correlated equilibria and communication in games. Complex Soc. Behav. Syst.: Game Theory Agent-Based Models, 107–118 (2020)
4. Myerson, R.B.: Game Theory: Analysis of Conflict. Harvard University Press, Cambridge (1997)
5. Hart, S.: Adaptive heuristics. Econometrica **73**(5), 1401–1430 (2005)
6. Hart, S., Mas-Colell, A.: A simple adaptive procedure leading to correlated equilibrium. Econometrica **68**(5), 1127–1150 (2000)
7. Hart, S., Mas-Colell, A.: A reinforcement procedure leading to correlated equilibrium. Econ. Essays, 181–200 (2001)
8. Foster, D.P., Vohra, R.V.: Calibrated learning and correlated equilibrium. Games Econom. Behav. **21**(1–2), 40–55 (1997)
9. Fudenberg, D., Levine, D.K.: The Theory of Learning in Games. The MIT Press, vol. 1, no. 0262061945 (1998)
10. Cesa-Bianchi, N., Lugosi, G.: Prediction, Learning, and Games. Cambridge University Press, USA (2006)
11. Foster, D., Young, H.P.: Regret testing: learning to play Nash equilibrium without knowing you have an opponent. Theor. Econ. **1**(3), 341–367 (2006)
12. Young, H.P.: Learning by trial and error. Games Econom. Behav. **65**(2), 626–643 (2009)
13. Boussaton, O., Cohen, J., Tomasik, J., Barth, D.: On the distributed learning of Nash equilibria with minimal information. In: 2012 6th International Conference on Network Games, Control and Optimization (NetGCooP). IEEE, pp. 30–37 (2012)
14. Frihauf, P., Krstic, M., Basar, T.: Nash equilibrium seeking in noncooperative games. IEEE Trans. Autom. Control **57**(5), 1192–1207 (2011)
15. Germano, F., Lugosi, G.: Global Nash convergence of foster and young's regret testing. Games Econom. Behav. **60**(1), 135–154 (2007)
16. Hart, S., Mas-Colell, A.: Uncoupled dynamics do not lead to Nash equilibrium. Am. Econ. Rev. **93**(5), 1830–1836 (2003)
17. Marden, J.R., Young, H.P., Arslan, G., Shamma, J.S.: Payoff-based dynamics for multiplayer weakly acyclic games. SIAM J. Control. Optim. **48**(1), 373–396 (2009)
18. Pradelski, B.S., Young, H.P.: Learning efficient Nash equilibria in distributed systems. Games Econom. Behav. **75**(2), 882–897 (2012)
19. Ariel, I., Babichenko, Y.: Average Testing and the Efficient Boundary. Center for the study of Rationality (2011)
20. Marden, J.R., Young, H.P., Pao, L.Y.: Achieving pareto optimality through distributed learning. SIAM J. Control. Optim. **52**(5), 2753–2770 (2014)
21. Blackwell, D., et al.: An analog of the minimax theorem for vector payoffs. Pac. J. Math. **6**(1), 1–8 (1956)
22. Perchet, V.: Université Paris-Diderot, Laboratoire de Probabilités et Modèles Aléatoires, UMR 7599, 8 place FM/13, Paris, "Approachability, regret and calibration: Implications and equivalences," J. Dyn. Games, vol. 1, no. 2, pp. 181–254 (2014)
23. Greenwald, A., Hall, K., Serrano, R.: Correlated q-learning. In: ICML, vol. 3, pp. 242–249 (2003)

24. Borowski, H.P., Marden, J.R., Shamma, J.S.: Learning to play efficient coarse correlated equilibria. Dyn. Games Appl. **9**(1), 24–46 (2019)
25. Marden, J.R.: Selecting efficient correlated equilibria through distributed learning. Games Econom. Behav. **106**, 114–133 (2017)
26. Celli, A., Marchesi, A., Farina, G., Gatti, N.: No-regret learning dynamics for extensive-form correlated and coarse correlated equilibria. CoRR, vol. abs/2004.00603 (2020)
27. Farina, G., Celli, A., Marchesi, A., Gatti, N.: Simple uncoupled no-regret learning dynamics for extensive-form correlated equilibrium. CoRR, vol. abs/2104.01520 (2021)
28. Jin, H., Guo, H., Su, L., Nahrstedt, K., Wang, X.: Dynamic task pricing in multi-requester mobile crowd sensing with markov correlated equilibrium. In: IEEE INFOCOM 2019-IEEE Conference on Computer Communications. IEEE, pp. 1063–1071 (2019)
29. Hu, Q., Nigam, Y., Wang, Z., Wang, Y., Xiao, Y.: A correlated equilibrium based transaction pricing mechanism in blockchain. In: 2020 IEEE International Conference on Blockchain and Cryptocurrency (ICBC). IEEE, pp. 1–7 (2020)
30. Cigler, L., Faltings, B.: Reaching correlated equilibria through multi-agent learning. In: 10th Conference on Autonomous Agents and Multiagent Systems AAMAS, no. CONF (2011)
31. Young, H.P.: The evolution of conventions. Econometrica: J. Econometric Soc. pp. 57–84 (1993)
32. Dolan, R.J.: Incentive mechanisms for priority queuing problems. Bell J. Econ. 421–436 (1978)
33. Lykouris, T., Syrgkanis, V., Tardos, É.: Learning and efficiency in games with dynamic population. In: Proceedings of the 27th Annual ACM-SIAM Symposium on Discrete algorithms. SIAM, pp. 120–129 (2016)
34. Ackermann, H., Röglin, H., Vöcking, B.: Pure Nash equilibria in player-specific and weighted congestion games. Theoretical Comput. Sci. **410**(17), 1552–1563 (2009)
35. Rosenthal, R.W.: A class of games possessing pure-strategy Nash equilibria. Internat. J. Game Theory **2**(1), 65–67 (1973)

Cooperative Game Theoretic Analysis
of Shared Services

Anirban Mitra[1], Manu K. Gupta[1($\boxtimes$)], and N. Hemachandra[2]

[1] Indian Institute of Technology Roorkee, Roorkee 247667, Uttarakhand, India
{anirban_m,manu.gupta}@ms.iitr.ac.in
[2] Indian Institute of Technology Bombay, Mumbai 400076, Maharashtra, India
nh@iitb.ac.in

Abstract. Shared services are increasingly popular among firms and are often modeled as multi-class queuing systems. Several priority scheduling rules are possible to schedule customers from different classes. These scheduling rules can be static, where a class has strict priority over the other class, or can be dynamic based on delay and certain weights for each class. An interesting and important question is how to fairly allocate the waiting cost for shared services.

In this paper, we address the above problem using the solution concepts of cooperative game theory. We first appropriately define worth functions for each player (class), each coalition, and the grand coalition for multi-class M/G/1 queue with non-preemptive priority. It turns out that the worth function of the grand coalition follows Kleinrock's conservation law. We fully analyze the 2−class game and obtain the fair waiting cost allocations from several cooperative games' solution concepts viewpoints. These include Shapley value, the core, and nucleolus. We prove the 2−class game is convex which implies that the core is nonempty and the Shapley value allocation belongs to the core. Cooperative game-theoretic solutions capture fairness. We characterize the closed-form expression for these scheduling policies as bringing out various fairness aspects amongst scheduling policies. We consider Delay dependent priority (DDP) rule to determine fair scheduling policies from the Shapley value and the core-based allocation. We present extensive numerical experiments by partitioning the stability region for 2-class queues in three sub-regions.

Keywords: Cooperative game theory · Multi-class queueing systems · Dynamic priority scheduling · Shapley value · Nucleolus · The core · Achievable region · Delay dependent priority rule

1 Introduction

We consider the problem of fair scheduling in a queuing system where a server caters to several classes of customers. Customer's arrival to each class follows

E. Hyytiä and V. Kavitha (Eds.): VALUETOOLS 2022, LNICST 482, pp. 33–47, 2023.
https://doi.org/10.1007/978-3-031-31234-2_3

Poisson process and a single server provide service to each class with non-preemptive priority and general service time distribution. In order to facilitate customer service, different priority scheduling rules are possible. These include static priority where one class of customers has strict high priority over the other class of customers. On the other hand, we can also have dynamic priority rules which may be dependent on the number in the queue or the delay of customers in each class. An important question in this setup is how the total cost can be fairly divided among its participants. This paper focuses on characterizing fair scheduling policies (fair waiting cost allocation) based on several solution concepts from cooperative game theory.

We first define an appropriate N-class game where the worth functions of each player, coalition, and the grand coalition are in terms of mean waiting time weighted by the load factors of each class. We then consider several solution concepts including the core, Shapely value, and nucleolus for fair waiting cost allocation. The core provides the set of coalitional and collectively rational allocations whereas the Shapley value is based on marginal utility and nucleolus minimizes the maximum dissatisfaction. We completely characterize these solution concepts for the 2-class game by first proving it to be convex and then deriving the closed-form expressions for allocations. We note that the class with a higher load factor results in higher Shapley value allocations. This is intuitive as a class that brings the higher load in the system gets allocated the higher waiting cost for a solution concept (Shapley value) which is based on marginal utility. For this game, Shapley value and nucleolus turn out to be the same. We also find the addition of Shapley value and the core allocations are the same as right hand side of Kleinrock's conservation law [1].

We consider Delay Dependent Priority (DDP) rule to determine fair scheduling policy. Delay dependent priority was first introduced by Kleinrock [2] and the mean waiting time in multi-class M/G/1 queue was derived under the DDP scheduling rule. A scheduling rule is *complete* if it covers all possible vectors of mean waiting time which are achievable. A set of all scheduling policies are obviously complete, however, one is interested in finding parameterized policies that are complete [3]. The completeness of DDP and its implications are discussed in [4]. DDP prioritizes each class based on the delay and a certain predefined weight parameter for each class. We now briefly explain the mechanism of DDP for two class queues. Let b_1 and b_2 be the weights associated with classes 1 and 2 respectively. Let $\beta := b_2/b_1$ be the ratio of these weights. Suppose $\beta = 0.75$, it means $b_2 = 0.75 b_1$ i.e. the DDP priority scheduling prioritize queue class 2, 0.75 times than queue class 1. We utilize this delay dependent priority parameter and obtain fair scheduling policies with respect to the several solution concepts discussed above. We determine fair scheduling policy parameters associated with Shapley value ($\beta^{Shapley}$) and the core (β^{Core}).

We consider the entire region of stability for 2-class queues and decompose it appropriately in three sub-regions. In each sub-region, we identify the fair scheduling policy along with the closed-form expression ($\beta^{Shapley}$). This enables us to identify the sub-region where global FCFS should be the fair scheduling policy and also the sub-regions where a class should be given higher dynamic priority over the others. We present our understanding through numerical illustrations for different stability regions.

1.1 Related Literature

Several papers discussed the application of cooperative game theory to multi-class single server queues. These included either optimized service capacity [5–7] or fixed service capacity [8,9]. In an optimized service system of a single-server queueing game, each player is associated with a customer arrival stream and an M/M/1 queue operated by a group of players, which provides service to the members of arrival streams [10]. Gonzalez et al. [5] considered a cost-allocation problem of shared medical services. They assumed any coalition optimizes it's own service rate with respect to constraints of sojourn time. Under this assumption, they defined core allocation. Garcia-Sanz et al. [6] analyzed variations of the model proposed by Gonzalez et al. [5]. They considered more generic constraints of sojourn time and constraints on the mean waiting time of a queue. Yu et al. [7] considered game theoretic settings to analyze capacity sharing between different independent firms. Further, they modeled facilities as queueing systems. They showed conditions under which capacity sharing can be beneficial to the firms.

In the fixed service capacity of a single-server queueing game, each player has it's service capacity endowment and this can be modeled as a potential service rate [10]. Anily and Haviv [8] considered M/M/1 queueing systems and modeled it as a TU game when servers merge their capacities or each coalition of players pools these endowments into a single-server M/M/1 queueing setup. They analyzed the value of that coalition. Another paper Anily et al. [9] analyzed models with single-server situations for fixed network form. They also discussed redistribution of combined service capacity in network structure of M/M/1 queueing system. To the best of our knowledge, single server queues have not been analyzed for general service time distribution which we address in this paper. Another significant advancement in this paper includes the analysis of several game-theoretic solution concepts whereas literature often deals with a single solution concept [5,11,12].

Along with these several papers also discussed game-theoretic model in the context of resource pooling. Resource pooling has been analyzed by Armony et al. [13] and Liu et al. [11]. Armony et al. [13] developed game-theoretic model to evaluate the performance of pooling when servers strategically selects their capacity. Liu and Yu [11] also designed a multi-server queueing game and described shared services. They used the concept of Polymatroidal structure and found lower priority firms get subsidized by higher priority firms also sometimes lower priority firms can get net positive rewards which incentivizes them to collaborate. In these papers researchers mainly focused on shared services between independent firms. They modeled this scenario as a queueing system and analyzed them using cooperative game theory.

This paper is organized as follows: Sect. 2 describes the game theoretic model of N-class queueing system. Section 3 completely analyzes 2-class queueing games and several solutions. Section 4 provides a summary and discusses relevant future research directions.

2   Model Description

In this section, we discuss a cooperative game theoretic model for multi-class queues. Let's consider a multi-class M/G/1 queue with N number of classes. Some of the classes may have a higher priority over the other classes. We consider *non-preemptive* priority rules where customers with higher priority may not interrupt service of lower priority customers and higher priority class customers have to wait till the service completion of lower priority customers. And these priorities may be static (strict) or dynamic (based on the number or delay of each class). One of the possibilities for static priority is the case where class 1 has strict (non-preemptive) priority over class 2, class 2 has strict priority over class 3 and so on. There are $N!$ such permutations possible. Let Π denote the set of all such scheduling policies and $\mathbb{E}(W_i^\pi)$ be the mean waiting time of class i under the policy $\pi \in \Pi$.

Let the class i customers arrive according to the Poisson process with the rate λ_i, $i = 1, 2, \cdots, N$; let μ be the finite service rate for each class of customers. The load factor for class i will be $\rho_i = \lambda_i/\mu$ and $\rho = \sum_{i=1}^{N} \rho_i$. We model the above multi-class queue as N-player cooperative game, described below. In this game, each player corresponds to a class of multi-class queuing systems. We refer N player cooperative game as N-class game in this paper.

2.1   N-class Game

We model the N-class queueing system as a Transferable Utility (TU) game with each class being considered as a player. Let $(\mathcal{P}, v)$ be a TU game with $\mathcal{P} = \{1, \cdots, N\}$ as the set of players and $v : 2^N \to \mathbb{R}$ as the worth functions of players. $v(\{S\})$ represents the worth of coalition $S, S \subseteq \mathcal{P}$. From the properties of TU game, the worth function of the null set is zero, i.e., $v(\{\phi\}) = 0$. We define the worth function of player i (class i), the worth function of a possible coalition set $S \subseteq \mathcal{P}$, and the worth function of the grand coalition $\mathcal{G}$ as follows:

$$v(\{i\}) = \left(\rho_i \sum_{\pi \in \mathcal{N}_i} \mathbb{E}(W_i^\pi) \right), \tag{1}$$

$$v(\{S\}) = \frac{\sum\limits_{i \in S} [\rho_i \sum\limits_{\pi \in \mathcal{N}_S} \mathbb{E}(W_i^\pi)]}{|S|!}, S \subseteq \mathcal{P}, \tag{2}$$

$$v(\{\mathcal{G}\}) = \frac{\sum\limits_{i \in N} [\rho_i \sum\limits_{\pi \in \Pi} \mathbb{E}(W_i^\pi)]}{|\mathcal{G}|!}, \tag{3}$$

where $\mathcal{N}_i \subset \Pi$ are the set of policies such that player i has the highest priority and $\mathcal{N}_S$ will be the set of policies where players in set S have higher priority,

$\mathcal{N}_S = \cup_{\{i \in S\}} \mathcal{N}_i$. We now illustrate the scheduling policies in $\mathcal{N}_i, i = 1, \cdots, N$ and $\mathcal{N}_S$ for 2−class and 3−class games.

1. For a 2−class game $\mathcal{N}_1$ is a set of policies where player 1 has higher priority, $\mathcal{N}_1 = \{12\}$. Similarly, $\mathcal{N}_2$ will be $\{21\}$. Now consider the set $S = \{1, 2\}$, $\mathcal{N}_S$ is a set of policies where players 1 and 2 have higher priorities, $\mathcal{N}_S = \{12, 21\}$. Here policy 12 indicates that class 1 has higher static priority over class 2 and vice-versa for 21.
2. For 3−class game, $\mathcal{N}_1 = \{123, 132\}$, $\mathcal{N}_2 = \{213, 231\}$ and $\mathcal{N}_3 = \{312, 321\}$. Consider $S = \{1, 2\}$. Thus, $\mathcal{N}_S$ will be the set of policies such that class 1 or 2 has the highest priority. For this game, $\mathcal{N}_{\{1,2\}} = \{123, 132, 213, 231\}$. Similarly, $\mathcal{N}_{\{2,3\}} = \{213, 231, 312, 321\}$ and $\mathcal{N}_{\{3,1\}} = \{312, 321, 123, 132\}$.

2.2 Importance of Worth Functions in N-class Game

We determine the worth function of an individual class by the sum of mean waiting times under the policies where the class has the highest priority. This is because of the selfish nature of the individual players. Further, this sum is multiplied by the load factor of that class. The load factor multiplication ensures that a player can only value policies that give it an absolute priority.

Another important aspect of our worth function of a coalition $(S \subset \mathcal{G})$ is that we consider weighted average waiting time under the scheduling policies $(\pi \in \mathcal{N}_S)$ where classes in a coalition are given higher priority. We are considering the highest priorities of players in the coalition because of the selfish nature of players in the coalition. The weights are given in terms of the load factor of the respective class. This is also in line with the worth function of the individual players.

For the grand coalition instead of taking participants of the coalition, we consider all the players in the game. Federgruen and Groenevelt [12] analyzed the performance of a queuing system by considering priority class queues where several leagues are formed. These leagues are different subsets of N. In the above game description, the leagues have similarities to the coalition. We now present the motivation behind the above worth functions. The grand coalition in Eq. (3) can be rewritten as follows since $|\Pi| = N!$.

$$v(\{\mathcal{G}\}) = \frac{\rho_1 \left[\mathbb{E}(W_1^{\pi_1}) + \cdots + \mathbb{E}(W_1^{\pi_{N!}}) \right] + \cdots + \rho_N \left[(\mathbb{E}(W_N^{\pi_1}) + \cdots + \mathbb{E}(W_N^{\pi_{N!}}) \right]}{|\mathcal{G}|!},$$

on rewriting the above expression by collecting the mean waiting time for each scheduling policy $\pi_1, \pi_2, \cdots, \pi_{N!}$, we have

$$v(\{\mathcal{G}\}) = \frac{\left[\rho_1 \mathbb{E}(W_1^{\pi_1}) + \cdots + \rho_N \mathbb{E}(W_N^{\pi_1}) \right] + \cdots + \left[\rho_1 \mathbb{E}(W_1^{\pi_{N!}}) + \cdots + \rho_N \mathbb{E}(W_N^{\pi_{N!}}) \right]}{|\mathcal{G}|!}.$$

From Kleinrock's conservation law [1], we have

$$\sum_{i=1}^{N} \rho_i \mathbb{E}(W_i^{\pi}) = \frac{\rho W_0}{1 - \rho} \ \forall \ \pi \in \Pi, \tag{4}$$

where, $W_0 = \sum_{i=1}^{N} \frac{\lambda_i}{2}[\sigma^2 + \frac{1}{\mu^2}]$ and σ^2 is variance of service time. We can now further simplify $v(\{\mathcal{G}\})$ using the above conservation law:

$$v(\{\mathcal{G}\}) = \frac{N!(\rho W_0)}{N!(1-\rho)} = \frac{\rho W_0}{1-\rho},$$

which is the right-hand side of Kleinrock's conservation law in Eq. (4). Therefore, we can say that the worth of the grand coalition is independent of scheduling policies.

We intend to explore several solution concepts from cooperative game theory and find out a fair scheduling policy for each solution concept in the above game. We now illustrate the results with the 2−class game in the next section.

3   2-class Game Illustration

In this section, we consider a 2−class game, i.e., $N = 2$. The set of players is $\mathcal{P} = \{1, 2\}$ and there are a total 2! scheduling policies. Let $\pi_1 = \{12\}$ and $\pi_2 = \{21\}$ be these two scheduling policies where player 1 (class 1) and player 2 (class 2) have strict priorities respectively. Note that $\Pi = \{\pi_1, \pi_2\}$. Let $v(\{1\})$, $v(\{2\})$ and $v(\{12\})$ are the worth functions for players 1, 2, and the grand coalition $\mathcal{G}$ respectively. By using the definition of N-class game from Eq. (1)-(3) worth functions of player 1, player 2 and, the grand coalition are as follows:

$$v(\{1\}) = \rho_1 \mathbb{E}(W_1^{12}), \tag{5}$$

$$v(\{2\}) = \rho_2 \mathbb{E}(W_2^{21}), \tag{6}$$

$$v(\{12\}) = \frac{\rho_1 \left[\mathbb{E}(W_1^{12}) + \mathbb{E}(W_1^{21})\right] + \rho_2 \left[\mathbb{E}(W_2^{12}) + \mathbb{E}(W_2^{21})\right]}{2}. \tag{7}$$

We now show below that the worth function of the grand coalition is higher than the addition of individual worth functions, i.e.,

$$v(\{12\}) > v(\{1\}) + v(\{2\}).$$

This implies that there is an incentive for players to collaborate. The mean waiting time expressions for class 1 and class 2 under policy $\{12\}$ and $\{21\}$ are as follows (see [14]):

$$\mathbb{E}(W_1^{12}) = \frac{W_0}{(1-\rho_1)} \quad \text{and} \quad \mathbb{E}(W_1^{21}) = \frac{W_0}{(1-\rho_2)(1-\rho)}, \tag{8}$$

$$\mathbb{E}(W_2^{21}) = \frac{W_0}{(1-\rho_2)} \quad \text{and} \quad \mathbb{E}(W_2^{12}) = \frac{W_0}{(1-\rho_1)(1-\rho)}. \tag{9}$$

Now, from the above equations we got the followings:

$$v(\{1\}) = \frac{\rho_1 W_0}{(1-\rho_1)}, \quad v(\{2\}) = \frac{\rho_2 W_0}{(1-\rho_2)}, \quad v(\{12\}) = \frac{\rho W_0}{(1-\rho)}.$$

We have,

$$v(\{1\}) + v(\{2\}) = \frac{\rho W_0 - \rho_1 \rho_2 W_0}{(1 - \rho) + \rho_1 \rho_2}.$$

Therefore, $v(\{12\}) > v(\{1\}) + v(\{2\})$ as $\rho_1 > 0, \rho_2 > 0$ and $W_0 > 0$.

Convexity of 2-Class Game: We prove below that the 2−class game is convex. A TU game is convex if it follows supermodularity, which is

$$v(\{C \cup D\}) + v(\{C \cap D\}) \geq v(\{C\}) + v(\{D\}), \ \forall \ C, \ D \subseteq \mathcal{P}.$$

For the above 2−class game, we verify all the possible subsets of C and D $(C \subset D, D \subset C, C = D, C \cap D = \phi)$. It follows that, $v(\{C \cup D\}) + v(\{C \cap D\}) \geq v(\{C\}) + v(\{D\})$. Therefore, we can say the 2−class game is convex. Now we explore the core in the next subsection.

3.1   The Core

The core is a solution concept from cooperative game theory which includes all the possible allocations which are coalitional and collectively rational. It follows from the convexity of the game that the core is non-empty [15] (see page 424). The following proposition presents the complete characterization of all allocations in the core for the 2−class game.

Proposition 1. *For 2-class game, the core, $\mathcal{C}(\mathcal{P}, v)$, is non-empty and a set given by:*

$$\mathcal{C}(\mathcal{P}, v) = \left\{ (x_1, x_2) : \frac{\rho_1 W_0}{(1 - \rho_1)} \leq x_1 \leq \frac{\rho_1 W_0}{(1 - \rho_2)(1 - \rho)}, \ x_1 + x_2 = \frac{\rho W_0}{(1 - \rho)} \right\}.$$

Proof. See Appendix A

Remark 1. *In the 2-class game, the addition of core allocations is right hand side of Kleinrock's conservation law, i.e., $x_1 + x_2 = \dfrac{\rho W_0}{1 - \rho}$.*

We now explore the Shapley value solution concept for this 2−class game.

3.2   Shapley Value

Shapley value is an axiomatic solution concept in cooperative game theory that faithfully provides the marginal contribution of each player. The following proposition provides the Shapley value allocation for the 2−class game.

Proposition 2. *For the 2-class game, the Shapley value allocation for class 1, $\phi_1(v)$, and class 2, $\phi_2(v)$, are respectively given by*

$$\phi_1(v) = \frac{W_0 \rho_1}{2} \left[\frac{\rho \rho_2 + 2(1 - \rho)}{(1 - \rho_1)(1 - \rho_2)(1 - \rho)} \right], \tag{10}$$

$$\phi_2(v) = \frac{W_0 \rho_2}{2} \left[\frac{\rho \rho_1 + 2(1 - \rho)}{(1 - \rho_1)(1 - \rho_2)(1 - \rho)} \right]. \tag{11}$$

Proof. See Appendix A

Corollary 1. *In the 2-class game, the player with a higher load factor gets the higher Shapley value allocation and vice-versa.*

Proof. From Eqs. (10) and (11), we note that the Shapley values are dependent on the load factor of the respective and the other player. We also note that the denominator of Shapley values is the same and non-negative as $0 < \rho_1 < 1$ and $0 < \rho_2 < 1$ from the stability of queues. If $\rho_1 > \rho_2$ then $\phi_1 > \phi_2$. Similarly, if $\rho_2 > \rho_1$ then $\phi_2 > \phi_1$. Therefore, the corollary holds.

Corollary 2. *In the 2-class game, the addition of Shapley values is right hand side of the Kleinrock's conservation law, i.e., $\phi_1(v) + \phi_2(v) = \dfrac{\rho W_0}{1 - \rho}$.*

Proof. The result immediately follows from Proposition 2.

3.3   Fair Scheduling Policies

A fair scheduling policy is one that results in a fair mean waiting time for each class. The fairness of mean waiting times can be determined by the cooperative game-theoretic solution concepts. We exploit Remark 1 and Corollary 2 to obtain a fair scheduling policy from the core and Shapley value-based solution concepts respectively in the 2−class game.

Shapley Value-Based Fair Scheduling Policy. Note that the Kleinrock's conservation law for two classes is given by (under the scheduling policy π):

$$\rho_1 \mathbb{E}(W_1^\pi) + \rho_2 \mathbb{E}(W_2^\pi) = \frac{\rho W_0}{1 - \rho}. \tag{12}$$

From Corollary 2, we have

$$\phi_1(v) + \phi_2(v) = \frac{\rho W_0}{1 - \rho}. \tag{13}$$

The above expression can be rewritten as follows in view of the comparison of the above two.

$$\rho_1 \hat{\phi}_1(v) + \rho_2 \hat{\phi}_2(v) = \frac{\rho W_0}{1 - \rho}, \tag{14}$$

where $\hat{\phi}_1(v) = \dfrac{W_0[\rho\rho_2 + 2(1 - \rho)]}{2(1 - \rho_1)(1 - \rho_2)(1 - \rho)}$ and $\hat{\phi}_2(v) = \dfrac{W_0[\rho\rho_1 + 2(1 - \rho)]}{2(1 - \rho_1)(1 - \rho_2)(1 - \rho)}$.

We are interested in exploring a scheduling policy $\pi^{Shapley}$ that schedules the customers in such a way that the mean waiting times for class 1 and class 2 under the scheduling policy $\pi^{Shapley}$ becomes $\hat{\phi}_1(v)$ and $\hat{\phi}_2(v)$ respectively. We exploit Delay dependent priority (DDP) queues to determine $\pi^{Shapley}$. DDP queues are the dynamic priority rules based on the delay of customers in queues [2]. The delay dependent priority scheduling is shown to be complete, i.e., it achieves all possible vectors of mean waiting times for 2−class queue (see [4]) under non-preemptive, non-anticipating and work conserving scheduling policy. Thus, we use DDP to find $\pi^{Shapley}$. The average waiting times for class 1 and class 2 under DDP scheduling policy is as follows [2,4,16–18]:

$$\mathbb{E}[W_1^{DDP}(\beta)] = \frac{W_0(1 - \rho(1 - \beta))}{(1 - \rho)(1 - \rho_1(1 - \beta))}1_{\{\beta \leq 1\}} + \frac{W_0}{(1 - \rho)(1 - \rho_2(1 - \frac{1}{\beta}))}1_{\{\beta > 1\}},$$
(15)

$$\mathbb{E}[W_2^{DDP}(\beta)] = \frac{W_0}{(1 - \rho)(1 - \rho_1(1 - \beta))}1_{\{\beta \leq 1\}} + \frac{W_0(1 - \rho(1 - \frac{1}{\beta}))}{(1 - \rho)(1 - \rho_2(1 - \frac{1}{\beta}))}1_{\{\beta > 1\}},$$
(16)

where $1_{\{.\}}$ is an indicator function and β is a parameter that determines the scheduling policy. $\beta := b_2/b_1$ where b_1 and b_2 are the weights associated with class 1 and class 2 respectively. $b_1 = 0$ implies strict higher priority to class 2 and it indicates $\beta = \infty$. On the other hand, $b_2 = 0$ implies strict higher priority to class 1 and it indicates $\beta = 0$. It has been shown in [4] that $0 \leq \beta \leq \infty$ achieves all possible vectors of mean waiting time, i.e., completeness of DDP. The following proposition finds the fair DDP scheduling policy parameter ($\beta^{Shapley}$) that schedules according to $\pi^{Shapley}$.

Proposition 3. *In the 2-class game, the DDP scheduling parameter $\beta^{Shapley}$ that achieves the fair scheduling policy $\pi^{Shapley}$ is given by:*

$$\beta^{Shapley} = \frac{(2 - \rho)(1 - \rho_1)}{\rho\rho_1 + 2(1 - \rho)}1_{\{\rho_1 \geq \rho_2\}} + \frac{\rho\rho_2 + 2(1 - \rho)}{(2 - \rho)(1 - \rho_2)}1_{\{\rho_1 < \rho_2\}}.$$
(17)

Proof. See Appendix A

We have the following interpretation of the above proposition.

1. When load factors are equal, i.e., $\rho_1 = \rho_2$, $\beta^{Shapley}$ turns out to be 1. This implies global FCFS scheduling policy.
2. When load factor for class 1 is higher than that of class 2, i.e., $\rho_1 > \rho_2$, $0 < \beta^{Shapley} < 1$. This implies class 1 has higher dynamic priority than class 2.
3. When the load factor for class 2 is higher than that of class 1, i.e., $\rho_2 > \rho_1$, $1 < \beta^{Shapley} < \infty$. This implies class 2 has a higher dynamic priority than class 1.
4. At the extreme case when class 1 achieves the highest load factor ($\rho_1 \to 1$) then $\beta^{Shapley} \to 0$. This implies static high priority to class 1.
5. At another extreme case when class 2 achieves the highest load factor ($\rho_2 \to 1$) then $\beta^{Shapley} \to \infty$. This implies static high priority to class 2.

In Fig. 1, we discuss the fair scheduling policy allocation based on Shapley value for the entire stability region ($\rho_1 + \rho_2 < 1$). This stability region is divided into three sub-regions: 1) $\rho_1 > \rho_2$ 2) $\rho_1 < \rho_2$ 3) $\rho_1 = \rho_2$. The stability region

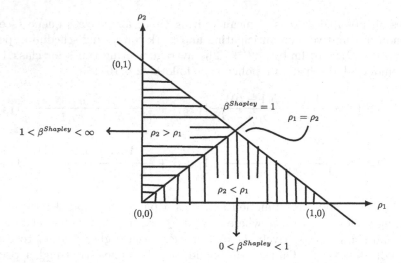

Fig. 1. Fair scheduling policy based on Shapley value, $\beta^{Shapley}$, within the stability region ($\rho_1 + \rho_2 < 1$)

$\rho_1 > \rho_2$ is shown by the bottom triangle. In this sub-region, $0 < \beta^{Shapley} < 1$, indicates higher dynamic priority to class 1. Another sub-region ($\rho_1 < \rho_2$) indicates the upper triangle in Fig. 1. Inside this sub-region ($1 < \beta^{Shapley} < \infty$), indicates higher dynamic priority to class 2. The third sub-region indicates a line ($\rho_1 = \rho_2$). In this sub-region, $\beta^{Shapley} = 1$ which implies global FCFS scheduling policy.

We now present the numerical experiments to illustrate the above. In Fig. 2, we illustrate the above point (1) where both the classes have equal load factors ($\rho_1 = \rho_2$). In this case, we observe $\beta^{Shapley} = 1$ and it coincides with global FCFS scheduling policy. The parameter settings are mentioned in the caption. In all the figures, square and cross represent the scheduling policies corresponding to $\beta^{Shapley}$ and global FCFS respectively. Figure 3 illustrates the above point (2) where $\rho_1 > \rho_2$. In this case, $\beta^{Shapley}$ turns out to be 0.54 which is between 0 and 1 as expected. Note that the mean waiting time corresponding to the global FCFS scheduling policy is shifting towards policy 21 ($\beta = \infty$). This is expected as the implication of increased load factor from class 1 implies global FCFS to behave in the same way as policy 21. Figure 4 illustrates the case where $\rho_2 > \rho_1$. In this case, $\beta^{Shapley}$ turns out to be 3.24 which is larger than 1 as expected. Note that the mean waiting time corresponds to the scheduling policy $\beta^{Shapley}$ is the middle point of the waiting times corresponding to policies 12 and 21. This can be verified mathematically from the expression of $\hat{\phi}_i(v), i = 1, 2$, and the mean waiting time expressions in (8) and (9).

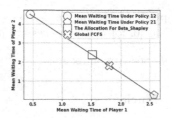

Fig. 2. Policy illustration for $\rho_1 = \rho_2$. Parameter settings: $\lambda_1 = \lambda_2 = 2$ and $\mu = 5$.

Fig. 3. Policy illustration for $\rho_1 > \rho_2$. Parameter settings: $\lambda_1 = 3$, $\lambda_2 = 1$ and $\mu = 5$.

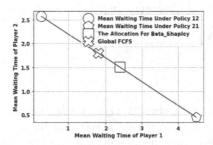

Fig. 4. Policy illustration for $\rho_1 < \rho_2$. Parameter settings: $\lambda_1 = 1, \lambda_2 = 3.8$ and $\mu = 5$.

Core Based Fair Scheduling Policy. Note that Kleinrock's conservation law for two classes is given by (under the scheduling policy π):

$$\rho_1\mathbb{E}(W_1^\pi) + \rho_2\mathbb{E}(W_2^\pi) = \frac{\rho W_0}{1 - \rho}. \tag{18}$$

From Remark 1, we have

$$x_1 + x_2 = \frac{\rho W_0}{1 - \rho}. \tag{19}$$

The above expression can be rewritten as follows in view of the comparison of the above two.

$$\rho_1\hat{x}_1 + \rho_2\hat{x}_2 = \frac{\rho W_0}{1 - \rho}, \tag{20}$$

where $\frac{W_0}{(1 - \rho_1)} \leq \hat{x}_1 \leq \frac{W_0}{(1 - \rho_2)(1 - \rho)}$ and $\hat{x}_2 = \frac{1}{\rho_2}\frac{\rho W_0}{(1-\rho)} - \frac{\rho_1\hat{x}_1}{\rho_2}$. We are interested in exploring a scheduling policy π^{Core} that schedules the customers in such a way that the mean waiting times for class 1 and class 2 under the scheduling policy π^{Core} becomes $\hat{x}_1$ and $\hat{x}_2$ respectively. We again consider DDP scheduling policy since it is complete. The following proposition finds the range of fair DDP scheduling policy parameter (β^{Core}) that schedules according to π^{Core}.

Proposition 4. *In the 2-class game, the range of DDP scheduling parameter* $\beta^{Core} \in [0, \infty]$ *that achieves the fair scheduling policy* π^{Core}.

Proof. See Appendix A

3.4   Nucleolus

Nucleolus is a solution concept in cooperative game theory which minimizes the maximum excess (unhappiness) of the most unhappy coalition, the second most unhappy coalition, and so on. Since the core is non-empty (see proposition 1), nucleolus belongs to the core and it is unique [15] (see page 455).

Proposition 5. *For the 2-class game nucleolus is the Shapley value.*

Proof. See Appendix A

4   Discussion

We considered a generic multi-class M/G/1 queuing system and designed a cooperative game theoretic setup to obtain a fair scheduling policy. We completely characterized the 2-class game using solution concepts such as Shapley value, the core, and nucleolus. We showed Shapley value and nucleolus to be the same for 2−class game. Also, the waiting cost allocations by the Shapley value and the core respect Kleinrock's conservation law.

The major contribution of our paper is to determine fair scheduling policy by exploiting Kleinrock's delay dependent priority for 2−class queues. We partition the entire stability region into three parts: 1) $\rho_1 > \rho_2$, 2) $\rho_1 < \rho_2$ and 3) $\rho_1 = \rho_2$. And obtain a fair scheduling scheme in each sub-region. We obtain a closed-form expression of fair scheduling policy parameter associated with Shapley value $(\beta^{Shapley})$ and a range of β associated with the core (β^{Core}).

This model can be extended in several ways. Firstly, we can extend this model to N-class queueing system with different service rates/distributions for each class and explore a fair scheduling policy for this. Secondly, we can consider a queueing network, where multiple servers are present with multiple queue classes. In this complex scenario, obtaining a fair scheduling policy is another interesting future avenue.

A   Proofs

Proof of Proposition 1: It follows that for any convex game the core is non-empty and the nucleolus belongs to the core [15] (See page 424 and 455). As we already proved this is a Convex Game. so, the core is non-empty and the nucleolus belongs to the core. Also, Shapley value belongs to the core. From [15] (see page 416) the core, $\mathcal{C}(\mathcal{P}, v) = \{x = (x_1, \cdots, x_n) \in \mathbb{R}^n : \sum_{i=1}^{n} x_i = v(\{N\}); \sum_{i \in C} x_i \geq$

$v(\{C\}), \forall\ C \subseteq \mathcal{P}\}$. For 2$-$class game the core is $\mathcal{C}(\mathcal{P}, v) = \{x = (x_1, x_2) \in \mathbb{R}^2 : \sum_{i=1}^{2} x_i = v(\{N\}); \sum_{i \in C} x_i \geq v(\{C\}), \forall\ C \subseteq \mathcal{P}\}$. For this 2$-$class game by using Eqs. (1)-(3) we simplify write $x_1 \geq \dfrac{\rho_1 W_0}{(1 - \rho_1)}, x_2 \geq \dfrac{\rho_2 W_0}{(1 - \rho_2)}, x_1 + x_2 \geq \dfrac{\rho W_0}{(1 - \rho)}, x_2 = \dfrac{\rho W_0}{(1 - \rho)} - x_1$. From these expressions we get Proposition 1. ∎

Proof of Proposition 2: It follows that there exists exactly one mapping $\phi :$ $\mathbb{R}^{2^N - 1} \to \mathbb{R}^N$ that satisfies all three Axioms (Symmetry, Linearity, and Carrier) [15] (see page 432). This mapping satisfies

$$\phi_i(v) = \sum_{C \subseteq \mathcal{P} \backslash \{i\}} \frac{|C|!(N - |C| - 1)!}{N!} \Big\{ v(C \cup \{i\}) - v(C) \Big\} \ \forall\ i \in \mathcal{P},\ v \in \mathbb{R}^{2^N - 1}$$

where N is the total number of players. The above expression for $\phi_i(v)$ gives the expected contribution of player i to the worth of any coalition and is called Shapley value. For this 2$-$class game all the possible coalitions are $(\{\phi\}), (\{1\}), (\{2\})$ and $(\{12\})$. From the above expression, the Shapley values of player 1 and player 2 are:

$$\phi_1(v) = \frac{1}{2} \left[v(\{1\}) + v(\{12\}) - v(\{2\}) \right],$$

$$\phi_2(v) = \frac{1}{2} \left[(v(\{2\}) + v(\{12\}) - v(\{1\})) \right].$$

Now from Eqs. (1, 2, 3) and mean waiting time expressions we simplify the Shapley value of player 1 and player 2 as given in the proposition. ∎

Proof of Proposition 3: Using Eqs. (18) and (20) we can write $\hat{\phi}_1 = \mathbb{E}(W_1^\beta)$ and $\hat{\phi}_2 = \mathbb{E}(W_2^\beta)$. From Eqs. (15) and (16) mean waiting time for class 1 and class 2 under DDP are as follows:

$$\mathbb{E}[W_1^{DDP}(\beta)] = \frac{W_0(1 - \rho(1 - \beta))}{(1 - \rho)(1 - \rho_1(1 - \beta))} 1_{\{\beta \leq 1\}} + \frac{W_0}{(1 - \rho)(1 - \rho_2(1 - \frac{1}{\beta}))} 1_{\{\beta > 1\}},$$

$$\mathbb{E}[W_2^{DDP}(\beta)] = \frac{W_0}{(1 - \rho)(1 - \rho_1(1 - \beta))} 1_{\{\beta \leq 1\}} + \frac{W_0(1 - \rho(1 - \frac{1}{\beta}))}{(1 - \rho)(1 - \rho_2(1 - \frac{1}{\beta}))} 1_{\{\beta > 1\}},$$

Now by comparing $\hat{\phi}_1$ and $\hat{\phi}_2$ with the mean waiting time of class 1 and class 2 under DDP for $\beta \leq 1$ we get the following:

$$\frac{W_0[\rho \rho_2 + 2(1 - \rho)]}{2(1 - \rho_1)(1 - \rho_2)(1 - \rho)} = \frac{W_0(1 - \rho(1 - \beta^{Shapley}))}{(1 - \rho)(1 - \rho_1(1 - \beta^{Shapley}))}$$

and

$$\frac{W_0[\rho \rho_1 + 2(1 - \rho)]}{2(1 - \rho_1)(1 - \rho_2)(1 - \rho)} = \frac{W_0}{(1 - \rho)(1 - \rho_1(1 - \beta^{Shapley}))}$$

Similarly, for $\beta > 1$ we get the following:

$$\frac{W_0[\rho\rho_2 + 2(1-\rho)]}{2(1-\rho_1)(1-\rho_2)(1-\rho)} = \frac{W_0}{(1-\rho)(1-\rho_2(1-\frac{1}{\beta^{Shapley}}))}$$

and

$$\frac{W_0[\rho\rho_1 + 2(1-\rho)]}{2(1-\rho_1)(1-\rho_2)(1-\rho)} = \frac{W_0(1-\rho(1-\frac{1}{\beta^{Shapley}}))}{(1-\rho)(1-\rho_2(1-\frac{1}{\beta^{Shapley}}))}$$

Compiling all the results we get the outcome mentioned in Proposition 3.   ∎

Proof of Proposition 4: From Eq. (15) and (16) mean waiting time for class 1 and class 2 under DDP are as follows:

$$\mathbb{E}[W_1^{DDP}(\beta)] = \frac{W_0(1-\rho(1-\beta))}{(1-\rho)(1-\rho_1(1-\beta))}1_{\{\beta \leq 1\}} + \frac{W_0}{(1-\rho)(1-\rho_2(1-\frac{1}{\beta}))}1_{\{\beta>1\}},$$

$$\mathbb{E}[W_2^{DDP}(\beta)] = \frac{W_0}{(1-\rho)(1-\rho_1(1-\beta))}1_{\{\beta \leq 1\}} + \frac{W_0(1-\rho(1-\frac{1}{\beta}))}{(1-\rho)(1-\rho_2(1-\frac{1}{\beta}))}1_{\{\beta>1\}},$$

For the 2-class game The Core expression we got, $x_1 \geq \frac{\rho_1 W_0}{(1-\rho_1)}, x_2 \geq \frac{\rho_2 W_0}{(1-\rho_2)}, x_1 + x_2 \geq \frac{\rho W_0}{(1-\rho)}, x_2 = \frac{\rho W_0}{(1-\rho)} - x_1$. Now by comparing the mean waiting time for class 1 under DDP with Core allocation of class 1 (x_1) and mean waiting time for class 2 under DDP with Core allocation of class 2 (x_2) we get the following:

$$\frac{W_0}{(1-\rho)(1-\rho_1(1-\beta^{Core}))} \geq \frac{W_0}{(1-\rho_1)}, \beta^{Core} \leq 1$$

$$\frac{W_0}{(1-\rho)(1-\rho_2(1-\frac{1}{\beta^{Core}}))} \geq \frac{W_0}{(1-\rho_2)}, \beta^{Core} > 1$$

After simplifying the above inequalities we get the ranges of β as mentioned in this proposition.   ∎

Proof of Proposition 5: Let's assume Nucleolus is Shapley value (ϕ_1, ϕ_2). Now excess of coalition 1, $e(1, \phi_1) = v(1) - \phi_1$ and excess of coalition 2, $e(2, x) = v(2) - \phi_2$. Excess of the grand coalition, $e(12, \phi) = 0$. We found $e(1, \phi_1) = e(2, \phi_2) = \frac{-\rho_1\rho_2 W_0(2-\rho)}{2(1-\rho_1)(1-\rho_2)(1-\rho)}$. Now suppose there are any other allocations (x_1^*, x_2^*), that can further reduce $e(1, \phi_1)$ and $e(2, \phi_2)$. It means $v(\{1\}) - x_1^* < v(\{1\}) - \phi_1$ and $v(\{2\}) - x_2^* < v(\{2\}) - \phi_2$. This implies $x_1^* > \phi_1$ and $x_2^* > \phi_2$ which cannot be true as $\phi_1 + \phi_2 = \frac{\rho W_0}{1-\rho}$. Thus Shapley value is Nucleolus.

References

1. Kleinrock, L.: A conservation law for a wide class of queueing disciplines. Naval Res. Logistics Q. **12**(2), 181–192 (1965)
2. Kleinrock, L.: A delay dependent queue discipline. Naval Res. Logistics Q. **11**(3–4), 329–341 (1964)
3. Mitrani, I., Hine, J.H.: Complete parameterized families of job scheduling strategies. Acta Informatica **8**(1), 61–73 (1977)
4. Gupta, M.K., Hemachandra, N., Venkateswaran, J.: Some parameterized dynamic priority policies for two-class M/G/1 queues: completeness and applications. ACM Trans. Model. Perform. Eval. Comput. Syst. (TOMPECS) **5**(2), 1–37 (2020)
5. González, P., Herrero, C.: Optimal sharing of surgical costs in the presence of queues. Math. Methods Oper. Res. **59**(3), 435–446 (2004)
6. García-Sanz, M.D., Fernández, F.R., Fiestras-Janeiro, M.G., García-Jurado, I., Puerto, J.: Cooperation in markovian queueing models. Eur. J. Oper. Res. **188**(2), 485–495 (2008)
7. Yu, Y., Benjaafar, S., Gerchak, Y.: Capacity sharing and cost allocation among independent firms with congestion. Prod. Oper. Manag. **24**(8), 1285–1310 (2015)
8. Anily, S., Haviv, M.: Cooperation in service systems. Oper. Res. **58**(3), 660–673 (2010)
9. Anily, S., Haviv, M.: Homogeneous of Degree One Games are Balanced with Applications to Service Systems. Tel Aviv University, Faculty of Management, The Leon Recanati Graduate (2011)
10. Karsten, F., Slikker, M., Van Houtum, G.-J.: Resource pooling and cost allocation among independent service providers. Oper. Res. **63**(2), 476–488 (2015)
11. Liu, H., Yu, Y.: Incentives for shared services: multiserver queueing systems with priorities. Manuf. Serv. Oper. Manag. **24**(3), 1751–1759 (2022)
12. Federgruen, A., Groenevelt, H.: M/G/c queueing systems with multiple customer classes: characterization and control of achievable performance under nonpreemptive priority rules. Manage. Sci. **34**(9), 1121–1138 (1988)
13. Armony, M., Roels, G., Song, H.: Pooling queues with strategic servers: the effects of customer ownership. Oper. Res. **69**(1), 13–29 (2021)
14. Gelenbe, E., Mitrani, I.: Analysis and Synthesis of Computer Systems, vol. 4. World Scientific, Singapore (2010)
15. Narahari, Y.: Game Theory and Mechanism Design, vol. 4. World Scientific, Singapore (2014)
16. Kleinrock, L.: Queueing Systems, vol. 1. Wiley-Interscience, Hoboken (1975)
17. Kanet, J.J.: A mixed delay dependent queue discipline. Oper. Res. **30**(1), 93–96 (1982)
18. Sinha, S.K., Rangaraj, N., Hemachandra, N.: Pricing surplus server capacity for mean waiting time sensitive customers. Eur. J. Oper. Res. **205**(1), 159–171 (2010)

Queueing Models

System Content Analysis for a Two-Class Queue Where Service Times in a Busy Period Depend on the Presence of Class-2

Sara Sasaninejad[✉][iD], Joris Walraevens, Hossein Moradi,
and Sabine Wittevrongel

SMACS Research Group, Department of Telecommunications and Information
Processing, Ghent University, Ghent, Belgium
{Sara.Sasaninejad,Joris.Walraevens,Hossein.Moradi,
Sabine.Wittevrongel}@ugent.be

Abstract. Since many real-world queueing systems are meant to incorporate heterogeneous customers, the analysis of multi-class queueing models has been an area of active research. A review of the associated models shows, however, that multi-class queueing systems in which service times depend on the presence of one certain class of customers have not yet been extensively analyzed. To address this research gap, we consider an infinite-capacity single-server discrete-time queueing system with two classes of customers (say *class-1* and *class-2*). We assume that the scheduling discipline in our work is FCFS. We assume that if we have at least one *class-2* customer during an ongoing busy period (until the system becomes empty), the service time distributions of all the customers change to the service time distribution of a *class-2* customer. By further considering the number of customer arrivals of each class to be independent and identically distributed (with a general probability distribution) from slot to slot, we perform the system content analysis by means of a generating function based approach. The results of this analysis reveal that the incorporation of such an interdependency in the service process significantly affects the resulting system content, as compared to a model where the service times are completely attached to the customer classes.

Keywords: Multi-class queueing systems · Dependent service times · System content

1 Introduction

Multi-class queueing models have been widely studied in the queueing theory literature. Such multi-class models allow to take into account nonidentical behaviors of different classes of customers entering a queueing system at the same time [1]. In multi-class queueing systems, various classes of customers can also receive

E. Hyytiä and V. Kavitha (Eds.): VALUETOOLS 2022, LNICST 482, pp. 51–66, 2023.
https://doi.org/10.1007/978-3-031-31234-2_4

different treatments [2]. Some studies on multi-class systems in the literature mainly focus on considering different kinds of class-dependent arrival character-istics for customers (e.g., [3–6]). Other studies focus more on class-dependent service time specifications (e.g., [7–10]) or consider different kinds of queueing disciplines that allow the preferential treatment of a certain class of customers (e.g., [11–15]). In our paper, we focus on a special kind of service time speci-fication where a particular interdependency is introduced between the service time distributions of different customers, namely by letting the service time dis-tribution be dependent on the presence of a certain class of customers in the system during the ongoing busy period. To the best of the authors' knowledge, no analysis of a multi-class queueing system with such interdependency has been reported so far in the literature.

To address the indicated research gap, we work in a discrete-time setting. This means that time is assumed to be divided into time slots of equal length and, therefore, the service time of a customer is defined by the number of slots of service that the customer requires [16]. We consider a two-class system in which the service time distribution varies depending on the presence of *class-2* customers during an ongoing busy period. To be more specific, during the ongoing busy period, if there were no *class-2* customers in our queueing system, then all customers would have a service time distribution of *type-1*. However, as soon as at least one *class-2* customer is or has been present in the system during the busy period, then as long as the system does not become empty, all customers will have a service time distribution of *type-2*. The scheduling discipline in our work is FCFS.

This research is initially motivated by the lack of analytic models considering differences among various types of vehicles in traffic. As a case in point, we know that the presence of a freight vehicle during a busy period leads to a slowdown for all vehicles sharing the same road. To mathematically model such a phenomenon in this paper, we first develop an analytical technique to derive the distribution and moments of the system content in a two-class queueing system with the non-classical service process explained above. Then, in order to evaluate the effect of the particular interdependency between service times, we compare the obtained results in terms of the mean system content for our model to those of a corresponding conventional two-class queueing model represented in [17], where service times are completely attached to the customer classes.

The organization of the paper is as follows. Section 2 explains the specific assumptions of our considered two-class queueing model and states the main system equations describing the behavior of the system. Section 3 presents our performed analysis to obtain an expression for the probability generating func-tion of the system content in steady state. Section 4 illustrates the obtained results through some numerical examples. Section 5 enumerates the main con-clusions.

2   Queueing Model and System Equations

As is mentioned earlier, we assume two classes of customers (i.e., *class-1* and *class-2* customers) arriving in an infinite-capacity single-server queueing system (defined in the discrete-time domain) that serves the customers in FCFS order. The random variable $a_{j,k}$ represents the number of arrivals of *class-j customers* ($j = 1, 2$) in the kth slot. The numbers of customer arrivals of both classes are assumed to be independent and identically distributed (with a general probability distribution) from slot to slot and are characterized by the joint probability mass function

$$a(m, n) \triangleq \Pr[a_{1,k} = m, \, a_{2,k} = n], \tag{1}$$

and the joint probability generating function (PGF)

$$A(z_1, z_2) \triangleq \mathrm{E}[z_1^{a_{1,k}} z_2^{a_{2,k}}] = \sum_{m=0}^{\infty} \sum_{n=0}^{\infty} \Pr[a_{1,k} = m, \, a_{2,k} = n] z_1^m z_2^n. \tag{2}$$

The marginal PGF of the number of *class-1* (*class-2*) customer arrivals per slot is given by $A_1(z) = A(z, 1)$ ($A_2(z) = A(1, z)$). The PGF of the total number of *class-1* and *class-2* customer arrivals is given by $A_T(z) = A(z, z)$. The arrival rate λ_j for *class-j* is given by $A_j'(1)$ (recall that $j = 1$ or $j = 2$).

Each customer has a service time requirement of a given number of slots. This service time can start (only) at slot boundaries. As explained in Sect. 1, the service process depends on the presence of *class-2* customers during an ongoing busy period. During the ongoing busy period, if there were no *class-2* customers in the queueing system, all customers (of *class-1*) have a service time distribution of *type-1*, characterized by the PGF $S_1(z)$. Otherwise, as soon as at least one *class-2* customer is or has been present in the system during the ongoing busy period, all customers (both those of *class-1* and *class-2*) that are still to be taken into service during the busy period before the system becomes vacant, will have a service time distribution of *type-2*, characterized by the PGF $S_2(z)$. Note that *class-2* customers will therefore always have a service time PGF $S_2(z)$, while the service time PGF for a *class-1* customer can be either $S_1(z)$ or $S_2(z)$ depending on the presence of a *class-2* customer during the ongoing busy period.

We now define the random variable X_k as the total number of customers in the system at the beginning of slot k. Furthermore, we introduce R_k as the remaining service time (expressed as a number of slots) of the in-service customer (if any) at the beginning of slot k (we assume $R_k = 0$ if $X_k = 0$). Note that $R_k \geq 1$ if $X_k > 0$. Finally, we define the random variable I_k as the indicator of having had a *class-2* customer in the system during the ongoing busy period. More specifically, $I_k = 1$ if during the ongoing busy period there is or has already been at least one *class-2* customer in the system at the beginning of slot k and $I_k = 0$ otherwise. With these definitions, the vector (I_k, R_k, X_k) is easily seen to constitute a three-dimensional Markovian state description of the system at the beginning of slot k. Indeed, we can establish a set of system equations that describe the relationship between the vectors (I_k, R_k, X_k) and

$(I_{k+1}, R_{k+1}, X_{k+1})$. To do so, depending on the values of I_k, X_k and $a_{2,k}$, we distinguish five different cases:

- If $I_k = 0$ and $a_{2,k} > 0$ then $I_{k+1} = 1$.
- If $I_k = 0$ and $a_{2,k} = 0$ then $I_{k+1} = 0$.
- If $I_k = 1$ and $X_k > 0$ then $I_{k+1} = 1$.
- If $I_k = 1$, $X_k = 0$ and $a_{2,k} > 0$ then $I_{k+1} = 1$.
- If $I_k = 1$, $X_k = 0$ and $a_{2,k} = 0$ then $I_{k+1} = 0$.

If we now introduce the random variables S_1 and S_2 with PGFs $S_1(z)$ and $S_2(z)$ respectively, then the following state equations can be written for these five different cases:

- Case 1: If $I_k = 0$ and $a_{2,k} > 0$ then $I_{k+1} = 1$.
    - If $R_k = 0$ (and, hence, $X_k = 0$):

$$\begin{cases} X_{k+1} = a_{1,k} + a_{2,k}, \\ R_{k+1} = S_2. \end{cases} \tag{3}$$

    - If $R_k = 1$ (and, hence, $X_k > 0$):

$$\begin{cases} X_{k+1} = X_k - 1 + a_{1,k} + a_{2,k}, \\ R_{k+1} = S_2. \end{cases} \tag{4}$$

    - If $R_k > 1$ (and, hence, $X_k > 0$):

$$\begin{cases} X_{k+1} = X_k + a_{1,k} + a_{2,k}, \\ R_{k+1} = R_k - 1. \end{cases} \tag{5}$$

- Case 2: If $I_k = 0$ and $a_{2,k} = 0$ then $I_{k+1} = 0$.
    - If $R_k = 0$ (and, hence, $X_k = 0$):

$$\begin{cases} X_{k+1} = a_{1,k}, \\ R_{k+1} = \begin{cases} 0 & \text{if } a_{1,k} = 0, \\ S_1 & \text{if } a_{1,k} > 0. \end{cases} \end{cases} \tag{6}$$

    - If $R_k = 1$ (and $X_k > 0$):

$$\begin{cases} X_{k+1} = X_k - 1 + a_{1,k}, \\ R_{k+1} = \begin{cases} 0 & \text{if } X_k = 1 \text{ and } a_{1,k} = 0, \\ S_1 & \text{if } X_k > 1 \text{ or } a_{1,k} > 0. \end{cases} \end{cases} \tag{7}$$

    - If $R_k > 1$ (and $X_k > 0$):

$$\begin{cases} X_{k+1} = X_k + a_{1,k}, \\ R_{k+1} = R_k - 1. \end{cases} \tag{8}$$

– Case 3: If $I_k = 1$ and $X_k > 0$ then $I_{k+1} = 1$.
  • If $R_k = 1$:

$$\begin{cases} X_{k+1} = X_k - 1 + a_{1,k} + a_{2,k}, \\ R_{k+1} = \begin{cases} 0 & \text{if } X_k = 1 \text{ and } a_{1,k} + a_{2,k} = 0, \\ S_2 & \text{if } X_k > 1 \text{ or } a_{1,k} + a_{2,k} > 0. \end{cases} \end{cases} \quad (9)$$

  • If $R_k > 1$:

$$\begin{cases} X_{k+1} = X_k + a_{1,k} + a_{2,k}, \\ R_{k+1} = R_k - 1. \end{cases} \quad (10)$$

– Case 4: If $I_k = 1$, $X_k = 0$ and $a_{2,k} > 0$ then $I_{k+1} = 1$; we only have $R_k = 0$.

$$\begin{cases} X_{k+1} = a_{1,k} + a_{2,k}, \\ R_{k+1} = S_2. \end{cases} \quad (11)$$

– Case 5: If $I_k = 1$, $X_k = 0$ and $a_{2,k} = 0$ then $I_{k+1} = 0$; we only have $R_k = 0$.

$$\begin{cases} X_{k+1} = a_{1,k}, \\ R_{k+1} = \begin{cases} 0 & \text{if } a_{1,k} = 0, \\ S_1 & \text{if } a_{1,k} > 0. \end{cases} \end{cases} \quad (12)$$

3 Queueing Analysis

The goal of this section is to derive an expression for the PGF of the system content at the beginning of a slot in steady state. To perform the analysis, we first define $P_k(x, z)$ as the joint PGF of the vector (R_k, X_k) by

$$P_k(x, z) - \mathrm{E}[x^{R_k} z^{X_k}] = \sum_{i=0}^{\infty} \sum_{j=0}^{\infty} \Pr[R_k = i, X_k = j] x^i z^j, \quad (13)$$

where $\mathrm{E}[.]$ indicates the expected value of the expression within the square brackets.

Furthermore, we introduce the partial PGFs $P_{i,k}(x, z)$ as

$$P_{i,k}(x, z) = \mathrm{E}[x^{R_k} z^{X_k} | I_k = i] \Pr[I_k = i] \quad , \text{i=0,1.} \quad (14)$$

Clearly, the joint PGF $P_k(x, z)$ can then be expressed as $P_k(x, z) = P_{0,k}(x, z) + P_{1,k}(x, z)$. Since $R_k = 0$ if and only if $X_k = 0$, we have also

$$P_{i,k}(x, 0) = P_{i,k}(0, 0), \quad \text{for all } x, \quad (15)$$

which will be used later in the analysis.

The next step in our analysis is now to derive relationships between the functions $P_{0,k}(x, z)$ and $P_{1,k}(x, z)$ for slot k and the functions $P_{0,k+1}$ and $P_{1,k+1}$ for slot $k + 1$ by using the system equations shown in Eqs. (3) to (12). We note that case 2 and case 5 of the system equations lead to $I_{k+1} = 0$. Accordingly, we can express $P_{0,k+1}(x, z)$ in terms of $P_{0,k}(x, z)$ and $P_{1,k}(x, z)$ based on cases 2 and 5. We proceed as follows:

$$
\begin{aligned}
P_{0,k+1}(x, z) =&\, \mathrm{E}[x^{R_{k+1}} z^{X_{k+1}} | I_{k+1} = 0]\,\Pr[I_{k+1} = 0] \\
=&\, \Pr[I_k = R_k = X_k = 0]\,\Pr[a_{1,k} = a_{2,k} = 0] \\
&+ \Pr[I_k = R_k = X_k = 0]\,\Pr[a_{1,k} > 0, a_{2,k} = 0] \\
&\quad \mathrm{E}[x^{S_1} z^{a_{1,k}} | a_{2,k} = 0, a_{1,k} > 0] \\
&+ \Pr[I_k = 0, R_k = X_k = 1]\,\Pr[a_{1,k} = a_{2,k} = 0] \\
&+ \Pr[I_k = 0, R_k = 1, X_k - 1 + a_{1,k} > 0, a_{2,k} = 0] \\
&\quad \mathrm{E}[x^{S_1} z^{X_k - 1 + a_{1,k}} | I_k = 0, R_k = 1, X_k - 1 + a_{1,k} > 0, a_{2,k} = 0] \\
&+ \Pr[I_k = 0, R_k > 1, X_k > 0]\,\Pr[a_{2,k} = 0] \\
&\quad \mathrm{E}[x^{R_k - 1} z^{X_k + a_{1,k}} | I_k = 0, R_k > 1, X_k > 0, a_{2,k} = 0] \\
&+ \Pr[I_k = 1, R_k = X_k = 0]\,\Pr[a_{1,k} = a_{2,k} = 0] \\
&+ \Pr[I_k = 1, R_k = X_k = 0]\,\Pr[a_{1,k} > 0, a_{2,k} = 0] \\
&\quad \mathrm{E}[x^{S_1} z^{a_{1,k}} | a_{2,k} = 0, a_{1,k} > 0],
\end{aligned}
\tag{16}
$$

where we also used the independence of (I_k, R_k, X_k) and $(a_{1,k}, a_{2,k})$ at places.

We can further work out Eq. (16) by using the definitions (2) and (14). This leads to

$$
\begin{aligned}
P_{0,k+1}(x, z) =&\, P_{0,k}(0,0)A(0,0) \\
&+ P_{0,k}(0,0)\big[A(z,0) - A(0,0)\big]S_1(x) \\
&+ F_{0,k}(0)A(0,0) \\
&+ \big[F_{0,k}(z)A(z,0) - F_{0,k}(0)A(0,0)\big]S_1(x) \\
&+ \frac{A(z,0)}{x}\big[P_{0,k}(x,z) - xzF_{0,k}(z) - P_{0,k}(0,0)\big] \\
&+ P_{1,k}(0,0)A(0,0) \\
&+ P_{1,k}(0,0)\big[A(z,0) - A(0,0)\big]S_1(x),
\end{aligned}
\tag{17}
$$

where the function $F_{i,k}(z)$ is defined as

$$
F_{i,k}(z) = \mathrm{E}[z^{X_k - 1} | I_k = i, R_k = 1, X_k > 0]\,\Pr[I_k = i, R_k = 1, X_k > 0].
\tag{18}
$$

In a similar way, we can also express $P_{1,k+1}(x, z)$ in terms of $P_{0,k}(x, z)$ and $P_{1,k}(x, z)$, by noting that cases 1, 3 and 4 of the system equations all lead to

$I_{k+1} = 1$. As a result, we then obtain

$$
\begin{aligned}
P_{1,k+1}(x, z) =& \mathrm{E}[x^{R_{k+1}} z^{X_{k+1}} | I_{k+1} = 1] \Pr[I_{k+1} = 1] \\
=& \Pr[I_k = R_k = X_k = 0] \Pr[a_{2,k} > 0] \mathrm{E}[x^{S_2} z^{a_{1,k}+a_{2,k}} | a_{2,k} > 0] \\
& + \Pr[I_k = 0, R_k = 1, X_k > 0] \Pr[a_{2,k} > 0] \\
& \quad \mathrm{E}[x^{S_2} z^{X_k-1+a_{1,k}+a_{2,k}} | I_k = 0, R_k = 1, X_k > 0, a_{2,k} > 0] \\
& + \Pr[I_k = 0, R_k > 1, X_k > 0] \Pr[a_{2,k} > 0] \\
& \quad \mathrm{E}[x^{R_k-1} z^{X_k+a_{1,k}+a_{2,k}} | I_k = 0, R_k > 1, X_k > 0, a_{2,k} > 0] \\
& + \Pr[I_k = R_k = X_k = 1] \Pr[a_{1,k} = a_{2,k} = 0] \\
& + \Pr[I_k = R_k = 1, X_k - 1 + a_{1,k} + a_{2,k} > 0] \\
& \quad \mathrm{E}[x^{S_2} z^{X_k-1+a_{1,k}+a_{2,k}} | I_k = R_k = 1, X_k - 1 + a_{1,k} + a_{2,k} > 0] \\
& + \Pr[I_k = 1, R_k > 1, X_k > 0] \\
& \quad \mathrm{E}[x^{R_k-1} z^{X_k+a_{1,k}+a_{2,k}} | I_k = 1, R_k > 1, X_k > 0] \\
& + \Pr[I_k = 1, R_k = X_k = 0] \Pr[a_{2,k} > 0] \mathrm{E}[x^{S_2} z^{a_{1,k}+a_{2,k}} | a_{2,k} > 0].
\end{aligned}
\tag{19}
$$

With the definitions (2), (14) and (18), Eq. (19) then simplifies into

$$
\begin{aligned}
P_{1,k+1}(x, z) =& P_{0,k}(0,0) \big[A(z, z) - A(z, 0) \big] S_2(x) \\
& + S_2(x) F_{0,k}(z) \big[A(z, z) - A(z, 0) \big] \\
& + \frac{A(z, z) - A(z, 0)}{x} \big[P_{0,k}(x, z) - xz F_{0,k}(z) - P_{0,k}(0,0) \big] \\
& + F_{1,k}(0) A(0,0) \\
& + S_2(x) \big[F_{1,k}(z) A(z, z) - F_{1,k}(0) A(0,0) \big] \\
& + \frac{A(z, z)}{x} \big[P_{1,k}(x, z) - xz F_{1,k}(z) - P_{1,k}(0,0) \big] \\
& + P_{1,k}(0,0) \big[A(z, z) - A(z, 0) \big] S_2(x).
\end{aligned}
\tag{20}
$$

Given the above calculations, Eq. (17) provides a relationship between the functions $P_{0,k}$, $P_{1,k}$ and $P_{0,k+1}$ and Eq. (20) provides a relationship between $P_{0,k}$, $P_{1,k}$ and $P_{1,k+1}$. Once a steady state is reached, the functions $P_{i,k}$ and $F_{i,k}$ ($i = 0, 1$) converge to limiting functions (for k going to infinity):

- $P_0(x, z) = \lim_{k \to \infty} P_{0,k}(x, z) = \lim_{k \to \infty} P_{0,k+1}(x, z)$,
- $P_1(x, z) = \lim_{k \to \infty} P_{1,k}(x, z) = \lim_{k \to \infty} P_{1,k+1}(x, z)$,
- $F_0(z) = \lim_{k \to \infty} F_{0,k}(z) = \lim_{k \to \infty} F_{0,k+1}(x, z)$,
- $F_1(z) = \lim_{k \to \infty} F_{1,k}(z) = \lim_{k \to \infty} F_{1,k+1}(x, z)$.

Under the assumption of stationary distributions and after some simplifications, Eq. (17) can be rewritten as

$$
\begin{aligned}
P_0(x, z) = \frac{1}{x - A(z,0)} \Big\{ &\big[(xS_1(x) - 1)A(z,0) - xA(0,0)(S_1(x) - 1)\big] P_0(0,0) \\
&+ \big[xS_1(x)A(z,0) - xA(0,0)(S_1(x) - 1)\big] P_1(0,0) \\
&+ \big[xA(0,0)(1 - S_1(x))\big] F_0(0) \\
&+ \big[xA(z,0)(S_1(x) - z)\big] F_0(z) \Big\}.
\end{aligned}
$$

$$(21)$$

The same approach holds for Eq. (20) that after some simplifications can be rewritten as

$$
\begin{aligned}
P_1(x, z) = \frac{1}{(x - A(z,z))(x - A(z,0))} \Big\{ &\Big[\big((S_1(x) - S_2(x))A(z,0) \\
&+ (1 - S_1(x))A(0,0) + xS_2(x) - 1)x(A(z,z) - A(z,0))\big) \Big] P_0(0,0) \\
&+ \Big[-x(S_1(x) - S_2(x))A(z,0)^2 + \big((xS_1(x) - xS_2(x) + 1)A(z,z) \\
&- x((1 - S_1(x))A(0,0) + xS_2(x))\big)A(z,0) \\
&+ \Big((1 - S_2(x))A(0,0) + xS_2(x) - 1\Big)xA(z,z)\Big] P_1(0,0) \\
&+ \big[xA(0,0)(1 - S_1(x))(A(z,z) - A(z,0))\big] F_0(0) \\
&+ \Big[\big((S_2(x) - S_1(x))A(z,0) + x(z - S_2(x))\big)(A(z,0) - A(z,z))x\Big] F_0(z) \\
&+ \big[xA(0,0)(1 - S_2(x))(A(z,0) + x)\big] F_1(0) \\
&+ \big[xA(z,z)(z - S_2(x))(A(z,0) - x)\big] F_1(z) \Big\}.
\end{aligned}
$$

$$(22)$$

In Eqs. (21) and (22), $F_0(z)$ and $F_1(z)$ are unknown functions and $P_0(0,0)$, $P_1(0,0)$, $F_0(0)$, and $F_1(0)$ are the unknown constants that should still be determined. We now explain the derivation of these unknowns in three subsequent steps. In the first step, to find $P_0(0,0)$ and $P_1(0,0)$, we use Eq. (15). Imposing this condition in Eq. (21) for $z = 0$, we obtain

$$
P_0(0,0)\big[1 - A(0,0)\big] = A(0,0)\big[F_0(0) + P_1(0,0)\big].
$$

$$(23)$$

Similarly, by applying Eq. (15) in Eq. (22) for $z = 0$, we find

$$
P_1(0,0) = F_1(0)A(0,0).
$$

$$(24)$$

Notice that in Eqs. (23) and (24), $P_0(0,0)$ and $P_1(0,0)$ are derived based on $F_0(0)$ and $F_1(0)$.

In the second step, we find the functions $F_0(z)$ and $F_1(z)$. Given definition (14), we know that the partial PGF $P_0(x, z)$ must be bounded for all possible values of x and z, such that $|x| < 1$ and $|z| < 1$. Specifically, this should hold for $x = A(z,0)$ and $|z| < 1$, since $|A(z,0)| < 1$ for all such z. Therefore, if we choose $x = A(z,0)$ in Eq. (21), the denominator vanishes. Then the same must be true for the numerator of Eq. (21) (in which we have considered both Eqs. (23) and (24)). This way, we can find $F_0(z)$ in terms of $F_0(0)$ and $F_1(0)$:

$$F_0(z) = \frac{S_1(A(z,0))A(0,0)}{A(z,0)\big(1 - A(0,0)\big)\big(S_1(A(z,0) - z\big)}$$
$$\left[\big(1 - A(z,0)\big)F_0(0) + \big(A(0,0) - A(z,0)\big)F_1(0)\right].$$

(25)

Similarly, in Eq. (22), we can see that if $x = A(z,0)$ and/or $x = A(z,z)$, the denominator of Eq. (22) becomes zero. If we substitute x with $A(z,0)$ in the numerator of Eq. (22), we see that the numerator becomes zero as well. However, if we choose $x = A(z,z)$, the denominator of Eq. (22) becomes zero but the numerator does not automatically become zero. Again, we know that with respect to Eq. (14), $P_1(x,z)$ must be bounded for all possible values of x and z such that $|x| < 1$ and $|z| < 1$. Therefore, the numerator of Eq. (22) should become zero if we choose $x = A(z,z)$. After some calculations and using the Eqs. (21)-(25), we can find $F_1(z)$ in terms of $F_0(0)$ and $F_1(0)$ as

$$F_1(z) =$$
$$\frac{1}{A(z,z)A(z,0)(-1 + A(0,0))(z - S_2(A(z,z)))(z - S_1(A(z,0)))}$$
$$\left\{\left[-\big(-(A(z,0) - A(z,z))(zA(z,0) - S_1(A(z,0)))S_2(A(z,z))\right.\right.$$
$$\left.+ z(A(z,0) - 1)(A(z,0)S_1(A(z,z)) - A(z,z)S_1(A(z,0))))A(0,0)\right]F_0(0)$$
$$\left[A(0,0)(((-A(z,0) + A(z,z)A(0,0))S_1(A(z,0)) - (-A(z,0)\right.$$
$$+ A(z,z) - 1 + A(0,0))A(z,0)z)S_2(A(z,z))$$
$$\left.+ z(A(0,0) - A(z,0))(A(z,0)S_1(A(z,z)) - A(z,z)S_1(A(z,0))))\right]F_1(0)\right\}.$$

(26)

In the last step, we determine the two remaining unknown constants $F_0(0)$ and $F_1(0)$. To this end, we first utilize the normalization condition, which should be met for $P_0(x,z) + P_1(x,z)$. Accordingly, $P_0(1,1) + P_1(1,1)$ should be equal to 1 in order to have a normalized distribution. After applying $P_0(1,1) + P_1(1,1) = 1$ and using L'Hôp ital's rule (twice), we find

$$P_0(1,1) + P_1(1,1) =$$

$$\frac{1}{[(-1+S_2'(1))(\lambda_1+\lambda_2)(-1+S_1(A(1,0)))(-1+A(0,0))]}$$

$$\cdot \left\{ [F_0(0) + F_1(0)] [S_1(A(1,0)) - (S_1'(1) - S_2'(1))A(1,0)] \right. \tag{27}$$

$$F_1(0) [(S_1'(1) - S_2'(1))A(0,0) - 1]$$

$$\left. + F_0(0) [S_1'(1) - S_2'(1) - 1] \right\} A(0,0) = 1,$$

in which λ_1 is the arrival rate of *class-1* customers and λ_2 is the arrival rate of *class-2* customers. Eq. (27) provides a first relationship between $F_0(0)$ and $F_1(0)$. To arrive at a second relation between these unknowns, we now focus our attention on the PGF $X(z)$ of the total number of customers in the system at the beginning of a slot in steady state. According to the equations developed above, $X(z)$ can easily be found as $X(z) = P(1,z) = P_0(1,z) + P_1(1,z)$.

Setting $x = 1$ in Eqs. (21) and (22) and using the results shown in Eqs. (23)–(26), we obtain

$$X(z) =$$

$$\frac{A(0,0)(z-1)}{[(z - S_2(A(z,z)))(z - S_1(A(z,0)))(-1+A(0,0))(A(z,z) - 1)]}$$

$$\left\{ [F_0(0) + F_1(0)] \left[\left((A(z,z) - 1)S_1(A(z,0)) - z(A(z,z) - A(z,0)) \right) \right. \right.$$

$$\left. S_2(A(z,z)) - zS_1(A(z,z))A(z,0) \right] + F_1(0) \left[(-z(-1+A(0,0)) \right.$$

$$\left. S_2(A(z,z)) + zS_1(A(z,z))A(0,0) \right] + F_0(0) \left[zS_1(A(z,z)) \right] \right\}.$$

$$\tag{28}$$

We know that the PGF $X(z)$ must be bounded for all possible values of z with $|z| \leq 1$. Note that the denominator of the right-hand side of Eq. (28) has a unique zero inside the complex unit circle; this can be proved by Rouché's theorem. Let us define this unique zero by z_r; it is characterized by the following equation:

$$z_r - S_1(A(z_r, 0)) = 0, \quad \text{with} \quad |z_r| < 1. \tag{29}$$

Since $X(z)$ is analytic inside the complex unit circle, the numerator of $X(z)$ should also be zero for $z = z_r$. This property leads to

$$\left[\left(-F_0(0) - F_1(0) \right) A(z_r, 0) + F_1(0)A(0,0) + F_0(0) \right] A(0,0)z_r(z_r - 1)$$

$$\left(S_1(A(z_r, z_r)) - S_2(A(z_r, z_r)) \right) = 0, \tag{30}$$

which is the second relationship between $F_0(0)$ and $F_1(0)$ we were looking for. The two last unknown constants $F_0(0)$ and $F_1(0)$ can then be found by solving

Eqs. (27) and (30) (two equations and two unknowns). Accordingly,

$$F_0(0) =$$

$$\frac{-\Big(A(0,0) - A(z_r,0)\Big)\Big(-1 + S_1(A(1,0))\Big)\Big(S_1'(1)\lambda_1 + S_2'(1)\lambda_2 - 1\Big)}{A(0,0)\Big((S_1'(1) - S_2'(1))\Big(A(1,0) - A(z_r,0)\Big) + 1 - S_1(A(1,0))\Big)}$$

(31)

and

$$F_1(0) =$$

$$\frac{\Big(A(z_r,0) - 1\Big)\Big(-1 + S_1(A(1,0))\Big)\Big(S_1'(1)\lambda_1 + S_2'(1)\lambda_2 - 1\Big)}{A(0,0)\Big((S_1'(1) - S_2'(1))\Big(A(1,0) - A(z_r,0)\Big) + 1 - S_1(A(1,0))\Big)}.$$

(32)

With the results for $F_0(0)$ and $F_1(0)$, the expressions for $P_0(x,z)$, $P_1(x,z)$ and $X(z)$ are now completely determined. Based on the PGF $X(z)$, we can then also calculate moments of the system content. In particular, we can calculate the average number of customers in the system $E[X]$ by

$$E[X] = \frac{dX(z)}{dz}\bigg|_{z=1}.$$

(33)

4   Numerical Results

In this section, we present some numerical examples to illustrate how the considered interdependency in the service process impacts the average system content. To do so, we assume here that the total number of customer arrivals is independent and identically distributed from slot to slot and follows a Bernoulli distribution, i.e., $A_T(z) = 1 - \lambda + \lambda z$, where λ is the total arrival rate. Moreover, we assume that each arrival belongs to one of the two classes with a given probability, independently from customer to customer. Let α be the probability that an arriving customer is a *class-2* customer; $1 - \alpha$, then, indicates the probability that an arriving customer belongs to *class-1*. Under these assumptions, the joint PGF $A(z_1, z_2)$ of the arrival process becomes

$$A(z_1, z_2) = 1 - \lambda + \lambda(\alpha z_2 + (1 - \alpha)z_1),$$

(34)

In Sect. 3, we obtained Eqs. (28), (31), (32), and (33) to calculate the PGF and the average value of the total number of customers in the system at the beginning of a slot in steady state. Based on these equations, the average number of customers in the system depends on (1) the arrival rate of each type of customers (i.e., α and λ in Eq. (34)) and (2) the two types of service time distributions (i.e., the PGFs $S_1(z)$ and $S_2(z)$). To study the basic effects of these parameters, we further focus on the case where all service times have a fixed length of (dependent on their type) either S_1 or S_2 slots, i.e., we consider $S_1(z) = z^{S_1}$ and $S_2(z) = z^{S_2}$. In order to show the effects of these parameters on the average number of customers in the system, Figs. 1 and 2 are developed. Figure 1 illustrates the change of the average system content with respect to the parameter λ by assuming in (a) $S_1 = 1$, $S_2 = 2$ and in (b) $S_1 = 2$, $S_2 = 1$. Figure 2 presents the change of the average system content with respect to the parameter α by assuming in (a) $S_1 = 1$, $S_2 = 2$, and in (b) $S_1 = 2$, $S_2 = 1$.

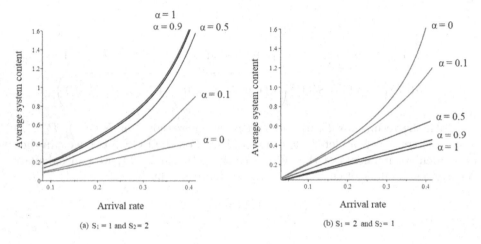

(a) $S_1 = 1$ and $S_2 = 2$

(b) $S_1 = 2$ and $S_2 = 1$

Fig. 1. Average system content versus arrival rate λ in case of (a) $S_1 = 1$, $S_2 = 2$ and (b) $S_1 = 2$, $S_2 = 1$

First, it is trivial to see in all the above figures that the average number of customers in the system increases in case of higher arrival rates (as expected). In Fig. 1(a) and Fig. 2(a), for the case of $S_1 = 1$ and $S_2 = 2$ (i.e., in case service times are twice as long when at least one *class-2* customer has been present in the system during the ongoing busy period), we see that a higher α as well as a higher λ results in an increase in the average number of customers in the system. Notice that a higher α means a higher probability of having a *class-2* customer in the system during the ongoing busy period and relatively more *class-2* customers on average. Given the imposed interdependency between service times and since $S_2 > S_1$, this result is also expected. On the contrary, in Fig. 1(b) and Fig. 2(b), we evaluate the case where $S_1 = 2$ and $S_2 = 1$, meaning that the service times are longer when no *class-2* customers have been present in the system. Accordingly, a higher α leads typically to a shorter service time for more customers. Therefore, we see a lower average system content for higher α in this case.

To compare our results with a conventional two-class model in which service times of different classes of customers are independent and completely attached to the customer classes, we use [17] in which the authors presented a multi-class

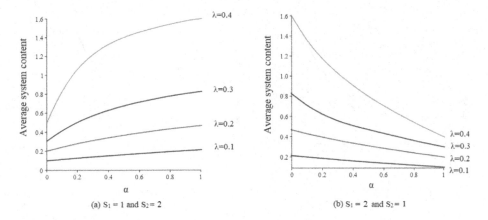

Fig. 2. Average system content versus α in case of (a) $S_1 = 1$, $S_2 - 2$ and (b) $S_1 = 2$, $S_2 = 1$

queueing model with a general arrival distribution and general service times. In Fig. 3, we compare the results of the model presented in [17] to those from our model, again considering the Bernoulli arrival distribution of Eq. (34) and fixed-length service times. For the conventional model, the latter means that all *class-1* customers receive a service time of S_1 slots, while the service time of *class-2* customers equals S_2 slots. Figure 3 shows that the conventional model cannot, in general, provide accurate estimations of the average system content in case there exists interdependency between the service times of different classes.

There are two different cases considered in Fig. 3. The first case compares the average system contents of the two models when $S_1 = 1$ and $S_2 = 2$. The same comparison is also carried out for $S_1 = 1$ and $S_2 = 5$ in the second case. Our comprehensive evaluation takes into account a range of α values. From Fig. 3, the following conclusions can be drawn:

- The effect of considering interdependency between service times of different classes of customers will vanish when α (the percentage of *class-2* customers) equals 0 or 1. When $\alpha = 0$, the model simplifies to a conventional queueing system where all customers have service time S_1. When $\alpha = 1$, the model simplifies to a conventional queueing system with service time S_2 for all customers.
- When $0 < \alpha < 1$, (see, for example, $\alpha = 0.1$, $\alpha = 0.5$, and $\alpha = 0.9$ in Fig. 3), our developed model shows higher average system contents compared to the conventional model.
- When $0 < \alpha < 1$, as the ratio of S_2 to S_1 increases, the mentioned differences become more tangible.

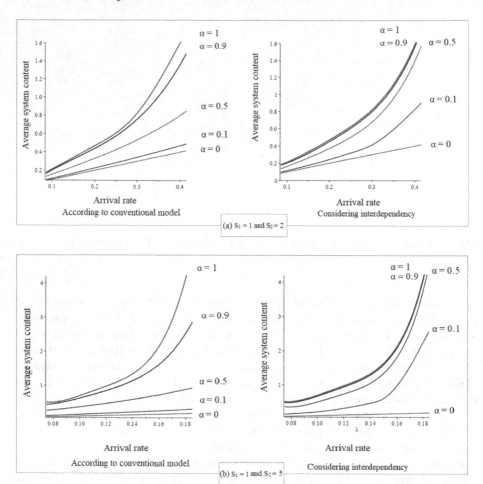

Fig. 3. Comparison between average system contents versus arrival rate λ calculated from a conventional model and from our developed formulas, for (a)$S_1 = 1$, $S_2 = 2$ and (b)$S_1 = 1$, $S_2 = 5$

5   Conclusions

In this paper, we have presented a discrete-time queueing model for evaluating the behavior of a multi-class queueing system in which service times are affected by the presence of a certain class of customers during an ongoing busy period. In this respect, we defined two different classes of customers (labeled by *class-1* customers and *class-2* customers) and two different types of service time distributions (with PGFs $S_1(z)$ and $S_2(z)$). When a *class-2* customer is or has been present during the current busy period, all service times for all customers will change to PGF $S_2(z)$. Otherwise, customer service times will have PGF $S_1(z)$. Under these assumptions, we developed an analytical formulation describing the average system content using a generating function technique. The carried out analysis confirms that the incorporation of heterogeneity of customers along with their associated service times whose values depend on the presence of a certain class of customers leads to considerable accuracy improvements over a conventional model where interdependency between the service times is not considered.

We are currently in the process of investigating the delay (average delay) a given class of customer (using this model) may tolerate.

Acknowledgments. This work was supported in part by an EOS grant from the Belgian Research Councils FWO and FNRS (grant number 30452698) and in part by a research project from the Flemish Research Council FWO (grant number 3G051118).

References

1. De Clercq, S., Steyaert, B., Bruneel, H.: Queue content analysis in a 2-class discrete-time queueing system under the slot-bound priority service rule. Math. Prob. Eng. **2012** (2012)
2. De Clercq, S., Laevens, K., Steyaert, B., Bruneel, H.: A multi-class discrete-time queueing system under the FCFS service discipline. Ann. Oper. Res. **202**(1), 59–73 (2013)
3. Baetens, J., Steyaert, B., Claeys, D., Bruneel, H.: Analysis of a batch-service queue with variable service capacity, correlated customer types and generally distributed class-dependent service times. Perform. Eval. **135**, 102012 (2019)
4. Walraevens, J., Bruneel, H., Fiems, D., Wittevrongel, S.: Delay analysis of multi-class queues with correlated train arrivals and a hybrid priority/FIFO scheduling discipline. Appl. Math. Model. **45**, 823–839 (2017)
5. Van Houdt, B., Blondia, C.: The delay distribution of a type k customer in a first-come-first-served MMAP [K]/PH[K]/1 queue. J. Appl. Probab. **39**, 213–223 (2002)
6. De Clercq, S., Walraevens, J.: Delay analysis of a two-class priority queue with external arrivals and correlated arrivals from another node. Ann. Oper. Res. **293**(1), 57–72 (2020)
7. Takine, T.: Single-server queues with Markov-modulated arrivals and service speed. Queueing Syst. **49**(1), 7–22 (2005)
8. Wittevrongel, S., Feyaerts, B., Bruneel, H., De Vuyst, S.: Delay characteristics in place-reservation queues with class-dependent service times. J. Ind. Manage. Optim. **15**(1), 37–58 (2019)
9. Boxma, O.J., Takine, T.: The M/G/1 FIFO queue with several customer classes. Queueing Syst. **45**(3), 185 (2003)
10. Kim, B., Kim, J.: Stability of a multi-class multi-server retrial queueing system with service times depending on classes and servers. Queueing Syst. **94**(1), 129–146 (2020)
11. Miller, R.G., Jr.: Priority queues. Ann. Math. Stat. **31**(1), 86–103 (1960)
12. Maertens, T., Walraevens, J., Bruneel, H.: Priority queueing systems: from probability generating functions to tail probabilities. Queueing Syst. **55**(1), 27–39 (2007)
13. Walraevens, J., Steyaert, B., Bruneel, H.: A preemptive repeat priority queue with resampling: performance analysis. Ann. Oper. Res. **146**(1), 189–202 (2006)

14. Fiems, D., Walraevens, J., Bruneel, H.: Performance of a partially shared priority buffer with correlated arrivals. In: Mason, L., Drwiega, T., Yan, J. (eds.) ITC 2007. LNCS, vol. 4516, pp. 582–593. Springer, Heidelberg (2007). https://doi.org/10.1007/978-3-540-72990-7_52

15. Maertens, T., Walraevens, J., Bruneel, H.: On priority queues with priority jumps. Perform. Eval. **63**(12), 1235–1252 (2006)

16. De Muynck, M., Bruneel, H., Wittevrongel, S.: Analysis of a queue with general service demands and correlated service capacities. Ann. Oper. Res. **293**(1), 73–99 (2020)

17. Bruneel, H., Kim, B.G.: Discrete-time models for communication systems including ATM. Kluwer Academic Publishers, Boston (1993)

Asymptotic Analysis of Modified Erlang-B System with Sensing Time and Stochastic Loss of Secondary Users

Kazuma Abe[1] and Tuan Phung-Duc[2]($\boxtimes$)

[1] Graduate School of Science and Technology, University of Tsukuba, 1-1-1, Tennoudai, Tsukuba, Ibaraki, Japan
abe.kazuma.su@alumni.tsukuba.ac.jp
[2] Institute of Systems and Information Engineering, University of Tsukuba, Tsukuba, Japan
tuan@sk.tsukuba.ac.jp

Abstract. This paper considers a modified Erlang-B model for cognitive radio networks with both primary users (PUs) and secondary users (SUs). PUs have absolute priority over SUs, and are blocked whenever all channels are used by other PUs upon their arrivals. SUs must sense an idle channel upon their arrivals. If, after sensing, an SU finds an idle channel, it can occupy the channel immediately; otherwise, the SU may either sense again or leave the system forever. Under Poisson arrival assumptions (both PUs and SUs) and exponential sensing and service times, we formulate the system as a three-dimensional Markov chain, and consider an asymptotic regime when the sensing rate is extremely low. We prove that a scaled version of the number of sensing SUs converges to a deterministic process. Furthermore, we prove that the deterministic process has a unique stationary point which we use to approximate the mean number of sensing SUs and the distribution of the states of the channels. Numerical examples reveal that these approximations are highly accurate when the sensing rate is low.

Keywords: Retrial Queue · Cognitive wireless networks (CRN) · Erlang-B model · ODE

1 Introduction

Today's communication network carries very high traffic, making it essential to allocate limited resources efficiently. Therefore, cognitive radio networks (CRN) are expected to play a vital role in developing and expanding next-generation networks that address the bandwidth shortage problem. In CRN, unlicensed devices or users can transmit on the channels of licensed devices or users to satisfy their own spectrum demands as long as they ensure that the interference thus

E. Hyytiä and V. Kavitha (Eds.): VALUETOOLS 2022, LNICST 482, pp. 67–80, 2023.
https://doi.org/10.1007/978-3-031-31234-2_5

caused does not interrupt the activities of the licensed users. These unlicensed users are known as secondary users (SUs), and licensed users are called primary users (PUs).

Three types of spectrum-sharing paradigms for cognitive radio networks are widely discussed [5]: overlay access, underlay access and interweave access. In overlay access, an SU cooperatively relays PU transmissions, permitting the SU to transmit its own data concurrently with a PU. Underlay access allows the SU to transmit simultaneously with a PU, provided that the interference quantity at the PU receiver due to SU transmissions is below some certain predefined threshold. In interweave access, the SUs can use a channel only when it is not occupied by any PU.

In this paper, we focus on interweave access. SUs must sense the available channels before using the frequency bands. If an SU discovers an idle channel after sensing, it can access the channel and start transmission; otherwise, the SU must sense again until it finds an idle channel later or leave the system.

Queueing systems for cognitive radio networks were extensively studied [9]. The SU sensing process is similar to the retrial process in queueing systems. In these systems, arriving customers are blocked when the servers are already fully occupied. These blocked customers instead enter a virtual waiting room called the orbit (the sensing pool in CRN), and try repeatedly after a random waiting time until they obtain a server. For example, [11] is based on a multi-server retrial queue. [13] considered a model with a stochastic choice of channels and a finite number of simultaneously sensing users (i.e., a finite sensing pool). [3] considered the assumption that a newly arriving priority customer is queued in the buffer when all channels are busy with other priority customers. In [10], the size of the sensing pool is infinite.

In this paper, applying the asymptotic method [4,6–8] to our model, we focus on the situation where it takes SUs a long time to sense channel availability. In this case, the number of SUs in the sensing pool diverges, but a scaled version of this number converges to a deterministic process. The limiting results are used to approximate the mean number of sensing SUs and the distribution of the channel states.

It turns out that the main results for the lossless model in [1] can be extended to the current model. In particular, the stability of the deterministic process coincides with that of the system's underlying Markov chain. Furthermore, the uniqueness of the stationary solution of the deterministic process is guaranteed, which is further used to approximate the mean number of sensing SUs in the steady state.

The paper consists of six sections. In Sect. 2, we introduce the mathematical model and preliminary analysis. We consider the first-order approximation of our model in Sect. 3. In Sect. 4, we prove the main results for the stability condition and the uniqueness of the stationary solution of the deterministic process. Section 5 compares simulation results with the approximation obtained in Sect. 3. We conclude with a summary synthesis in Sect. 6.

2   Model Description

In this section, we describe an Erlang-B system with two types of users. PUs and SUs arrive at the system of c servers according to Poisson processes with rates λ_1 and λ_2, respectively. The service times are exponentially distributed with parameters μ_1 and μ_2, for PUs and SUs respectively. The arrival processes of both user types and the service times are assumed to be mutually independent. If all of the c channels are occupied by other PUs, a newly arriving PU is blocked. Hence, the model can be treated as Erlang-B from PU's point of view. Arriving SUs must enter the sensing pool and sense for available channels. The sensing times of the SUs follow the exponential distribution with rate σ and do not depend on other SUs. When an SU finishes sensing and cannot find an available channel, there is a probability p that SU will stay in the pool for another sensing; otherwise, it leaves the system with probability $1 - p$. When a new PU arrives at the system where all c channels are occupied by other SUs and PUs, the PU terminates the transmission of an SU (if exists) and uses that channel. The interrupted SU must enter the sensing pool to sense again. The sensing pool is assumed infinite.

The model analyzed in [1] is the same as ours with $p = 1$. Note that the service time distribution of an interrupted SU is the same as that of a newly arrived SU because of the memorylessness property of exponential distributions.

Let us denote:

- $n_1(t)$: the number of PUs occupying channels at time t,
- $n_2(t)$: the number of SUs occupying channels at time t,
- $i(t)$: the number of SUs staying at the sensing pool at time t.

Let $P(n_1, n_2, i, t) = P\{n_1(t) = n_1, n_2(t) = n_2, i(t) = i\}$ be the joint probability distribution of the process $\{(n_1(t), n_2(t), i(t)) \mid t \geq 0\}$. Under the assumptions of the model, the process is a three-dimensional Markov chain. The transition rates from a state $x = (n_1, n_2, i)$ to another state y $(x \neq y)$ are given as follows.

$$q_{x,y} = \begin{cases} \lambda_1 & \text{if } y = (n_1 + 1, n_2, i), n_1 + n_2 \leq c - 1, \\ \lambda_1 & \text{if } y = (n_1 + 1, n_2 - 1, i + 1), n_1 + n_2 = c, n_2 \geq 1, \\ \lambda_2 & \text{if } y = (n_1, n_2, i + 1), \\ n_1 \mu_1 & \text{if } y = (n_1 - 1, n_2, i), n_1 \geq 1, \\ n_2 \mu_2 & \text{if } y = (n_1, n_2 - 1, i), n_2 \geq 1, \\ i\sigma & \text{if } y = (n_1, n_2 + 1, i - 1), n_1 + n_2 \leq c - 1, \\ (1 - p)i\sigma & \text{if } y = (n_1, n_2, i - 1), n_1 + n_2 = c, 0 \leq p \leq 1 \\ 0 & \text{otherwise.} \end{cases}$$

The purpose of the paper is to obtain the scaling limits of $(n_1(t), n_2(t))$ and $i(t)$. We solve this problem via the first-order approximation under the asymptotic condition when the sensing time is long: $\sigma \to 0$.

The Kolmogorov forward equations are:

(i) $n_1 + n_2 = 0$

$$\frac{dP(0,0,i,t)}{dt} = -(\lambda_1 + \lambda_2 + i\sigma)P(0,0,i,t) + \lambda_2 P(0,0,i-1,t)$$
$$+ \mu_1 P(1,0,i,t) + \mu_2 P(0,1,i,t).$$

(ii) $1 \le n_1 + n_2 \le c - 1$

$$\frac{dP(n_1,n_2,i,t)}{dt} = -(\lambda_1 + \lambda_2 + n_1\mu_1 + n_2\mu_2 + i\sigma)P(n_1,n_2,i,t)$$
$$+ \lambda_2 P(n_1,n_2,i-1,t) + \lambda_1 P(n_1-1,n_2,i,t)$$
$$+ (n_1+1)\mu_1 P(n_1+1,n_2,i,t)$$
$$+ (n_2+1)\mu_2 P(n_1,n_2+1,i,t)$$
$$+ (i+1)\sigma P(n_1,n_2-1,i+1,t).$$

(iii) $n_1 + n_2 = c, n_2 \ge 1$

$$\frac{dP(n_1,n_2,i,t)}{dt} = -(\lambda_1 + \lambda_2 + (1-p)i\sigma + n_1\mu_1 + n_2\mu_2)P(n_1,n_2,i,t)$$
$$+ \lambda_1\{P(n_1-1,n_2,i,t) + P(n_1-1,n_2+1,i-1,t)\}$$
$$+ \lambda_2 P(n_1,n_2,i-1,t) + (1-p)(i+1)\sigma P(n_1,n_2,i+1,t)$$
$$+ (i+1)\sigma P(n_1,n_2-1,i+1,t).$$

(iv) $n_1 = c$

$$\frac{dP(c,0,i,t)}{dt} = -(\lambda_2 + (1-p)i\sigma + c\mu_1)P(c,0,i,t) + \lambda_2 P(c,0,i-1,t)$$
$$+ (1-p)(i+1)\sigma P(n_1,0,i+1,t)$$
$$+ \lambda_1\{P(c-1,0,i,t) + P(c-1,1,i-1,t)\}.$$

We use the convention that $P(n_1,n_2,i,t) = 0$ for $n_1 < 0$ or $n_2 < 0$ or $i < 0$ and let $j = \sqrt{-1}$ for denote imaginary number. We define the partial characteristic function as

$$H(n_1,n_2,s,t) = \sum_{i=0}^{\infty} e^{jsi} P(n_1,n_2,i,t).$$

We obtain the following differential equations:

(i) $n_1 + n_2 = 0$

$$\frac{\partial H(0,0,s,t)}{\partial t} = -(\lambda_1 + \lambda_2)H(0,0,s,t) + e^{js}\lambda_2 H(0,0,s,t)$$
$$+ \mu_1 H(1,0,s,t) + \mu_2 H(0,1,s,t) + j\sigma\frac{\partial H(0,0,s,t)}{\partial s}. \qquad (1)$$

(ii) $1 \le n_1 + n_2 \le c - 1$

$$\frac{\partial H(n_1, n_2, s, t)}{\partial t} = -(\lambda_1 + \lambda_2 + n_1\mu_1 + n_2\mu_2)H(n_1, n_2, s, t)$$
$$+ e^{js}\lambda_2 H(n_1, n_2, s, t) + \lambda_1 H(n_1 - 1, n_2, s, t)$$
$$+ (n_1 + 1)\mu_1 H(n_1 + 1, n_2, s, t)$$
$$+ (n_2 + 1)\mu_2 H(n_1, n_2 + 1, s, t)$$
$$+ j\sigma \frac{\partial H(n_1, n_2, s, t)}{\partial s} - e^{-js}j\sigma \frac{\partial H(n_1, n_2 - 1, s, t)}{\partial s}. \quad (2)$$

(iii) $n_1 + n_2 = c, n_2 \ge 1$

$$\frac{\partial H(n_1, n_2, s, t)}{\partial t} = -(\lambda_1 + \lambda_2 + n_1\mu_1 + n_2\mu_2)H(n_1, n_2, s, t)$$
$$+ e^{js}\lambda_2 H(n_1, n_2, s, t) + \lambda_1\{H(n_1 - 1, n_2, s, t)$$
$$+ e^{js}H(n_1 - 1, n_2 + 1, s, t)\}$$
$$+ j(1 - p)\sigma(1 - e^{-js})\frac{\partial H(n_1, n_2, s, t)}{\partial s}$$
$$- e^{-js}j\sigma \frac{\partial H(n_1, n_2 - 1, s, t)}{\partial s}. \quad (3)$$

(iv) $n_1 = c$

$$\frac{\partial H(c, 0, s, t)}{\partial t} = -(\lambda_2 + c\mu_1)H(c, 0, s, t) + e^{js}\lambda_2 H(c, 0, s, t)$$
$$+ j(1 - p)\sigma(1 - e^{-js})\frac{\partial H(n_1, n_2, s, t)}{\partial s}$$
$$+ \lambda_1\{H(c - 1, 0, s, t) + e^{js}H(c - 1, 1, s, t)\}. \quad (4)$$

By adopting linear finite difference operators $\mathbf{A}$, $\mathbf{B}$, $\mathbf{C}$, $\mathbf{I}_0$, $\mathbf{I}_1$, $\mathbf{I}_2$, we can rewrite (1)–(4) as follows.

$$\frac{\partial \mathbf{H}(s, t)}{\partial t} = \{\mathbf{A} + e^{js}(\lambda_1\mathbf{B} + \lambda_2\mathbf{C})\}\mathbf{H}(s, t)$$
$$+ \{\mathbf{I}_0 - e^{-js}\mathbf{I}_1 + (1 - p)(1 - e^{-js})\mathbf{I}_2\}j\sigma \frac{\partial \mathbf{H}(s, t)}{\partial s}, \quad (5)$$

where $\mathbf{H}(s, t)$ is a $(c+1) \times (c+1)$ top-left triangle matrix whose (n_1, n_2) element is $H(n_1, n_2, s, t)$ for $n_1 \ge 0$, $n_2 \ge 0$, $n_1 + n_2 \le c$. Operators in (5) are defined as:

$$\mathbf{AH}(s,t)_{n_1,n_2} = \begin{cases} -(\lambda_1 + \lambda_2)H(0,0,s,t) + \mu_1 H(1,0,s,t) + \mu_2 H(0,1,s,t), \\ \quad (n_1 + n_2 = 0), \\ -(\lambda_1 + \lambda_2 + n_1\mu_1 + n_2\mu_2)H(n_1,n_2,s,t) \\ \quad + \lambda_1 H(n_1-1,n_2,s,t) + (n_1+1)\mu_1 H(n_1+1,n_2,s,t) \\ \quad + (n_2+1)\mu_2 H(n_1,n_2+1,s,t), \quad (1 \le n_1 + n_2 \le c-1), \\ -(\lambda_1 + \lambda_2 + n_1\mu_1 + n_2\mu_2)H(n_1,n_2,s,t) \\ \quad + \lambda_1 H(n_1-1,n_2,s,t), \quad (n_1+n_2 = c), \\ -(\lambda_2 + c\mu_1)H(c,0,s,t) + \lambda_1 H(c-1,0,s,t), \quad (n_1 = c). \end{cases}$$

$$\mathbf{BH}(s,t)_{n_1,n_2} = \begin{cases} H(n_1-1,n_2+1,s,t), & (n_1+n_2 = c, n_2 \ge 1), \\ 0, & (\text{otherwise}). \end{cases}$$

$$\mathbf{CH}(s,t)_{n_1,n_2} = H(n_1,n_2,s,t), \quad (0 \le n_1 + n_2 \le c)$$

$$\mathbf{I_0 H}(s,t)_{n_1,n_2} = \begin{cases} H(n_1,n_2,s,t), & (n_1+n_2 \le c-1), \\ 0, & (\text{otherwise}). \end{cases}$$

$$\mathbf{I_1 H}(s,t)_{n_1,n_2} = \begin{cases} H(n_1,n_2-1,s,t), & (1 \le n_2 \le c), \\ 0, & (\text{otherwise}). \end{cases}$$

$$\mathbf{I_2 H}(s,t)_{n_1,n_2} = \begin{cases} H(n_1,n_2,s,t), & (n_1+n_2 = c), \\ 0, & (\text{otherwise}). \end{cases}$$

Summing (1)-(4), we obtain

$$\left\{ \frac{\partial}{\partial t} \sum_{n_1+n_2 \le c} H(n_1,n_2,s,t) \right\} = (e^{js} - 1)\left\{ \lambda_1 \sum_{\substack{n_1+n_2=c \\ n_2 \ge 1}} H(n_1,n_2,s,t) \right.$$

$$\left. + \lambda_2 \sum_{n_1+n_2 \le c} H(n_1,n_2,s,t) + e^{-js} j\sigma \sum_{n_1+n_2 \le c-1} \frac{\partial H(n_1,n_2,s,t)}{\partial s} \right\}$$

$$+ (1-p)(1-e^{-js}) j\sigma \sum_{n_1+n_2=c} \frac{\partial H(n_1,n_2,s,t)}{\partial s}. \quad (6)$$

Let $\mathbf{S_1}$ be the summing operator for the elements with $n_1 + n_2 = c$ and $n_2 \ge 1$, $\mathbf{S_2}$ and $\mathbf{S_3}$ be those for the elements with $n_1 + n_2 \le c-1$ and with $n_1 + n_2 = c$ respectively. Furthermore, let $\mathbf{S}$ be the total summing operator. We hence rewrite (6) in the following form

$$\frac{\partial}{\partial t}[\mathbf{SH}(s,t)] = (e^{js} - 1)\left\{ \lambda_1 \mathbf{S_1 H}(s,t) + \lambda_2 \mathbf{SH}(s,t) + e^{-js} j\sigma \frac{\partial}{\partial s}[\mathbf{S_2 H}(s,t)] \right\}$$

$$+ (1-p)(1-e^{-js}) j\sigma \frac{\partial}{\partial s}[\mathbf{S_3 H}(s,t)]. \quad (7)$$

3   First-Order Approximation

In this section, we solve the system of equations (5) and (7) using the first-order analysis under the asymptotic condition, $\sigma \to 0$. Here, we put the following substitutions for the sensing rate and time:

$$\sigma = \epsilon, \ \tau = \epsilon t, \ s = \epsilon \omega, \ \mathbf{H}(s,t) = \mathbf{F}(\omega, \tau, \epsilon).$$

Then, we have the following equations:

$$
\epsilon \frac{\partial \mathbf{F}(\omega, \tau, \epsilon)}{\partial \tau} = \{\mathbf{A} + e^{j\epsilon\omega}(\lambda_1 \mathbf{B} + \lambda_2 \mathbf{C})\}\mathbf{F}(\omega, \tau, \epsilon)
$$
$$
+ j\{(\mathbf{I_0} - e^{-j\epsilon\omega}\mathbf{I_1}) + (1-p)(1 - e^{-j\epsilon\omega})\mathbf{I_2}\}\frac{\partial \mathbf{F}(\omega, \tau, \epsilon)}{\partial \omega}, \tag{8}
$$

$$
\epsilon \frac{\partial}{\partial \tau}[\mathbf{SF}(\omega, \tau, \epsilon)] = (e^{j\epsilon\omega} - 1)\{\lambda_1 \mathbf{S_1} \mathbf{F}(\omega, \tau, \epsilon) + \lambda_2 \mathbf{SF}(\omega, \tau, \epsilon)
$$
$$
+ e^{-j\epsilon\omega}j\mathbf{S_2}\mathbf{F}(\omega, \tau, \epsilon)\} + (1-p)(1 - e^{-j\epsilon\omega})j\frac{\partial}{\partial \omega}\mathbf{S_3}\mathbf{F}(\omega, \tau, \epsilon). \tag{9}
$$

Lemma 1. The following equality holds as $\sigma \to 0$.

$$
\lim_{\sigma \to 0} \mathbb{E}[e^{j\omega\sigma i(\frac{\tau}{\sigma})}] = e^{j\omega x(\tau)}, \tag{10}
$$

where $x(\tau)$ is a solution of

$$
x'(\tau) = a(x) = (\lambda_1 \mathbf{S_1} + \lambda_2 \mathbf{S})\mathbf{R} - x(\mathbf{S_2}\mathbf{R} + (1-p)\mathbf{S_3}\mathbf{R}). \tag{11}
$$

Here, $\mathbf{R} = \mathbf{R}(x)$ is a left-top triangle matrix which is a solution of the following system

$$
\{\mathbf{A} + \lambda_1 \mathbf{B} + \lambda_2 \mathbf{C} - x(\tau)(\mathbf{I_0} - \mathbf{I_1})\}\mathbf{R} = 0, \tag{12}
$$

and satisfies the normalization condition of a probability distribution

$$
\mathbf{SR} = \sum_{n_1 + n_2 \leq c} R(n_1, n_2, x) = 1. \tag{13}
$$

From (12) and (13), $R(n_1, n_2, x)$ is the steady-state probability of a Markov chain at state (n_1, n_2). The associated transition diagram is illustrated in Fig. 1 (for simplicity, we show the case of $c = 4$). It follows from (12) that this Markov chain represents the corresponding loss system, where the arrival rates of PUs and SUs are λ_1 and x, respectively. It is noted that the Markov chain is independent of p.

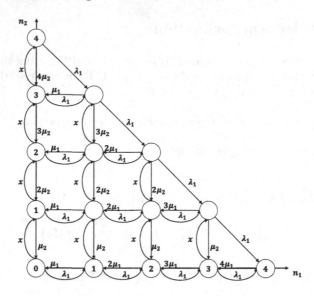

Fig. 1. Transitions among states of the Markov chain.

Proof. Denoting $\lim_{\epsilon \to 0} \mathbf{F}(\omega, \tau, \epsilon) = \mathbf{F}(\omega, \tau)$ and taking the limit $\epsilon \to 0$ in (8), we have

$$(\mathbf{A} + \lambda_1 \mathbf{B} + \lambda_2 \mathbf{C})\mathbf{F}(\omega, \tau) + (\mathbf{I}_0 - \mathbf{I}_1)j\frac{\partial \mathbf{F}(\omega, \tau)}{\partial \omega} = 0. \tag{14}$$

Due to the structure of (14), similar to the scalar case, we find the solution of (14) in the form

$$\mathbf{F}(\omega, \tau) = \mathbf{R}e^{j\omega x(\tau)}, \tag{15}$$

where $\mathbf{R}$ is a left-top triangle matrix and $x(\tau)$ is a scalar function which represents the asymptotic value of the normalized number of SUs in the sensing pool, i.e., $\sigma i(\frac{\tau}{\sigma})$. Substituting (15) into (14), we obtain (12). Because $\mathbf{R}$ encodes the stationary distribution of a Markov chain, it satisfies (13). Taking the limit $\epsilon \to 0$ in (9) yields

$$\mathbf{S}\frac{\partial \mathbf{F}(\omega, \tau)}{\partial \tau} = j\omega \left\{ \lambda_1 \mathbf{S_1}\mathbf{F}(\omega, \tau) + \lambda_2 \mathbf{S}\mathbf{F}(\omega, \tau) + j\frac{\partial}{\partial \omega}[\mathbf{S_2}\mathbf{F}(\omega, \tau)] \right\}$$

$$+(1 - p)j\omega \cdot j\frac{\partial}{\partial \omega}[\mathbf{S_3}\mathbf{F}(\omega, \tau)]. \tag{16}$$

Substituting (15) into (16), we obtain (11). Since the scalar function $x(\tau)$ is the asymptotic value of the normalized number of SUs in the sensing pool $\sigma i(\frac{\tau}{\sigma})$, (10) holds.

For clarity, we can rewrite the explicit form of (11) as follows.

$$a(x) = \lambda_1 \sum_{\substack{n_1+n_2=c \\ n_2 \geq 1}} R(n_1, n_2, x) + \lambda_2$$

$$- x \left\{ \sum_{n_1+n_2 \leq c-1} R(n_1, n_2, x) + (1-p) \sum_{n_1+n_2=c} R(n_1, n_2, x) \right\}.$$

Using the first-order analysis, we construct an approximation to the mean of the number of sensing SUs and compare the approximation with simulation results in Sect. 5.

4 Main Results

In this section, we consider the necessary stability condition. The system can be shown always stable when probability $p < 1$ via the theory of Lyapunov functions [2,12]. In this paper, we show that the limit condition $\lim_{x \to \infty} a(x) < 0$ is consistent with the stability condition by the Lyapunov function approach.

Theorem 1 (Stability condition). When $p < 1$, the system is always stable for all parameters, which coincides with $\lim_{x \to \infty} a(x) < 0$.

Proof. From (11), we rewrite the function $a(x)$ as below:

$$
\begin{aligned}
a(x) &= (\lambda_1 \mathbf{S_1} + \lambda_2 \mathbf{S}) \mathbf{R}(x) - x(\mathbf{S_2} \mathbf{R}(x) + (1-p) \mathbf{S_3} \mathbf{R}(x)) \\
&= \lambda_1 \{ 1 - \mathbf{S_2} \mathbf{R}(x) - R(c,0,x) \} + \lambda_2 - x(\mathbf{S_2} \mathbf{R}(x) + (1-p) \mathbf{S_3} \mathbf{R}(x)) \\
&= \lambda_1 (1 - \pi_c) + \lambda_2 - (\lambda_1 + x) \mathbf{S_2} \mathbf{R}(x) - x(1-p) \mathbf{S_3} \mathbf{R}(x). \quad (17)
\end{aligned}
$$

Here, π_c is Erlang-B formula for PUs and is given as follows:

$$\pi_c = \frac{\frac{\lambda_1^c}{c! \mu_1^c}}{\sum_{k=0}^{c} \frac{\lambda_1^k}{k! \mu_1^k}}.$$

We note that π_c does not depend on x. The third term of (17), $(\lambda_1 + x) \mathbf{S_2} \mathbf{R}(x)$ indicates the incoming flow of the two types of users successfully entering the system without blocking and interrupting. In other words, the third term expresses the arrival rate that increases the number of users in the channels (the throughput of all users).

Moreover, the fourth term $x(1-p)\mathbf{S_3R}(x)$ diverges to infinity as $x \to \infty$ since $\mathbf{S_3R}(x)$ means the blocking probability and increases to 1 as $x \to \infty$. Hence, $\lim\limits_{x\to\infty} a(x) < 0$ holds for all parameters with $p < 1$. Therefore, $a(x)$ decreases with the increase in x, and thus the theorem is proved.

Next, we study the uniqueness of the fixed point κ such that $a(\kappa) = 0$, to derive the stationary solution of $x(\tau)$ for our model with $p < 1$. This point also plays a pivotal role in determining the asymptotic number of SUs in the orbit.

Theorem 2 (Uniqueness).
When $p < 1$, the solution of $a(x) = 0$ is unique.

Proof. It is obvious that $a(0) > 0$ and $\lim\limits_{x\to\infty} a(x) < 0$ from (11) and Theorem 1. From the intermediate value theorem, there is at least one value κ in $(0, \infty)$ for which $a(\kappa) = 0$. We prove that this equation has a unique solution κ.

In Eq. (17), the latter two terms represent the throughput of all users and the rate of SUs being blocked and leaving the orbit. As a consequence, $a(x)$ monotonically decreases as x increases.

5   Numerical Experiment

In this section, we carry out some numerical experiments to evaluate the model's performance. We set the service rates to $\mu_1 = 4$, $\mu_2 = 20$ and $c = \{1, 5\}$ and investigate the impact of λ_1 and λ_2. Under these same service rates, we also evaluate performance, comparing results from simulations with those from the asymptotic method. All of the experimental simulations here are run for 10^6 time steps, which is sufficient to converge to their corresponding numerical solutions. The simulation results in all the figures are denoted by "Sim."

Figures 2 and 3 show the average number of SUs in the orbit against the arrival rate of PUs for $c = \{1, 5\}$. Here, the mean number of SUs in the orbit is approximated by

$$\mathbb{E}[N_{\text{orbit}}] \approx \frac{\kappa}{\sigma}.$$

We can see that the larger the probability p is, the more SUs there are in the orbit. This trend is due to the higher chances that an SU continues to stay in the orbit when it gets blocked. In Fig. 3, there are small differences between each p when λ_1 is small. In contrast, the bigger λ_1 is, the bigger the differences are. Because the number of SUs in the orbit is fewer when p is lower, and more channels are available to allocate, they have more chances to occupy the channel on first arriving. The greater the probability p is, the bigger the differences become because the number of sensing SUs increases and an SU is more likely to be blocked.

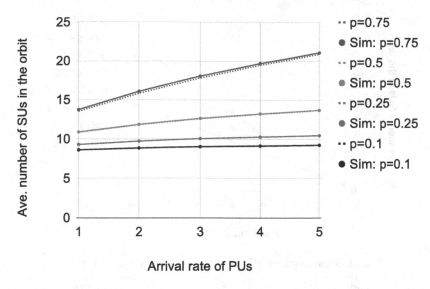

Fig. 2. Mean number SUs in the orbit versus λ_1, for $\sigma = 1.0$, $c = 1$.

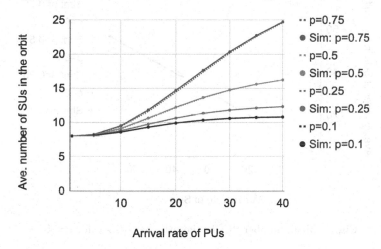

Fig. 3. Mean number SUs in the orbit versus λ_1, for $\sigma = 1.0$, $c = 5$.

Figures 4 and 5 show the average number of SUs in the orbit against their arrival rate. When λ_2 is small, the difference between the values for each p also becomes smaller, and the difference is more significant with larger λ_2. Furthermore, we can interpret that the crowding of the orbit increases the demand upon available channels when the probability is high.

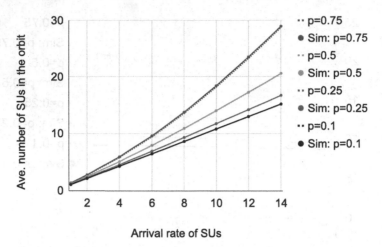

Fig. 4. Mean number SUs in the orbit versus λ_2, for $c = 1$.

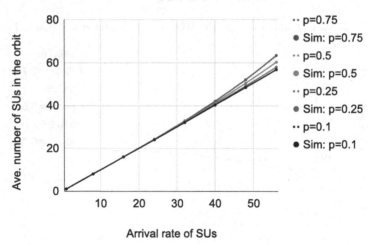

Fig. 5. Mean number SUs in the orbit versus λ_2, for $c = 5$.

Finally, we compare the transition of the behavior between simulations and $x(\frac{\tau}{\sigma})$ in Fig. 6. We can see that the simulation results evolve around $x(\frac{\tau}{\sigma})$ over time. We can see that $x(\cdot)$ is appropriate enough to approximate the normalized number of SUs in the orbit.

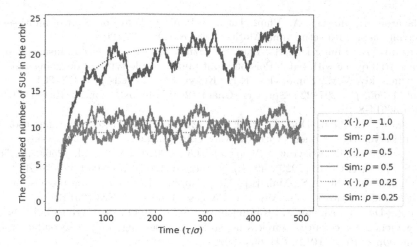

Fig. 6. The transition of the normalized number of SUs in the orbit for $\lambda_1 = 1$, $\lambda_2 = 8$, $\mu_1 = 4$, $\mu_2 = 20$, $\sigma = 0.1$, $c = 1$.

6   Concluding Remark

We analyzed the behavior of secondary users in a modified Erlang-B system using the asymptotic approach under $\sigma \to 0$. We derived the probability distribution of the states of occupied servers under first-order approximation. Using the method of asymptotic analysis, we obtained the stability condition, which is consistent with previous work. Besides, we showed the uniqueness of the fixed point κ such that $a(\kappa) = 0$ to derive the stationary solution of $x(\tau)$ for our model with $p < 1$. We also performed some numerical experiments to investigate the distribution of the states of servers and the number of SUs in the orbit.

Acknowledgement.   The research of Tuan Phung-Duc was supported in part by JSPS KAKENHI Grant Number 21K11765.

References

1. Abe, K., Phung-Duc, T.: Diffusion limit of a modified Erlang-B system with sensing time of secondary users. Annals Oper. Res. 1–22 (2022)
2. Falin, G., Templeton, J.G.: Retrial Queues, vol. 75. CRC Press, Boca Raton (1997)
3. Gómez-Corral, A., Krishnamoorthy, A., Narayanan, V.C.: The impact of self-generation of priorities on multi-server queues with finite capacity. Stoch. Model. **21**(2–3), 427–447 (2005)
4. Moiseev, A., Nazarov, A., Paul, S.: Asymptotic diffusion analysis of multi-server retrial queue with hyper-exponential service. Mathematics **8**(4), 531 (2020)
5. Nasser, A., Al Haj Hassan, H., Abou Chaaya, J., Mansour, A., Yao, K.: Spectrum Sensing for a cognitive radio: recent advances and future challenge. Sensors **21**(7), 2408 (2021)

6. Nazarov, A., Moiseev, A., Phung-Duc, T., Paul, S.: Diffusion limit of multi-server retrial queue with setup time. Mathematics 8(12), 2232 (2020)
7. Nazarov, A., Phung-Duc, T., Paul, S., Lizura, O.: Asymptotic-diffusion analysis for retrial queue with batch Poisson input and multiple types of outgoing calls. In: Vishnevskiy, V.M., Samouylov, K.E., Kozyrev, D.V. (eds.) DCCN 2019. LNCS, vol. 11965, pp. 207–222. Springer, Cham (2019). https://doi.org/10.1007/978-3-030-36614-8_16
8. Nazarov, A., Phung-Duc, T., Paul, S., Lizyura, O.: Diffusion approximation for multiserver retrial queue with two-way communication. In: Vishnevskiy, V.M., Samouylov, K.E., Kozyrev, D.V. (eds.) DCCN 2020. LNCS, vol. 12563, pp. 567–578. Springer, Cham (2020). https://doi.org/10.1007/978-3-030-66471-8_43
9. Palunčlć, F., Alfa, A.S., Maharaj, B.T., Tsimba, H.M.: Queueing models for cognitive radio networks: a survey. IEEE Access 6, 50801–50823 (2018)
10. Phung-Duc, T., Akutsu, K., Kawanishi, K., Salameh, O., Wittevrongel, S.: Queueing models for cognitive wireless networks with sensing time of secondary users. Ann. Oper. Res. 310(2), 641–660 (2022)
11. Phung-Duc, T., Kawanishi, K.: Multiserver retrial queue with setup time and its application to data centers. J. Ind. Manage. Optim. 15(1), 15–35 (2019)
12. Phung-Duc, T.: Retrial queueing models: a survey on theory and applications. arXiv preprint arXiv:1906.09560 (2019)
13. Salameh, O., De Turck, K., Bruneel, H., Blondia, C., Wittevrongel, S.: Analysis of secondary user performance in cognitive radio networks with reactive spectrum handoff. Telecommun. Syst. 65(3), 539–550 (2017)

A Product-Form Solution for a Two-Class $Geo^{Geo}/D/1$ Queue with Random Routing and Randomly Alternating Service

Arnaud Devos[✉][iD], Michiel De Muynck, Herwig Bruneel[iD],
and Joris Walraevens[iD]

Department of Telecommunications and Information Processing (EA07),
Ghent University - UGent, Sint-Pietersnieuwstraat 41, 9000 Gent, Belgium
{Arnaud.Devos,MichielR.DeMuynck,Herwig.Bruneel,Joris.Walraevens}@ugent.be

Abstract. We analyze a discrete-time queueing system, consisting of two queues and a single server. The server randomly distributes its time between the two queues. Service times of any customer of either queue are deterministically equal to 1 time slot. In general, the joint analysis of such a two-queue system turns out to be very hard. In this paper, we assume that the total number of arrivals into the system constitutes a series of i.i.d. random variables with common geometric distribution. Each arriving customer is routed probabilistically to a queue. By means of a state-of-the-art approach, we obtain a closed-form expression of the steady-state joint PGF of the number of customers present ("system contents") in both queues, at the beginning of a random slot. We find that the joint PGF is of product form, which proves that the system contents in both queues are independent. We provide an additional intuitive stochastic explanation for this remarkable result. We discuss several model extensions using the stochastic analysis.

Keywords: Two-class queueing model · Non-work-conserving · Product-form solution

1 Introduction

Two-class queueing systems have received great attention in the queueing literature over the last decades. On the one hand, this is partially because these models can be used for many practical applications. On the other hand, the analysis of such a model usually provides formidable mathematical difficulties which are of interest in their own right. The latter is also the scope and focus of this work. In the most common two-class queueing models, the scheduling disciplines (e.g. global first-come-first-served [7], fixed priority and round robin) depend on the number of customers present in the system, typically to keep the system work-conserving. However, some multi-class queueing models with

© ICST Institute for Computer Sciences, Social Informatics and Telecommunications Engineering 2023
Published by Springer Nature Switzerland AG 2023. All Rights Reserved
E. Hyytiä and V. Kavitha (Eds.): VALUETOOLS 2022, LNICST 482, pp. 81–95, 2023.
https://doi.org/10.1007/978-3-031-31234-2_6

a non-work-conserving scheduler have been studied in the past, as well. See for example [4,8,11,16] and references therein. Besides possible practical motivations, a non-work-conserving scheduler usually has the (mathematical) benefit that the per-class queues can be analyzed relatively easily when viewed in isolation [8,16]. Unfortunately, a joint analysis of both per-class queues is still considered to be notoriously difficult, or even impossible, if one is interested in a closed-form solution [8,16]. Notice that a joint analysis is for instance necessary if one is interested in joint performance measures such as the correlation coefficient between the two queue contents, or the variance of the total queue content. In an earlier paper [9], we studied a discrete-time two-class model with the following non-work conserving scheduling discipline: at each service opportunity, the server is willing to serve queue 1 (resp. queue 2) with probability α (resp. $1 - \alpha$). If the server chooses an empty queue, no-one gets service in that time slot. For this model, we were also confronted with the notorious problem of solving a functional equation [6], which we were unable to solve exactly. However, for the same service model, but for Bernoulli distributed numbers of class-1 and class-2 arrivals per time slot, we found a closed-form analysis in [10]. In [9], we assume that the numbers of per-slot class-1 and class-2 arrivals have a *generic* distribution. The surprising result of [10] has made us question if there exist other arrival processes such that a closed-form analysis is feasible. The answer is yes: we have in particular found a product-form solution for the case that the total numbers of arrivals to the queueing system during consecutive slots are independent geometrically distributed random variables and customers are probabilistically routed to one of the two queues (independently from customer to customer). This analysis is the subject of this paper.

The outline of the paper is as follows. In Sect. 2, the mathematical model is presented. Some preliminaries are given in Sect. 3. In Sect. 4, we analyze the joint system contents by using tools from complex analysis. Alternatively and complementarily, an intuitive stochastic analysis is presented in Sect. 5. Finally, we discuss several extensions for this model in Sect. 6.

2   Mathematical Model

We review the model of [9] in this section. We consider a discrete-time single-server system with two infinite waiting rooms. Time is assumed to be slotted, i.e. the time axis is divided into fixed-length intervals referred to as (time) slots. New customers may enter the system at an given (continuous) point on the time axis, but services can only start and end at slot boundaries. There are two types of customers arriving to the system, namely customers of class 1 (resp. class 2) joining queue 1 (resp. queue 2). We assume that the *total* numbers of newly generated arrivals during consecutive slots are independent and geometrically distributed with mean λ_T. More specifically,

$$a_T(n) \triangleq \Pr[n \text{ customer arrivals in one slot}],$$

$$= \frac{1}{1 + \lambda_T} \left(\frac{\lambda_T}{1 + \lambda_T} \right)^n, \quad n = 0, 1, \ldots. \tag{1}$$

One easily verifies that this arrival process corresponds to a batch arrival process with geometrically distributed inter-arrival times and the batch sizes are geometrically distributed (see for example [2, Chapter 1]).

An arriving customer is routed to queue j with probability $\frac{\lambda_j}{\lambda_T}$, $j = 1, 2$. In particular, note that

$$\lambda_1 + \lambda_2 = \lambda_T. \tag{2}$$

A simple calculation shows that

$$a(n_1, n_2) \triangleq \Pr[n_1 \text{ class-1 arrivals and } n_2 \text{ class-2 arrivals in one slot}]$$

$$= \frac{1}{1 + \lambda_T} \left(\frac{\lambda_T}{1 + \lambda_T} \right)^{n_1 + n_2} \binom{n_1 + n_2}{n_1} \left(\frac{\lambda_1}{\lambda_T} \right)^{n_1} \left(\frac{\lambda_2}{\lambda_T} \right)^{n_2}. \tag{3}$$

The joint probability generating function is then given by

$$A(z_1, z_2) = \sum_{n_1=0}^{\infty} \sum_{n_2=0}^{\infty} a(n_1, n_2) z_1^{n_1} z_2^{n_2}$$

$$= \frac{1}{1 + \lambda_1 + \lambda_2 - \lambda_1 z_1 - \lambda_2 z_2}. \tag{4}$$

The service times of customers equal one slot. At the beginning of every time slot, the single server randomly selects either queue 1 or queue 2 to serve. This selection occurs independently of the system state and is modeled by a single parameter α $(0 < \alpha < 1)$, that is defined as

$$\alpha = \Pr[\text{server is available to class-1 customers during a slot}].$$

This directly means that the server is available to class-2 customers during a slot with probability $1 - \alpha$. Moreover, it is assumed that the state of the server (available to either class-1 or class-2 customers) during a certain slot is independent of the state of the server during previous slots, and also of the other random variables present in the model. Notice that when the server is available to an empty queue, no service occurs in that slot, even when the other queue is non-empty. Hence, the system is not work-conserving.

Finally, since we are interested in a stochastic equilibrium, it is required that (see Equation (5) in [9])

$$\lambda_1 < \alpha \quad \text{and} \quad \lambda_2 < 1 - \alpha. \tag{5}$$

3   Preliminaries

In this section, we write down the fundamental functional equation for the joint PGF of the steady-state system contents. Next, we provide the marginal PGFs of the system contents, as these are readily obtained.

3.1   The Functional Equation

In order to analyze the above queueing model, let $u_{1,k}$ and $u_{2,k}$ denote the numbers of class-1 and class-2 customers in the system at the beginning of slot k. It is easy to see that $(u_{1,k}, u_{2,k})$ is a discrete-time Markov chain with state space

$$\mathcal{S} = \{0, 1, \ldots\}^2.$$

We assume the stationary distribution of this stochastic process exists, see also (5). Therefore, we define the limiting joint probability mass function (pmf)

$$p(n_1, n_2) \triangleq \lim_{k \to \infty} \Pr[u_{1,k} = n_1, u_{2,k} = n_2], \quad (n_1, n_2) \in \mathcal{S}. \tag{6}$$

The balance equations read as follows:

$$
\begin{aligned}
p(n_1, n_2) = {} & \alpha \sum_{j=0}^{n_2} a(n_1, n_2 - j)p(0, j) \\
& + \alpha \sum_{i=0}^{n_1} \sum_{j=0}^{n_2} a(n_1 - i, n_2 - j)p(i + 1, j) \\
& + (1 - \alpha) \sum_{i=0}^{n_1} a(n_1 - i, n_2)p(i, 0) \\
& + (1 - \alpha) \sum_{i=0}^{n_1} \sum_{j=0}^{n_2} a(n_1 - i, n_2 - j)p(i, j + 1).
\end{aligned}
\tag{7}
$$

Now let us define the joint PGF

$$U(z_1, z_2) \triangleq \sum_{n_1=0}^{\infty} \sum_{n_2=0}^{\infty} p(n_1, n_2) z_1^{n_1} z_2^{n_2}. \tag{8}$$

It follows from Eq. (7) that

$$K(z_1, z_2)U(z_1, z_2) = A(z_1, z_2)[(1 - \alpha)(z_2 - 1)z_1 U(z_1, 0) + \alpha(z_1 - 1)z_2 U(0, z_2)], \tag{9}$$

with

$$K(z_1, z_2) = z_1 z_2 - [(1 - \alpha)z_1 + \alpha z_2]A(z_1, z_2). \tag{10}$$

Equation (9) is in accordance with the functional equation obtained in Section 2.1 in [9]. Recall that in this work we assume that $A(z_1, z_2)$ is given by (4), in contrast to [9] (where the exact form of $A(z_1, z_2)$ is not specified).

3.2   The Marginal PGFs

In this section, we define the pmf $p_i(n)$, $i = 1, 2$, of the number of class-i customers in the system at the beginning of a random slot in steady state, i.e.,

$$p_i(n) = \lim_{k \to \infty} \Pr[u_{i,k} = n] \qquad n = 0, 1, \ldots. \tag{11}$$

The marginal PGF $U_1(z)$ of the number of class-1 customers in the system at the beginning of a random slot in steady state can be easily deducted from (9) by choosing $\{z_1 = z, z_2 = 1\}$, which results in

$$U_1(z) \triangleq \sum_{n=0}^{\infty} p_1(n)z^n \tag{12}$$

$$= U(z, 1)$$

$$= \frac{\alpha - \lambda_1}{\alpha - \lambda_1 z}. \tag{13}$$

The reader will recognize the expression above as the PGF of a geometrically distributed random variable with parameter $\frac{\lambda_1}{\alpha}$. Hence the pmf $p_1(n)$ is given by

$$p_1(n) = \left(1 - \frac{\lambda_1}{\alpha}\right)\left(\frac{\lambda_1}{\alpha}\right)^n, \quad n = 0, 1, \ldots. \tag{14}$$

It easily follows that the radius of convergence of (12), say τ_1, is equal to

$$\tau_1 = \frac{\alpha}{\lambda_1}. \tag{15}$$

For reasons of symmetry, we have that

$$U_2(z) \triangleq \sum_{n=0}^{\infty} p_2(n)z^n \tag{16}$$

$$= U(1, z)$$

$$= \frac{1 - \alpha - \lambda_2}{1 - \alpha - \lambda_2 z} \tag{17}$$

and

$$p_2(n) = \left(1 - \frac{\lambda_2}{1 - \alpha}\right)\left(\frac{\lambda_2}{1 - \alpha}\right)^n, \quad n = 0, 1, \ldots. \tag{18}$$

The radius of convergence of (16), say τ_2, is given by

$$\tau_2 = \frac{1 - \alpha}{\lambda_2}. \tag{19}$$

4   Complex-Analytic Analysis

Two-class queueing models often give rise to the problem of solving a functional equation similar to (9). In the pioneering paper [12], a solution technique for such equations is demonstrated. It was shown that the solution can be found as the solution of a boundary-value problem for analytic functions. This technique is nowadays considered as the state-of-the art technique for dealing with such equations, and this technique goes nowadays by the name of the *boundary-value method*. A more detailed contribution of the analysis of such functional equations was later provided in [5,13]. The method that we employ in this work covers the same principle ideas as the one of the boundary-value method, which we now describe below.

In order to obtain the joint PGF $U(z_1, z_2)$ for arbitrary values (z_1, z_2) from (9), the partial PGFs $U(z_1, 0)$ and $U(0, z_2)$ have to be obtained, which is the non-straightforward objective of the analysis. It is worth mentioning that substitution of $\{z_1 = z, z_2 = 0\}$ or $\{z_1 = 0, z_2 = z\}$ into (9) always leads to the tautology "$0 = 0$". The crucial part of the analysis is studying the function K, which is referred to as the *kernel* of the functional equation. This is because whenever a zero $(\hat{z}_1, \hat{z}_2)$ of K lies inside the region of convergence of the PGF $U(z_1, z_2)$, this relates $U(\hat{z}_1, 0)$ with $U(0, \hat{z}_2)$. More precisely, for any $(\hat{z}_1, \hat{z}_2)$ which lies inside the region of convergence of $U(\cdot, \cdot)$ such that $K(\hat{z}_1, \hat{z}_2) = 0$ and $A(\hat{z}_1, \hat{z}_2) \neq 0$, we have that

$$(1 - \alpha)(\hat{z}_2 - 1)\hat{z}_1 U(\hat{z}_1, 0) + \alpha(\hat{z}_1 - 1)\hat{z}_2 U(0, \hat{z}_2) = 0,$$

which gives us an equation in terms of $U(\hat{z}_1, 0)$ and $U(0, \hat{z}_2)$.

Therefore, we will first discuss the regions of convergence of the PGFs of interest. Next, we investigate the kernel K. We emphasize that the function K has the same structure as the one in [15]. Therefore the analysis of the kernel K is comparable to the one in [15]. The difference between [15] and our work is that the RHS of the functional equation does not have the same structure. Hence, at some point in the analysis, a different approach is used (in comparison with [15]).

4.1   Regions of Convergence

The boundary function $U(\cdot, 0)$ is defined by

$$U(z, 0) = \sum_{n=0}^{\infty} p(n, 0) z^n, \tag{20}$$

the power series of the horizontal boundary probabilities. Similarly, the boundary function $U(0, \cdot)$ is defined by

$$U(0, z) = \sum_{n=0}^{\infty} p(0, n) z^n, \tag{21}$$

the power series of the vertical boundary probabilities. We now investigate for which values of z these two infinite series converge. To accomplish this, we observe that for every $n = 0, 1, \ldots$

$$p(n, 0) \leq \sum_{j=0}^{\infty} p(n, j)$$
$$= p_1(n).$$

Hence, the radius of convergence of (12) is a lower bound for the radius of convergence of (20). Analogously, the radius of convergence of (16) is a lower bound for the radius of convergence of (21). Recall that we have determined the radius of convergence τ_1 (resp. τ_2) of (12) (resp. (16)) in the Sect. 3.2.

Next, we investigate the joint PGF $U(z_1, z_2)$. For any z_2 with modulus smaller than or equal to 1, we have

$$
\begin{aligned}
|U(z_1, z_2)| &\leq \sum_{i=0}^{\infty} \sum_{j=0}^{\infty} p(i,j)|z_1|^i |z_2|^j \\
&\leq \sum_{i=0}^{\infty} \sum_{j=0}^{\infty} p(i,j)|z_1|^i \\
&= \sum_{i=0}^{\infty} p_1(i)|z_1|^i \\
&= U_1(|z_1|).
\end{aligned}
$$

From the fact that the radius of convergence of $U_1(z)$ is given by τ_1, we further obtain that

$$|U(z_1, z_2)| < \infty, \quad \text{if } |z_1| < \tau_1, |z_2| \leq 1.$$

For reasons of symmetry, we can similarly prove that

$$|U(z_1, z_2)| < \infty, \quad \text{if } |z_1| \leq 1, |z_2| < \tau_2.$$

In summary, we have shown that:

Lemma 1

(i) $U(z, 0)$ converges absolutely for $|z| < \tau_1$,
(ii) $U(0, z)$ converges absolutely for $|z| < \tau_2$,
(iii) $U(z_1, z_2)$ converges absolutely for $|z_1| < \tau_1, |z_2| \leq 1$,
(iv) $U(z_1, z_2)$ converges absolutely for $|z_1| \leq 1, |z_2| < \tau_2$.

4.2   Analysis of the Kernel $K(z_1, z_2)$

In this subsection, we investigate the zeros of the kernel K. We have that

$$
\begin{aligned}
&K(z_1, z_2) = 0 \\
\Leftrightarrow\; & \frac{-z_1^2 z_2 \lambda_1 - z_1 z_2^2 \lambda_2 + z_1 z_2 \lambda_1 + z_1 z_2 \lambda_2 + z_1 \alpha - z_2 \alpha + z_1 z_2 - z_1}{-\lambda_1 z_1 - \lambda_2 z_2 + \lambda_1 + \lambda_2 + 1} = 0 \\
\Leftrightarrow\; & -z_1^2 z_2 \lambda_1 - z_1 z_2^2 \lambda_2 + z_1 z_2 \lambda_1 + z_1 z_2 \lambda_2 + z_1 \alpha - z_2 \alpha + z_1 z_2 - z_1 = 0 \\
\Leftrightarrow\; & z_1 z_2 \left(-z_1 \lambda_1 - z_2 \lambda_2 + \lambda_1 + \lambda_2 + \frac{\alpha}{z_2} - \frac{\alpha}{z_1} + 1 - \frac{1}{z_2} \right) = 0.
\end{aligned}
$$

The left-hand side in the equation above has the same form as the kernel that is studied in [15]. We now proceed as per [15] to analyze the solutions of this equation. Letting

$$H_1(z_1) = \alpha + \lambda_1 - \lambda_1 z_1 - \frac{\alpha}{z_1}, \tag{22}$$

$$H_2(z_2) = 1 - \alpha + \lambda_2 - \lambda_2 z_2 - \frac{1-\alpha}{z_2}, \tag{23}$$

we see that

$$H_1(z_1) + H(z_2) = 0 \Rightarrow K(z_1, z_2) = 0.$$

For complex values of z_1, we will only observe that for $z_1 = \sqrt{\frac{\alpha}{\lambda_1}} e^{\pm i\theta}$, $H_1(z_1)$ is real and equal to

$$\alpha + \lambda_1 - \sqrt{\lambda_1 \alpha} 2\cos(\theta).$$

Moreover, we have that

$$\alpha + \lambda_1 - \sqrt{\lambda_1 \alpha} 2\cos(\theta) > 0, \tag{24}$$

since

$$\alpha + \lambda_1 - \sqrt{\lambda_1 \alpha} 2\cos(\theta) \geq \alpha + \lambda_1 - \sqrt{\lambda_1 \alpha} 2$$
$$= (\sqrt{\alpha} - \sqrt{\lambda_1})^2$$
$$> 0.$$

We are ready to prove the following lemma.

Lemma 2. *For values $z_1 = \sqrt{\frac{\alpha}{\lambda_1}} e^{\pm i\theta}$, there is a unique $z_2 =: y(z_1) \in \,]0,1[$ such that*

$$H_1(z_1) + H_2(y(z_1)) = 0.$$

Proof. For $x \in [0,1]$, $H_2(x)$ increases monotonically from $-\infty$ at $x = 0$ to 0 at $x = 1$. Moreover, we have that

$$H_1\left(\sqrt{\frac{\alpha}{\lambda_1}} e^{\pm i\theta}\right) > 0,$$

cf. (24). In particular, $H_2(x)$ is continuous in $]0,1[$. By virtue of the intermediate value theorem, there is a unique value z_2 in the interval $]0,1[$ such that

$$H_2(z_2) = -H_1\left(\sqrt{\frac{\alpha}{\lambda_1}} e^{\pm i\theta}\right).$$

4.3   Analytic Continuation of $U(z, 0)$ and $U(0, z)$

We can now proceed to determine the functions $U(z, 0)$ and $U(0, z)$ and hence solve the functional equation (9). To accomplish this, it is crucial to note that

$$y(z) = y(\bar{z}), \quad |z| = \sqrt{\frac{\alpha}{\lambda_1}},$$

with y defined in the previous subsection. The reason why the equality above holds, is simply because

$$H_1\left(\sqrt{\frac{\alpha}{\lambda_1}}e^{i\theta}\right) = \alpha + \lambda_1 - \sqrt{\lambda_1\alpha}2\cos(\theta)$$

$$= \alpha + \lambda_1 - \sqrt{\lambda_1\alpha}2\cos(-\theta)$$

$$= H_1\left(\sqrt{\frac{\alpha}{\lambda_1}}e^{-i\theta}\right).$$

Further, since $\frac{\alpha}{\lambda_1} > 1$ it obviously holds that

$$\sqrt{\frac{\alpha}{\lambda_1}} = \sqrt{\tau_1} < \tau_1$$

Due to the inequality above and the fact that $y(z) \in {]}0,1{[}$, we have that $U(z, y(z))$ remains finite by virtue of Lemma 1 on page 7. Hence, substituting $\{z_1 = z, z_2 = y(z)\}$, $|z|^2 = \frac{\alpha}{\lambda_1}$ into the functional equation (9) yields

$$(1-\alpha)(y(z)-1)zU(z,0) + \alpha(z-1)y(z)U(0,y(z)) = 0,$$

and substitution of $(\bar{z}, y(z))$ for values of z such that $|z|^2 = \frac{\alpha}{\lambda_1}$ yields

$$(1-\alpha)(y(z)-1)\bar{z}U(\bar{z},0) + \alpha(\bar{z}-1)y(z)U(0,y(z)) = 0.$$

Eliminating $U(0, y(z))$ gives us

$$(\bar{z}-1)zU(z,0) = (z-1)\bar{z}U(\bar{z},0), \quad |z| = \sqrt{\frac{\alpha}{\lambda_1}}. \tag{25}$$

Finally, when multiplying both sides of the relation above by z and using the relations $z\bar{z} = \frac{\alpha}{\lambda_1} \leftrightarrow |z| = |\bar{z}| = \sqrt{\frac{\alpha}{\lambda_1}}$ we find that

$$z\left(\frac{\alpha}{\lambda_1} - z\right)U(z,0) = \frac{\alpha}{\lambda_1}(z-1)U\left(\frac{\alpha}{\lambda_1}z^{-1},0\right), \quad |z| = \sqrt{\frac{\alpha}{\lambda_1}}. \tag{26}$$

This functional equation for $U(\cdot,0)$ can for instance be solved as follows. Let us substitute the series expression (20) into (26), we obtain that

$$z\left(\frac{\alpha}{\lambda_1} - z\right)\sum_{n=0}^{\infty}p(n,0)z^n = \frac{\alpha}{\lambda_1}(z-1)\sum_{n=0}^{\infty}p(n,0)\left(\frac{\alpha}{\lambda_1}\right)^n z^{-n},$$

which can be rewritten as

$$\sum_{n=1}^{\infty}\frac{\alpha}{\lambda_1}p(n-1,0)z^n - \sum_{n=2}^{\infty}p(n-2,0)z^n - \sum_{n=0}^{\infty}\left(\frac{\alpha}{\lambda_1}\right)^{n+2}p(n+1,0)z^{-n}$$

$$-\frac{\alpha}{\lambda_1}p(0,0)z + \sum_{n=0}^{\infty}\left(\frac{\alpha}{\lambda_1}\right)^{n+1}p(n,0)z^{-n} = 0.$$

This equation is valid for z-values such that $|z| = \sqrt{\frac{\alpha}{\lambda_1}}$. Hence, by multiplying by appropriate powers of z and integrating over the positively oriented complex circle centered at 0 with radius $\sqrt{\tau_1}$, we may identify the coefficients of equal (positive or negative) powers of z of the above equation. We obtain that

$$p(n,0) = \frac{\lambda_1}{\alpha} p(n-1,0), \qquad n = 1,2,\ldots.$$

Solving this elementary difference equation yields

$$p(n,0) = \left(\frac{\lambda_1}{\alpha}\right)^n p(0,0).$$

Finally, using the condition $\sum_{n=0}^{\infty} p(n,0) = p_2(0) = 1 - \frac{\lambda_2}{1-\alpha}$ gives us

$$p(0,0) = \frac{(\alpha - \lambda_1)(1 - \alpha - \lambda_2)}{\alpha(1-\alpha)}.$$

Hence, the probabilities $p(n,0)$ $(n = 0,1,\ldots)$ are completely determined. A simple calculation then shows that $U(z,0)$ is given by the following rational function

$$U(z,0) = \frac{\left(1 - \frac{\lambda_2}{1-\alpha}\right)(\alpha - \lambda_1)}{\alpha - \lambda_1 z}. \tag{27}$$

For reasons of symmetry, it can be shown that $U(0,z)$ is given by

$$U(0,z) = \frac{\left(1 - \frac{\lambda_1}{\alpha}\right)(1 - \alpha - \lambda_2)}{1 - \alpha - \lambda_2 z}. \tag{28}$$

The reader might have noticed that

$$U(z_1,0) = U_1(z_1)U_2(0) \text{ and that } U(0,z_2) = U_1(0)U_2(z_2).$$

This suggests that the steady-state system contents are statistically independent.

4.4   The Joint PGF

If we substitute the expressions (27) and (28) for $U(z,0)$ and $U(0,z)$, respectively, into the functional equation for $U(z_1,z_2)$, we get

$$U(z_1,z_2) = \frac{(\alpha - \lambda_1)(1 - \alpha - \lambda_2)}{(\alpha - \lambda_1 z_1)(1 - \alpha - \lambda_2 z_2)}. \tag{29}$$

We can conclude that $U(z_1,z_2) = U(z_1,1)U(1,z_2)$, i.e., the steady-state system contents are indeed statistically independent. We emphasize that this is a striking result. This result is primarily obtained through a complex-analytic analysis. In Sect. 5, we provide a more intuitive and stochastic analysis of the system contents to obtain the same result.

4.5   The Steady-State Joint Probabilities

The joint probability mass function $p(n_1, n_2)$ of the numbers of class-1 and class-2 customers is thus easily obtained because the joint pmf can be factorized as

$$p(n_1, n_2) = p_1(n_1)p_2(n_2).$$

We obtain that, using (14) and (18),

$$p(n_1, n_2) = \frac{(\alpha - \lambda_1)(1 - \alpha - \lambda_2)}{\alpha(1 - \alpha)} \left(\frac{\lambda_1}{\alpha}\right)^{n_1} \left(\frac{\lambda_2}{1 - \alpha}\right)^{n_2}. \tag{30}$$

5   Intuitive Stochastic Analysis

We now present an intuitive explanation of the mutual independence of the two system contents in the model under study. We have assumed that the total numbers of arrivals during consecutive slots constitute a sequence of i.i.d. geometric random variables. Observing the system contents from slot to slot thus implies that the system contents can increase to any level, since there is a non-zero probability of having $n \in \mathbb{N}$ arrivals during a slot. However, note that a geometric random variable can be viewed as the outcome of a sequence of independent and identical Bernoulli experiments. In this case, the two possible outcomes of the Bernoulli experiments are "a customer arrives" and "no customer arrives". Note that "no customer arrives" implies the end of arrivals in a slot. Because we assume that an arriving customer is randomly routed to a queue with fixed probabilities, independently from customer to customer, we thus have that the arrivals constitute a sequence of independent events. These events are the following

(i)   A class-1 customer arrives;
(ii)   A class-2 customer arrives;
(iii)   End of arrivals in a slot.

The probability of having event (i), event (ii) or event (iii) (at a given point in time) is independent of the events that have occurred before. These three probabilities can be computed, but the exact expressions are not needed for the remainder of this section. Note that we have introduced an explicit sequence of arrivals in a slot, but that the total numbers of arrivals per class are given by the distribution (3). As a consequence, and because of the randomly alternating service discipline studied in this paper, changes of the *system contents* can be represented by a sequence of independent events, which are the following

1.   A class-1 customer arrives;
2.   A class-2 customer arrives;
3.   A new slot begins and a class-1 customer is served (if any);
4.   A new slot begins and a class-2 customer is served (if any).

Again, the probability of having event 1, event 2, event 3 or event 4 (at a given point in time) is independent of the events that have occurred before. These four probabilities can be computed, but the exact expressions are not needed for the remainder of this section. The evolution of the system contents can for instance be described by means of a sequence of numbers, taken from the set $\{1, 2, 3, 4\}$, where the numbers corresponds to the events as described above. For example, a slot with two class-1 arrivals, one class-2 arrival, followed by a slot with a class-1 service could be "represented" by the sequence 1123. Important to note is that we now assume that services in a slot happen before arrivals. However, it is not difficult to see that this again boils down to the model we studied earlier.

Let v_1 (resp. v_2) denote the number of class-1 customers (resp. class-2 customers) in the system (right after the *occurrence* of an event $\in \{1, 2, 3, 4\}$), when a stochastic equilibrium has been reached. In such an equilibrium, the system contents are represented by an **infinite** sequence, say ω, of numbers of the set $\{1, 2, 3, 4\}$. It is easy to see that the random variable v_1 is completely determined by the events 1 and 3, while v_2 is completely determined by the events 2 and 4: for given ω, only the numbers 1 and 3 (resp. 2 and 4) are sufficient and necessary to determine v_1 (resp. v_2). Now it can be seen that information of v_2 (and hence information about the occurrences of the events 2 and 4 in ω) gives us no information about v_1. Even knowing the exact order and amount of $2s$ and $4s$ in the infinite sequence ω provides us no information about the (number and order of) $1s$ and $3s$ in ω, and v_1 is solely determined by the latter. Similarly, information about v_1 (and hence information about the occurrences the events 1 and 3 in ω) gives us no information about v_2. From this reasoning, we may conclude that v_1 and v_2 are independent random variables. Finally, because the beginning of slots are just moments after specific events, the stationary system contents of class 1 and class 2 at the beginning of slots, u_1 and u_2, are also independent because of the BASTA property (Bernoulli-Arrivals-See-Time-Averages [14]).

6　Direct Extensions of the Queueing Model

Inspired by the intuitive explanation for the product-form result, we studied several extensions to our queueing model such that the system contents remain independent.

6.1　Multiple Arrivals

Consider the queueing model as described in Sect. 3.2, but with the following (more general) form for $A(z_1, z_2)$:

$$A(z_1, z_2) = \frac{1}{1 + \mu_1 + \mu_2 - \mu_1 L_1(z_1) - \mu_2 L_2(z_2)}, \tag{31}$$

with $L_1(z)$ and $L_2(z)$ being PGFs, but not specified. Note that the case where

$$L_1(z) = L_2(z) = z$$

corresponds to the arrival PGF (4). We can apply the same reasoning as per Sect. 5. The only difference is that the events 1 and 2 should be replaced by

1. *A number L_1 of class-1 customer arrive*;
2. *A number L_2 of class-2 customer arrive.*

The number of arriving customers L_1 (resp. L_2) is distributed according to the PGF $L_1(z)$ (resp. $L_2(z)$). Because the events are still independent, we can again conclude that the steady-state system contents at the beginning of a random slot are independent, which implies that $U(z_1, z_2) = U(z_1, 1)U(1, z_2)$. Hence,

$$U(z_1, z_2) = \frac{(\alpha - \lambda_1)(1 - \alpha - \lambda_2)(z_1 - 1)(z_2 - 1)A_1(z_1)A_2(z_2)}{(z_1 - A_1(z_1)[\alpha + (1 - \alpha)z_1])(z_2 - A_2(z_2)[1 - \alpha + \alpha z_2])}, \tag{32}$$

with

$$A_i(z) = \frac{1}{1 + \mu_i - \mu_i L_i(z)}, \quad i = 1, 2,$$

the PGF of the number of class-i arrivals in a slot. It can be checked that this solution indeed satisfies the functional equation (9).

6.2   Multiple Servers

Consider the queueing model as described in Sect. 3.2. Instead of serving one class-i customer during a slot (if any), we now assume that the number of available servers for class-i customers (if class i is chosen to be served) is distributed according to a distribution with PGF $S_i(z)$, $i = 1, 2$. Note that the case where

$$S_1(z) = S_2(z) = z$$

corresponds to the original model. We can apply the same reasoning as per Sect. 5. The only difference is that the events 3 and 4 should be replaced by

3. A new slot begins and a *number* of class-1 customers are served (if any);
4. A new slot begins and a *number* of class-2 customers are served (if any).

The maximum number of served customers of class 1 (resp. class 2) is distributed according to the PGF $S_1(z)$ (resp. $S_2(z)$). Because the events are still independent, we can again conclude that the system contents are independent. We emphasize that the analysis of the marginal system contents for this model is more difficult as compared to the analysis of Sect. 3.2, since a queue in isolation is now a multi-server queue with a variable number of (available) servers. However, several special cases have been studied, such as the cases where the number of available servers never exceeds a certain maximum [1, Section 5], or is geometrically distributed [3].

6.3 Multiple Queues

Consider the queueing model as described in Sect. 3.2, but with an arbitrary number N different customer classes, each with their own queue. The single server is allocated to queue j with probability α_j, $j = 1, \ldots, N$ and $\sum_{j=1}^{N} \alpha_j = 1$. As in Sect. 3.2, we assume that there is a single arrival stream of customers to the system, described by means of a sequence of i.i.d. geometric random variables during the consecutive slots (1). An arriving customer is of class j with probability $\frac{\lambda_j}{\lambda_T}$, $j = 1, 2, \ldots, N$. Each queue is stable as long as $\lambda_j < \alpha_j$.

It is not difficult to see that we may extend the reasoning as in Sect. 5 to multiple queues. We may thus conclude again that the N steady-state system contents are independent at the beginning of a random slot. To the best of our knowledge, this result is one of the few explicit results that exist for the steady-state joint analysis of more than two queues.

Obviously, combining some/all the extensions leads to a product-form solution as well.

References

1. Bruneel, H.: A general model for the behaviour of infinite buffers with periodic service opportunities. Eur. J. Oper. Res. **16**(1), 98–106 (1984)
2. Bruneel, H., Kim, B.G.: Discrete-Time Models for Communication Systems Including ATM. Kluwer Academic Publisher, Boston (1993)
3. Bruneel, H., Wittevrongel, S., Claeys, D., Walraevens, J.: Discrete-time queues with variable service capacity: a basic model and its analysis. Ann. Oper. Res. **239**(2), 359–380 (2016). https://doi.org/10.1007/s10479-013-1428-y
4. Al Hanbali, A., de Haan, R., Boucherie, R.J., van Ommeren, J.: Time-limited polling systems with batch arrivals and phase-type service times. Ann. Oper. Res. **198**(1), 57–82 (2012). https://doi.org/10.1007/s10479-011-0846-y
5. Cohen, J.W., Boxma, O.J.: Boundary Value Problems in Queueing System Analysis. North-Holland, Amsterdam (1983)
6. Cohen, J.W.: Boundary value problems in queueing theory. Queueing Syst. **3**(2), 97–128 (1988). https://doi.org/10.1007/BF01189045
7. De Clercq, S., Laevens, K., Steyaert, B., Bruneel, H.: A multi-class discrete-time queueing system under the FCFS service discipline. Ann. Oper. Res. **202**(1), 59–73 (2013). https://doi.org/10.1007/s10479-011-1051-8
8. de Haan, R., Boucherie, R.J., van Ommeren, J.: A polling model with an autonomous server. Queueing Syst. **62**(3), 279–308 (2009). https://doi.org/10.1007/s11134-009-9131-z
9. Devos, A., Walraevens, J., Fiems, D., Bruneel, H.: Approximations for the performance evaluation of a discrete-time two-class queue with an alternating service discipline. Ann. Oper. Res. **310**(2), 477–503 (2022). https://doi.org/10.1007/s10479-020-03776-5
10. Devos, A., Walraevens, J., Fiems, D., Bruneel, H.: Analysis of a discrete-time two-class randomly alternating service model with Bernoulli arrivals. Queueing Syst. **96**, 133–152 (2020). https://doi.org/10.1007/s11134-020-09663-x
11. Dvir, N., Hassin, R., Yechiali, U.: Strategic behaviour in a tandem queue with alternating server. Queueing Syst. **96**, 205–244 (2020). https://doi.org/10.1007/s11134-020-09665-9

12. Fayolle, G., Iasnogorodski, R.: Two coupled processors: the reduction to a Riemann-Hilbert problem. Zeitschrift für Wahrscheinlichkeitstheorie und verwandte Gebiete **47**(3), 325–351 (1979). https://doi.org/10.1007/BF00535168
13. Fayolle, G., Malyshev, V.A., Iasnogorodski, R.: Random Walks in the Quarter-Plane. Springer, Heidelberg (1999). https://doi.org/10.1007/978-3-642-60001-2
14. Halfin, S.: Batch delays versus customer delays. Bell Syst. Tech. J. **62**(7), 2011–2015 (1983)
15. Konheim, A.G., Meilijson, I., Melkman, A.: Processor-sharing of two parallel lines. J. Appl. Probab. **18**(4), 952–956 (1981)
16. Saxena, M., Boxma, O., Kapodistria, S., Queija, R.: Two queues with random time-limited polling. Probab. Math. Stat. **37**(2), 257–289 (2017)

Applications

Short Term Wind Turbine Power Output Prediction

Sándor Kolumbán[1], Stella Kapodistria[2](✉), and Nazanin Nooraee[3]

[1] Department of Mathematics and Computer Science of the Hungarian Line,
Babeş-Bolyai University, Cluj-Napoca, Romania
[2] Department of Mathematics and Computer Science, Eindhoven University
of Technology, P.O. Box 513, 5600 MB Eindhoven, The Netherlands
s.kapodistria@tue.nl
[3] MSD, Eindhoven, The Netherlands

Abstract. In the wind energy industry, it is of great importance to
develop models that accurately forecast the power output of a wind turbine, as such predictions are used for wind farm location assessment
or power pricing and bidding, monitoring, and preventive maintenance.
As a first step, and following the guidelines of the existing literature,
we use the *supervisory control and data acquisition* (SCADA) data to
model the *wind turbine power curve* (WTPC). We explore various parametric and non-parametric approaches for the modeling of the WTPC,
such as parametric logistic functions, and non-parametric piecewise linear, polynomial, or cubic spline interpolation functions. We demonstrate
that all aforementioned classes of models are rich enough (with respect
to their relative complexity) to accurately model the WTPC, as their
mean squared error (MSE) is close to the MSE lower bound calculated
from the historical data. However, all aforementioned models, when it
comes to forecasting, seem to have an intrinsic limitation, due to their
inability to capture the inherent auto-correlation of the data. To avoid
this conundrum, we show that adding a properly scaled ARMA modeling layer increases short-term prediction performance, while keeping
the long-term prediction capability of the model. We further enhance
the accuracy of our proposed model, by incorporating additional environmental factors that affect the power output, such as the ambient
temperature and the wind direction.

Keywords: Wind turbine power curve modeling · parametric and
non-parametric modeling techniques · probabilistic forecasting ·
SCADA data

The authors acknowledge the Daisy4offshore consortium for the provision of the data.
The work of Sándor Kolumbán and Stella Kapodistria is supported by NWO through
the Gravitation-grant NETWORKS-024.002.003. Sándor Kolumbán also received funding from the Institute for Complex Molecular Systems (ICMS) in Eindhoven. Furthermore, the research of Stella Kapodistria was partly done in the framework of the
TKI-WoZ: Daisy4offshore project.

E. Hyytiä and V. Kavitha (Eds.): VALUETOOLS 2022, LNICST 482, pp. 99–132, 2023.
https://doi.org/10.1007/978-3-031-31234-2_7

1   Introduction

Wind turbine power curves (WTPC) are used for the modeling of the power output of a single wind turbine. Such models are needed in i) Wind power pricing and bidding: Electricity is a commodity which is traded similarly to stocks and swaps, and its pricing incorporates principles from supply and demand. ii) Wind energy assessment and prediction: Wind resource assessment is the process by which wind farm developers estimate the future energy production of a wind farm. iii) Choosing a wind turbine: WTPC models aid the wind farm developers to choose the generators of their choice, which would provide optimum efficiency and improved performance. iv) Monitoring a wind turbine and for preventive maintenance: A WTPC model can serve as a very effective performance monitoring tool, as several failure modes can result in power generation outside the specifications. As soon as an imminent failure is identified, preventive maintenance (age or condition based) can be implemented, which will reduce costs and increase the availability of the asset. v) Warranty formulations: Power curve warranties are often included in contracts, to insure that the wind turbine performs according to specifications. Furthermore, service providers offer warranty and verification testing services of whether a turbine delivers its specified output and reaches the warranted power curve, while meeting respective grid code requirements. See, e.g., [13,21,27] and the references therein for the aforementioned applications. Thus it is pivotal to construct accurate WTPC models. However, this is a difficult problem, as the output power of a wind turbine varies significantly with wind speed and every wind turbine has a very unique power performance curve, [14].

In this paper, we create an accurate WTPC model based on a real dataset and suggest practical and scientific improvements on the model construction. We initially construct a *static* model (in which the regressor(s) and the regressand(s) are considered to be independent identically distributed (i.i.d.) random variables) for the WTPC and demonstrate how various parametric and non-parametric approaches are performing from both a theoretical perspective, and also with regard to the data. In particular, we explore parametric logistic functions, and the non-parametric piecewise linear interpolation technique, the polynomial interpolation technique, and the cubic spline interpolation technique. We demonstrate that all aforementioned classes of models are rich enough to accurately model the WTPC, as their mean squared error (MSE) is close to a theoretical MSE lower bound. Within each non-parametric model class, we select the best model by rewarding MSEs close to the theoretical bound, while simultaneously penalizing for overly complicated models (i.e., models with many unknown parameters), using the Bayesian information criterion (BIC), see [20]. We demonstrate that such a static model, even after incorporating information on the wind speed and the available environmental factors, such as wind angle and ambient temperature, does not fully capture all available information. To this end, we propose in this paper, to enhance the static model with a *dynamic* layer (in which the regressor(s) is considered to be inter-correlated e.g., time series or stochastic processes), based on an autoregressive-moving-average (ARMA) modeling layer.

1.1   Contribution of the Paper

In this paper, based on a real dataset, we explore a hybrid approach for the wind turbine power output modeling consisting of the static model plus the dynamic layer. This approach: i) provides a very accurate modeling approach; ii) is very useful for accurate short and long-term predictions; iii) indicates that, within the cut-in wind speed (3.5 m/s) and the rated output wind speed (15 m/s), the conditional distribution of the power output is Gaussian. We consider that points i)–ii) mentioned above will contribute directly to the practice, as the accurate modeling and forecasting capabilities are of utter importance. We follow the straightforward and industrially accepted approach of first estimating the WTPC, then extending this model with additional modeling layers. Although, there are various ways of modeling the WTPC, we argue, that above a given level of modeling flexibility, the exact choice is not important. The presented approach relies on available predictions of the environmental conditions. Furthermore, point *iii)* mentioned above will greatly benefit the literature, as it is the first stepping stone towards proving that random power injections from wind energy in the electric grid can be accurately modeled using a Gaussian framework, see [15,16]. All in all, in this paper, we provide a new dataset collected from a wind turbine, and use it to show how to accurately model and forecast power output. Since the features of the used SCADA data are common among other types of turbines, the conclusions of the paper remain valid for other turbines as well. The analysis presented in this paper is scientifically and practically relevant, and contributes substantially from both the modeling and forecasting aspect, while providing a thorough overview of sound statistical methods. All results presented in the paper are motivated scientifically (when appropriate and possible) and are supported by real data.

1.2   Paper Outline

In Sect. 2, we treat the WTPC modeling: First, in Sect. 2.1, we present a simple static WTPC modeling approach, which models the power output as a function of the wind speed, using both parametric and non-parametric approaches; parametric logistic models (Sect. 2.1), non-parametric piecewise linear models (Sect. 2.1), polynomial models (Sect. 2.1), and spline models (Sect. 2.1). In Sect. 2.2, we compare the various modeling classes and determine criteria for model selection. In Sect. 3, we enhance the static model at hand by incorporating additional factors, such as the wind angle and the ambient temperature. Analyzing the residuals of the enhanced static model, we are motivated to introduce a dynamic Gaussian layer in our model, cf. Sect. 4, which produces very accurate short-term predictions, cf. Sect. 4.3. We conclude the paper with some remarks in Sect. 5. Finally, in the appendix, Sect. A, we describe the raw data and provide all information on how the data was cleaned.

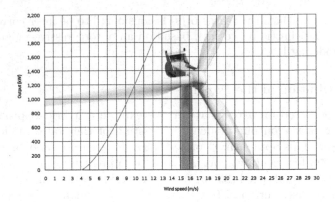

Fig. 1. WTPC of the V80-2.0MW (picture from [26])

2 Power Curve Modeling and Its Limitations

When it comes to pricing wind power, assessing the possible location for a wind turbine installation or to forecasting short-term (expected) power generation for supply purposes, the main tool proposed in the literature is the WTPC. Such a curve is used to describe the relationship between the steady wind speed and the produced power output of the turbine. The shape of the WTPC for the type of wind turbines of interest to this study is depicted in Fig. 1, while the fitted curve based on the cleaned data is depicted in Fig. 2.

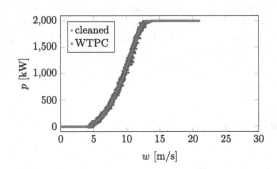

Fig. 2. The power output p against wind speed w for the cleaned training dataset together with an estimated WTPC

The WTPC, in ideal (laboratory) conditions, is given by the International Standard or the manufacturer, cf. [6,26], but such curves can change over time due to environmental changes or due to component wear. This makes it paramount to estimate the power curve for each turbine individually, so these tailor-made WTPCs may be used for power generation forecasting, decision under uncertainty, and monitoring.

The literature dealing with the topic of WTPC modeling techniques is extensive and covers many fields, see, e..g., [3, 10, 12, 13, 23] and the references therein. The majority of this work is focused on obtaining the best parametric or non-parametric model for the power curve of a turbine based on the available data. To this purpose, different approaches are compared using various criteria. However, as we point out in this paper by comparing the various model classes proposed in the literature, obtaining a parametric or non-parametric estimate of the WTPC is of limited value. Although Fig. 2 indicates an "appropriate" fitted model to the power output using the wind speed, there are apparent remaining residuals that are not explained by the fitted power curve. Investigating the statistical properties of the residuals reveals features that should be taken into account in the modeling. The remaining residuals can be explained by the fact that it might be needed to use additional regressors (besides the wind speed) to explain the power output, and can be attributed to the fact that the homoscedasticity assumption is not valid, i.e. the variance of the residuals is not constant and the residuals are highly correlated. These two issues can be partly overcome by considering machine learning and artificial intelligence approaches, see, e..g., [5, 17, 25] and the references therein. However, the drawback in these approaches is that the models are not interpretable, that they require a trove of data for their training, and that they cannot be easily transferred to model the WTPC of another wind turbine. For these reasons, we strongly believe that, contrary to the existing literature, the focus should shift to obtaining models that are interpretable, that can be easily extended to various regressors, and that can capture the heteroscedastic nature of the data. Such models should not only be ranked according to the regular modeling power, but also according to their computational complexity and their numerical robustness.

2.1   Power Curve Modeling Classes

In this section, we present and compare various model classes proposed in the literature. Firstly, we introduce some notation in Sect. 2.1 that allows us to describe in a uniform manner the models belonging to different model classes. Thereafter, we describe how to calculate the estimates for each model class. For all model classes, we assume that the value of the power curve is constant below 3.5 m/s taking the estimated power output value at 3.5 m/s. Similarly, in the wind speed range between 15 m/s and 25 m/s, the power output curve is constant taking the estimated power output value at 15 m/s. Above the cut-out speed 25 m/s, the power output is set to zero as the turbine should not operate. Thus, this part of the curve is not estimated, as in addition the cleaned dataset does not contain any observations in this range. These limitations need to be incorporated into the estimation procedure of the specific models, the details of which are presented in Sect. 2.1. We note that the chosen 15 m/s as an upper bound, for the rated speed, is lower than the value suggested by the manufacturer (see Sect. A), but the data validate our choice.

We consider both parametric and non-parametric models and compare the various model classes using the mean squared error (MSE) value, while within a class (for the non-parametric models) we select a model taking into account the complexity associated with it; non-parametric model classes (e.g. polynomial or spline models) have a nested structure, where the nesting levels correspond to complexity levels within the class (e.g. degree of polynomial or knot points of splines). The selection procedure of a model within a class is presented in Sect. 2.1.

Modeling and Least Squares Estimation. A power curve is a functional relation between the wind speed, w, and the power generation, p. We define this functional relation as

$$p = \mathcal{M}_\theta(w), \tag{1}$$

where $\mathcal{M}_\theta(\cdot)$ is a function belonging to the model class parametrized by a vector of parameters $\theta \in \mathbb{R}^{n_\theta}$, with n_θ the dimension of the parameter vector depending on the model class $\mathcal{M}$. In the next sections, we consider various parametric and non-parametric model classes: logistic models $\mathcal{G}_\theta(\cdot)$ in Sect. 2.1, piecewise linear models $\mathcal{L}_\theta(\cdot)$ in Sect. 2.1, polynomial models $\mathcal{P}_\theta(\cdot)$ in Sect. 2.1, and spline models $\mathcal{S}_\theta(\cdot)$ in Sect. 2.1.

Given a dataset containing a series of wind speed and power output pairs, $(w_k, p_k)_{1 \leq k \leq N}$ with N the total number of observations, we define the least squares estimate within a model class as

$$\hat{\theta} = \arg\min_\theta \frac{1}{N} \sum_{k=1}^{N} (p_k - \mathcal{M}_\theta(w_k))^2. \tag{2}$$

In order to shorten notation, the power output given by the least-squares estimated model at a given time is going to be denoted as $\hat{p} = \mathcal{M}_{\hat{\theta}}(w)$, where the model class $\mathcal{M}$ is always going to be clear from the context.

One important conclusion of the paper is that WTPC modeling has significant limitations. In order to show this, we introduce some elementary facts about least squares estimates related to quantized data (as the SCADA data are quantized to one decimal digit, as described in Sect. A).

Proposition 1 (Lower bound for MSE). *Irrespective of the model structure that is used to fit a model to the training data, if the training data are quantized in the regressor then there is a minimal attainable MSE and that can be calculated based on the data.*

Let the samples be $(x_k, y_k)_{1 \leq k \leq N}$ and consider a model $y = \mathcal{M}_\theta(x)$, with least squares estimate

$$\hat{\theta} = \arg\min_\theta \frac{1}{N} \sum_{k=1}^{N} (y_k - \mathcal{M}_\theta(x_k))^2.$$

Let $\mathcal{X}$ be the set of all appearing values of x, i.e. $\mathcal{X} = \bigcup_{k=1}^{N}\{x_k\}$, then the minimal attainable MSE value can be calculated as

$$\min_{\theta} \frac{1}{N} \sum_{k=1}^{N}(y_k - \mathcal{M}_{\theta}(x_k))^2 \geq \frac{1}{N} \sum_{x \in \mathcal{X}} \sum_{k=1}^{N} \mathbb{1}_{\{x_k=x\}} (y_k - \bar{y}_x)^2, \tag{3}$$

with

$$\bar{y}_x = \frac{\sum_{k=1}^{N} \mathbb{1}_{\{x_k=x\}} y_k}{\sum_{k=1}^{N} \mathbb{1}_{\{x_k=x\}}}, \tag{4}$$

and $\mathbb{1}_{\{\cdot\}}$ an indicator function taking value 1, if the event in the brackets is satisfied, and 0, otherwise.

Proof. The MSE can be written as

$$\frac{1}{N} \sum_{k=1}^{N}(y_k - \mathcal{M}_{\theta}(x_k))^2 = \frac{1}{N} \sum_{x \in \mathcal{X}} \sum_{k=1}^{N} \mathbb{1}_{\{x_k=x\}} (y_k - \mathcal{M}_{\theta}(x))^2.$$

The right hand side of the above equation can be bounded by calculating lower bounds to each group of summands involving the same regressor value x. Given x, let $z_x = \mathcal{M}_{\theta}(x)$, then the corresponding group of summands can be written as

$$S_x := \frac{1}{N} \sum_{k=1}^{N} \mathbb{1}_{\{x_k=x\}} (y_k - z_x)^2.$$

The derivative of S_x with respect to z_x is

$$\frac{\partial}{\partial z_x} S_x = -\frac{2}{N} \sum_{k=1}^{N} \mathbb{1}_{\{x_k=x\}} (y_k - z_x)$$

$$= 2\frac{z_x}{N} \sum_{k=1}^{N} \mathbb{1}_{\{x_k=x\}} - \frac{2}{N} \sum_{k=1}^{N} \mathbb{1}_{\{x_k=x\}} y_k.$$

Solving the optimality condition $\frac{\partial}{\partial z_x} S_x = 0$ for z_x reveals that the minimum is obtained at (4). Thus, the lower bound is attained if $\forall x \in \mathcal{X} : \mathcal{M}_{\theta}(x) = \bar{y}_x$.

The lower bound given in (3) is always true, but it is not necessarily a tight bound. If every regressor's value, x, appears only once in the data, then this bound would be 0, which is trivial for a sum of squares. The bound will give a nonzero value in the case of observations with $|\mathcal{X}| < N$, where $|\mathcal{X}|$ denotes the cardinality of the set $\mathcal{X}$. In our case, when considering $\mathcal{X} = \{3.5, 3.6, \ldots, 14.9, 15\}$, with $|\mathcal{X}| = 116$ and $N = 12849$, the bound is non-zero.

Constrained Model. In order to keep the notation and the calculations simple, without loss of generality, we estimate the corresponding parameters and choose the best WTPC model (within a class), only for wind speeds in the range [3.5, 15].

To this end, we consider a slightly modified model: For a model $\mathcal{M}_\theta$ determined by the parameter vector θ, from the model class $\mathcal{M}$, we define the constrained model $\overline{\mathcal{M}}_\theta$ as

$$
\begin{aligned}
\overline{\mathcal{M}}_\theta(w) = \mathcal{M}_\theta\big(3.5 \cdot \mathbb{1}\{w < 3.5\} + w \cdot \mathbb{1}\{3.5 \le w < 15\} \\
+ 15 \cdot \mathbb{1}\{15 \le w < 25\}\big) - \mathcal{M}_\theta(0) \cdot \mathbb{1}\{25 \le w\}.
\end{aligned}
\tag{5}
$$

The argument of $\mathcal{M}_\theta$ is constructed such that for wind values smaller than 3.5 the model $\overline{\mathcal{M}}_\theta$ will result in the same power output values as $\mathcal{M}_\theta(3.5)$, for values $w \in [3.5, 15)$ the model $\overline{\mathcal{M}}_\theta$ results in the same power output as $\mathcal{M}_\theta$, for values $w \in [15, 25)$ the model $\overline{\mathcal{M}}_\theta$ results in the same power output as $\mathcal{M}_\theta(15)$, and for wind values above 25 the predicted power output is zero. Considering the constrained model, we can estimate the parameters of the model as usual after a slight transformation of the training data: for all observations with $w < 3.5$ the value of w is changed to 3.5, for all observations with $w \in [15, 25)$ the value of w is changed to 15, and all observations with $w \ge 25$ are ignored. Then, this transformed dataset is used for the parameter estimation.

Logistic Models. Logistic models have been widely used in growth curve analysis and their shape resembles that of a WTPC under the cut-out speed. For this reason, they were recently applied to model WTPCs, see [8,13]. [12] present an overview of parametric and non-parametric models for the modeling of the WTPC, and state that the 5-parameter logistic (5-PL) function is superior in comparison to the other models under consideration. However, as we show in the sequel, this statement should be viewed with skepticism and perhaps should be interpreted as the result of a comparison only within models with the same number of parameters (parametric models) or same level of complexity (non-parametric models).

In this section, we apply a different formulation of the logistic model from the one used in [12], so as to improve fitness. The 5-PL model used in [13] is given as follows

$$
p = \theta_5 + \frac{\theta_1 - \theta_5}{\left(1 + \left(\frac{w}{\theta_2}\right)^{\theta_3}\right)^{\theta_4}}.
\tag{6}
$$

In this model, parameters θ_1 and θ_5 are the asymptotic minimum and maximum, respectively, parameter θ_2 is the inflection point, parameter θ_3 is the slope and θ_4 governs the non-symmetrical part of the curve. However, this type of 5-PL does not describe the asymmetry as a function of the curvature, see [18]. As an alternative, [24] proposed a technique which can handle the curvature in the extreme regions. We apply this technique with a slight modification to fit a logistic model to the WTPC. The general form of the model is presented in Eq. (7)

$$p = \mathcal{G}_\theta(w)$$

$$= \theta_1 + \frac{\theta_4 - \theta_1}{1 + exp\left[-\left\{\theta_2(w - \theta_3) + \theta_\ell(w - \theta_3)^2 \mathbb{1}_{[3.5, \theta_3)}(w) + \theta_u(w - \theta_3)^2 \mathbb{1}_{[\theta_3, 15]}(w)\right\}\right]},$$
$$(7)$$

with $\mathbb{1}_A(w)$ denoting the indicator function taking value 1 when $w \in A$, for a given set A, and zero otherwise. We substitute the term $(w - \theta_3)^2 \mathbb{1}_{[3.5, \theta_3)}(w)$ in (7) with $(w - \theta_3)^4 \mathbb{1}_{[3.5, \theta_3)}(w)$, so as to capture more accurately the curvature in the left tail of the WTPC, cf. Fig. 2. For this reason, we refer to this model as the modified Stukel model (mStukel).

In Table 1, we present the MSE and BIC for the 5-PL model and the mStukel model according to (5). As it is evident from the results presented in Table 1, the mStukel model drastically improves the fitness of the WTCP. The parameter estimates, $\hat{\theta}^{(g)}$, of the mStukel model with the corresponding standard errors are given in Table 2.

Table 1. MSE and BIC for the fitted models on the training and validation datasets

Models	Training dataset		Validation dataset
	MSE	BIC	MSE
5-PL	1554.2700	131000	1650.7300
mStukel	884.4321	123710	1020.3800

Table 2. Parameter estimates (StandardError) for the mStukel logistic model on the training dataset

Parameter	Training set
$\hat{\theta}_1$	−30.8580 (1.3187)
$\hat{\theta}_2$	0.5845 (0.0010)
$\hat{\theta}_3$	9.6481 (0.0032)
$\hat{\theta}_4$	2010.46 (1.2119)
$\hat{\theta}_u$	0.1602 (0.0019)
$\hat{\theta}_\ell$	−0.0010 (0.00004)

Piecewise Linear Model Class. Piecewise linear models are not particularly appealing for practical use for many reasons, but they are very useful as benchmarks. We include piecewise linear models so they can serve as a benchmark non-parametric model class and because, as it is shown in the sequel, cf. Proposition 2, this class can achieve the bound of the MSE.

Let the piecewise linear function be defined as follows

$$p = \mathcal{L}_{\theta^{(\ell)}}(w) = \theta + \sum_{k=0}^{m-1} \mathbb{1}\{s_k \leq w\}(w - s_k)\theta_k. \tag{8}$$

The parameter vector $\theta^{(\ell)}$ consists of the (height) parameter θ and the segment slope parameters θ_k, $k = 0, 1, \ldots, m - 1$. The splitting points $s_0, \ldots, s_{m-1}$ should be defined beforehand. Throughout the paper, we use equidistant splitting points on the interval $[3.5, 15]$ and we estimate the parameters of the constrained model $\bar{\mathcal{L}}_{\theta^{(\ell)}}$ defined in Sect. 2.1.

The piecewise linear model can achieve the bound of the MSE on the training data. This is due to the quantized nature of the values of the data to one decimal digit. Thus, using 116 splitting points for the piecewise linear model, we can cover the entire range of wind values in $[3.5, 15]$. In this case, the least-squares estimate of the power output is given as the average of the power values of samples given the value of the wind speed, thus attaining the lower bound of the MSE on the training data.

Proposition 2 (Piecewise linear model attaining the MSE lower bound). *For a scalar dataset with one dimensional regressors with $|\mathcal{X}| = m + 1$ a piecewise linear model of order m with split points $\mathcal{X}$ attains the minimal MSE bound given in Proposition 1.*

Proof. For $|\mathcal{X}| = 1$ the only parameter to be estimated is θ, which should be chosen as $\bar{y}$, cf. Proposition 1.

The rest of the proof is based on induction on the cardinality of the set $\mathcal{X}$, denoted by $|\mathcal{X}|$. Let $\left(x^{(i)}\right)_{0 \leq i \leq m}$ be the ordered values of $\mathcal{X}$, such that $x^{(0)} < x^{(1)} < \cdots < x^{(m)}$ and lets assume that the parameters $\theta, \theta_0, \ldots, \theta_{m-2}$ are chosen such that the linear model with these parameters attains the minimal MSE on the restricted dataset having regressors $\mathcal{X} \setminus \{x^{(m)}\}$. To prove the statement, we need to show that θ_{m-1} can be chosen such that $\mathcal{L}_\theta(x^{(m)}) = \bar{y}_{x^{(m)}}$. From the definition of the piecewise linear function

$$\mathcal{L}_{\theta^{(\ell)}}(x^{(m)}) = \theta + \sum_{k=0}^{m-2} (x^{(m)} - x^{(k)})\theta_k + (x^{(m)} - x^{(m-1)})\theta_{m-1}.$$

Solving this equation for θ_{m-1}, we get that

$$\theta_{m-1} = \frac{\bar{y}_{x^{(m)}} - \theta - \sum_{k=0}^{m-2}(x^{(m)} - x^{(k)})\theta_k}{x^{(m)} - x^{(m-1)}},$$

which concludes the proof.

It can be stated in general that once a model structure has enough degrees of freedom to assign the estimates $\mathcal{M}_\theta(w)$ independently to every wind value $w \in \mathcal{X}$, then the lower bound for the MSE value can be attained.

Piecewise linear model classes, with a fixed number of splitting points equidistantly chosen in an interval, are not properly nested, if $m = 1, 2, \ldots$. Proper nesting is achieved, if $m = 2^0, 2^1, 2^2, \ldots$, or if some other exponential series is chosen. The parameters $\hat{\boldsymbol{\theta}}_m^{(\ell)}$ of a model belonging to the fixed choice of m can be estimated for different values of m, but then the problem reduces to optimally choosing m, which is a model selection problem.

The other reason, why it is instructive to examine the properties of the piecewise linear model structure, is that, assuming Gaussian residuals, the combined variance of the estimated parameters can be calculated analytically. This is visualized in Fig. 3 as the trace of the estimated covariance matrix of the parameters is shown against the complexity of the model class m. This shows the generic features of model selection problems.

For very small values of m the modeling error is big, so the estimated variance of those few estimated parameters is going to be big (combination of modeling error and variance from noise), so the sum is going to be a sum of few but large in absolute value entries. Values of m that correspond to a model class that can properly model the data will result in a sum that contains more summand terms, but with smaller in absolute value entries. The variance of the parameters in this case is expected to be small for two reasons: *i)* the modeling error is reduced or eliminated; *ii)* a small number of parameters needs to be estimated from the data. For higher values of m the number of summands will increase and so will the corresponding absolute values of the entries. This is because the modeling error was already minimized and a higher number of parameters needs to be estimated from the data, which increases their variance. This heuristic results in a quasiconvex shape of the MSE as a function of the complexity parameter m (a.k.a. the model order). The goal of model selection is to define how an optimal model order $\hat{m}$ should be chosen. This question arises in the case of all non-parametric model classes and our approach is based on the BIC, see Sect. 2.1.

As it can be seen in Fig. 3, the trace of the estimated covariance matrix of the parameters is quasiconvex shaped, as it decreases in the beginning and then it increases rapidly when the model order is increased. If this is compared to the decrease of the MSE shown in Fig. 4, we see that going above a given complexity level just adds unnecessary uncertainty to the estimation without improving the modeling precision. This trade-off should be balanced by the model selection algorithm. Using model selection based on the BIC, see Sect. 2.1, the optimal number of linear segments turns out to be $m = 13$. The parameters of the estimated model are given in Table 3. The MSE of this model on the training data is 815.5127, while on the validation set it is 974.6084.

Polynomial Model Class. A univariate polynomial model of degree m of the power function is given as

$$p = \mathcal{P}_{\boldsymbol{\theta}}(w) = \sum_{i=0}^{m} \theta_i w^i. \tag{9}$$

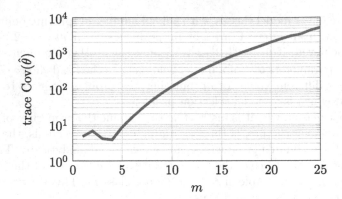

Fig. 3. The sum of the parameter variances for the piecewise linear model assuming Gaussian residuals

Table 3. Estimated parameters of a piecewise linear model with $m = 13$ segments

$t_k = 3.5 + k\frac{15-3.5}{13}$, $k = 0, \ldots, 12$			
Parameter	**Training set**	**Parameter**	**Training set**
$\hat{\theta}$	-8.3398	$\hat{\theta}_0$	0.8929
$\hat{\theta}_1$	95.4169	$\hat{\theta}_2$	17.8948
$\hat{\theta}_3$	42.1545	$\hat{\theta}_4$	58.0053
$\hat{\theta}_5$	38.8957	$\hat{\theta}_6$	60.8006
$\hat{\theta}_7$	47.2667	$\hat{\theta}_8$	6.8485
$\hat{\theta}_9$	-68.7682	$\hat{\theta}_{10}$	-207.2188
$\hat{\theta}_{11}$	-94.4818	$\hat{\theta}_{12}$	4.8853

The formulation given in (9) should be adapted to take into account the constrained model $\overline{\mathcal{P}}$ defined in Sect. 2.1. However, even after the transformation to the constrained model, and the reduction of the wind range to practically $[3.5, 15]$, we have to note that estimating the parameters θ_i, $i = 0, \ldots, m$, of the polynomial model is a numerically difficult problem. This is due to the fact that, e.g., for a polynomial model of degree $m = 14$, the coefficient matrix of the parameters includes entries corresponding to values $1, 15, 15^2, \ldots, 15^{14}$. Inverting such a matrix is numerically unstable due its high condition number, cf. [2].

To overcome the numerical stability issues, one of the simplest techniques is to rescale the argument w of the polynomial, so higher powers of the argument will still remain numerically tractable. With this change, we redefine the polynomial model as

$$\mathcal{P}_{\boldsymbol{\theta}(p)}(w) = \bar{p} + d_p \sum_{i=0}^{m} \theta_i \left(\frac{w - \bar{w}}{d_w}\right)^i, \tag{10}$$

where the polynomial parameter vector $\boldsymbol{\theta}^{(p)}$ contains the coefficients of the polynomial $\mathcal{P}$ as well as the scaling parameters $\bar{w}$, $\bar{p}$, d_w, d_p. $\bar{w}$ and $\bar{p}$ denote the sample averages of the wind speed (w), and the sample average of the power output (p), respectively, while d_w and d_p denote the sample standard deviation of the wind speed (w), and of the power output (p), respectively. The model order parameter for polynomial models is the degree of the polynomial, m.

Polynomial models are not performing well according to the literature. This is the result of a combination of factors: Firstly, they are not capable of capturing the flat plateau on the left and the right tail of WTPC. Once this obvious drawback is compensated by considering the constrained model, polynomial models drastically increase their fitness. Secondly, there are various numerical difficulties associated with the estimation of the parameters of polynomial models. Unfortunately, this issue constitutes a significant drawback especially at higher model orders, as we show in Sect. 2.2.

Estimating (in the least squares sense) the coefficients of a polynomial with degree $m = 14$ results in the parameters presented in Table 4. The choice of degree $m = 14$ is explained in Sect. 2.1. The MSE of this model on the training data is 812.2287, while on the validation set it is 969.8870.

Note, that the polynomial coefficients in Table 4 are reported with 15 decimal digits, as we take into account the support of the wind values $[3.5, 15]$ and the maximum degree of the polynomial model: this is due to the fact that for example for the polynomial of degree $m = 14$ the leading coefficient of the polynomial, $\hat{\theta}_{14}$, is multiplied with $\left(\frac{w-7.241154953692900}{3.092009009051451}\right)^{14}$ for $w \in [3.5, 15]$. This illustrates that the estimation of the polynomial coefficients is numerically sensitive, which is not the case for the other discussed non-parametric model classes.

Spline Model Class. Splines provide a universal family for approximating smooth functions. A spline is defined by a series of knot points and by polynomials representing its value between the knot points in a continuous way [19]. Formally a cubic B-spline is given by a triplet of parameters $\boldsymbol{\theta}^{(s)} = (m, \boldsymbol{k}, \boldsymbol{\alpha})$,

Table 4. Estimated parameters of a polynomial model with degree $m = 14$

Par.	Training set	Par.	Training set
$\hat{p}$	1012.7	$\hat{w}$	7.241154953692900
$\hat{d}_p$	601.0210490157367	$\hat{d}_w$	3.092009009051451
$\hat{\theta}_0$	-1.083983804472287	$\hat{\theta}_8$	0.913785265115761
$\hat{\theta}_1$	1.027493542215327	$\hat{\theta}_9$	0.158488326138962
$\hat{\theta}_2$	0.437620131289974	$\hat{\theta}_{10}$	-0.462562253267288
$\hat{\theta}_3$	-0.258311524269187	$\hat{\theta}_{11}$	0.100868720012586
$\hat{\theta}_4$	0.152839963020718	$\hat{\theta}_{12}$	0.068782606353010
$\hat{\theta}_5$	0.837258874326937	$\hat{\theta}_{13}$	-0.034900832592028
$\hat{\theta}_6$	-0.693269004241413	$\hat{\theta}_{14}$	0.004495461408312
$\hat{\theta}_7$	-0.791866808461089		

where $m \in \mathbb{N}_+$ is the number of basis functions used, $k \in \mathbb{R}^{m+4}$ is a vector of knot points in nondecreasing order, $\alpha \in \mathbb{R}^m$ is the vector of coefficients for the basis functions $B_{i,k,3}$ defined by the Cox-de Boor recursion [4]

$$
\begin{aligned}
B_{i,k,0}(x) &= \mathbb{1}_{[k_i, k_{i+1})}(x), \ i = 1, \dots, m+3, \\
B_{i,k,d}(x) &= \frac{x - k_i}{k_{i+d} - k_i} B_{i,k,d-1} \\
&+ \frac{k_{i+d+1} - x}{k_{i+d+1} - k_{i+1}} B_{i+1,k,d-1}, \ d = 1, 2, 3, \\
i &= 1, \dots, m+3-d.
\end{aligned}
\tag{11}
$$

A cubic B-spline model for the WTPC is given as

$$
p = \mathcal{S}_{\theta^{(s)}}(w) = \sum_{i=1}^{m} \alpha_i B_{i,k,3}(w).
\tag{12}
$$

The complexity of cubic spline models is defined by the number of basis functions m. If the knot points k are fixed then the parameters α can be estimated analytically in the least-squares sense, but this cannot be done simultaneously with the location of the knots [7]. We use a simple suboptimal procedure to find the estimates, which performs the estimation in two rounds. In the first round the knot points are equidistantly chosen in the $[3.5, 15]$ interval and the parameters α are estimated. In the second round, new knot points are calculated, based on the data and the first round estimates, using the MATLAB® routine *newknt*, which reallocates the knot points to allow a better estimation of α. Then α is estimated for the second time.

The estimated parameters $\hat{\theta}^{(s)}$ of a cubic spline using $m = 17$ B-splines are

$$
\begin{aligned}
\hat{\alpha} = [&- 8.0336698 \ - 7.2559215 \ - 23.865741 \\
&78.529492 \ 156.55003 \ 272.98557 \\
&452.80144 \ 690.69908 \ 1022.923 \ 1400.7208 \\
&1721.1444 \ 1921.2212 \ 1998.4378 \ 1992.549 \\
&2005.308 \ 1997.8069 \ 2000.3969]
\end{aligned}
\tag{13}
$$

with knot points

$$
\begin{aligned}
\hat{k} = [&3.5 \ 3.5 \ 3.5 \ 3.5 \ 4.4247 \ 5.2668 \ 5.9855 \\
&6.7569 \ 7.6994 \ 8.6481 \ 9.7265 \\
&10.8994 \ 11.6831 \ 12.3575 \ 12.9990 \\
&13.6470 \ 14.323515 \ 15 \ 15 \ 15].
\end{aligned}
\tag{14}
$$

An interesting feature of the resulting $\hat{k}$ is that its first four entries and last four entries coincide. As it can be deduced from Eq. (11), the multiplicity of the knot points shows how smooth is the function at the specific knot point.

The two endpoints (due to their high multiplicity) indicate that the higher order derivatives are zero at the endpoints of the support [3.5, 15], so the estimated WTPC is flat at the left and right tails of the support. This is expected and desired, since the support was chosen so that the WTPC outside this support is constant (left and right tail of the WTPC).

B-splines are zero outside the range defined by the knot points, so a proper power function estimate is obtained by transforming $\mathcal{S}$ to the constrained model $\overline{\mathcal{S}}$ defined in Sect. 2.1. The MSE of the model $\overline{\mathcal{S}}$, with the parameters given above, evaluated on the training data, is 811.9171, while on the validation set, it is 969.5854.

We note that [22] developed a much more evolved procedure for the selection of the number of the knot points, as well as for the selection of the location of the knot points, but such a complicated model choice does not improve more than 1% the modeling fit, which is insignificant if compared to the improvements achieved by incorporating the wind direction and the ambient temperature, and by the addition of the dynamic layer.

Model Selection Based on BIC. In the case of non-parametric models, the model class consists of subclasses indexed by the complexity parameter m (a.k.a. model order), i.e., piecewise linear models with an increasing number of segments, polynomial models with an increasing degree, or spline models with an increasing number of basis functions. The appropriate model order should be selected in a way that adheres to the principle of parsimony: Goodness-of-fit must be balanced against model complexity in order to avoid overfitting–that is, to avoid building models that in addition to explain the data, they also explain the independent random noise in the data at hand, and, as a result, fail in out-of-sample predictions.

There are several approaches for selecting a model, among others the AIC [1] or the BIC [20]. Although AIC can be asymptotically optimal under certain conditions, BIC penalizes the model complexity stronger. Therefore we use the BIC for the selection of the models reported in the previous sections. The BIC is defined as

$$\mathrm{BIC}(\hat{\boldsymbol{\theta}}_m) = \ln(N)n_{\hat{\theta}} - 2\ln(\hat{L}),$$

where N is the number of data samples used to estimate $\hat{\boldsymbol{\theta}}_m$, $n_{\hat{\theta}}$ is the number of estimated parameters and $\hat{L}$ is the estimated likelihood of the observations assuming the model with estimated parameters $\hat{\boldsymbol{\theta}}_m$.

Assuming a Gaussian noise model $p_k = \mathcal{M}_{\tilde{\theta}}(w_k) + \varepsilon_k$, $k = 1, \ldots, N$, where $\varepsilon_k \overset{\text{i.i.d.}}{\sim} \mathcal{N}(0, \sigma^2)$, we get that the BIC can be written as

$$\mathrm{BIC}(\tilde{\boldsymbol{\theta}}) = \ln(N)n_{\hat{\theta}} + N\ln(2\pi\sigma^2) + \frac{\sum_{i=1}^{N}\varepsilon_i^2}{\sigma^2}.$$

If the parameters $\hat{\boldsymbol{\theta}}_m$ of a model from the subclass with complexity m are estimated using the training data, then the MSE on the training data, say MSE_m, is an asymptotically unbiased estimator for the unknown variance σ^2. Thus, evaluating the BIC on the training data yields that

$$\mathrm{BIC}(\hat{\boldsymbol{\theta}}_m) \approx \ln(N)n_{\hat{\boldsymbol{\theta}}_m} + N\ln(\mathrm{MSE}_m) + N\ln(2\pi) + 1.$$

Models with different complexity are compared using the $\mathrm{BIC}(\hat{\boldsymbol{\theta}}_m)$ and the model complexity is estimated as

$$\hat{m} = \arg\min{}_m \mathrm{BIC}(\hat{\boldsymbol{\theta}}_m),$$

resulting in the final estimate

$$\hat{\boldsymbol{\theta}} = \hat{\boldsymbol{\theta}}_{\hat{m}}.$$

Using this procedure, we obtain that for the piecewise linear models, the optimal number of segments is 13, for the cubic spline models the optimal number of basis functions is 17, while for the polynomial models the optimal degree is 14.

2.2   Comparison of Models from Different Classes

Figures 4 and 5 depict the behavior of the MSE as a function of the complexity for the different model structures on the training and the validation datasets, respectively. The goal of this section is to summarize the remarks that can be made based on these figures. Since, the mStukel logistic model has a fixed number of complexity parameters m (a.k.a. fixed model order), its MSE is depicted in Figs. 4 and 5 as a constant function in m, taking values 884.4321 and 1020.3800, on the training and validation sets, respectively.

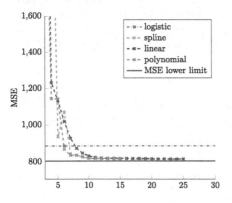
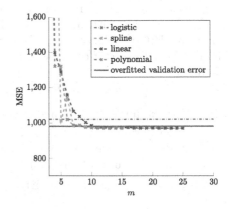

Fig. 4. The MSE on the training set   **Fig. 5.** The MSE on the validation set

The logistic model class, due to its parametric nature, only contains models that have a specific shape similar to what is expected from the WTPC. This is the reason why it performs relatively well, if compared to other models with matching complexity ($m = 6$), especially when compared to the piecewise linear and the spline models. The main advantage of parametric models is that they have a pre-defined shape that matches the data, and they can describe the model with a much smaller number of parameters. As a result they can be used in case the data sparsely covers the support. However, in our case, due to the large amount of data covering densely the full support of the wind values, such advantage does not become apparent.

As stated in Proposition 1, we can calculate the MSE lower bound based on the data. Regardless of the model class, the MSE converges to that limit, as the complexity parameter tends to infinity, $m \to \infty$. Moreover, for some of the model classes we investigate, convergence will occur with finite complexity, e.g., piecewise linear models converge at $m = 116$, cf. Sect. 2.1. Similar complexity values can be calculated for the other model classes. It is important to note that the MSE converges rapidly to the lower bound for small values of m, while for large values of m, convergence seems to slow down significantly. As it can be seen in Fig. 4, this happens in the range $m \in [10, 15]$, depending on the model class.

As expected, when considering a very complicated model, then the validation error has the tendency to increase in comparison to the optimal complexity model. The solid line in Fig. 5 depicts the validation error of the model that attains the lower limit of the estimation error. As it is visible in the figure, this overfitting error is really small in comparison to the validation error of model orders around the optimal order (the validation error of the most overfitted model is 955.9658 that is approximately 1% worse than the validation errors of the different models). This shows that the data are fully covering the support [3.5, 15] of the wind speed for the constrained model, and that, in our case, overfitting issues are of minor importance, as such overfitting does not impact significantly the validation error.

The model orders selected by the BIC, cf. Sect. 2.1, are all under $m = 20$, so they result in relatively simple models. They require more parameters than the logistic model, but the comparison based on the BIC indicates that the extra flexibility of these models is needed. This is not unexpected, given the provided improvement in terms of the modeling error.

Here we can underline one of the main messages of the paper: non-parametric models seem to be more suitable for the WTPC modeling than parametric models. This is mainly due to the relatively simple shape of the WTPC and the large amount of available data that can be used for the estimation of models with high complexity.

Another advantage for non-parametric models is that their shape does not depend significantly on the knowledge of the cut-in speed and the rated speed. As long as a lower bound for the cut-in speed and an upper bound for the rated speed are known, these models obtain the right shape between the two values. Whereas, for parametric models these two values are either chosen beforehand, which impacts the model significantly, or they need to be estimated, which impacts significantly the difficulty of estimation (e.g., non-convexity, non-uniqueness, etc.).

Based on the above remark, that non-parametric models provide a better fit for the WTPC, we now turn our attention to the natural question on how to choose between the various classes of non-parametric models. This question is treated in the sequel in more detail.

In what follows, the goal is to show that in theory it should not matter which non-parametric model class we choose to estimate the WTPC, however practical considerations can still result in arguments against particular model classes. The main objective, when considering a model class, should be the numerical robustness of the estimation procedure that can provide the corresponding estimates.

The polynomial model structure is evaluated only up to degree $m = 15$, cf. Figs. 4 and 5. This is because estimating higher order polynomials is numerically infeasible, as we already mentioned in Sect. 2.1. When it comes to estimation of splines with fixed knot points k, the estimates of the coefficients α can be obtained in a numerically reliable way. Similarly for piecewise linear models, given the split points (t_k), the estimation is numerically reliable. Due to the simple shape of the WTPC, the allocation of these points is not particularly important. What could be gained by the optimal choice of these points is on the one hand negligible, as it can be seen from Fig. 4, and on the other hand it can be mitigated by adding extra parameters.

In order to illustrate that the choice of the model class is almost irrelevant, we define a measure of comparison for models from different model classes, say $\mathcal{M}_{\theta_i}(\cdot)$, $i = 1, 2$, as follows

$$\Delta_{\theta_1, \theta_2} = \frac{\mathbb{E}(\mathcal{M}_{\theta_1}(W) - \mathcal{M}_{\theta_2}(W))^2}{\min\left\{\mathbb{E}(P - \mathcal{M}_{\theta_1}(W))^2, \mathbb{E}(P - \mathcal{M}_{\theta_2}(W))^2\right\}}, \tag{15}$$

with W and P denoting the random wind speed and the random power output, respectively. $\Delta_{\theta_1, \theta_2}$ measures what is the expected difference between predictions made by the two models θ_1 and θ_2 relative to the modeling error of the better of the two. This quantity is evaluated empirically both on the training and on the validation data using the models estimated earlier and the obtained values are reported in Table 5. The difference between the logistic and the selected spline model $\Delta_{\hat{\theta}^{(g)}, \hat{\theta}^{(s)}}$ is approximately 10%, the difference between the piecewise linear and spline models $\Delta_{\hat{\theta}^{(\ell)}, \hat{\theta}^{(s)}}$ is under 1%, and $\Delta_{\hat{\theta}^{(p)}, \hat{\theta}^{(s)}}$ gets even smaller when it comes to the polynomial and spline models. This indicates that optimizing the model selection with regard to the class is not expected to provide significant improvements. As there is no significant difference between the various non-parametric WTPC model classes, from this point onward, we restrict our analysis to the spline model given in Sect. 2.1.

In the next sections, we address two points of concern: $i)$ we discuss how to improve the WTPC model by incorporating more environmental variables, such

Table 5. The relative difference between models of different classes

Parameter	Training set	Validation set
$\Delta_{\hat{\theta}(g),\hat{\theta}(s)}$	0.0884	0.0715
$\Delta_{\hat{\theta}(\ell),\hat{\theta}(s)}$	0.0059	0.0048
$\Delta_{\hat{\theta}(p),\hat{\theta}(s)}$	0.0005	0.0004

as the relative wind angle and the ambient temperature, and *ii)* we explore if the residuals of the model are Gaussian and investigate how to incorporate the natural autocorrelation of the data into the model by specifying that the power output variable depends linearly on its own previous values and on a stochastic term. In Sect. 3, we discuss the results of incorporating more environmental variables into the power estimation, while in Sect. 4, we explore the possibility of estimating the power output based on previous measurements in time.

3 Including More Physical Parameters

From a physical perspective the power output can be model as

$$p = \frac{1}{2}\rho\pi R^2 C_p(\lambda,\beta)w^3, \tag{16}$$

with p the power captured by the rotor of a wind turbine, ρ the air density, R the radius of the rotor determining its swept area, C_p the power coefficient which is a function of the blade-pitch angle β and the tip-speed ratio λ, and w the wind speed, see [9, Eq. (2)]. Thus, although wind speed is the most relevant factor determining the power output, it is evident from (16) that other environmental or turbine specific factors impact the power output. One way to improve the modeling and forecasting capabilities of the WTPC model is to incorporate additional relevant parameters according to the physical first principle arguments. In accordance to our available data, we illustrate the additional benefits of incorporating two additional environmental parameters: the relative incidence angle of the wind with respect to the rotor plane, say ϕ, and the ambient temperature recorded on the exterior of the wind turbine nacelle, say T.

The new signals are incorporated into (12) as follows

$$p = \mathcal{F}_{\theta(f)}(w,\phi,T) = \mathcal{S}_{\theta(s)}\left(w\cdot|\cos(\phi)|^{c_\phi}\right)\left(1 + c_T\left(T - \bar{T}\right)\right), \tag{17}$$

with ϕ and T the relative incidence angle and the ambient temperature, $\bar{T}$ the average temperature obtained by the training data, and $c_\phi \geq 0$ and c_T are parameters to be estimated from the data.

The inclusion of these factors can be argued based on heuristic arguments as follows: As a rough approximation, it can be stated that power generation is only achieved by the perpendicular component of the wind speed to the rotor plane of the turbine. This perpendicular component is mathematically represented by $w\cdot\cos(\phi)$. The introduction of the absolute value of the cos term ensures that the direction of the wind is not changed. Furthermore, the inclusion of the $c_\phi \geq 0$ parameter in the $|\cos(\phi)|^{c_\phi}$ term makes sure that the wind is not amplified (i.e., the wind speed cannot get a multiplier greater than one). Regarding the inclusion of the temperature factor, this is motivated by the inherent physical relation of the temperature and the air density, as well as the prominent role of air density in the physical expression of the power output, cf. (16). Without assuming any specific functional form for this dependence, the parameter c_T can be thought of as the partial derivative of this relationship around the average temperature $\bar{T}$.

Using the B-spline WTPC model $\hat{\boldsymbol{\theta}}^{(s)}$ with complexity $m = 17$, with estimated parameters $\hat{k}$ and $\hat{\alpha}$ given in Sect. 2.1, we can estimate the value of c_ϕ and c_T in the least squares sense. In Table 6, we provide the MSE values of the model (17), where the parameters are estimated or fixed to zero in different combinations. Fixing either c_ϕ or c_T is equivalent to omitting the corresponding modeling aspect. This allows us to see the impact of the different environmental parameters on the power generation. The first line contains the baseline, the MSE value of the WTPC model with only the wind factor. The other lines contain the MSE values corresponding to WTPC models generalized to include only the incidence angle; only the relative temperature; or both the angle and the temperature. In the remainder of the paper, $\hat{\boldsymbol{\theta}}^{(f)}$ denotes the combination of the B-spline WTPC model $\hat{\boldsymbol{\theta}}^{(s)}$ generalized to include the two environmental factors, with estimates $\hat{c}_\phi = 1.0115$ and $\hat{c}_T = -0.0050$. For this reason, when needed, we shall illustrate this by writing $\hat{\boldsymbol{\theta}}^{(f)} = (\hat{\boldsymbol{\theta}}^{(s)}, \hat{c}_\phi, \hat{c}_T)$.

Table 6. The MSE values of models given in (17) with different modeling complexity

c_ϕ parameter	c_T parameter	MSE on training set	MSE on validation set
$c_\phi = 0$	$c_T = 0$	811.9171	969.5854
$\hat{c}_\phi = 0.4279$	$c_T = 0$	810.1959	943.8046
$c_\phi = 0$	$\hat{c}_T = -0.0047$	690.5758	798.9763
$\hat{c}_\phi = 1.0115$	$\hat{c}_T = -0.0050$	681.6206	753.7712

From Table 6, it is evident that the inclusion of the incidence angle does not improve significantly the model. This is evident by the difference between the MSE values of the two models captured in the first and second line, respectively, of the table, or similarly in the third and fourth line. This difference is smaller than one percent. This is not because the incidence angle is not relevant for power generation, but because the automatism in the turbine keeps the nacelle facing the most beneficial direction with regard to the power output. Figure 6 depicts the empirical density function of the incidence angle ϕ and it shows that the incidence angle is tightly concentrated around 0°, which indicates that the wind is almost always nearly perpendicular to the rotor plane. Contrary, the inclusion of the temperature, with estimated parameter c_T, adds more than 15%

in the modeling precision. Figure 7 depicts the values of the ambient temperature for the training set (red) and the validation set (blue). Moreover, the negative sign of $\hat{c}_T$ matches the physical insight that increasing the temperature leads to a decrease of the air density at constant pressure.

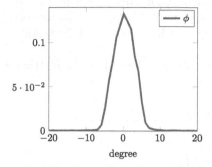

Fig. 6. Empirical density of the incidence angle in degrees

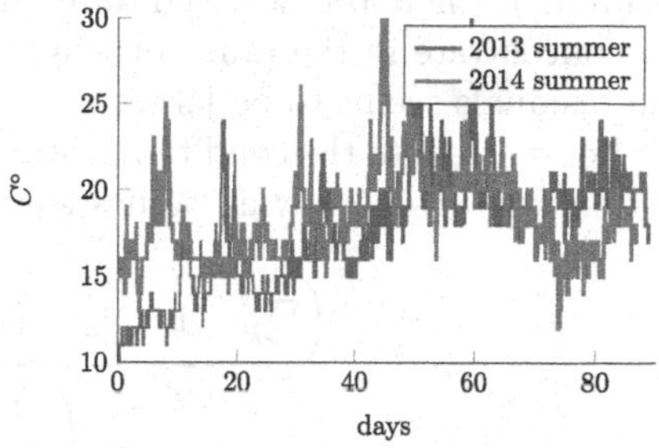

Fig. 7. The temperature variation during the training and the validation period (Color figure online)

All in all, the impact of the temperature is much larger than that of the incidence angle because the turbine mechanisms cannot influence the temperature, as they can the incidence angle. According to (16), besides the wind speed and the air density (in the form of temperature in our case, due to temperature data availability) there seem to be no other important environmental factors, that may affect the power generation significantly and that can be predicted well. In the next section we investigate the residuals of the model with the environmental factors and model the power output by adding a time series layer that allows for a significant short-term forecasting improvement.

4   Predicting Power Output Using Time Series

The effect of the modeling error can be compensated, to some extent, by modeling the residual power output with a stochastic process that has a time scale, which is much slower than that of the wind turbine mechanics. This is based on the intuition that the power output reacts quickly to environmental changes (time scale of minutes), but the environment changes in a slower rate (if there is strong wind, that will last for a few hours with a high probability).

In order to model the power output more accurately, we need to understand the statistical properties of the residuals, which are obtained as follows

$$r = p - \mathcal{F}_{\hat{\theta}(f)}(w, \phi, T) = p - \hat{p}, \tag{18}$$

where $\hat{p}$ is a brief notation for $\mathcal{F}_{\hat{\theta}(f)}(w, \phi, T)$.

The standard deviation of the distribution of the residual, conditioned on the wind speed value, is shown in Fig. 8. It is apparent from the figure, that the standard deviation of the residuals is relatively small below the cut-in speed and above the rated speed, but this is not the case between these values. Thus, the WTPC model (even enhanced with the environmental factors) does not explain fully the power output leaving only the inherent randomness (captured by the residuals). Therefore, we need to further enhance the WTPC model. To this end, we concentrate in the range of wind values for which the standard deviation of the residuals seems to be large.

Let σ_w denote the conditional standard deviation of the residuals r restricted to observations with wind values equal to w

$$\sigma_w = \frac{\left(\sum_{k=1}^N \mathbb{1}_{\{w_k=w\}} \left(p_k - \mathcal{F}_{\hat{\theta}(f)}(w_k, \phi_k, T_k)\right)^2\right)^{1/2}}{\left(\sum_{k=1}^N \mathbb{1}_{\{w_k=w\}}\right)^{1/2}}.$$

The rescaled residual signal r' is defined as

$$r' = \frac{r}{\sigma_w}.$$

Figure 9 depicts the conditional distribution of the rescaled residual samples in the full wind speed range, while Fig. 10 concentrates on the range [3.5, 15]. There are some remarkable features that should be emphasized.

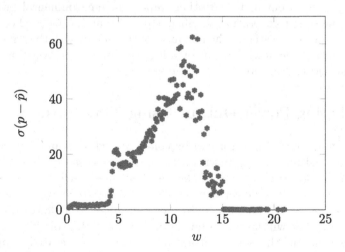

Fig. 8. The standard deviation of the residuals $p - \hat{p}$ with respect to the wind speed

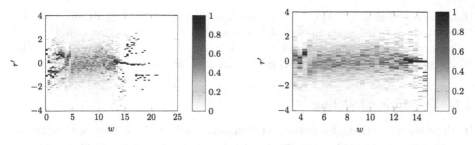

Fig. 9. Wind support $[0, 25]$ **Fig. 10.** Wind support $[3.5, 15]$

In Fig. 9, it is notable that the rescaled residuals outside the range defined by the cut-in speed and the rated speed have distinctive patterns. These patterns are partly caused by the fact that the data are quantized and partly caused by the fact that we are rescaling the residuals, which in this case means that we are dividing with a standard deviation close to zero, see Fig. 8 for the values of the standard deviation of the residuals.

In Fig. 10, it is notable that the rescaled residuals have very similar conditional densities for different wind speed values between the cut-in speed and the rated speed, i.e. in the range $[3.5, 15]$ the conditional distribution of the residuals given the wind speed is (approximately) independent of the wind speed. Thus, the wind speed is (approximately) independent from the rescaled residuals. This indicates that the WTPC captures most of the wind dependence in this range except for the variance.

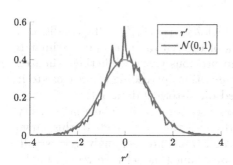

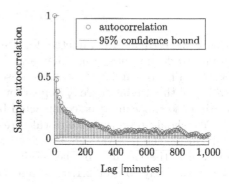

Fig. 11. The marginal density (blue) of the rescaled residuals conditioned on $w \in [3.5, 15]$ and the density of the standard Gaussian distribution (red) (Color figure online)

Fig. 12. The sample autocorrelation of the rescaled residual

As it can be seen in Fig. 11, the empirical density of the rescaled residuals inside the restricted wind speed interval resembles a Gaussian density. Combining this result with the fact that the residual is independent of the wind speed between the cut-in speed and the rated speed, we can reasonably assume that the rescaled residuals can be modeled using a Gaussian stochastic process. Motivated by this result, in Sect. 4.1, we model the rescaled residuals r' using an autoregressive moving-average (ARMA) model. This model can capture the inherent autocorrelation observed in the data, cf. Fig. 12.

4.1 Dynamic Modeling

In all previous sections, for reasons of simplicity and for the clarity of the exposition, we suppressed the time index from the notation. This was also in accordance with the static models we investigated for modeling the WTPC. In this section, we further improve on the previous static models by incorporating a dynamic aspect satisfying also the Gaussian behavior of the rescaled residuals. This will additionally permit us to increase the short-term forecasting potential of our model. To this purpose, we reinstate the subscript t (indicating the time dependence) to all variables and consider for modeling purposes an ARMA(q_1, q_2) model, with q_1 autoregressive terms (with coefficients a_i, $i = 1, \ldots, q_1$) and q_2 moving-average terms (with coefficients c_i, $i = 1, \ldots, q_2$), i.e.,

$$r'_t = 1 + \varepsilon_t + \sum_{i=1}^{q_1} a_i r'_{t-i} + \sum_{i=1}^{q_2} c_i \varepsilon_{t-i}. \qquad (19)$$

Taking into account the above model for the rescaled residuals, in the sequel, based on historical data till a given time τ, we develop the forecasting model for the power output

$$p_t = \mathcal{F}_{\boldsymbol{\theta}(f)}(w_t, \phi_t, T_t) + \sigma_{w_t} r'_t, \ t \geq \tau, \qquad (20)$$

where the estimated parameters for the model $\mathcal{F}_{\boldsymbol{\theta}(f)}(w_t, \phi_t, T_t)$, the conditional standard deviation σ_w, and the parameters of the ARMA model are estimated based on historical data (e.g. same season in previous year), while the estimated values of the driving noise ε_t depend on observations preceding t, but close to it in time, so this cannot be constructed based on historical data only.

We should note that the rescaled residuals seem to have a Gaussian density only inside the interval $[3.5, 15]$ of the wind speed values. Outside of this range of values, the variance of the residuals is constant and seemingly very small. Thus, similarly to Sect. 2.1, we define the constrained model with regard to the rescaled residuals as follows

$$
\begin{aligned}
p_t = \ &\mathcal{F}_{\boldsymbol{\theta}(f)}(w_t, \phi_t, T_t) \\
&+ \mathbb{1}\{g_\ell \leq w_t \leq g_u\}\sigma_{w_t} r'_t \\
&+ (1 - \mathbb{1}\{g_\ell \leq w_t \leq g_u\})e_t,
\end{aligned}
\qquad (21)
$$

with $3.5 \leq g_\ell < g_u \leq 15$. The values g_ℓ and g_u will be determined, so as to ensure that within the interval $[g_\ell, g_u]$ the conditional distribution of the rescaled residuals is Gaussian. Furthermore, e_t is a Gaussian noise source, such that for every finite set of indexes $\{t_1, \ldots, t_N\}$ the corresponding components are independent and identically normally distributed. Moreover, e_t is independent from the driving noise behind the rescaled residual signal, ε_t.

It needs to be mentioned that the noise ε_t cannot be obtained from the data using the model given in (21). To overcome this issue, we assume that the noise ε_t and the rescaled residual process starts at zero at the beginning of the measurement time line, i.e. ε_t and r'_t are zero, for $t < 0$, and assume that it stays "frozen" while the wind is outside the interval $[g_\ell, g_u]$. For the latter, we equivalently glue together consecutive periods of time for which the wind is within the desired range $[g_\ell, g_u]$.

The parameters of the constrained model described in Eq. (21) are: *i)* the parameters of the $\mathcal{F}_{\theta^{(f)}}(w_t, \phi_t, T_t)$ model; *ii)* the parameters of the wind speed dependent residual rescaling factors σ_w; *iii)* the parameters of the ARMA(q_1, q_2) model, say θ_{ARMA}: $\{a_1, \ldots, a_{q_1}\}$ and $\{c_1, \ldots, c_{q_2}\}$. So the full parameter vector θ of the model consists of $\theta^{(f)}$, σ_w, $\{a_1, \ldots, a_{q_1}\}$ and $\{c_1, \ldots, c_{q_2}\}$.

As it is visible in Fig. 9, the conditional distribution of the rescaled residuals conditioned on the wind speed is not Gaussian on the full wind speed support. In order to determine the lower and upper limits of the Gaussian range, g_ℓ and g_u, we performed the Anderson-Darling test to find the p-values for the conditional distributions that show how likely it is that the rescaled residuals, given the wind speed values, are samples from a standard normal distribution. Figure 13 shows the p-values of the test, along with the wind speed value boundaries that we used for later calculations. In particular, with relatively high confidence (p-value > 0.05) we cannot reject the hypothesis that the samples come from a standard normal distribution for $g_\ell = 5.4$ and $g_u = 13.6$, while outside these bounds the hypothesis can be rejected with extremely high confidence (p-value ≈ 0).

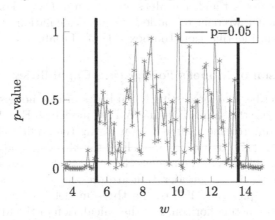

Fig. 13. The p-value of the Anderson-Darling test for standard normality performed on the conditional distribution of the rescaled residuals

Having decided on the values g_ℓ and g_u, we describe below the procedure for estimating the parameters θ of the model described in Eq. (21). First, we estimate the parameters of the $\mathcal{F}_{\theta^{(f)}}(w_t, \phi_t, T_t)$ model, next we estimate the parameters σ_w of the rescaled residuals, last we estimate the parameters of the

Table 7. ARMA model parameters belonging to different orders

Model order	model parameters				
$q_1 = 0, q_2 = 5$	$c_1 = 0.4188$	$c_2 = 0.2941$	$c_3 = 0.2379$	$c_4 = 0.1738$	$c_5 = 0.1085$
$q_1 = 5, q_2 = 0$	$a_1 = 0.4125$	$a_2 = 0.1271$	$a_3 = 0.0824$	$a_4 = 0.0375$	$a_5 = 0.0248$
$q_1 = 5, q_2 = 5$	$a_1 = 1.3982$	$a_2 = -0.3649$	$a_3 = -0.1556$	$a_4 = 0.3187$	$a_5 = -0.2043$
	$c_1 = -0.9894$	$c_2 = 0.0847$	$c_3 = 0.1463$	$c_4 = -0.2927$	$c_5 = 0.0901$

ARMA model. This is indicated by the data, as the distribution of the rescaled residuals r'_t is symmetric around zero and it is independent of the wind w_t. All in all, this procedure is mathematically described as

$$\hat{\theta} = \arg_\theta \left(\min_{\theta_{\text{ARMA}}} \min_{\sigma_w} \min_{\theta^{(f)}} \frac{1}{N} \sum_{k=1}^{N} (p_k - \hat{p}_k)^2 \right), \qquad (22)$$

where the prediction $\hat{p}_k$ is obtained in accordance to Eq. (21) and N is the total number of observations. Note that as $N \to \infty$, $\hat{\theta}$ converges to the least square estimate obtained by optimizing for every parameter simultaneously, instead of the proposed sequential optimization. This follows from the fact that the residuals $p_k - \mathcal{F}_{\theta^{(f)}}(w_t, \phi_t, T_t)$ are symmetric around zero.

The estimated parameters $\hat{\theta}$ are calculated as follows: For $\hat{\theta}^{(f)} = (\hat{\theta}^{(s)}, \hat{c}_\phi, \hat{c}_T)$, we use the estimated parameters for the B-spline model $\hat{\theta}^{(s)}$ given in Sect. 2.1, and the environmental coefficients $\hat{c}_\phi$ and $\hat{c}_T$ given in Sect. 3. For the rescaled residuals, $\hat{\sigma}_w$ is estimated in a non-parametric way for every appearing wind value in the dataset and the values are shown in Fig. 8. For the parameters of the ARMA model, we refer to Table 7. For the calculation of the parameters, we use the System Identification Toolbox [11] of Matlab.

4.2   Comparison of Model's Forecasting Capabilities

This section describes the forecasting capabilities of the models outlined above. In particular, we use the simple B-spline WTPC model, cf. Eq. (12), as a baseline to underline the improvement offered by utilizing the additional environmental regressors, cf. Eq. (17), as well as modeling the variance and the correlations remaining in the residuals of the model, cf. Eq. (21). The corresponding parameters for the models under consideration are presented in Sects. 2.1, 4.1, and 3, respectively. We depict the MSE of the three models in Figs. 14 and 15 as a function of the forecasting horizon. For the calculation of the MSE as a function of the forecasting horizon, we need to note that although the sampling frequency of the data is every $\delta = 10$ min, the forecasting horizon can receive any positive continuous value. Keeping this in mind, we define the MSE, given the forecasting horizon h, as follows

$$\text{MSE}_h = \frac{1}{N - \lceil h/\delta \rceil} \sum_{k=\lceil h/\delta \rceil}^{N} \left(p_k - \hat{p}_{k|k-\lceil h/\delta \rceil} \right)^2, \qquad (23)$$

where for the prediction of the k-th value, $\hat{p}_{k|k-\lceil h/\delta \rceil}$, it is required to provide as an input the wind speed values $w_1, w_2, \ldots, w_k$, the temperature values $T_1, T_2, \ldots, T_k$, the angle values $\phi_1, \phi_2, \ldots, \phi_k$, and the power output values $p_1, \ldots, p_{k-\lceil h/\delta \rceil}$, i.e., we predict from the $k - \lceil h/\delta \rceil$ power output values the future, given perfect future information of the explanatory values.

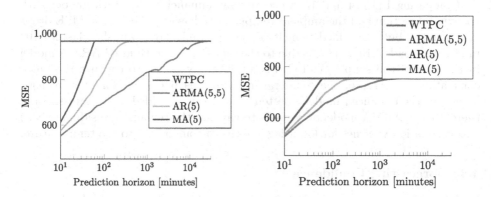

Fig. 14. Simple WTPC

Fig. 15. WTPC enhanced with temperature and angle

As shown in Figs. 14–15, the two static WTPC models, cf. Eqs. (12) and (17), given the wind speed, angle and temperature, have a constant MSE regardless of the forecasting horizon. Contrary, the dynamic ARMA(q_1, q_2) models permit a significant reduction of the MSE, especially for short-term forecasting in the range of 1 to 50, 1 to 10^2, or 1 to 10^3 min, depending on the values of the (q_1, q_2) parameters. Naturally, as the prediction horizon increases the added benefit of knowing the power output values from the past is getting less and less valuable. Furthermore, the least effective is the moving-average MA(q_2) model structure, since it utilizes information only from the past q_2 samples. So if the prediction horizon reaches this limit, no past information is used. As the unconditional expectation of the zero mean Gaussian process is zero, the expectation of the rescaled residuals will also be zero. This can be seen in Figs. 14 and 15, in which the MSE value of the MA(5) model becomes equal to that of the corresponding static WTPC model for prediction horizons $h > 5 \cdot \delta = 50$ min. While, for the same value of the forecasting horizon, the ARMA(5, 5) model has a reduced MSE value by 17% compared to the corresponding static WTPC model. In contrast to the short-term forecasting characteristics, the advantages of the dynamic models versus the static models disappear in the long-term. Thus, the dynamic WTPC model with the ARMA layer can be used for both short-term and long-term forecasting, as for short horizons it outperforms the static WTPC, while for longer horizons has the same performance as the static counterpart model. This result is evident in light of Figs. 14 and 15 as the various MSE values of the dynamic models converge to the MSE value of the corresponding static WTPC model.

We need to note that since the autocorrelation of the rescaled residuals (calculated using the enhanced WTPC model), cf. Fig. 12, is significant for a long period of time (more than 400 min), estimating higher order ARMA models would reduce the MSE value in comparison to the corresponding static model but this effect will vanish for time horizons longer than the autocorrelation length of the rescaled residuals.

Comparing Figs. 14 and 15, we note that enhancing the static model with the wind direction and the ambient temperature has two effects: the MSE drops significantly, but the added benefit of the dynamic layer vanishes faster (10^3 minutes instead of 10^4). This is due to the fact that the estimated ARMA model in the case of the simple WTPC was additionally trying to capture the autocorrelation structure of the temperature, which is persistent for lengthy lags. While, in the enhanced model, the temperature is provided as a regressor and therefore the ARMA model only needs to capture the remaining residual, whose autocorrelation vanishes for lower lag lengths in comparison to the temperature.

4.3   Forecasting Confidence

In this section, we are interested in investigating the performance of the dynamic model in terms of its forecasting ability. To this purpose, we visualize a power output trajectory in Fig. 16 and depict the difference between the prediction and the actual measurements in Fig. 17. In both figures, we define time 0 to be the starting point of the forecasting horizon and we assume that the wind speed, temperature and relative angle values are known also during the forecasting period, while the power output values are known only till time 0. For the creation of the figures, we consider both the static and the dynamic WTPC model and plot their predictions together with the corresponding prediction intervals. The prediction interval of the static WTPC model has a constant width, while the dynamic model has a varying width depending on the value of the wind speed. The 95% confidence band for predicted power production trajectory $\hat{p}_{k|0}$ was calculated based on the ARMA model and the wind dependent scaling factor.

For the static model, the fixed width interval is a result of calculating the variance of the residuals using the static WTPC model with the $p - \hat{p} = p - \mathcal{F}_{\hat{\theta}(f)}(w, \phi, T)$, cf. (17), as two times the standard deviation of the residuals can be used as an approximation for the 95% confidence region of the prediction. This calculation on our data results in a standard deviation for the residuals equal to 12.4925. However, for this to hold it should be the case that the residuals are normally distributed and independent of the wind speed, but as we have already shown this is not the case. Note that the variance of the residuals for the static model is calculated using observations covering the support of the wind speed values $[0, 25]$, thus simultaneously taking into account the part for which the static model is very accurate, $[0, g_\ell) \cup (g_u, 25]$, and the part in which it is highly inaccurate, $[g_\ell, g_u]$. As a result, the estimate for the variance of the residuals is overly conservative in $[0, g_\ell) \cup (g_u, 25]$, while it seems to underestimate the variance in $[g_\ell, g_u]$. This is clearly visible in Fig. 17 as during the first half of the forecasting horizon the wind speed was in $[0, g_\ell) \cup (g_u, 25]$, while in the second half it is $[g_\ell, g_u]$.

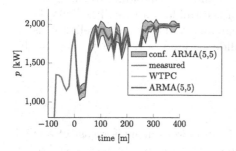
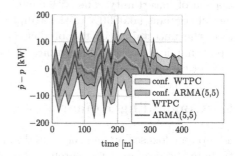

Fig. 16. Typical prediction trajectory with the corresponding 95% confidence bound

Fig. 17. The difference between the prediction and the actual measured power

For the dynamic model, cf. (21), the variance of the power estimate $\hat{p}_{k|k-\lceil h/\delta\rceil}$ can be calculated by considering the unknown random variables of $(\varepsilon_\ell)_{k-\lceil h/\delta\rceil<\ell\leq k}$, which drive the rescaled residual stochastic process $r'_{k|k-\lceil h/\delta\rceil}$, see (19). We know that the variance of $r'_{k|k-\lceil h/\delta\rceil}$ is monotonically increasing with the prediction distance $\lceil h/\delta\rceil$ and it has a bounded limit, since the ARMA model is stable (every solution $z \in \mathbb{C}$ of the $1 - \sum_{i=1}^{q_1} a_i z^{-1} = 0$ characteristic equation has absolute value less than 1). If we assume that ε_t is an i.i.d. Gaussian signal, then the variance of the power predictions can be calculated from the ARMA model and the wind dependent rescaling σ_{w_t}. The fact that the dynamic model results in a confidence band with varying width is initially surprising as the width might even shrink in size over time. The explanation for this result is that the proposed dynamic model contains a wind speed dependent scaling. This scaling factor has very small uncertainty when the wind speed is outside the interval $[g_\ell, g_u]$, i.e., for wind speed values outside the interval $[g_\ell, g_u]$, the variance is smaller in comparison to the corresponding value calculated over the full support. As it can be seen in Fig. 16, the wind value region, in which the width of the confidence band shrinks corresponds to wind speed values above the wind value g_u (the wind speed is not depicted directly but this can be inferred from the power curve and the shown measured power). In this region of wind values, predictions are more accurate and the confidence band becomes narrower than the corresponding confidence band of the static WTPC model. While, for wind values inside the interval $[g_\ell, g_u]$, it can be seen that the confidence band of the dynamic model gets wider and may even contain the confidence interval of the static WTPC model. The increased width of the confidence band is due to the combined effect of predicting values further into the future as well as the changes in the wind speed, that also effect the rescaling factor.

The confidence band of the static WTPC model contains 100% of the samples. To illustrate how imprecise the uncertainty estimate belonging to the

WTPC model is, we can calculate the maximal confidence level for which the empirical confidence is not 100%. The 41.0701% confidence band contains 99.9920% percent of the validation data, which shows a significant underestimation of uncertainty. The 95% confidence band corresponding to the dynamic model contains 96.0990% of the samples in the validation time line. This shows that the uncertainty of the predictions can be evaluated quite reliably using the dynamic model, as the empirical confidence level is relatively close to the theoretical one.

5   Concluding Remarks

The paper focuses on the short- and long-term power output forecast of a wind turbine based on past measurements of the wind speed, power output and other environmental factors, as well as perfect knowledge of the future wind speed, angle, and ambient temperature. We showed that the parametrization of the WTPC is not a key factor in improving prediction performance. The reason behind this is that for any model with a sufficiently rich structure (in the case of non-parametric models that implies sufficiently high complexity) we can achieve MSE values close to the lower bound, as long as we have sufficient data to estimate all the unknown parameters at hand. This is not a problem in our case, as we have a trove of data, making it more important to consider models that have a rich enough structure and the unknown parameters can still be estimated with high numerical accuracy, e.g. the polynomial based models suffer from numerical instability issues. Given the available data we have at our disposal, our conclusion is that the B-spline model with a sufficiently high number of knots provides a good modeling choice, as it can capture every detail of a WTPC and it can be estimated in a numerically stable way. Of course, if the data were sparse but the wind speed still covered the range of 3.5 m/s, 15 m/s], a better option would be a logistic model as such models maintain the shape of the WTPC.

The error between the actual power generation values and those predicted by the WTPC have special characteristics that open up possibilities for better modeling. Below the cut-in speed and above the rated speed of the turbine the predictions are quite accurate. However, in the middle range of the wind speed this is no longer true. We have shown that, on the dataset at hand, a proper rescaling of these residuals can transform the residual signal into a Gaussian signal. Modeling this Gaussian rescaled residual as a stochastic time series allowed us to improve significantly the predictions. The proposed model structure was able to improve up to 40% in predicting the power output of the wind turbine on short-term predictions, while the long-term prediction capabilities of the model are identical to that of the WTPC.

A   Appendix: Data

The goal of this section is to describe the features of the data used in this study. The data was obtained by the supervisory control and data acquisition (SCADA) system of a wind turbine operator in the Netherlands. The data was collected from an off-shore Vestas V80-2.0MW wind turbine, with a rated capacity of 2MW. Vestas V80-2.0MW joins the grid connection at a wind speed of 4 m/s, has a rated actual power output of 2 MW (typically achieved) at a wind speed of 16 ms, and it is disconnected at a wind speed of 25 ms. See Fig. 1 for a depiction of the theoretical WTPC. These are suggested values offered by the manufacturer, but they might change due to wear of the turbine or due to installation or geographic circumstances.

The data used for the analysis presented in this paper spans across two years and the dataset contains recordings of the environmental conditions, as well as the physical state, and power output of the turbine.

There are two important features of SCADA datasets, which are not specific to the data of our study but are common amongst SCADA datasets recorded throughout the wind industry. One of these is the 10 min reported frequency of the SCADA observations; although the signals of interest are collected at a relatively high frequency, only processed observations calculated on a 10 min window are recorded in the SCADA databases. These processed signals contain the average, maximum, minimum and standard deviation of the wind speed, and the power output amongst other quantities of interest. The second important feature is that the data are strongly quantized due to the rounding of the reported number. As a result, the observations are recorded up to one decimal digit. Some of our finding are consequences of these two properties which correspond to the quasi industry standard. Because of this, we expect that our results are also applicable to similar data coming from other wind turbine operators or wind turbine service providers.

A.1   Description of the Raw Dataset

All graphs and figures were produced using two seasonal parts of the available dataset. Throughout the paper, we refer to the data recorded between June 1, 2013, and August 31, 2013, as the training data, and the corresponding period of year 2014 as the validation data. Although, we have access to the full two year data set, we choose to restrict our analysis in a specific season of the year, as this reduces seasonality effects, while still maintaining a significant amount of data, and it permits a full decoupling between the training and the validation data. It is important to note that the results presented in the paper still hold when we perform the same analysis using the full year 2013 as training data and the data from 2014 for validation.

The dataset contains observations of various signals every 10 min. Some of the signals contained in the dataset are the ambient wind speed, say w_t, the relative direction of the wind speed with respect to the nacelle, say ϕ_t, the ambient temperature, say T_t, and the power output produced by the turbine, say p_t, at time t, $t \geq 0$. Besides the aforementioned continuous valued signals, there are some nominal variables with a discrete support, such as the variable pertaining to the different operational states of the turbine. Such variables help to identify time periods during which the turbine is out of use (maintenance, free run, blades turned into low resistance position) or if the wind turbine is in a state different from normal operational condition.

In the first part of the paper, we suppress the subscript t as we deal with static models, while in the second part of the paper we deal with dynamic models, and we, therefore, reinstate the subscript t notation.

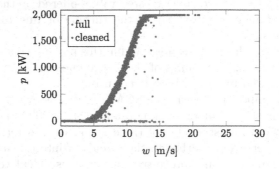

Fig. 18. The power output, p, against the wind speed, w, in the raw (red) and the cleaned (blue) dataset from 2013 (Color figure online)

A.2   Cleaning the data

The quality of the available SCADA data is extremely good, nevertheless it requires some pre-processing before creating the forecasting models. We list below the cleaning rules implemented in this study, according to which we disregard observations:

1. Missing entries (NAs): there are a few timestamps that are completely missing from the 10 min sampling sequence.
2. Incomplete entries (IN): if one or more of the signal values, e.g., the power output, the wind speed, etc., are missing from a data record, then the full record corresponding to this time stamp is discarded.
3. Not normal operation (NNO): based on the value of the state variables we can disregard states that do not correspond to normal operational conditions, e.g. free rotation of the wind turbine without connection to the grid, derated operation, etc.

Table 8. Summary report of the data cleaning

Year	2013	2014
Total number of observations	13248	13248
Number of NAs, IN, & NNO observations	255	445
Number of outliers	144	165
Total number of observations after cleaning	12849	12638
Percentage of observations kept after cleaning	97%	95.4%

4. Outliers: Firstly, all observations of wind power corresponding to the same wind speed are grouped together and the corresponding box plot is generated. Then, for every given wind speed value, all points with power generation outside the whiskers of the box plot (i.e., all observations falling outside the interval $(Q_1 - 3\text{IQR}, Q_3 + 3\text{IQR})$) are discarded.

Table 8 contains the summary report of the data cleaning procedure. It shows that approximately 5% of the original data is discarded, still leaving a trove of data to be used for estimation purposes. The scatter plot of the power output, p, against the wind speed, w, is shown in Fig. 18. In this figure, we have color-characterized the training data by depicting in red the raw data, and in blue the cleaned dataset used for the analysis.

References

1. Akaike, H.: A new look at the statistical model identification. IEEE Trans. Autom. Control **19**(6), 716–723 (1974)
2. Belsley, D.A., Kuh, E., Welsch, R.E.: Regression Diagnostics: Identifying Influential Data and Sources of Collinearity, vol. 571. Wiley, Hoboken (2005)
3. Carrillo, C., Obando Montaño, A., Cidrás, J., Díaz-Dorado, E.: Review of power curve modelling for wind turbines. Renew. Sustain. Energy Rev. **21**, 572–581 (2013)
4. De Boor, C.: A Practical Guide to Splines. Applied Mathematical Sciences, vol. 27, 1st edn. Springer, New York (1978)
5. Pelletier, F., Masson, C., Tahan, A.: Wind turbine power curve modelling using artificial neural network. Renew. Energy **89**, 207–214 (2016)
6. IEC 61400 12-1, E.: Wind turbines - part 12-1: Power performance measurements of electricity producing wind turbines. Technical report, 88/244/FDIS (2005)
7. Kang, H., Chen, F., Li, Y., Deng, J., Yang, Z.: Knot calculation for spline fitting via sparse optimization. Comput.-Aided Design **58**, 179–188 (2015). Solid and Physical Modeling 2014
8. Kusiak, A., Zheng, H., Song, Z.: On-line monitoring of power curves. Renew. Energy **34**(6), 1487–1493 (2009)
9. Lee, G., Ding, Y., Genton, M.G., Xie, L.: Power curve estimation with multivariate environmental factors for inland and offshore wind farms. J. Am. Stat. Assoc. **110**(509), 56–67 (2015)
10. Li, S., Wunsch, D.C., O'Hair, E., Giesselmann, M.G.: Comparative analysis of regression and artificial neural network models for wind turbine power curve estimation. J. Sol. Energy Eng. **123**, 327–332 (2001)
11. Ljung, L.: System Identification Toolbox User's Guide. The MathWorks Inc. (2010)
12. Lydia, M., Kumar, S.S., Selvakumar, A.I., Prem Kumar, G.E.: A comprehensive review on wind turbine power curve modeling techniques. Renew. Sustain. Energy Rev. **30**, 452–460 (2014)
13. Lydia, M., Selvakumar, A., Kumar, S., Kumar, G.: Advanced algorithms for wind turbine power curve modeling. IEEE Trans. Sustain. Energy **4**(3), 827–835 (2013)
14. Manwell, J.F., McGowan, J.G., Rogers, A.L.: Wind Energy Explained: Theory, Design and Application. Wiley, Hoboken (2010)
15. Nesti, T., Nair, J., Zwart, A.P.: Reliability of dc power grids under uncertainty: a large deviations approach. arXiv preprint arXiv:1606.02986 (2016)

16. Nesti, T., Zocca, A., Zwart, A.P.: Line failure probability bounds for power grids. arXiv preprint arXiv:1611.02338 (2016)
17. R. Lázaro, N.Y., Melero, J. (eds.): Wind turbine power curve modelling using Gaussian mixture copula, ANN regressive and BANN. In: The Science of Making Torque from Wind (TORQUE 2022) Journal of Physics: Conference Series (2022)
18. Ricketts, J., Head, G.: A five-parameter logistic equation for investigating asymmetry of curvature in baroreflex studies. Am. J. Physiol. **277**(2), 441–454 (1999)
19. Schumaker, L.: Spline Functions: Basic Theory. Cambridge Mathematical Library, 3rd edn. (2007)
20. Schwarz, G.: Estimating the dimension of a model. Ann. Stat. **6**(2), 461–464 (1978)
21. Shi, J., Qu, X., Zeng, S.: Short-term wind power generation forecasting: direct versus indirect ARIMA-based approaches. Int. J. Green Energy **8**(1), 100–112 (2011)
22. Shokrzadeh, S., Jafari Jozani, M., Bibeau, E.: Wind turbine power curve modeling using advanced parametric and nonparametric methods. IEEE Trans. Sustain. Energy **5**(4), 1262–1269 (2014)
23. Sohoni, V., Gupta, S.C., Nema, R.K.: A critical review on wind turbine power curve modelling techniques and their applications in wind based energy systems. J. Energy **2016**, 18 p., 8519785 (2016). https://doi.org/10.1155/2016/8519785
24. Stukel, T.: Generalized logistic models. J. Am. Stat. Assoc. **83**(402), 426–431 (1988)
25. Tümse, S., İlhan, A., Bilgili, M., Şahin, B.: Estimation of wind turbine output power using soft computing models. Energy Sour. Part A: Recovery Util. Environ. Effects **44**(2), 3757–3786 (2022)
26. Vestas: Vestas Manual: V80-2.0 MW, V90–1.8/2.0 MW, V100-1.8 MW (2011)
27. Widén, J., et al.: Variability assessment and forecasting of renewables: a review for solar, wind, wave and tidal resources. Renew. Sustain. Energy Rev. **44**, 356–375 (2015)

A Domain Specific Language for the Design of Artificial Intelligence Applications for Process Engineering

Lelio Campanile[1], Luigi Piero Di Bonito[1], Marco Gribaudo[2], and Mauro Iacono[1(✉)]

[1] Dip. di Matematica e Fisica, Università degli Studi della Campania "L. Vanvitelli", viale Lincoln 5, 81100 Caserta, Italy
{lelio.campanile,luigipiero.dibonito,mauro.iacono}@unicampania.it
[2] Dip. di Elettronica, Informatica e Bioingegneria Politecnico di Milano, via Ponzio 51, 20133 Milan, Italy
marco.gribaudo@polimi.it
https://www.deib.polimi.it/ita/home, https://www.matfis.unicampania.it

Abstract. Processes in chemical engineering are frequently enacted by one-of-a-kind devices that implement dynamic processes with feedback regulations designed according to experimental studies and empirical tuning of new devices after the experience obtained on similar setups. While application of artificial intelligence based solutions is largely advocated by researchers in several fields of chemical engineering to face the problems deriving from these practices, few actual cases exist in literature and in industrial plants that leverage currently available tools as much as other application fields suggest. One of the factors that is limiting the spread of AI-based solutions in the field is the lack of tools that support the evaluation of the needs of plants, be those existing or to-be settlements. In this paper we provide a Domain Specific Language based approach for the evaluation of the basic performance requirements for cloud-based setups capable of supporting chemical engineering plants, with a metaphor that attempts to bridge the two worlds.

Keywords: Artificial intelligence · process engineering · domain specific language · performance evaluation · cloud computing

1 Introduction

Current regulations for the safeguard of the environment require a strict optimization of plants that implement chemical processes, in order to reduce waste, pollution and risk and to optimize the efficiency of each stage and each subsystem. The nature of these plants, that include components with non-linear behavior and that may be one-of-a-kind elements of a chemical plant, challenges the consolidated tuning and control techniques and suggests the application of ad-hoc, self-adapting and time-variant controls, possibly considering a bal-

© ICST Institute for Computer Sciences, Social Informatics and Telecommunications Engineering 2023
Published by Springer Nature Switzerland AG 2023. All Rights Reserved
E. Hyytiä and V. Kavitha (Eds.): VALUETOOLS 2022, LNICST 482, pp. 133–146, 2023.
https://doi.org/10.1007/978-3-031-31234-2_8

anced tuning of parameters at both the subsystem and the system level. Domain experts of the process engineering field advocate the exploitation of consolidated approaches that may match these needs, based on Artificial Intelligence (AI), or, even more interesting, Explainable (XAI) or Trustworthy AI (TAI), that are novel in this sector and are still at a very experimental level.

Besides the extremely important problem of the adaptation of existing approaches and the possible discovery of new solutions, another problem is the evaluation and planning of the resources needed to implement the chosen AI-based solution. Cost parameters are of paramount importance in a market that is generally oriented to mass production, as the effort in training and applying the AI-based solution should be carefully taken into account and should actually lower the overall running costs of the plant. In fact, while domain experts have full control and expertise on design, maintenance and running costs of the plant, the evaluation of the same parameters on AI systems, that is an issue for computer systems engineers and software engineers as well, is generally far from their core professional interest.

The cost of the AI component of the system might be estimated considering the number of signals to be monitored, the frequency of sampling, the amount and intensity of control actions that are needed and the AI algorithms that are chosen, so that apparently the problem might be considered of secondary importance and solvable by an external intervention; but the nature, the dynamicity, the need for possible reconfigurations during ordinary operations, the multiplicity of use, the specificity of each single process plant and component make the problem not trivial, so that one should consider that the integration between the process engineers and the AI engineers in the team would benefit of the availability of design tools that allow a profitable and natural dialogue between the two parts.

In order to support (and promote) AI applications in the management, control and optimization of process plants, we propose a Domain Specific Language (DSL) for the description of sensitive parts of plants and the IT resources to be used to design the system and to implement the solution. The DSL aims at describing the setup of the system with the purpose of evaluating the needed amount of resources that allows to match the requirements of the plant and to quantify the needed amount of resources needed for the training or retraining phase of the plant, in order to guide the decision process for resource planning (private local cloud or public cloud, choice of commercial offer, costs evaluation). The DSL is oriented to provide a visual representation that is familiar both to process engineers and to IT engineers, to ease the collaboration and avoid specification errors and mismatches, with the goal of minimizing the design effort for both the parts of the team and to lower the communication barrier.

This paper is organized as follows: Sect. 2 describes the application domain; Sect. 3 provides related works; Sect. 4 describes the proposed DSL; Sect. 5 presents a case study; conclusions close the paper.

2   The Application Domain

A chemical plant is an industrial process plant that produces or processes chemicals on a large scale. The general objective of a chemical plant is to create new material wealth through chemical or biological transformation and separation of materials. Chemical plants use specialized equipment, units and technologies in the processes of production, treatment and separation of substances. Classic examples of applications may include polymer, pharmaceutical, food and some beverage production, petroleum refineries or bio-refineries, natural gas processing and biochemical plants, water and wastewater treatment plants. A chemical plant sees the use of different types of equipment, which are mainly fluid systems (e.g., chemical reactors, heat exchangers, liquid-gas, gas-liquid, liquid-liquid contact systems, tanks and separators) and auxiliaries for handling fluids and solids (e.g., piping, pumps, compressors, augers).

Chemical processes can be divided in two main categories: continuous processes and batch processes. Continuous processing plants, as the name implies, operate in an uninterrupted and continuous manner. Following the start-up phase of the plant, it is run in a more or less constant and, hopefully, totally optimum condition. Because the process should be in this ideal condition the majority of the time. Nonetheless, even the steady-state is changing with time. The most prevalent reasons of process operating point variations include changes in process product demand, changes in reactor/separator yield, heat exchanger clogging, and so on. Batch or discontinuous processes have a fixed time. These operations are frequently initiated on demand in order to produce the needed amount of product. Many processes in the food and biochemistry industries, such as fermentation processes, are of this sort. Because the specific chemicals must be produced seldom and frequently in extremely tiny quantities, running the facilities continuously would be financially unsustainable.

Chemical plants are often supplied with sophisticated equipment and a multiplicity of sensors. Sensors primary function is to give data for process monitoring and control. However, approximately two decades ago, academics began to use the huge volumes of data observed and kept in the process sector to construct predictive models. Data-driven models are more related to reality and better explain genuine process conditions since they are based on measurable data within process plants and so depict real process conditions. The primary, and still dominating, application area for these datasets is the prediction of process variables that can only be determined at low sample rates or by off-line analysis. Because these variables are frequently connected to process quality, they are critical for process management and monitoring. For these reasons, it is critical to give more information on these variables at a greater sample frequency and/or with a smaller financial cost. The industry is evolving toward a concept defined as "online prediction" with the use of soft sensors, with the goal of conducting process monitoring and process fault diagnosis. These duties involve detecting the state of the process and determining the source of any divergence from normal circumstances.

As a result, soft sensors can assist process operators in making faster, smarter, and more efficient decisions in order to ensure the long-term growth of the process sector since that many unions and governments have proposed innovative/sustainable manufacturing development plans in recent years. For example, in terms of Process Engineering, the ONU Sustainable Development Goals of clean water and sanitation, cheap and clean energy, responsible consumption and production, climate action, life below water, and life on land must be met by 2030. These objectives could only be met by incorporating smart systems into industrial manufacturing. The process sector has collected a massive quantity of data as a result of the extensive use of distributed control systems during the last few decades. While constructing first-principles models for more complicated processes is becoming more difficult, data-driven process modeling, monitoring, prediction, and control have received a lot of attention in recent years. Later, the process sector grew increasingly aware of the need of extracting knowledge from data, but these data are too large and complex for human modeling. The need for an automated method to model complex systems is increasing. Machine learning algorithms will be crucial in data mining and analytics in the process sector.

2.1   Process Measurements and Control

Process measurements include the application of metrology concepts to the process at hand. The goal is to collect values for the present process conditions and make this information available in a way that can be used by the control system, process operators, or management information systems. The expression measured variable or process variable refers to the process condition under consideration. Process measurements are classified into two types:

1. Constant measurements: a level measuring device that determines the liquid level in a tank is an example of a continuous measurement (e.g., in meters);
2. Measurements that are discrete: a level switch, which displays the presence or absence of liquid at the spot where the level switch is located, is an example of a discrete measurement.

Several process control applications in continuous processes rely on continuous measurements. Several process control applications in batch operations use both discrete and continuous measurements.

Temperature, pressure, flow rate, level, and composition measurement equipment, as well as online physical property measuring techniques, are the most common types of measurement devices utilized in the process industries. Chemical composition is typically the most difficult online measurement. A chemical composition analysis system may easily cost more than 100,000 dollar, and many composition analyzers used for process monitoring and control involve chemical conversion of one or more sample components prior to quantitative measurement. The sampling system includes all of the necessary equipment to provide a clean representative sample of a process stream to a process analyzer and dispose of that sample. When the analyzer is part of an automated control loop, the sampling system's trustworthiness is just as crucial as the analyzer's or control equipment's. Modern control systems allow for physical separations of several hundred meters between the measuring equipment, the control unit, and the final control element. The measured variable must be transmitted from the measuring device to the control unit, and the controller output must be transmitted from the control unit to the final control element. To make electronic transmission systems less sensitive to interference from magnetic fields, current rather than voltage is employed for the transmission signal. The signal has a range of 4 to 20 mA. There can only be one transmitter in each circuit or "current loop". For most measurement variable transmissions, the lower range is 4 mA and the maximum range is 20 mA [10]. In the process industry, these signals are frequently recorded using a data logger at various collection rates, resulting in a dataset that may be utilized in digital technologies for process control. In terms of database dimension, it is dependent on data logger performance in terms of acquisition rates, so:

- for lower limit an acquisition rate equal to 1 kHz can be considered: this limit primarily depends on both economic factors defined by data logger price and characteristic time of the considered process;
- for upper limit acquisition rates between 0.005–1 Hz can be considered: an analog signal from a traditional sensor is a continuous transmission signal ranging from 4 to 20 mA, but an analog/digital signal from an analyzer might be affected by a delay time determined by the working principle of the analyzer.

3   Related Works

3.1   AI and Chemical Process Plants

A classic example used in literature about the application of AI techniques to supervision and control of chemical process plants is the Tennessee Eastman Process, because of the availability of a large and consistent public dataset. Different applications of machine learning for fault diagnosis and identification based on the Tennessee Eastman Process dataset have been studied, such as in the papers analyzed in the following. [9,12,15] propose a new fault identification and diagnosis methods for manufacturing processes based on AI methodologies (i.e. Bayesian Neural Networks, Auto-associative Neural Networks, Generative Adversarial Networks), which enables (1) fault detection in nonlinear processes and (2) direct identification of faults using easy-to-interpret identification diagrams and fault propagation path analysis. One issue is that the usual dataset used for monitoring the Tennessee Eastman process has just a limited number of data samples, which might be quite restrictive for deep learning analysis. Some implemented datasets of these studies, are 500 times larger than the average datasets and large enough for deep learning. In Fault Diagnosis application, another issue could be the absence of data from essential sensors readings due to hardware or network issues. Results show that these AI methodologies can reduce the impact on problem detection and identification even in the face of repeatedly missing reading from sensors that are important to the monitoring system proper operation.

In [5, 7, 14] other examples of Fault Diagnosis applications in the field of process engineering are given, which do not consider the Tennessee Eastman process as a case study. In these studies, other process engineering equipment (such as chemical reactors and separation units) was analyzed in order to develop AI-based methodologies that can improve the performance of the online monitoring system of the units.

3.2 DSL for Performance Evaluation

A comprehensive survey on the use of DSL in the field of Model Driven Engineering (MDE) can be found in [1]. While in the MDE approach exploits metamodeling for the automatic generation of software implementations and/or system configurations, the SIMTHE*Sys* framework [13] supports the definition of DSL for the specification of performance oriented models that may be evaluated by means of different analytical or simulation-based approaches. For example, the SIMTHE*Sys* approach has been used to define DSL for Big Data systems in [2], for multicore CPU and GPU based computing architectures in [6], for lambda computing architectures in [11] and for cloud computing systems in [3], in all cases to support the design and dimensioning of systems in the target domains: these papers have inspired this one.

4   Design of the PE-AI-Perf DSL

We decided to use as running example the Tennessee Eastman process as an example that may support the design choices in designing the PE-AI-Perf DSL, in order to contextualize our work and guide the reader in getting familiar with the domain modeling problems. This example is considered by domain experts to be able to provide a sufficiently complete and sufficiently complex presentation of the target systems, and some quantitative references are provided as well to suggest the terms of the general problem.

4.1   Process Description

The Tennessee Eastman process model is a realistic simulation of a chemical plant that is extensively used as a reference for control and monitoring studies. The procedure is detailed in [8], and the FORTRAN code is available on the internet. Figure 1 depicts the process flow diagram, which includes five primary units: reactor, condenser, compressor, separator, and stripper.

The reaction yields two products from four reactants. An inert and a by-product are also present, for a total of eight components labeled as A, B, C, D, E, F, G, and H. The technique provides for a total of 53 measurements, 41 which are of process variables and 12 which are controlled variables. The Tennessee

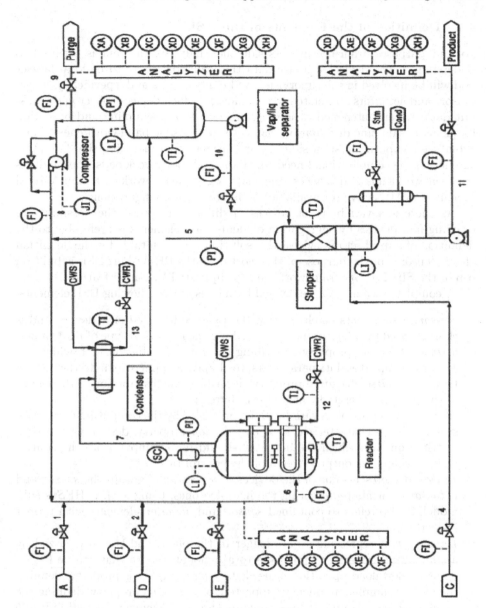

Fig. 1. The Tennessee Eastman Process Process Flow Diagram in [8].

Eastman Process simulation includes 21 preprogrammed defects (classes/labels) with a variety of disturbance types and locations and under typical working conditions, the system is in production mode, with a sample period of 3 min.

4.2   Definition of the Elements of the DSL

For our purposes, from the process side the analysis of a plant is oriented to understand which devices produce data that will contribute to build a dataset and will be involved in the supervision and control tasks and, specifically, which sensors and actuators are related to each device, which devices collect and transmit data: we are interested in identifying data types, sampling and operation frequencies, sampling distribution, dataset size, possible bandwidth constraints. From the computing system side, we are interested in modeling the data storage needs, the computational needs of the AI solutions workloads, the bindings between workloads and devices, the mapping between workloads and Virtual Machines (VM), active (or available) VMs and their configurations.

As there is a variability of devices in different projects, the possibility of building new devices by aggregation of elementary elements is preferable to the definition of a fixed set of devices (this solution is also suitable for the definition of soft sensors, for the purpose of this work). As the PE-AI-Perf DSL is built on top of the SIMTHE*Sys* framework, this is supported by native features.

A complete scenario can be defined by means of the following DSL elements:

- *Sensor*: it represents an elementary data source installed on a device, and is characterized by a *type* property, describing the numerical type of read values, a *timedistribution* property, describing the time distribution with which the sensor is sampled and its parameters, to shape the input stream to the control task, and a *sizedistribution* property, describing the distribution of the length of the packets generated (measured in bytes);
- *Actuator*: it represents a variable to be produced by the computing part of the system, and is characterized by a *distribution* property, describing the time distribution with which the actuator should receive input from the control task, to shape the output stream of the control task;
- *Device*: it represents one of the devices of a plant, and groups the *sensor* and *actuator* elements representing the installed ones; being a SIMTHE*Sys* submodel, it also refers to contained *sensor* and *actuator* elements with proper properties;
- *Datalogger*: it represents a data logger in the plant, and is characterized by a *storagesize* property, defining the total amount of data that can be logged before a download operation is needed, a *maxsamplefreq* property, defining the highest sampling frequency supported, a *maxinputs* property, defining the number of available input lines to connect *sensor* elements, a *netbandwidth* property, defining the maximum connection bandwidth on the computer network used to interface with the computing architecture of the system;
- *NetworkConnection*: it represents the connection between the plant plane and the data center, being it local to the site or remotely connected, and is characterized by a *totalbandwidth* property, defining the maximum connection bandwidth on the computer network used to interface with the computing architecture of the system, a *technology* property that describes the relevant technical parameters of the connection;

– *Workload*: it represents a single AI solution used for a device or a set of devices, and is characterized by an *requiredCPU* property, defining the computing needs for a single run of the algorithm on a single input in terms of the number of CPU operations, a *requiredGPU* property, defining the computing needs on a GPU in terms of the number of GPU operations;
– *VM*: it represents a virtual machine available to run a *workload*, and is characterized by a *cores* property, defining the number of available virtual cores, a *corespeed* property, defining the operational speed of a core, a *GPUs* property, defining the number of available GPUs, a *GPUspeed* property, defining the operational speed of a core, a *totalstorage* property, defining the amount of the available storage;
– *MapArc*: it represents the mapping between a *Device* and a *Datalogger*, a *Datalogger* and a *NetworkConnection*, a *NetworkConnection* and a *Workload*, a *Workload* and a *VM*;
– *BindArc*: it represents the mapping between a *Workload* and a *Device*, to specify which *Device* elements are related to a *Workload* element. This arc is characterized by a *weight* property, used to define how many instances of the corresponding data are required to run on instance of the considered workload.

Graphical symbols for the elements are depicted in Fig. 2.

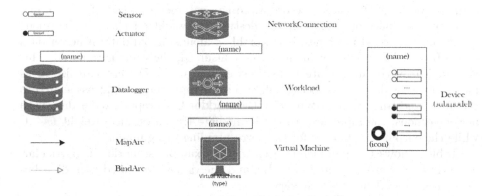

Fig. 2. The symbols for the language elements.

5   A Case Study

In this preliminary work, we do not consider *Actuators*, and we consider that all data produced by *Sensors* at a *Device* is aggregate and transmitted as single data blocks thorough the *Network Connections*. We also focus on workloads that can be entirely run on CPU, disregarding the GPUs. To simplify the description of the semantics of the resulting model, we perform an intermediate translation of the considered case study into a conventional GSPN/QN model, that we analyze using JMT - Java Modelling Tools [4]. Figure 4 shows the result of this translation process for the DSL model shown in Fig. 3. We also do not consider storage and focus on network and computation requirements.

The equivalent GSPN/QN model is characterized by $\#D + \#W$ classes, one for each *Device* ($\#D$ in total), and for each *Workload* (up to $\#W$). Each *Device* is converted in a QN source, that produces jobs of the corresponding class, at the arrival rate defined in the *timedistribution* parameter of the DSL object.

Dataloggers are converted into FCFS single server queues, where the service time of each class is derived from the *sizedistribution* of the sensor, and the *netbandwidth* property of the logger. Similarly, *NetworkConnection* DSL nodes are converted into processor sharing single server queues, where the service time of each class is derived from the *sizedistribution* of the sensor, and the *totalbandwidth* property of the router.

VirtualMachines are transformed into multiple server processor sharing queues, where the number of servers corresponds to the *cores* parameter of the node. Service time distributions are computed from the *corespeed* parameter of the node and from the *requiredCPU* parameter of the workload.

Workload nodes creates a GSPN submodel with one place and two immediate transitions, that aggregates all the data coming from the sensors and required by the considered algorithm. In particular, following the connections defined by the corresponding *BindArcs*, the immediate transitions ending with _T consume one or more tokens of the classes according to the parameter *weight* of the binding arcs, and produces one token of the destination workload class in the queue modeling the virtual machines. It is worthless analyzing old data: if newer data arrive before the previous value has been consumed, the value is replaced. This is modeled by the immediate transitions ending with _D, that can fire in as many modes as data types. Let as call w the corresponding weight associated to the arc connecting the data type with the workload. To replace older data with newer versions, the input arcs to the immediate transition have weight $w + 1$, while the output arcs have w for the corresponding firing mode.

Table 1 shows the parameters used in the example scenario. In particular, execution times are measured in ECU[1], and the values associated with distribution parameters define their average.

We start studying the effect of the number of VMs deployed in the cloud on both the response time and throughput of the system: results are shown in Fig. 5. With a single VM the system is unstable, and the response time tends to the infinity. In this case, the throughput of the system reduces, due to the full utilization of the cloud. System begins being stable with at least two VMs: in this case, however, queuing occurs very frequently, affecting the response time.

---

[1] The ECU, EC2 Computing Unit, is a measure defined by Amazon to compare computing power of a VM with respect to its reference VM on Amazon AWS cloud, that can be considered as equivalent to a 1.0–1.2 GHz 2007 Intel Xeon or AMD Opteron CPU; it is now less popular than when it was introduced, but we consider it fit to the context and the purpose of this paper.

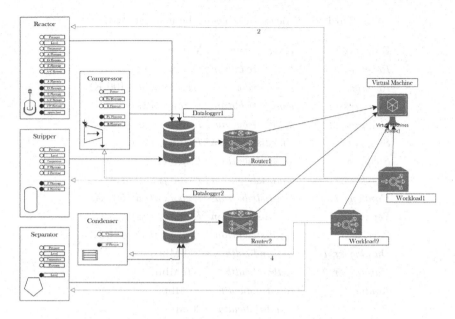

Fig. 3. The model for the example plant (online in-the-loop operations).

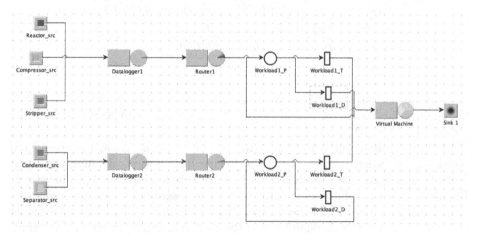

Fig. 4. The equivalent QN-PN model for the example plant.

With 4, 8 or 16 VMs response time stabilizes respectively to around 2 s and 1 s for both workloads, reaching performances very close to the considered service times. For this reason, a configuration with 4 VMs seems to be the one with the optimal tradeoff between performance and cost.

Throughput however, although becoming stationary, only reaches around 0.31 and 0.38 executions per second for both workloads. This is severely reduced with respect to the expected 0.5 executions per second which could be achieved with the considered data generation rate. Analyzing the firing modes of the drop

Table 1. Process variables to be manipulated.

Element	Parameter	Value
Reactor	timedistribution	$Erlang_4$ (1 s)
Reactor	sizedistribution	Exponential (100 KB)
Compressor	timedistribution	$Erlang_4$ (2 s)
Compressor	sizedistribution	Exponential (150 KB)
Stripper	timedistribution	$Erlang_4$ (2 s)
Stripper	sizedistribution	Exponential (200 KB)
Condenser	timedistribution	$Erlang_4$ (0.5 s)
Condenser	sizedistribution	Exponential (50 KB)
Separator	timedistribution	$Erlang_4$ (2 s)
Separator	sizedistribution	Exponential (100 KB)
Datalogger 1	netbandwidth	100 Mbps
Datalogger 2	netbandwidth	100 Mbps
Router 1	totalbandwidth	20 Mbps
Router 2	totalbandwidth	20 Mbps
Workload 1	requiredCPU	$Exponential (2\ ECU \cdot s)$
Workload 2	requiredCPU	$Exponential (1\ ECU \cdot s)$
Virtual Machine	cores	4
Virtual Machine	corespeed	1 ECU

transitions (Workload1_D and Workload2_D), we can see that around 19.5% of readings for Workload 1, and around 12% of the second workload are lost, regardless of the VM settings.

This problem is due to the jittering in the incoming data: the considered coefficient of variation $c_v = 0.5$ of the Erlang distributions defining the inter-arrival times of the data produced by the sensors is too high, and produces very frequently cases in which some data needs to be discarded to maintain only the most updated samples. Figure 6 shows the effect of varying the coefficient of variation on both the throughput and the probability of dropping some input. When it reduces below 1/16, the effect of jittering becomes negligible, and almost all input readings can be used for controlling the system. It is also interesting to note that Workload 1 is more affected by the problem since it requires the fusion of a larger number of sources, thus increasing the effect of jittering.

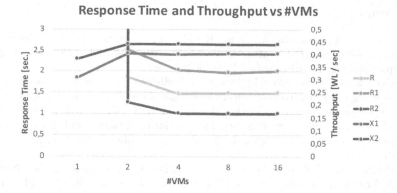

Fig. 5. Response time and throughput as function of the number of VMs deployed.

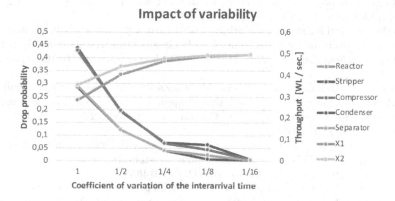

Fig. 6. Drop rate as function of the Coefficient of variation.

6   Conclusion and Future Work

In this paper we presented a DSL for the description of a computing architecture needed to implement an AI-based control system for the processes in chemical plants, oriented to performance evaluation and to support designers in defining and choosing a suitable cloud-based solution. We leveraged our previous results on DSL to obtain a user-friendly description that lowers the barrier between the two fields of chemical engineering and computer science and engineering practice. Future works include the definition of more complex and concurrent solutions for larger plants and more critical processes and a campaign to validate the approach and the solution with companies.

Acknowledgements. This work has been partially funded by the internal competitive funding program "VALERE: VAnviteLli pEr la RicErca" of Università degli Studi della Campania "Luigi Vanvitelli" and is part of the research activity developed within Industrial Ph.D. Programme PON 2014-2020.

References

1. Abouzahra, A., Sabraoui, A., Afdel, K.: Model composition in model driven engineering: a systematic literature review. Inf. Softw. Technol. **125**, 106316 (2020). https://doi.org/10.1016/j.infsof.2020.106316
2. Barbierato, E., Gribaudo, M., Iacono, M.: Modeling apache hive based applications in big data architectures. In: Proceedings of the 7th International Conference on Performance Evaluation Methodologies and Tools, ValueTools 2013, pp. 30–38. ICST (Institute for Computer Sciences, Social-Informatics and Telecommunications Engineering), ICST, Brussels (2013). https://doi.org/10.4108/icst.valuetools.2013.254398
3. Barbierato, E., Gribaudo, M., Iacono, M., Jakobik, A.: Exploiting CloudSim in a multiformalism modeling approach for cloud based systems. Simul. Modell. Pract. Theory **93**, 133–147 (2018)
4. Bertoli, M., Casale, G., Serazzi, G.: JMT: performance engineering tools for system modeling. SIGMETRICS Perform. Eval. Rev. **36**(4), 10–15 (2009). http://doi.acm.org/10.1145/1530873.1530877
5. Bhakte, A., Pakkiriswamy, V., Srinivasan, R.: An explainable artificial intelligence based approach for interpretation of fault classification results from deep neural networks. Chem. Eng. Sci. **250**, 117373 (2022). https://doi.org/10.1016/j.ces.2021.117373
6. Cerotti, D., Gribaudo, M., Iacono, M., Piazzolla, P.: Modeling and analysis of performances for concurrent multithread applications on multicore and graphics processing unit systems. Concurr. Comput. Pract. Exp. **28**(2), 438–452 (2016). https://doi.org/10.1002/cpe.3504
7. Dai, Y., Zhao, J.: Fault diagnosis of batch chemical processes using a dynamic time warping (DTW)-based artificial immune system. Ind. Eng. Chem. Res. **50**(8), 4534–4544 (2011). https://doi.org/10.1021/ie101465b
8. Downs, J.J., Vogel, E.F.: A plant-wide industrial process control problem. Comput. Chem. Eng. **17**(3), 245–255 (1993). https://doi.org/10.1016/0098-1354(93)80018-I
9. Dzaferagic, M., Marchetti, N., Macaluso, I.: Fault detection and classification in industrial IoT in case of missing sensor data. IEEE Internet Things J. **9**(11), 8892–8900 (2022). https://doi.org/10.1109/JIOT.2021.3116785
10. Green, D.W., Perry, R.H.: Perry's Chemical Engineers' Handbook, Eighth Edition, 8th edn. McGraw-Hill Education (2008). https://www.accessengineeringlibrary.com/content/book/9780071422949
11. Gribaudo, M., Iacono, M., Kiran, M.: A performance modeling framework for lambda architecture based applications. Futur. Gener. Comput. Syst. **86**, 1032–1041 (2017). https://doi.org/10.1016/j.future.2017.07.033
12. Heo, S., Lee, J.H.: Statistical process monitoring of the Tennessee Eastman process using parallel autoassociative neural networks and a large dataset. Processes **7**(7) (2019). https://doi.org/10.3390/pr7070411
13. Iacono, M., Gribaudo, M.: Element based semantics in multi formalism performance models. In: MASCOTS, pp. 413–416. IEEE (2010)
14. Liu, J., et al.: Explainable fault diagnosis of gas-liquid separator based on fully convolutional neural network. Comput. Chem. Eng. **155**, 107535 (2021). https://doi.org/10.1016/j.compchemeng.2021.107535
15. Sun, W., Paiva, A.R., Xu, P., Sundaram, A., Braatz, R.D.: Fault detection and identification using Bayesian recurrent neural networks. Comput. Chem. Eng. **141**, 106991 (2020). https://doi.org/10.1016/j.compchemeng.2020.106991

Regret-Optimal Online Caching
for Adversarial and Stochastic Arrivals

Fathima Zarin Faizal$^{(\boxtimes)}$, Priya Singh , Nikhil Karamchandani ,
and Sharayu Moharir

Indian Institute of Technology Bombay, Mumbai 400076, Maharashtra, India
180070018@iitb.ac.in
https://iitb.ac.in

Abstract. We consider the online caching problem for a cache of limited size. In a time-slotted system, a user requests one file from a large catalog in each slot. If the requested file is cached, the policy receives a unit reward and zero rewards otherwise. We show that a Follow the Perturbed Leader (FTPL)-based anytime caching policy is simultaneously regret-optimal for both adversarial and i.i.d. stochastic arrivals. Further, in the setting where there is a cost associated with switching the cached contents, we propose a variant of FTPL that is order-optimal with respect to time for both adversarial and stochastic arrivals and has a significantly better performance compared to FTPL with respect to the switching cost for stochastic arrivals. We also show that these results can be generalized to the setting where there are constraints on the frequency with which cache contents can be changed. Finally, we validate the results obtained on various synthetic as well as real-world traces.

Keywords: Online caching · algorithms · regret bounds

1 Introduction

The caching problem has been studied since the 1960s, initially motivated by memory management in computers [21]. More recently, there has been renewed interest motivated by Content Delivery Networks [3] used for applications such as Video-on-Demand services. Such applications rely on low latency to provide a good customer experience. The framework of this problem involves a library of L files and a cache located near the end-users that is capable of storing at most C files at any given time, the algorithmic challenge being to determine the most popular files to be stored in the cache.

Two types of arrival patterns have been considered in the existing literature and in our work. The first is known as the Independent Reference Model, where

This work is supported by a SERB grant on Leveraging Edge Resources for Service Hosting.

E. Hyytiä and V. Kavitha (Eds.): VALUETOOLS 2022, LNICST 482, pp. 147–163, 2023.
https://doi.org/10.1007/978-3-031-31234-2_9

request arrivals are generated by an i.i.d. stochastic process and the distribution of the request process is unknown to the policy. The second arrival model is the adversarial arrival model where we make no structural assumptions on the arrival process. Here, the arrival pattern is generated by an oblivious adversary who knows which caching policy is being used but is not aware of the sample path of decisions made by the policy. In both models, as we are focused on the online caching problem, requests are revealed causally and therefore caching decisions have to be made based on past arrival patterns without any explicit knowledge of future arrivals.

Various metrics have been used to characterize the performance of caching polices, including hit-rate and competitive ratio. Regret is a popular metric for online learning algorithms [9] and is defined as the difference between the reward incurred by the optimal stationary policy and the policy under consideration. Our broad goal is to determine if there exists caching policies that have order-optimal regret with respect to time for i.i.d. stochastic and adversarial arrivals and therefore robust to the nature of the arrival process. Polices that perform well in the adversarial setting are primarily focused on not performing horribly on any arrival sequence. This often leads to sub-optimal performance for specific arrival sequences. Similarly, policies designed for specific arrival processes or under some structural assumptions on the arrival process have poor performance in the adversarial setting as they have very poor performance for specific arrival processes which affects the worst-case performance of the policy. For instance, policies designed for the independent reference model would not be ideal when requests are not stationary.

Prediction with expert advice [9,16] and Online Convex Optimization [23] are well-known settings in online learning for which optimal algorithms have been found. Though the caching problem is equivalent to the prediction with expert advice setting with $\binom{L}{C}$ experts, $\binom{L}{C}$ is typically a very large number resulting in standard algorithms being computationally inefficient. Least Frequently Used (LFU), Least Recently Used (LRU) and First-in-First-Out (FIFO) are popular caching policies that have been shown to achieve optimal competitive ratio [4]. There are also results on the closed form stationary hit probabilities of these algorithms under the Independent Reference Model [6,22].

Under stochastic arrivals, LFU achieves order-optimal regret [8] but under adversarial arrivals, LFU, LRU and FIFO have been shown to have suboptimal regret [20]. A sublinear regret upper bound was proved for a gradient-based coded caching policy (OGA) under adversarial arrivals [20] while the first uncoded caching policy to be shown to achieve sublinear regret is the Follow The Perturbed Leader (FTPL) policy [7]. Proposed in [11], FTPL has also been shown to achieve order-optimal regret under adversarial arrivals by proving a lower bound on the regret using a balls-into-bins argument in [7]. An FTPL-based policy has also been shown to be regret-optimal for bipartite caching networks [19].

These policies do not consider the overhead of fetching files into the cache from the library each time the cache updates, called the *switching cost* [18]. An $\tilde{O}(C\sqrt{T})$ upper bound on the regret including the switching cost was shown for a variant of the Multiplicative-Weight policy (MW) under adversarial arrivals which is also more computationally efficient compared to the original MW algorithm naively applied to the caching problem. An upper bound of $\tilde{O}(\sqrt{CT})$ was shown for an FTPL-based policy which is also simpler to implement [18] and improves upon the earlier bound by a factor of $\Theta(\sqrt{C})$.

1.1 Our Contributions

We consider the following two settings: unrestricted switching, where the objective is to minimize the regret including the switching cost, and restricted switching, where the cache is allowed to update at certain fixed points only and the objective is to minimize regret. In Sect. 4, we consider the unrestricted switching setting and show that FTPL with an adaptive learning rate achieves order-optimal regret under stochastic arrivals even after including the switching cost, while FTPL with a constant learning rate cannot have order-optimal regret for both stochastic and adversarial arrivals. We also propose the Wait then FTPL (W-FTPL) policy that improves the bound on the switching cost from $\mathcal{O}(D)$ to $\mathcal{O}(\log D)$, where D is the per-file switching cost. In Sect. 5, we consider the restricted switching setting and prove a lower bound on the regret of any policy and an upper bound on the regret of FTPL. We show that FTPL acheives order-optimal regret under stochastic file requests and in a special case of this setting under adversarial file requests. Finally, in Sect. 6, we present the results of numerical experiments on synthetic as well as real-world traces that validate the results obtained. Due to a lack of space, the proofs of the theorems stated in this paper can be found in [1].

We thus show that FTPL with an adaptive learning rate applied to the online caching problem has order-optimal regret under stochastic and adversarial arrivals in the unrestricted switching and in a special case of the restricted switching setting.

2 Problem Formulation

We consider the classical content caching problem where a user requests files from a library that is stored in a back-end server. There is a cache that is capable of serving user requests at a lower cost but has a storage size that is typically considerably smaller than the library size. Time is slotted and in each time slot, the user requests at most one file. The sequence of events in a time slot is as follows. The cache may first update its contents, after which it receives a request for a file from the user. If the requested file is available in the cache, the cache is said to have a *hit* and the request is fulfilled locally by the cache, and otherwise a *miss*, in which case the file request is fulfilled by the back-end server.

Cache Configuration. We consider a cache of size C that stores files from a library $\mathcal{L}$ of size L. Usually, the cache size is much smaller than the library size, i.e., $C \ll L$. The file requested by the user at time t is denoted by x_t and is represented also in the form of the one-hot encoded vector $\mathbf{x}_t \in \{0,1\}^L$. For $\tau \geq 2$, we denote by $\boldsymbol{X}_\tau = \sum_{t=1}^{\tau-1} \boldsymbol{x}_t$ the L-length vector storing the cumulative sum of requests for each file till time slot $\tau - 1$. $\boldsymbol{X}_1$ is initialized to be the zero vector. Let C(t) denote the set of files cached in round t and let $\boldsymbol{y}_t \in \{0,1\}^L$ be a binary vector denoting the state of the cache at time t, such that $y_t = (y_t^1, y_t^2, \ldots, y_t^L)$ with $y_t^i = 1$ for $i \in C(t)$ and 0 otherwise.

File Requests. We consider two types of file requests: adversarial and stochastic. The file requests are said to be *adversarial* if no assumptions are made regarding the statistical properties of the file requests. We assume that the adversary is oblivious, i.e., the entire file request sequence is fixed before the first request is sent. The file requests are said to be *stochastic* if in each slot, the request is generated independently according to a popularity distribution $\boldsymbol{\mu} = (\mu_1, \ldots, \mu_L)$, where $\mathbb{P}(x_t = i) = \mu_i$ and $\sum_i \mu_i = 1$. Without loss of generality, we assume that $\mu_1 \geq \ldots \geq \mu_L$. As is the case in most real-world applications, the popularity distribution is assumed to be unknown to the caching policy beforehand.

Caching Policy. At the beginning of any given time slot $t \geq 2$, a caching policy $\pi(\cdot)$ maps the history of observations it has seen so far (denoted by $h(t)$) to a valid cache configuration C(t), i.e., $C(t) = \pi(h(t))$. In the first time slot, we assume that the cache stores C files randomly chosen from the library and that this does not incur any switch cost. We define T to be the time horizon of interest. When the file requests are adversarial, the optimal stationary policy is defined to be the caching policy that stores the top C files in hindsight, i.e., stores the C files that received the maximum number of requests till time T. When the file requests are stochastic, the optimal stationary policy is defined to be the caching policy that stores the files with the top C popularities in the cache, i.e., $C(t) = \mathcal{C} \ \forall t$, where $\mathcal{C} = \{1, \ldots, C\}$.

Reward and Switch Cost. At each time step, the policy obtains a reward of 1 unit when the requested file is available in the cache, i.e., a hit occurs, and a reward of 0 units otherwise. A caching policy that fetches a large number of files into the cache each time the cache updates is not ideal as fetching files into the cache causes latency and consumes bandwidth. Thus, we also consider the switch cost, i.e., the cost of fetching files from the back-end server into the cache. We assume that fetching a file into the cache from the server incurs a cost of D units.

Performance Metric. Policies are evaluated on the basis of the regret that they incur. Informally, the regret of a policy till time T is the difference between the net utility of the optimal stationary policy and the net utility the policy under consideration. The net utility of a policy till time T is the difference between the net reward accrued till T and the overall switch cost incurred till then. Stationary policies do not incur any switch cost and hence their net utility is determined by the overall number of hits they have till time T. As discussed in the next section, in some cases, we omit the switch cost.

Problem Settings. We consider the following two variations of the classical content caching problem:

1. **Setting 1:** Unrestricted switching with switching cost.
   In this setting, the system incurs a cost of D units every time a file is fetched from the back-end server to be stored in the cache. When following a policy

π on a request sequence $\{x_t\}_{t=1}^T$, the regret till time T for $\{x_t\}_{t=1}^T$ including the switching cost when the file requests are adversarial is defined as:

$$R_A^\pi(\{x_t\}_{t=1}^T, T, D) = \sup_{y \in \mathcal{Y}} \langle y, X_{T+1} \rangle - \sum_{t=1}^T \mathbb{E} \langle y_t, x_t \rangle + \frac{D}{2} \sum_{t=1}^{T-1} \mathbb{E} \|y_{t+1} - y_t\|_1,$$
(1)

where the expectation is with respect to any randomness introduced by the policy. The regret of a policy π till time T is defined as the worst-case regret over all possible request sequences, i.e.,

$$R_A^\pi(T, D) = \sup_{\{x_t\}_{t=1}^T} R_A^\pi(\{x_t\}_{t=1}^T, T, D).$$

When the file requests are stochastic, the regret including the switching cost after T time steps is defined as:

$$R_S^\pi(T, D) = \mathbb{E}\left[\sum_{t=1}^T \mathbb{1}\{x(t) \in \mathcal{C}\} - \mathbb{1}\{x(t) \in C(t)\}\right] + \frac{D}{2} \sum_{t=1}^{T-1} \mathbb{E} \|y_{t+1} - y_t\|_1,$$
(2)

where $\mathcal{C}$ denotes the set of files having the top C popularities. In the above expression, the expectation is taken with respect to the randomness in the file requests as well as any randomness introduced by the policy.

2. **Setting 2:** Restricted switching without switching cost.
   Here, the cache is allowed to change its contents only at $s + 1$ fixed time slots for some $1 \le s \le T$. To be precise, the cache is allowed to change its contents only at the beginning of the following time slots: $1, r_1 + 1, r_1 + r_2 + 1, \ldots, \sum_{i=1}^s r_i + 1$, where $1 < r_i \le T, 1 \le i \le s$ denotes the ith inter-switching period such that $\sum_{i=1}^s r_i = T$. Thus, within the time horizon T, the cache is allowed to update only at s fixed time slots. Note that the setting where the cache is allowed to change its contents only after every $1 \le r \le T$ requests, i.e., at time slots $1, r+1, \ldots, T+1$ and $s = \frac{T}{r}$ is a special case of this setting. For simplicity, we restrict our attention to the case where there is no switch cost, i.e., $D = 0$. When following a policy π, the regret after T time steps when the file requests are adversarial is:

$$R_A^\pi(T) = \sup_{y \in \mathcal{Y}} \langle y, X_{T+1} \rangle - \sum_{t=1}^T \mathbb{E} \langle y_t, x_t \rangle,$$
(3)

where the expectation is with respect to the randomness introduced by the policy. When the file requests are stochastic, the regret after T time steps is:

$$R_S^\pi(T) = \mathbb{E}\left[\sum_{t=1}^T \mathbb{1}\{x(t) \in \mathcal{C}\} - \mathbb{1}\{x(t) \in C(t)\}\right],$$
(4)

where $\mathcal{C}$ denotes the set of files having the top C popularities. In the above expression, the expectation is taken with respect to the randomness introduced by the policy and the file requests.

To distinguish between results including switching cost and those without switching cost, we use the notation $R_{(\cdot)}^\pi(T, D)$ for results involving the switch cost and $R_{(\cdot)}^\pi(T)$ for results without the switch cost.

The overall goal of this work is to characterize the optimal regret in the two settings mentioned above, for both adversarial and stochastic file requests. This entails proving scheme-agnostic lower bounds on the regret as well as designing policies whose regret is of the same order as these lower bounds. As we will see, these results will also highlight the impact of switching cost and intermittent switching on the optimal achievable regret.

3   Policies

In this section, we introduce and formalize policies whose optimality (or suboptimality) will be discussed in later sections.

3.1   Least Frequently Used (LFU)

The LFU algorithm (formally defined in Algorithm 1) keeps track of the number of times each file has been requested so far. At each time step t, the files with the C highest number of requests are cached. This policy is deterministic and thus performs poorly when faced with certain adversarial request sequences [20]. For the simplified case of $L = 2, C = 1$, one example is a round-robin request sequence of the form $1, 2, 1, 2, \ldots$ which would result in LFU obtaining essentially zero reward while the optimal stationary policy obtains a reward of $T/2$. For stochastic requests, it has been shown to achieve $\mathcal{O}(1)$ regret when switching is allowed at all time slots and when the algorithm incurs no switch cost [8].

Algorithm 1. LFU algorithm

1: **procedure** LFU(T)
2:     $c_t \leftarrow 0$
3:     **while** $t \leq T$ **do**
4:         $C_t \leftarrow \arg\max_C (c_t(1), \ldots, c_t(L))$
5:         Receive file request x_t
6:         $c_t(x_t) \leftarrow c_t(x_t) + 1$
7:     **end while**
8: **end procedure**

3.2   Follow the Perturbed Leader (FTPL)

The FTPL algorithm (formally defined in Algorithm 2) is a variation of the LFU algorithm and also keeps track of the number of times each file has been requested so far, but adds an independent Gaussian perturbation with mean 0 and standard deviation η_t (referred to as the learning rate) to the counts of each file in each time slot. At each time step t, the files with the C highest perturbed counts are cached. Special cases of this policy are known to achieve order-optimal regret under adversarial requests (with and without switch cost) [7,18]. We will henceforth refer to the FTPL algorithm with the learning rate η_t by FTPL(η_t).

Algorithm 2. FTPL algorithm

1: **procedure** FTPL($T, \{\eta_t\}_{t=1}^T$)
2:     $c_t \leftarrow \mathbf{0}$
3:     Sample $\gamma \sim \mathcal{N}(\mathbf{0}, \mathbf{I}_{L \times L})$
4:     **while** $t \leq T$ **do**
5:         $C_t \leftarrow \underset{C}{\arg\max}(c_t(1) + \eta_t \gamma(1), \ldots, c_t(L) + \eta_t \gamma(L))$
6:         Receive file request x_t
7:         $c_t(x_t) \leftarrow c_t(x_t) + 1$
8:     **end while**
9: **end procedure**

3.3   Wait Then FTPL (W-FTPL)

The algorithm that we propose, Wait then FTPL (formally defined in Algorithm 3), is a variant of the FTPL algorithm where the policy remains idle for an initial deterministic waiting period and then follows the normal FTPL algorithm. The motivation for this algorithm is to avoid the higher switch cost incurred initially by the FTPL algorithm under stochastic file requests until the policy has seen enough requests to have a good enough estimate of the underlying popularity distribution, while ensuring order optimal regret in the adversarial setting. We will henceforth refer to the W-FTPL algorithm with the learning rate η_t by W-FTPL(η_t).

Algorithm 3. W-FTPL algorithm

1: **procedure** W-FTPL($T, \{\eta_t\}_{t=1}^T, D, t'$)
2:     $c_t \leftarrow \mathbf{0}$
3:     Sample $\gamma \sim \mathcal{N}(\mathbf{0}, \mathbf{I}_{L \times L})$
4:     **while** $t \leq T$ **do**
5:         **if** $t > t'$ **then**
6:             $C_t \leftarrow \underset{C}{\arg\max}(c_t(1) + \eta_t \gamma(1), \ldots, c_t(L) + \eta_t \gamma(L))$
7:         **end if**
8:         Receive file request x_t
9:         $c_t(x_t) \leftarrow c_t(x_t) + 1$
10:     **end while**
11: **end procedure**

---

4 Setting 1: Unrestricted Switching with Switching Cost

In this section, we consider the setting where there is no limitation on the switching frequency of the cache and the objective is to minimize the regret including the switching cost, i.e., minimize regret as well as the number of fetches into the cache. We consider both stochastic and adversarial file request sequences and show that FTPL($\alpha\sqrt{t}$) and W-FTPL($\alpha\sqrt{t}$) are order-optimal under both types of file requests. While the FTPL(η) algorithm is order-optimal under adversarial requests for a particular value of η [7], we prove that the same does not hold true for stochastic file requests.

4.1 Adversarial Requests

In this section, we discuss the performance of the policies introduced in Sect. 3 under adversarial file requests. The key results of this section has been summarized in the following theorem:

Theorem 1. *Under adversarial requests, we have*

(a) *[7, Theorem 2] For any policy π and $L \geq 2C$,*

$$R_A^\pi(T, D = 0) \geq \sqrt{\frac{CT}{2\pi}} - \Theta\left(\frac{1}{\sqrt{T}}\right).$$

(b) *[20, Proposition 1] The regret of the LFU policy can be characterized as:*
$$R_A^{LFU}(T, 0) = \Omega(T).$$

(c) *[18, Theorem 4.1] The regret of FTPL($\alpha\sqrt{t}$) is upper bounded as:*
$$R_A^{FTPL(\alpha\sqrt{t})}(T, D) \leq c_1\sqrt{T} + c_2 \ln T + c_3,$$

where $c_1 = \mathcal{O}(\sqrt{\ln(Le/C)})$, and c_2, c_3 are small constants depending on L, C, D and α.
(d) *The regret of W-FTPL($\alpha\sqrt{t}$) is upper bounded as:*
$$R_A^{W\text{-}FTPL(\alpha\sqrt{t})}(T, D) \leq \mathcal{O}(\sqrt{T}).$$

Part (a) has been proved in [7] and provides a lower bound on the regret of any policy under adversarial requests.

As argued before, LFU performs poorly under adversarial requests. This is also seen for many popular classical caching algorithms like LRU and FIFO (refer [20]).

Part (c) has been proved in [18] and provides an $\mathcal{O}(\sqrt{T})$ upper bound on the regret including the switching cost of the FTPL($\alpha\sqrt{t}$) policy under adversarial requests, thus showing that this algorithm is order-optimal under adversarial requests. FTPL($\alpha\sqrt{T}$) has also been shown to be order-optimal under adversarial requests [7,18].

Part (d) provides an upper bound on the regret including the switching cost of W-FTPL($\alpha\sqrt{t}$) under adversarial requests. This result shows that W-FTPL($\alpha\sqrt{t}$) is order-optimal under adversarial requests. The proof of this result can be found in Appendix A.

4.2   Stochastic Requests

To find a policy that achieves order-optimal regret under stochastic and adversarial arrivals, we were motivated by [7,18] where the regret for FTPL with the learning rates $\alpha\sqrt{t}$ and $\alpha\sqrt{T}$ (α being some positive constant) under adversarial arrivals was characterized. In this section, we discuss the performance of these policies under stochastic file requests. The key results of this section has been summarized in the following theorem:

Theorem 2. *The file requests are stochastic i.i.d. with the popularity distribution* $\boldsymbol{\mu}$.

(a) [8, Theorem 1] When $D = 0$, *the regret of the LFU policy can be upper bounded as:*

$$R_S^{LFU}(T,0) < \min\left(\frac{16}{\Delta_{min}^2}, \frac{4\,C(L-C)}{\Delta_{min}}\right), \tag{5}$$

where $\Delta_{min} = \mu_C - \mu_{C+1}$.

(b) For $L = 2, C = 1$ *and* $D = 0$, *the regret of* $FTPL(\eta)$ *can be lower bounded as:*

$$R_S^{FTPL(\eta)}(T,0) \geq \frac{\eta e^{-\left(\frac{1+\eta}{\eta}\right)^2}}{4}.$$

(c) The regret of $FTPL(\alpha\sqrt{t})$ *is upper bounded as:*

$$R_S^{FTPL(\sqrt{t})}(T,D) \leq (1 + DC)\,t_0 + \left(1 + \frac{D}{\Delta_{min}}\right)\left(\frac{8}{\Delta_{min}} + \frac{32\alpha^2}{\Delta_{min}}\right),$$

where $t_0 = \max\left\{\frac{8}{\Delta_{min}^2}\log\left(L^3\right), \frac{32\alpha^2}{\Delta_{min}^2}\log\left(L^3\right)\right\}$.

(d) The regret of $W\text{-}FTPL(\alpha\sqrt{t})$ *is upper bounded as:*

$$R_S^{W\text{-}FTPL(\sqrt{t})}(T,D) \leq t' + \frac{16}{\Delta_{min}} + \frac{64\alpha^2}{\Delta_{min}} + 2L^3D\left(e^{-u(\log D)^{1+\beta}\Delta_{min}^2/8}\frac{8}{\Delta_{min}^2}\right.$$
$$\left. + e^{-u(\log D)^{1+\beta}\Delta_{min}^2/32\alpha^2}\frac{32\alpha^2}{\Delta_{min}^2}\right),$$

where $t' = \max\left\{\frac{8}{\Delta_{min}^2}\log\left(\frac{L^3}{2}\right), \frac{32\alpha^2}{\Delta_{min}^2}\log\left(\frac{L^3}{2}\right), u(\log D)^{1+\beta}\right\}$.

Part (a) of the above theorem has been proved in [8] and shows that the regret of LFU is $\mathcal{O}(1)$ when the file requests are stochastic. Thus, the regret of any policy that has order optimal regret under stochastic file requests should be $\mathcal{O}(1)$.

Part (b) gives a lower bound on the regret of the $FTPL(\eta)$ algorithm under stochastic file requests. Note that for all $\eta \geq 1$, we have

$$R_S^{FTPL(\eta)}(T) \geq \frac{\eta e^{-\left(\frac{1+\eta}{\eta}\right)^2}}{4} \geq \frac{\eta}{4e^4}.$$

This shows that the regret is $\Omega(\eta)$ for the FTPL(η) algorithm when the file requests are stochastic. Using $\eta = \alpha\sqrt{T}$, where α is a positive constant, from [7] which gave an $\mathcal{O}(\sqrt{T})$ upper bound for FTPL(η), we get that with the constant learning rate $\eta = \alpha\sqrt{T}$, the regret of FTPL(η) is $\Theta(\sqrt{T})$. Thus, while FTPL(η) is order-optimal under adversarial requests (see Sect. 4.1), it cannot simultaneously be order-optimal under adversarial and stochastic file requests. The proof of this result can be found in Appendix B.

Part (c) shows that FTPL($\alpha\sqrt{t}$), $\alpha > 0$ is order-optimal when the file requests are stochastic. While FTPL(η) with $\eta = \mathcal{O}(\sqrt{T})$ achieves $\Omega(\sqrt{T})$ regret, this result shows an $\mathcal{O}(1)$ upper bound on the regret of FTPL($\alpha\sqrt{t}$) including the switching cost, thus showing that this algorithm is order-optimal. Note that the upper bound grows linearly with the per-file switch cost D. The proof of this result can be found in Appendix C.

Recall that the Wait then FTPL($\alpha\sqrt{t}$) (W-FTPL($\alpha\sqrt{t}$)) algorithm is a variant of the FTPL($\alpha\sqrt{t}$) algorithm. The algorithm remains idle till time $t' = u(\log D)^{1+\beta}, u > 0$, and then normal FTPL($\alpha\sqrt{t}$) is followed. Part (d) proves an $\mathcal{O}(1)$ upper bound on the regret including the switching cost of this algorithm with respect to the horizon T under stochastic file requests, thus showing that this algorithm is order-optimal. The main improvement over the FTPL($\alpha\sqrt{t}$) algorithm is the $\mathcal{O}((\log D)^{1+\beta})$ upper bound on the regret including the switching cost for a large enough value of D under stochastic file requests, as compared to the upper bound $\mathcal{O}(D)$ for FTPL($\alpha\sqrt{t}$). The key idea behind remaining idle for an initial period that depends logarithmically on D is to avoid the higher switch cost incurred at the beginning by the FTPL($\alpha\sqrt{t}$) algorithm (refer to Sect. 6). The proof of this result can be found in Appendix D.

5   Restricted Switching

In this section, we consider the setting where the cache is allowed to update its contents only at $s + 1$ fixed number of time slots, where $s \in \mathbb{Z}, s \leq T$. The first point is at time slot 1, the second at time slot $r_1 + 1$, the third point is at time slot $r_1 + r_2 + 1$, and so on till the $s + 1^{\text{th}}$ point, which is at time slot $\sum_{i=1}^{s} r_i + 1$, where $r_i \in \mathbb{Z}, r_i \leq T, 1 \leq i \leq s$ and $\sum_{i=1}^{s} r_i = T$. Note that the cache is allowed to update its contents only s times till the time horizon T. Refer to Fig. 1 for an illustration of this setting. As a special case of this setting, we also consider the homogenous case where the cache is allowed to update only after every $r \in \mathbb{Z}$ requests, i.e., $s = \frac{T}{r}$. We study the regret performance of FTPL and also provide lower bounds on the regret incurred by any online scheme. In the homogenous case, we also show that FTPL($\sqrt{rt}$) achieves order-optimal regret.

5.1   Stochastic Requests

Theorem 3. *The file requests are stochastic i.i.d. with the popularity distribution μ. When cache updates are restricted to $s + 1$ fixed points defined by the inter-switching periods $\{r_i\}_{i=1}^{s}$ as outlined above,*

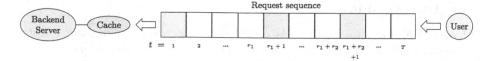

Fig. 1. The time slots where the cache is allowed to update its contents have been marked in yellow. (Color figure online)

(a) When $L = 2, C = 1$, for any online caching policy π, there exists a popularity distribution such that the popularities of the two files are greater than $1 > a > 0$ and the difference in the popularities is Δ, such that

$$R_S^\pi(T) \geq \frac{r_1 \Delta}{2} + \sum_{i=2}^s r_i \frac{\Delta}{4} \exp\left(-t_i \frac{\Delta^2}{a^2}\right).$$

(b) The regret of $FTPL(\alpha\sqrt{t})$ is upper bounded as:

$$R_S^{FTPL(\alpha\sqrt{t})}(T) \leq r_1 + 2 \sum_{j=1}^C \sum_{k=C+1}^L \sum_{i=2}^s r_i \Delta_{j,k} \left(e^{-t_i \Delta_{j,k}^2/8} + e^{-t_i \Delta_{j,k}^2/32\alpha^2}\right).$$

In part (a), we prove a fundamental lower bound on the regret of any policy π under stochastic file requests when cache updates are restricted to $s + 1$ fixed time slots. The proof of this result can be found in Appendix E. In part (b), we prove an upper bound on the regret of the $FTPL(\alpha\sqrt{t})$ policy when cache updates are restricted to $s + 1$ fixed time slots. The proof of this result can be found in Appendix F. We thus have that the $FTPL(\alpha\sqrt{t})$ policy has order-optimal regret in this setting under stochastic file requests. Next, we consider the special case where all r_i are equal to r, i.e., $s = T/r$.

Theorem 4. *The file requests are stochastic i.i.d. with the popularity distribution μ. When the cache is allowed to update only after every r requests,*

$$R_S^{FTPL(\alpha\sqrt{t})} \leq 1 + t_0' + 2\left(\frac{8}{\Delta_{\min}} + \frac{32\alpha^2}{\Delta_{\min}}\right).$$

where $t_0' = \max\left\{r, \frac{8}{\Delta_{\min}^2} \log\left(L^2\right), \frac{32\alpha^2}{\Delta_{\min}^2} \log\left(L^2\right)\right\}$.

In Theorem 4, we prove an $\mathcal{O}(\max\{r, \log L\})$ upper bound on the regret of the $FTPL(\alpha\sqrt{t})$ algorithm under stochastic file requests. While the order-optimality of this policy with respect to r follows from Theorem 3, we also note that the bound proved here improves upon the worst-case $\mathcal{O}(L^2)$ dependency in the upper bound proved in part (b) of Theorem 3 to $\mathcal{O}(\log L)$. The proof of this result can be found in Appendix G.

5.2   Adversarial Requests

Theorem 5. *Files are requested by an oblivious adversary. When cache updates are restricted to $s + 1$ fixed points defined by $\{r_i\}_{i=1}^s$ as outlined above,*

(a) For any online caching policy π and $L \geq 2C$,

$$R_A^\pi(T) \geq \frac{1}{2} \left(0.15 \sqrt{C \sum_{i=1}^s r_i^2 \left(1 - \frac{(C-1)\left(\sum_{i=1}^s r_i^4\right)}{2\left(\sum_{i=1}^s r_i^2\right)^2} \right)} - 0.6\, C \max_{1 \leq i \leq s} r_i \right).$$

(b) The regret of $FTPL(\alpha\sqrt{t})$ is upper bounded as:

$$R_A^{FTPL(\alpha\sqrt{t})}(T) \leq \mathcal{O}(\alpha\sqrt{T}) + \sqrt{\frac{2}{\pi}} \sum_{i=1}^s \frac{r_i^2}{\alpha \sqrt{\sum_{j=0}^{i-1} r_j}}.$$

The proof of this theorem can be found in Appendix H and Appendix I respectively. In part (a), we prove a lower bound on the regret of any policy π under adversarial file requests when cache updates are restricted to s fixed time slots. Note that a necessary condition for this bound to be meaningful is

$$4 \max_{1 \leq i \leq s} r_i \leq \sqrt{\sum_{i=1}^s r_i^2}. \tag{6}$$

When this bound is meaningful, we have that $R_A^\pi(T) = \Omega\left(\sqrt{C \sum_{i=1}^s r_i^2}\right)$ for any online caching policy π. When all the r_i's are equal, this condition translates to $r \leq T/16$. This condition does not hold if any of the r_i's is too large. For instance, when $s = 3$ and $r_1 = T/2, r_2 = r_3 = T/4$, this condition does not hold. When $\max_{1 \leq i \leq s} r_i$ and $\min_{1 \leq i \leq s} r_i$ are known, a sufficient condition for (6) to hold is:

$$\frac{\max_{1 \leq i \leq s} r_i}{\min_{1 \leq i \leq s} r_i} \leq \frac{\sqrt{s}}{4}.$$

We now discuss the special case where all r_i are equal to r, i.e., $s = T/r$. It follows from part (b) of Theorem 5 that $FTPL(\sqrt{rt})$ achieves a regret of $\mathcal{O}(\sqrt{rT})$. The following theorem provides a matching lower bound for this setting that proves that $FTPL(\sqrt{rt})$ is order-optimal, the proof of which can be found in Appendix J.

Theorem 6. *Files are requested by an oblivious adversary. When the cache is allowed to update only after every r requests, for any online caching policy π and $L \geq 2C$,*

$$R_A^\pi(T) \geq \begin{cases} \sqrt{\frac{CrT}{2\pi}} - \Theta\left(\frac{r\sqrt{r}}{\sqrt{T}}\right), & \text{when } r = o(T), \\ \Omega(T), & \text{when } r = \Omega(T). \end{cases}$$

6   Numerical Experiments

In this section, we present the results of numerical simulations for the various policies discussed in Sect. 3.

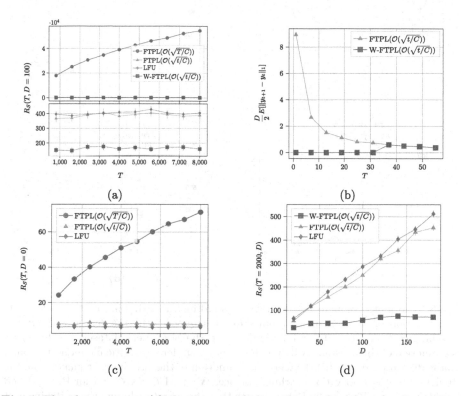

(a)   (b)

(c)   (d)

Fig. 2. The plots compare (a) the regret including the switching cost for $D = 100$ as a function of T, (b) the switching cost in each time slot for $D = 30, u = 5, \beta = 0.6$ as a function of T, (c) the regret as a function of T with $D = 0$, and (d) the regret including the switching cost for $T = 2000$ as a function of D, of various caching policies under stochastic file requests. $L = 10, C = 4$ for each of the plots and the popularity distribution is a dyadic distribution. Parts (a) and (c) show that the regret incurred by FTPL($\mathcal{O}(\sqrt{T})$) is increasing with T while FTPL($\mathcal{O}(\sqrt{t})$), W- FTPL($\mathcal{O}(\sqrt{t})$) and LFU have essentially constant regret. Part (b) shows that FTPL($\mathcal{O}(\sqrt{t})$) makes more switches at the beginning, thus motivating the W- FTPL($\mathcal{O}(\sqrt{t})$) algorithm. Part (d) shows that while the regret including the switching cost of LFU and FTPL($\mathcal{O}(\sqrt{t})$) increase linearly in D, it increases sublinearly for W-FTPL($\mathcal{O}(\sqrt{t})$).

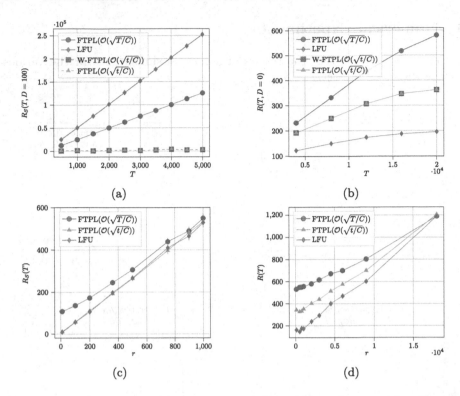

Fig. 3. The plots compare (a) the regret including the switching cost for $D = 100$ as a function of T on a round robin request sequence, (b) the regret without the switching cost, i.e., $D = 0$ as a function of T on the MovieLens dataset, (c) the regret as a function of the constant switching frequency r under stochastic file requests from a dyadic distribution, and (d) the regret as a function of the switching frequency r on the MovieLens dataset, of various caching policies. We used $L = 2, C = 1$ for Part (a) and $L = 10, C = 4$ for Part (c). In Part (a), note that the regret including the switching cost scales linearly with T for LFU, while W-FTPL($\mathcal{O}(\sqrt{t})$) and FTPL($\mathcal{O}(\sqrt{t})$) show better performance. In Part (c), the regret scales linearly with r for all the three algorithms as expected. The regret scales sublinearly with T in Part (b) and linearly with r in Part (d).

6.1   Setting 1 with Stochastic File Requests

Setup. We use $L = 10, C = 4$ throughout this section. The popularity distribution used is a dyadic distribution, i.e., for $1 \leq i \leq L - 1$, $\mu(i) = \frac{1}{2^i}$ and $\mu(L) = \frac{1}{2^{L-1}}$.

Results. Fig. 2a shows that the regret of FTPL including the switching cost increases with T, while it is essentially constant for FTPL($\mathcal{O}(\sqrt{t})$), W-FTPL($\mathcal{O}(\sqrt{t})$) and LFU. One can also observe that W- FTPL($\mathcal{O}(\sqrt{t})$) performs the best among all the four algorithms. In Fig. 2c, we plot only the regret as a function of T. Note that the same trend is observed here as well. Here, we omit plotting W- FTPL($\mathcal{O}(\sqrt{t})$) as its regret would be the same as that of FTPL($\mathcal{O}(\sqrt{t})$) in this case. Figure 2b shows that FTPL($\mathcal{O}(\sqrt{t})$) indeed makes more switches at the beginning, which is the motivation for the W-FTPL($\mathcal{O}(\sqrt{t})$) policy where no switches are made for an initial period. Figure 2d shows that the regret of LFU and FTPL($\mathcal{O}(\sqrt{t})$) grows linearly with D, while that of W-FTPL($\mathcal{O}(\sqrt{t})$) grows sublinearly with D.

6.2   Setting 1 with Adversarial File Requests

Setup. We consider a synthetic adversarial request sequence in Fig. 3a and a real-world trace in Fig. 3b. The synthetic adversarial request sequence used is $1, 2, 1, 2, \ldots$ for $L = 2, C = 1$, i.e., a round-robin request sequence. The real-world trace used is the first 20,000 rows of the MovieLens 1M dataset [2,12] which contains ratings for 2569 movies with timestamps that we model as requests to a CDN server of library size 2569 and a cache size of 25.

Results. Fig. 3a shows that under the round-robin request sequence, the regret including the switching cost of LFU scales linearly with T, while that of W-FTPL($\mathcal{O}(\sqrt{t})$) and FTPL($\mathcal{O}(\sqrt{t})$) scales sublinearly with T. Figure 3b shows that on the MovieLens dataset, the regret scales sublinearly with T for all the four algorithms.

6.3   Setting 2

Setup. We consider stochastic file requests drawn from a dyadic distribution for $L = 10, C = 4$ in Fig. 3c and file requests from the MovieLens dataset in Fig. 3d. We also used $T = 18000$ and chose r to be factors of T. There were 2518 unique movies in the first 18000 rows of the MovieLens dataset and we set the cache size to be 25.

Results. Figure 3c shows that when file requests are drawn from a dyadic popularity distribution, the regret of all three policies vary linearly with r. Figure 3d shows that on the MovieLens dataset, the regret scales linearly with r for all the three policies.

7   Conclusion

We have shown that FTPL($\mathcal{O}(\sqrt{t})$) achieves order-optimal regret even after including the switching cost under stochastic requests. Combining with prior results on the performance of FTPL, it is simultaneously order-optimal for both stochastic and adversarial requests. We also showed that FTPL(η) cannot possibly achieve order-optimal regret simultaneously under both stochastic and adversarial requests, while variants of this policy can individually be order-optimal under each type of request. We proposed the W-FTPL($\mathcal{O}(\sqrt{t})$) policy as a way of preventing the high switching cost incurred by FTPL at the beginning under stochastic file requests. We also considered the restricted switching setting, where the cache is allowed to update its contents only at specific pre-determined time slots and obtained a lower bound on the regret incurred by any policy. We proved an upper bound on the regret of $FTPL(\mathcal{O}(\sqrt{t}))$ and showed that it is order-optimal under stochastic file requests and in the homogenous restricted switching case under adversarial file requests.

This work motivates several directions for future work: (1) Bringing the upper and lower bounds closer in the general restricted switching setting would help in proving whether $FTPL(\mathcal{O}(\sqrt{t}))$ is order-optimal or not under adversarial file requests in this case too. (2) For the restricted switching setting, our results consider only the regret. Adding the switching cost too here would make the bounds complete.

References

1. https://github.com/fathimazarin/Valuetools2022_caching/blob/main/main.pdf
2. MovieLens 1M dataset. https://grouplens.org/datasets/movielens/. Accessed 8 Aug 2022
3. Aggarwal, C., Wolf, J.L., Yu, P.S.: Caching on the world wide web. 125 J. Distrib. Parallel Syst. (IJDPS) **2**(6), 94–107 (2000). https://doi.org/10.1109/69.755618
4. Albers, S.: Competitive Online Algorithms. BRICS, Shanghai (1996)
5. Alon, N., Spencer, J.: Appendix B: Paul Erdös. John Wiley and Sons, Ltd, New York (2008). https://doi.org/10.1002/9780470277331.app2
6. Aven, O.I., Coffman, E.G., Kogan, Y.A.: Stochastic Analysis of Computer Storage. Kluwer Academic Publishers, USA (1987)
7. Bhattacharjee, R., Banerjee, S., Sinha, A.: Fundamental limits of online network-caching. CoRR abs/2003.14085 (2020). https://doi.org/10.48550/arXiv.2003.14085
8. Bura, A., Rengarajan, D., Kalathil, D., Shakkottai, S., Chamberland, J.F.: Learning to cache and caching to learn: regret analysis of caching algorithms. IEEE/ACM Trans. Netw. **30**(1), 18–31 (2022). https://doi.org/10.48550/arXiv.2004.00472
9. Cesa-Bianchi, N., Lugosi, G.: Prediction, Learning, and Games. Cambridge University Press, Cambridge (2006). https://doi.org/10.1017/CBO9780511546921
10. Cohen, A., Hazan, T.: Following the perturbed leader for online structured learning. In: Bach, F., Blei, D. (eds.) Proceedings of the 32nd International Conference on Machine Learning. Proceedings of Machine Learning Research, PMLR, Lille, France, vol. 37, pp. 1034–1042, 07–09 July 2015
11. Hannan, J.: Approximation to Bayes risk in repeated play. In: Contributions to the Theory of Games, vol. 3, no. 2, 97–139 (1957). https://doi.org/10.1515/9781400882151
12. Harper, F.M., Konstan, J.A.: The Movielens datasets: history and context. ACM Trans. Interact. Intell. Syst. **5**(4), December 2015. https://doi.org/10.1145/2827872
13. Hoeffding, W.: Probability inequalities for sums of bounded random variables. J. Am. Stat. Assoc. **58**(301), 13–30 (1963). https://doi.org/10.1080/01621459.1963.10500830
14. Kaas, R., Buhrman, J.M.: Mean, median and mode in binomial distributions. Stat. Neerl. **34**(1), 13–18 (1980). https://doi.org/10.1111/j.1467-9574.1980.tb00681.x
15. Lattimore, T., Szepesvári, C.: Bandit Algorithms. Cambridge University Press, Cambridge (2020). https://doi.org/10.1017/9781108571401

16. Littlestone, N., Warmuth, M.K.: The weighted majority algorithm. Inf. Comput. **108**(2), 212–261 (1994). https://doi.org/10.1006/inco.1994.1009

17. Mourtada, J., Gaïffas, S.: On the optimality of the hedge algorithm in the stochastic regime. J. Mach. Learn. Res. **20**, 1–28 (2019). https://doi.org/10.48550/arXiv.1809.01382

18. Mukhopadhyay, S., Sinha, A.: Online caching with optimal switching regret. CoRR abs/2101.07043 (2021). https://doi.org/10.1109/ISIT45174.2021.9517925

19. Paria, D., Sinha, A.: Leadcache: regret-optimal caching in networks. In: Thirty-Fifth Conference on Neural Information Processing Systems, vol. 34, pp. 4435–4447 (2021). https://doi.org/10.48550/arXiv.2009.08228

20. Paschos, G.S., Destounis, A., Vigneri, L., Iosifidis, G.: Learning to cache with no regrets. In: IEEE INFOCOM 2019 - IEEE Conference on Computer Communications, pp. 235–243. IEEE Press (2019). https://doi.org/10.1109/INFOCOM.2019.8737446

21. Silberschatz, A., Galvin, P., Gagne, G.: Operating System Principles. John Wiley & Sons, Hoboken (2006)

22. Starobinski, D., Tse, D.: Probabilistic methods for web caching. Perform. Eval. **46**(2–3), 125–137, October 2001. https://doi.org/10.1016/S0166-5316(01)00045-1

23. Zinkevich, M.: Online convex programming and generalized infinitesimal gradient ascent. In: Proceedings of the 20th International Conference on Machine Learning (ICML-03), pp. 928–936 (2003)

Retrial Queues

Cyclic Retrial Queue for Building Data Transmission Networks

Anatoly Nazarov[1], Tuan Phung-Duc[2], Ksenia Shulgina[1(✉)],
Olga Lizyura[1], Svetlana Paul[1], and Dmitriy Shashev[3]

[1] Institute of Applied Mathematics and Computer Science, National Research Tomsk
State University, 36 Lenina ave., Tomsk 634050, Russia
shulgina19991999@mail.ru
[2] Faculty of Engineering Information and Systems, University of Tsukuba, 1-1-1
Tennodai, Tsukuba, Ibaraki 305-8573, Japan
tuan@sk.tsukuba.ac.jp
[3] Faculty of Innovative Technologies, National Research Tomsk State University,
36/3 Lenina ave., Tomsk 634050, Russia
dshashev@mail.tsu.ru

Abstract. This paper considers a mathematical model of a cyclic multiple access communication network. The model can be used to build specialized "flying" FANET data transmission networks. We consider a single server retrial queue for modeling one node in such network. The input consists of multiple Poisson processes with different arrival rates. Service and retrial rates depend on the origin flow. Thus, each flow has its own orbit for redial. Under the condition when the retrial rate is low, we obtain an asymptotic probability distribution of the number of customers in the orbits.

Keywords: cyclic queueing system · retrial queue · vacations · asymptotic analysis · diffusion approximation

1 Introduction

Special communication networks are destined to provide data transmission between a group of devices. In this paper, we discuss aspects of the organization of special FANET (Flying Ad-Hoc Networks) [1] by stochastic modeling. They are used to organize data transmission in a group of unmanned aerial vehicles (drones).

The actual topology for such communication networks can be a "star", the central node of which performs the functions of controlling groups of drones and is a common network resource. The central node can be a control center for a group of devices, a flight control center, a control room interacting with a group

---

This study was supported by the Tomsk State University Development Programme (Priority-2030).

E. Hyytiä and V. Kavitha (Eds.): VALUETOOLS 2022, LNICST 482, pp. 167–179, 2023.
https://doi.org/10.1007/978-3-031-31234-2_10

of drones. The presence of a network allows each drone to transmit data to the central node.

Resource sharing is a common problem, which can be solved by choosing a protocol for accessing network subscribers to a shared resource. We consider a cyclic protocol, which allocates each drone one time interval, during which it completely transmits data to the control center. Time windows are organized sequentially. Each time window is assigned to one drone. When using the random multiple access protocol, each drone randomly selects a window for transmitting information.

Retrial queues [2–5] are adequate mathematical models of random access protocols and polling systems [6,7] are for cyclic protocols.

In this paper, we intend to investigate a variant of a communication system with a group of drones as a queueing system. When a group of drones is on duty, monitoring the area or delivering cargo, the communication network is in a regular cyclic mode - each drone transmits the collected information in its segment of the cycle to the control center. We consider the cycle as the sum of access intervals to the common resource of each drone. A feature of the proposed model is that the durations of such intervals are random (in particular, they can be deterministic) and independent not only among themselves, but also do not depend on the incoming flows of requests and the duration of their service.

The aim of the paper is to determine the characteristics of the number of messages in orbits of the cyclic retrial queue. The problem is solved using the classical method of "system with server vacations" [8,9]. We have proposed algorithm for assigning access intervals independent of the incoming flow and the time of servicing requests. For our strategy, these times are independent, so the multidimensional probability distribution is factorized and the method of "server vacations" used in the work completely solves the problem.

Polling systems with retrial behavior are considered in papers [11–15]. The authors propose numerical analysis for gated or mixed service disciplines in such systems. We propose the analysis of the system using original method of asymptotic-diffusion analysis under low rate of retrial condition [16]. Our approach allows to build accurate enough approximation for the steady state distribution of the number of calls in the orbit.

The rest of the paper is structured as follows. In Sect. 2, we describe the structure of the model and define its parameters. Section 3 shows the derived Kolmogorov equations for the system state process. In Sects. 4, 5, we describe the main results and prove theorems about approximate diffusion process. In Sect. 6, we present the algorithm of calculation for the approximation of the steady state distribution of the number of customers in the orbit. Section 7 depicts the numerical example of using the derived formulas. Finally, Sect. 8 presents concluding remarks.

2   Mathematical Model

The group of N drones forms N Poisson flows of incoming packages (calls) with intensity λ_n for the n-th drone ($n = 1, \ldots, N$) to the control center (see Fig. 1).

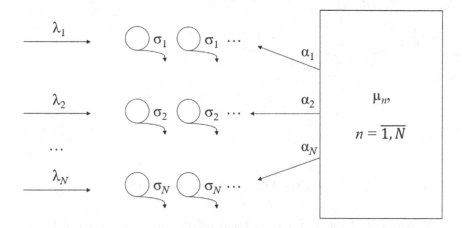

Fig. 1. Cyclic retrial queue

Calls of n-th flow form their own unlimited orbit. The pair of flow and orbit will be called the n-th RQ-system. The control center (server) visits retrial queues in a cyclic order, starting from the first and ending with N-th, then the cycle repeats. The time spent by the server at the n-th retrial queue follows the exponential distribution with mean $1/\alpha_n$, $n = 1, \ldots, N$. During this time, the server transmits packages from the incoming flow and corresponding orbit.

If a call of n-th flow detects the server busy or not connected, it instantly goes to n-th orbit and performs a random delay, otherwise the incoming customer is served. The retrial intervals follow the exponential distribution with mean $1/\sigma_n$, $n = 1, \ldots, N$, after which the call reapplies to the server. The service times of calls are exponentially distributed with mean $1/\mu_n$, $n = 1, \ldots, N$.

If the orbit is empty at the time the server arrives, or it has served all the calls that were in orbit, and no more new calls have arrived from the incoming flow, the server still remains connected to the retrial queue until the connection time expires. We study this cyclic system by decomposing it to N separated systems and analyze them as a retrial queue with vacation.

2.1 Modeling of Server Vacations

To study cyclic retrial queue, we consider the model with server vacations (see Fig. 2), which represents one node in our network.

Let us consider the first system with repeated calls with one server and an orbit of infinite capacity. The system receives the requests from a Poisson process with rate λ. The system operates in a cyclic mode whose cycle consists of two consecutive intervals. During the first interval, the server receives calls that come from the incoming flow during an exponentially distributed time with rate μ.

If an incoming call detects the server busy, it instantly goes into orbit, where it performs a random delay during the exponential time with parameter σ, after which it returns to the server.

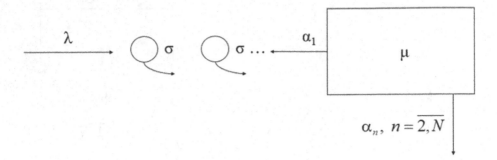

Fig. 2. Retrial queue with server vacations

The duration of the server connection follows the exponential distribution with mean $1/\alpha_1$. Upon the termination of the server connection time, the ongoing call (if any) is pushed to the orbit and retries to enter the server later.

After this interval, the server starts vacation, the duration of which consists of $N - 1$ phases. Each phase follows the exponential distribution with parameters α_n, $n = 2, \ldots, N$. During the vacation, the calls that came into the system accumulate in orbit and wait for the server to return.

The process $k(t)$ depicts the state of server at time t: $k(t) = 0$ if the server is free, $k(t) = 1$ if the server is busy servicing a call, $k(t) = n$ if the server is on the n-th phase of the vacation, $n = 2, \ldots, N$.

We also introduce the random process $i(t)$ as the number of calls in the orbit at time t.

3   Kolmogorov Equations

We are going to obtain the stationary distribution of the number of calls in the orbit. To this end, we study the two-dimensional Markov chain $\{k(t), i(t)\}$. For the probability distribution $P\{k(t) = k, i(t) = i\} = P_k(i, t)$, we compose the Kolmogorov system

$$\frac{\partial P_0(i,t)}{\partial t} = -(\lambda + i\sigma + \alpha_1)P_0(i,t) + \mu P_1(i,t) + \alpha_N P_N(i,t),$$

$$\frac{\partial P_1(i,t)}{\partial t} = -(\lambda + \mu + \alpha_1)P_1(i,t) + \lambda P_0(i,t) + \sigma(i+1)P_0(i+1,t) + \lambda P_1(i-1,t),$$

$$\frac{\partial P_2(i,t)}{\partial t} = -(\lambda + \alpha_2)P_2(i,t) + \alpha_1 P_1(i-1,t) + \alpha_1 P_0(i,t) + \lambda P_2(i-1,t),$$

$$\frac{\partial P_n(i,t)}{\partial t} = -(\lambda + \alpha_n)P_n(i,t) + \lambda P_n(i-1,t) + \alpha_{n-1}P_{n-1}(i,t), \quad n = 3, \ldots, N. \quad (1)$$

Because it is difficult to directly solve the above system of differential equations, we introduce partial characteristic functions, where $j = \sqrt{-1}$:

$$H_k(u,t) = \sum_{i=0}^{\infty} e^{jui} P_k(i,t), \quad k = 0, \ldots, N,$$

and transform (1) as follows for further research

$$\frac{\partial H_0(u,t)}{\partial t} = -(\lambda + \alpha_1)H_0(u,t) + j\sigma\frac{\partial H_0(u,t)}{\partial u} + \mu H_1(u,t) + \alpha_N H_N(u,t),$$

$$\frac{\partial H_1(u,t)}{\partial t} = (\lambda(e^{ju} - 1) - \mu - \alpha_1)H_1(u,t) + \lambda H_0(u,t) - j\sigma e^{-ju}\frac{\partial H_0(u,t)}{\partial u},$$

$$\frac{\partial H_2(u,t)}{\partial t} = (\lambda(e^{ju} - 1) - \alpha_2)H_2(u,t) + e^{ju}\alpha_1 H_1(u,t) + \alpha_1 H_0(u,t),$$

$$\frac{\partial H_n(u,t)}{\partial t} = (\lambda(e^{ju} - 1) - \alpha_n)H_n(u,t) + \alpha_{n-1}H_{n-1}(u,t), n = 3, \dots, N. \quad (2)$$

Summing up the equations in (2), we obtain

$$\frac{\partial H(u,t)}{\partial t} = (e^{ju} - 1)\left(j\sigma e^{-ju}\frac{\partial H_0(u,t)}{\partial u} + \alpha_1 H_1(u,t) + \lambda\sum_{n=1}^{N} H_n(u,t)\right). \quad (3)$$

Because the solution of (2–3) for arbitrary σ is difficult, we consider asymptotic solution under the condition $(\sigma \to 0)$.

4   First Step of Asymptotic-Diffusion Analysis

Introducing $\varepsilon = \sigma$ and performing the following substitution in (2–3)

$$\tau = t\varepsilon, u = \varepsilon w, H_k(u,t) = F_k(w,\tau,\varepsilon),$$

to obtain

$$\varepsilon\frac{\partial F_0(w,\tau,\varepsilon)}{\partial \tau} = -(\lambda + \alpha_1)F_0(w,\tau,\varepsilon) + j\frac{\partial F_0(w,\tau,\varepsilon)}{\partial w}$$

$$+\mu F_1(w,\tau,\varepsilon) + \alpha_N F_N(w,\tau,\varepsilon),$$

$$\varepsilon\frac{\partial F_1(w,\tau,\varepsilon)}{\partial \tau} = (\lambda(e^{j\varepsilon w} - 1) - \mu - \alpha_1)F_1(w,\tau,\varepsilon)$$

$$+\lambda F_0(w,\tau,\varepsilon) - je^{-j\varepsilon w}\frac{\partial F_0(w,\tau,\varepsilon)}{\partial w},$$

$$\varepsilon\frac{\partial F_2(w,\tau,\varepsilon)}{\partial \tau} = (\lambda(e^{j\varepsilon w} - 1) - \alpha_2)F_2(w,\tau,\varepsilon) + e^{j\varepsilon w}\alpha_1 F_1(w,\tau,\varepsilon) + \alpha_1 F_0(w,\tau,\varepsilon),$$

$$\varepsilon\frac{\partial F_n(w,\tau,\varepsilon)}{\partial \tau} = (\lambda(e^{j\varepsilon w} - 1) - \alpha_n)F_n(w,\tau,\varepsilon)$$

$$+\alpha_{n-1}F_{n-1}(w,\tau,\varepsilon), \ n = 3, \dots, N,$$

$$\varepsilon\frac{\partial F(w,\tau,\varepsilon)}{\partial \tau} = (e^{j\varepsilon w} - 1)\cdot$$

$$\cdot\left(je^{-j\varepsilon w}\frac{\partial F_0(w,\tau,\varepsilon)}{\partial w} + \alpha_1 F_1(w,\tau,\varepsilon) + \lambda\sum_{n=1}^{N} F_n(w,\tau,\varepsilon)\right). \quad (4)$$

Solving (4) for $\varepsilon \to 0$, we prove Theorem 1.

Theorem 1.

$$\lim_{\sigma \to 0} \mathbb{E} e^{jw\sigma i(\frac{\tau}{\sigma})} = e^{jwx(\tau)}, \tag{5}$$

where

$$x'(\tau) = -x(\tau)r_0 + \alpha_1 r_1 + \lambda \sum_{n=1}^{N} r_n.$$

Here, probabilities $r_k = r_k(x), k = 0, \ldots, N$ *are given by*

$$r_0(x) = \left[\frac{\mu + \alpha_1 + \lambda + x}{\mu + \alpha_1} + \sum_{n=2}^{N} \frac{\alpha_1(\mu + \alpha_1 + \lambda + x)}{\alpha_n(\mu + \alpha_1)} \right]^{-1},$$

$$r_1(x) = \frac{\lambda + x}{\mu + \alpha_1} r_0(x),$$

$$r_2(x) = \frac{\alpha_1(\mu + \alpha_1 + \lambda + x)}{\alpha_2(\mu + \alpha_1)} r_0(x),$$

$$r_n(x) = \frac{\alpha_1(\mu + \alpha_1 + \lambda + x)}{\alpha_n(\mu + \alpha_1)} r_0(x), \quad n = 3, \ldots, N.$$

Proof. Taking $\varepsilon \to 0$ in (4), we have

$$-(\lambda + \alpha_1)F_0(w, \tau) + j\frac{\partial F_0(w, \tau)}{\partial w} + \mu F_1(w, \tau) + \alpha_N F_N(w, \tau) = 0,$$

$$-(\mu + \alpha_1)F_1(w, \tau) + \lambda F_0(w, \tau) - j\frac{\partial F_0(w, \tau)}{\partial w} = 0,$$

$$-\alpha_2 F_2(w, \tau) + \alpha_1 F_1(w, \tau) + \alpha_1 F_0(w, \tau) = 0,$$

$$-\alpha_n F_n(w, \tau) + \alpha_{n-1}F_{n-1}(w, \tau) = 0, \quad n = 3, \ldots, N,$$

$$\frac{\partial F(w, \tau)}{\partial \tau} = jw \left(j\frac{\partial F_0(w, \tau)}{\partial w} + \alpha_1 F_1(w, \tau) + \lambda \sum_{n=1}^{N} F_n(w, \tau) \right), \tag{6}$$

where $F_k^{(2)}(w, \tau) = \lim_{\varepsilon \to 0} F_k^{(2)}(w, \tau, \varepsilon)$.

We will seek the solution of (6) in the form

$$F_k(w, \tau) = r_k(x)e^{jwx(\tau)}, \quad k = 0, \ldots, N, \tag{7}$$

where $x = x(\tau) = \lim_{\sigma \to 0} \sigma i(\tau/\sigma)$.

Substituting (7) into (6), we obtain

$$-(\lambda + \alpha_1 + x)r_0(x) + \mu r_1(x) + \alpha_N r_N(x) = 0,$$

$$-(\mu + \alpha_1)r_1(x) + (\lambda + x)r_0(x) = 0,$$

$$-\alpha_2 r_2(x) + \alpha_1 r_1(x) + \alpha_1 r_0(x) = 0,$$

$$-\alpha_n r_n(x) + \alpha_{n-1}r_{n-1}(x) = 0, \quad n = 3, \ldots, N,$$

$$x'(\tau) = -x(\tau)r_0(x) + \alpha_1 r_1(x) + \lambda \sum_{n=1}^{N} r_n(x). \tag{8}$$

System (8) together with normalization condition $\sum_{k=0}^{N} r_k(x) = 1$ determine $r_k(x)$

$$r_0(x) = \left[\frac{\mu + \alpha_1 + \lambda + x}{\mu + \alpha_1} + \sum_{n=2}^{N} \frac{\alpha_1(\mu + \alpha_1 + \lambda + x)}{\alpha_n(\mu + \alpha_1)} \right]^{-1},$$

$$r_1(x) = \frac{\lambda + x}{\mu + \alpha_1} r_0(x),$$

$$r_2(x) = \frac{\alpha_1(\mu + \alpha_1 + \lambda + x)}{\alpha_2(\mu + \alpha_1)} r_0(x),$$

$$r_n(x) = \frac{\alpha_1(\mu + \alpha_1 + \lambda + x)}{\alpha_n(\mu + \alpha_1)} r_0(x), \quad n = 3, \ldots, N. \tag{9}$$

Let us denote

$$a(x) = x'(\tau) = \lambda - \left(x - \frac{\alpha_1(\lambda + x)}{\mu + \alpha_1} + \lambda \right) r_0(x). \tag{10}$$

As we will see, $a(x)$ represents the drift coefficient of a certain diffusion process related to the scaled number of calls in the orbit. Thus, Theorem 1 is proven.

Corollary 1. *Stability condition in considered queue is given by*

$$\lim_{x \to \infty} a(x) < 0,$$

which is equivalent to

$$\lambda \left(\sum_{n=1}^{N} \frac{\alpha_1}{\alpha_n} \right) < \mu.$$

Proof. From explicit expressions of $r_k(x), k = 0, 1, \ldots, N$, we have

$$\lim_{x \to \infty} r_0(x) = \frac{\mu + \alpha_1}{1 + \sum_{k=2}^{N} \alpha_1/\alpha_n},$$

and

$$\lim_{x \to \infty} r_n(x) = \frac{\alpha_1}{\alpha_n(1 + \sum_{k=2}^{N} \alpha_1/\alpha_n)}, n = 1, 2 \ldots, N.$$

Plugging these limits into $\lim_{x \to \infty} a(x)$ and rearranging the result yields corollary 1.

It should be remarked that if $\alpha_n = \infty$ for $n = 2, 3, \ldots, N$, i.e., the server only serves queue 1, the stability condition is reduced to $\lambda < \mu$ which is consistent with the stability of the M/M/1 retrial queue.

5   Second Step of Asymptotic-Diffusion Analysis

In (2) and (3), we make the following substitutions:

$$H_k(u,t) = H_k^{(2)}(u,t)e^{j\frac{u}{\sigma}x(\sigma t)}, \ k = 0,\ldots,N.$$

and obtain the system of equations

$$\frac{\partial H_0^{(2)}(u,t)}{\partial t} + jux'(\sigma t)H_0^{(2)}(u,t) = -(\lambda + \alpha_1 + x(\sigma t))H_0^{(2)}(u,t)$$

$$+j\sigma\frac{\partial H_0^{(2)}(u,t)}{\partial u} + \mu H_1^{(2)}(u,t) + \alpha_N H_N^{(2)}(u,t),$$

$$\frac{\partial H_1^{(2)}(u,t)}{\partial t} + jux'(\sigma t)H_1^{(2)}(u,t) = (\lambda(e^{ju}-1) - \mu - \alpha_1)H_1^{(2)}(u,t)$$

$$+(\lambda + x(\sigma t)e^{-ju})H_0^{(2)}(u,t) - j\sigma e^{-ju}\frac{\partial H_0^{(2)}(u,t)}{\partial u},$$

$$\frac{\partial H_2^{(0)}(u,t)}{\partial t} + jux'(\sigma t)H_2^{(2)}(u,t) = (\lambda(e^{ju}-1) - \alpha_2)H_2^{(2)}(u,t)$$

$$+e^{ju}\alpha_1 H_1^{(2)}(u,t) + \alpha_1 H_0^{(2)}(u,t),$$

$$\frac{\partial H_n^{(2)}(u,t)}{\partial t} + jux'(\sigma t)H_n^{(2)}(u,t) = (\lambda(e^{ju}-1) - \alpha_n)H_n^{(2)}(u,t)$$

$$+\alpha_{n-1}H_{n-1}^{(2)}(u,t), n = 3,\ldots,N.$$

$$\frac{\partial H^{(2)}(u,t)}{\partial t} + jux'(\sigma t)H^{(2)}(u,t) = (e^{ju}-1)\left(-x(\sigma t)e^{-ju}H_0^{(2)}(u,t)\right.$$

$$\left.+j\sigma e^{-ju}\frac{\partial H_0^{(2)}(u,t)}{\partial u} + \alpha_1 H_1^{(2)}(u,t) + \lambda\sum_{n=1}^{N}H_n^{(2)}(u,t)\right). \tag{11}$$

The characteristic function of $i(t) - \frac{1}{\sigma}x(\sigma t)$ is given by $H^{(2)}(u,t)$. We make the following substitutions.

Denoting $\sigma = \varepsilon^2$ in (11) and substituting

$$\tau = \varepsilon^2 t, u = \varepsilon w, H_k^{(2)}(u,t) = F_k^{(2)}(w,\tau,\varepsilon), \ k = 0,\ldots,N,$$

we obtain

$$\varepsilon^2\frac{\partial F_0^{(2)}(w,\tau,\varepsilon)}{\partial\tau} + j\varepsilon wa(x)F_0^{(2)}(w,\tau,\varepsilon) = -(\lambda + \alpha_1 + x)F_0^{(2)}(w,\tau,\varepsilon)$$

$$+j\varepsilon\frac{\partial F_0^{(2)}(w,\tau,\varepsilon)}{\partial w} + \mu F_1^{(2)}(w,\tau,\varepsilon) + \alpha_N F_N^{(2)}(w,\tau,\varepsilon),$$

$$\varepsilon^2 \frac{\partial F_1^{(2)}(w,\tau,\varepsilon)}{\partial \tau} + j\varepsilon w a(x) F_1^{(2)}(w,\tau,\varepsilon) = (\lambda(e^{j\varepsilon w} - 1) - \mu - \alpha_1) F_1^{(2)}(w,\tau,\varepsilon)$$

$$+(\lambda + xe^{-j\varepsilon w}) F_0^{(2)}(w,\tau,\varepsilon) - j\varepsilon e^{-j\varepsilon w} \frac{\partial F_0^{(2)}(w,\tau,\varepsilon)}{\partial w},$$

$$\varepsilon^2 \frac{\partial F_2^{(2)}(w,\tau,\varepsilon)}{\partial \tau} + j\varepsilon w a(x) F_2^{(2)}(w,\tau,\varepsilon) = (\lambda(e^{j\varepsilon w} - 1) - \alpha_2) F_2^{(2)}(w,\tau,\varepsilon)$$

$$+ e^{j\varepsilon w} \alpha_1 F_1^{(2)}(w,\tau,\varepsilon) + \alpha_1 F_0^{(2)}(w,\tau,\varepsilon),$$

$$\varepsilon^2 \frac{\partial F_n^{(2)}(w,\tau,\varepsilon)}{\partial \tau} + j\varepsilon w a(x) F_n^{(2)}(w,\tau,\varepsilon) = (\lambda(e^{j\varepsilon w} - 1) - \alpha_n) F_n^{(2)}(w,\tau,\varepsilon)$$

$$+ \alpha_{n-1} F_{n-1}^{(2)}(w,\tau,\varepsilon), \ n = 3, \dots, N,$$

$$\varepsilon^2 \frac{\partial F^{(2)}(w,\tau,\varepsilon)}{\partial \tau} + j\varepsilon w a(x) F^{(2)}(w,\tau,\varepsilon) = (e^{j\varepsilon w} - 1) \left(-xe^{-j\varepsilon w} F_0^{(2)}(w,\tau,\varepsilon) \right.$$

$$\left. + j\varepsilon e^{-j\varepsilon w} \frac{\partial F_0^{(2)}(w,\tau,\varepsilon)}{\partial w} + \alpha_1 F_1^{(2)}(w,\tau,\varepsilon) + \lambda \sum_{n=1}^{N} F_n^{(2)}(w,\tau,\varepsilon) \right). \tag{12}$$

Solving this system, we obtain Theorem 2.

Theorem 2.

$$F_k^{(2)}(w,\tau) = \lim_{\varepsilon \to 0} F_k^{(2)}(w,\tau,\varepsilon), \ k = 0, \dots, N$$

are given by

$$F_k^{(2)}(w,\tau) = \Phi(w,\tau) r_k(x), \ k = 0, \dots, N$$

where $r_k(x)$ is given before and $\Phi(w,\tau)$ satisfies

$$\frac{\partial \Phi(w,\tau)}{\partial \tau} = a'(x) w \frac{\partial \Phi(w,\tau)}{\partial w} + \frac{(jw)^2}{2} b(x) \Phi(w,\tau). \tag{13}$$

$a(x)$ is obtained in (10) and

$$b(x) = a(x) + 2 \left(-xg_0(x) + \alpha_1 g_1(x) + \lambda \sum_{k=1}^{N} g_k(x) + xr_0(x) \right), \tag{14}$$

where the functions $g_k(x), \ k = 0, \dots, N$ are defined by an heterogeneous system:

$$-(\lambda + \alpha_1 + x) g_0 + \mu g_1 + \alpha_N g_N = a(x) r_0,$$

$$-(\mu + \alpha_1) g_1 + (\lambda + x) g_0 = a(x) r_1 - \lambda r_1 + xr_0,$$

$$-\alpha_2 g_2 + \alpha_1 g_1 + \alpha_1 g_0 = a(x) r_2 - \lambda r_2 - \alpha_1 r_1,$$

$$-\alpha_n g_n + \alpha_{n-1} g_{n-1} = a(x) r_n - \lambda r_n, \ n = 3, \dots, N,$$

$$\sum_{k=0}^{N} g_k = 0. \tag{15}$$

Proof. Let us use the following decomposition in (12)

$$F_k^{(2)}(w, \tau, \varepsilon) = \Phi(w, \tau)(r_k + j\varepsilon w f_k) + O(\varepsilon^2), \quad k = 0, \ldots, N. \qquad (16)$$

Substituting (16) into the first four equations of system (12), we obtain the following system in the limit by $\varepsilon \to 0$:

$$-(\lambda + \alpha_1 + x)f_0 + \mu f_1 + \alpha_N f_N = a(x)r_0 - \frac{\partial \Phi(w, \tau)/\partial w}{w\Phi(w, \tau)} r_0,$$

$$-(\mu + \alpha_1)f_1 + (\lambda + x)f_0 = a(x)r_1 - \lambda r_1 + x r_0 + \frac{\partial \Phi(w, \tau)/\partial w}{w\Phi(w, \tau)} r_0,$$

$$-\alpha_2 f_2 + \alpha_1 f_1 + \alpha_1 f_0 = a(x)r_2 - \lambda r_2 - \alpha_1 r_1,$$

$$-\alpha_n f_n + \alpha_{n-1} f_{n-1} = a(x)r_n - \lambda r_n, \quad n = 3, \ldots, N. \qquad (17)$$

We propose finding the solution as

$$f_k = Cr_k + g_k - \phi_k \frac{\partial \Phi(w, \tau)/\partial w}{w\Phi(w, \tau)}, \qquad (18)$$

and substitute in (17) to obtain two systems

$$-(\lambda + \alpha_1 + x)\phi_0 + \mu \phi_1 + \alpha_N \phi_N = r_0,$$

$$-(\mu + \alpha_1)\phi_1 + (\lambda + x)\phi_0 = -r_0,$$

$$-\alpha_2 \phi_2 + \alpha_1 \phi_1 + \alpha_1 \phi_0 = 0,$$

$$-\alpha_n \phi_n + \alpha_{n-1}\phi_{n-1} = a(x)\phi_n - \lambda \phi_n, \quad n = 3, \ldots, N. \qquad (19)$$

$$-(\lambda + \alpha_1 + x)g_0 + \mu g_1 + \alpha_N g_N = a(x)r_0,$$

$$-(\mu + \alpha_1)g_1 + (\lambda + x)g_0 = a(x)r_1 - \lambda r_1 + x r_0,$$

$$-\alpha_2 g_2 + \alpha_1 g_1 + \alpha_1 g_0 = a(x)r_2 - \lambda r_2 - \alpha_1 r_1,$$

$$-\alpha_n g_n + \alpha_{n-1}g_{n-1} = a(x)r_n - \lambda r_n, \quad n = 3, \ldots, N. \qquad (20)$$

We take into account the last equation of (12) with the substitution (16) up to $O(\varepsilon^3)$. Taking the limit by $\varepsilon \to 0$, we obtain

$$\frac{\partial \Phi(w, \tau)}{\partial \tau} = (jw)^2 \left(-a(x)\sum_{k=0}^{N} f_k + x r_0 - x f_0 + \alpha_1 f_1 + \lambda \sum_{n=1}^{N} f_n\right)\Phi(w, \tau)$$

$$+ j^2 w \frac{\partial \Phi(w, \tau)}{\partial w} r_0 + \frac{(jw)^2}{2}\left(-x r_0 + \alpha_1 r_1 + \lambda \sum_{n=1}^{N} r_n\right)\Phi(w, \tau). \qquad (21)$$

We will make a substitution (18) into (21) to obtain

$$\frac{\partial \Phi(w, \tau)}{\partial \tau} = (jw)^2 \left(x r_0 - x g_0 + \alpha_1 g_1 + \lambda \sum_{n=1}^{N} g_n\right)\Phi(w, \tau)$$

$$-(jw)^2(-x\phi_0 + \alpha_1\phi_1 + \lambda \sum_{n=1}^{N} \phi_n - r_0)\frac{\partial \Phi(w,\tau)/\partial w}{w}$$

$$+ \frac{(jw)^2}{2}(-xr_0 + \alpha_1 r_1 + \lambda \sum_{n=1}^{N} r_n)\Phi(w,\tau). \qquad (22)$$

We note that

$$-x\phi_0 + \alpha_1\phi_1 + \lambda \sum_{n=1}^{N} \phi_n - r_0 = a'(x).$$

We denote

$$b(x) = a(x) + 2\left(-xg_0(x) + \alpha_1 g_1(x) + \lambda \sum_{k=1}^{N} g_k(x) + xr_0(x) \right). \qquad (23)$$

We have

$$\frac{\partial \Phi(w,\tau)}{\partial \tau} = a'(x)w\frac{\partial \Phi(w,\tau)}{\partial w} + \frac{(jw)^2}{2}b(x)\Phi(w,\tau).$$

Theorem is proved.

Lemma 1. *The stationary probability density of the normalized and centered number of calls in the orbit is given by*

$$s(z) = \frac{C}{b(z)}exp\left\{ \frac{2}{\sigma} \int_0^z \frac{a(x)}{b(x)} \, dx \right\}, \qquad (24)$$

where C is subject to the normalization condition.

The proof of the Lemma 1 is described in paper [17].
We define a non-negative function $G(i)$ of discrete argument i in the form

$$G(i) = \frac{C}{b(\sigma i)}exp\left\{ \frac{2}{\sigma} \int_0^{\sigma i} \frac{a(x)}{b(x)} \, dx \right\}. \qquad (25)$$

After that, we construct an approximation $P_{dif}(i)$ of the probability distribution $P(i) = P\{i(t) = i\}$ of i calls in orbit for RQ-systems using the formula (24):

$$P_{dif}(i) = \frac{G(i)}{\sum\limits_{i=0}^{\infty} G(i)}. \qquad (26)$$

6 Algorithm of Calculation Probability Distribution $P_{dif}(i)$

1. Let us define the parameters of the system λ, σ, μ, and α_n, $n = 1, ..., N$.

2. We calculate $r_0(x)$ and determine probabilities $r_n(x)$, $n = 1, ..., N$ as functions of x using (9).
3. We substitute $r_n(x)$ into (10) and obtain drift coefficient $a(x)$.
4. We determine additional functions $g_n(x)$, $n = 0, ..., N$ as the solution of system (15) for each x.
5. Substituting $r_n(x)$ and $g_n(x)$ into (23), we obtain diffusion coefficient $b(x)$.
6. Having $a(x)$ and $b(x)$, we can calculate values $G(i)$.
7. Finally, we apply formula (26) to determine stationary probability distribution $P_{dif}(i)$ of the number of customers in the orbit.

7   Domain of Applicability of the Asymptotic-Diffusion Analysis

This section is devoted to determining the area of applicability of the obtained asymptotic-diffusion results. Comparing the asymptotic results with the pre-limit distribution obtained earlier in [10], we can determine the parameters, for which approximate probability distribution is close to the pre-limit one. Let us define the parameters of the system $\lambda = 1$, $\mu = 3$, $N = 5$, $\alpha_n = 0.2 \times n$, $n = 1, ..., N$.

Table 1 shows the values of Kolmogorov distance for various σ.

Table 1. Kolmogorov distance Δ.

	$\sigma = 0.5$	$\sigma = 0.1$	$\sigma = 0.05$	$\sigma = 0.01$	$\sigma = 0,005$
Δ	0.078	0.073	0.056	**0.049**	**0.037**

Analyzing the data of Table 1, we can say that the approximation accuracy increases with a decrease in σ. The given approximations are applicable for the Kolmogorov distance not exceeding 0.05. Values of accuracy, which we consider as satisfactory, are marked bold in Table 1. From the obtained values, we can conclude that the approximation of the asymptotic-diffusion analysis is applicable when $\sigma \leq 0.01$.

8   Conclusion

This paper presents a study of a cyclic retrial queue for a special data transmission network FANET. The analysis of the presented model is carried out by the method of asymptotic-diffusion analysis. Based on the results obtained, an approximation of the probability distribution of the number of calls in orbit was constructed. In the chapter on numerical analysis, the accuracy of the constructed approximation of the asymptotic-diffusion analysis is shown.

References

1. Khan, M.F., Yau, K.-L.A., Noor, R.M., Imran, M.A.: Routing schemes in FANETs: a survey. Sensors **20**, 38 (2020)
2. Artalejo, J.R.: Accessible bibliography on retrial queues: progress in 2000–2009. Math. Comput. Model. **51**(9–10), 1071–1081 (2010)
3. Artalejo, J.R.: A classified bibliography of research on retrial queues: progress in 1990–1999. TOP **7**(2), 187–211 (1999)
4. Artalejo, J.R., Gómez-Corral, A.: Retrial queueing systems: a computational approach. Springer, Heidelberg (2008). https://doi.org/10.1007/978-3-540-78725-9
5. Artalejo, J.R., Falin, G.I.: Standard and retrial queueing systems: a comparative analysis. Revista Matematica Complutense **15**, 101–129 (2002)
6. Vishnevskii, V., Semenova, O.: Sistemy pollinga: teoriya i primenenie v shirokopolosnykh besprovodnykh setyakh [Polling systems: theory and applications in broadband wireless networks], 312 p. Tekhnosfera Publ., Moscow (2007)
7. Vishnevskii, V., Semenova, O.: Mathematical research methods polling systems. Autom. Telemechanics **2**, 3–56 (2006)
8. Nazarov, A., Paul, S.: A cyclic queueing system with priority customers and T-strategy of service. Commun. Comput. Inf. Sci. **678**, 182–193 (2016)
9. Nazarov, A., Paul, S.: A number of customers in the system with server vacations. Commun. Comput. Inf. Sci. **601**, 334–343 (2015)
10. Nazarov, A.A., Paul, S.V., Klyuchnikova, P.N.: Research of a cyclic system with repeated calls. In: Distributed Computer and Telecommunication Networks: Control, Calculation, Communication (DCCN-2020), 14–18 September 2020, Moscow, Russia (2020)
11. Langaris, C.: A polling model with retrial customers. J. Oper. Res. Soc. Japan **40**(4), 489–508 (1997)
12. Langaris, C.: Gated polling models with customers in orbit. Math. Comput. Model. **30**(3–4), 171–187 (1999)
13. Langaris, C.: Markovian polling system with mixed service disciplines and retrial customers. TOP **7**, 305–322 (1999)
14. Boxma, O., Resing, J.: Vacation and polling models with retrials. In: Horváth, A., Wolter, K. (eds.) EPEW 2014. LNCS, vol. 8721, pp. 45–58. Springer, Cham (2014). https://doi.org/10.1007/978-3-319-10885-8_4
15. Abidini, M.A., Boxma, O., Resing, J.: Analysis and optimization of vacation and polling models with retrials. Perform. Eval. **98**, 52–69 (2016)
16. Moiseev, A., Nazarov, A., Paul, S.: Asymptotic diffusion analysis of multi-server retrial queue with hyper-exponential service. Mathematics **8**(4), 531 (2020)
17. Nazarov, A., Phung-Duc, T., Paul, S., Lizyura, O.: Diffusion limit for single-server retrial queues with renewal input and outgoing calls. Mathematics **10**(6), 948 (2022)

The Asymmetric Join the Shortest Orbit Queue: Analysis via a Dimensionality Reduction

Ioannis Dimitriou[(✉)] [iD]

University of Ioannina, 45110 Ioannina, Greece
`idimit@uoi.gr`

Abstract. In this work, we investigate the stationary behaviour of the asymmetric join the shortest queue system with a single server and two infinite capacity orbit queues. Arriving jobs that find the server busy, are forwarded to the least loaded orbit queue, and in case of a tie, they choose an orbit randomly. Orbiting jobs retry to connect with the server at different retrial rates, i.e., heterogeneous orbit queues. Our system is described by a Markov modulated two-dimensional random walk. By exploiting its special structure, its invariant measure is obtained in terms of the invariant measure of a non-modulated two-dimensional random walk by applying the compensation method.

Keywords: Asymmetric Join the Shortest Orbit Queue · Retrials · Compensation Method

1 Introduction

Our primary aim in this work is twofold. First, to investigate the stationary analysis of a certain class of non-homogeneous Markov-modulated random walks in the quarter plane, where modulation allows for a tractable analysis via a dimensionality reduction. In particular, by exploiting its special structure, the problem of deriving its invariant measure is reduced to the problem of solving for the invariant measure of a related non-homogeneous, **non**-modulated two dimensional random walk, which has a *complicated* boundary behaviour. The invariant measure of this standard non-homogeneous, **non**-modulated two dimensional random walk is derived by using the compensation method (CM) [3,5]. To accomplish this task, we consider a retrial system with two infinite capacity orbits and different retrieval rates, operating under the *join the shortest queue* strategy. This is the simplest queueing example, which can be described by such a Markov-modulated two-dimensional random walk. The approach we follow can be adapted to more complicated systems including finite priority lines in front of the server (i.e., priorities), the possibility of joining the priority line directly from the orbits, the case of Erlang arrivals etc.

Second, by application point of view, the simple retrial queueing network that we use has potential applications in the performance modelling of cooperative

E. Hyytiä and V. Kavitha (Eds.): VALUETOOLS 2022, LNICST 482, pp. 180–194, 2023.
https://doi.org/10.1007/978-3-031-31234-2_11

relay assisted wireless networks [15]. Such networks operate as follows: A finite number of source users transmit packets (i.e., the arrival stream) to a common destination node (i.e., the service station). We assume that the destination node can handle at most one job (e.g., due to limited memory capacity). Blocked jobs (i.e., jobs that find the service station occupied) are routed according to a cooperative policy to a finite number of relay nodes (i.e., the orbit queues) that assist the source users by retransmitting their blocked packets to the destination node. The cooperative policy among source users and relays refers to a strategy that dictates in which relay station a blocked job will be forwarded. In this work, we consider the join the shortest queue (JSQ) policy.

Cooperative relaying gives rise to pure wireless self-organizing networks without any need for base stations, and it can be employed in various applications of networked embedded systems, e.g., Cars use it to communicate directly with each other, for instance, to exchange reports on accidents, traffic jams, or bad road conditions. Autonomous robots may use it to build a wireless network in areas without infrastructure, e.g., in deserts and in space. This concept was mostly considered at the physical layer, based on information-theoretic considerations, e.g., [13], and have become a powerful technique to combat fading and attenuation in wireless networks. Recent works [14,16] shown that similar gains are achieved by network-layer cooperation, i.e., when relaying is assumed to take place at the protocol level avoiding physical layer considerations.

Thus, we consider a Markovian network with three nodes: the main service node where blocking is possible, and two delay nodes for repeated attempts. External arrivals are routed initially to the main service node. If the main service node is empty, the arriving job starts service immediately, and leaves the network after the service completion. Otherwise, the arriving blocked job is routed to the least loaded delay node. Each delay station is responsible to retransmit its blocked jobs to the main service station.

The standard (i.e., non-modulated) two dimensional JSQ problem was initially studied in [11,12], and further investigated by using generating functions in [7,10]. However, their analyses do not lead to an explicit characterization of the equilibrium probabilities. The CM introduced in [3–5] is an elegant and direct method to obtain explicitly the stationary distribution as infinite series of product form terms; see also [6,17]. In [1], the CM was used to analyze the JSQ policy in a two-queue system fed by Erlang arrivals. The queueing system in [1] is described by a multilayer random walk in the quarter plane; see also [18]. To our best knowledge, the works in [8,9] are the only that deal with the stationary analysis of retrial queues under the JSQ rule. In [8], the CM was applied for the symmetric (i.e., identical retrial rates), two orbit queue system with Poisson arrivals, by following the multilayer framework in [1]. Contrary to the work in [8], in this work, we are dealing with the asymmetric case (i.e., different retrial rates), which leads to a random walk in the half-plane. Moreover, our methodology is different since in this work the invariant measure is obtained in terms of the invariant measure of a standard non-modulated random walk, which is constructed by the original one through the dimensionality reduction.

In [9], exact tail asymptotics, and stationary approximations were investigated for the asymmetric two-orbit case, with additional dedicated Poisson streams that upon blocking, they forward their blocked jobs to specific orbits.

2   The System Model and the Equilibrium Equations

Consider a single server retrial system with two infinite capacity orbit queues. Jobs arrive at the system according to a Poisson process with rate $\lambda > 0$. If an arriving job finds the server idle, it starts service immediately. Otherwise, it is routed to the least loaded orbit queue. In case both orbit queues have the same occupancy, the blocked job is routed either to orbit 1 with probability q, or to orbit 2 with probability $1 - q$. Orbiting jobs of either type retry independently to occupy the server according to a constant retrial policy. More precisely, the first job in orbit queue 1 (resp. 2) retry after an exponentially distributed time period with rate α_1 (resp. α_2). Without loss of generality, let $\alpha_1 < \alpha_2$. Service times are independent and exponentially distributed with rate μ.

Let $Q_l(t)$ be the number of jobs stored in orbit l, $l = 1, 2$, at time t, and by $C(t)$ the state of the server, i.e., $C(t) = 1$, when it is busy and $C(t) = 0$ when it is idle at time t, respectively. $Y(t) = \{(Q_1(t), Q_2(t), C(t)); t \geq 0\}$ is an irreducible Markov process on $\{0, 1, \ldots\} \times \{0, 1, \ldots\} \times \{0, 1\}$. Denote by $Y = \{(Q_1, Q_2, C)\}$ its stationary version, and define the set of stationary probabilities $p_{i,j}(k) = \mathbb{P}(Q_1 = i, Q_2 = j, C = k)$. The equilibrium equations are as follows. Define the set of stationary probabilities

$$p_{i,j}(k) = \mathbb{P}(Q_1 = i, Q_2 = j, C = k).$$

Let J be a random variable indicating the orbit queue which an arriving blocked job joins. Clearly, J is dependent on the vector (Q_1, Q_2, C). Then, the equilibrium equations are

$$
\begin{aligned}
&p_{i,j}(0)(\lambda + \alpha_1 1_{\{i>0\}} + \alpha_2 1_{\{j>0\}})) = \mu p_{i,j}(1), \\
&p_{i,j}(1)(\lambda + \mu) = \lambda p_{i,j}(0) + \alpha_1 p_{i+1,j}(0) + \alpha_2 p_{i,j+1}(0) \\
&+\lambda[p_{i-1,j}(1)\mathbb{P}(J = 1|Q = (i-1,j,1))1_{\{i>0\}} \\
&+p_{i,j-1}(1)\mathbb{P}(J = 2|Q = (i,j-1,1))1_{\{j>0\}}],
\end{aligned}
\tag{1}
$$

where, $1_{\{E\}}$ the indicator function of the event E and

$$
\begin{aligned}
\mathbb{P}(J = l|Q = (Q_1, Q_2, 1)) &= \frac{\psi_l}{\sum_{k=1}^{2} \psi_k 1_{\{Q_k = Q_l\}}}, \\
\mathbb{P}(J = l|Q = (Q_1, Q_2, 0)) &= 0, \ l = 1, 2,
\end{aligned}
$$

where $\psi_l = \begin{cases} p, l = 1, \\ q, l = 2 \end{cases}$.

To apply the compensation method, we have to consider the following transformation: Let $X_1(t) = min\{Q_1(t), Q_2(t)\}$, $X_2(t) = Q_2(t) - Q_1(t)$. The system is described by a 3-dimensional continuous time Markov chain with state space $\{(m, n, k); m \geq 0, n \in \mathbb{Z}, k = 0, 1\}$. Let $q_{m,n}(k)$ be the equilibrium probability of being in state (m, n, k), and denote $\mathbf{q}_{m,n} = (q_{m,n}(0), q_{m,n}(1))^T$, with $\mathbf{x}^T$ the transpose of a vector $\mathbf{x}$. Its matrix transition diagram is given in Fig. 1. The equilibrium equations are as follows:

$$
\begin{aligned}
(\mathbf{A}_{0,0} + (\alpha_1 + \alpha_2)\mathbf{M})\mathbf{q}_{m,n} + \mathbf{A}_{0,-1}\mathbf{q}_{m,n+1} + \mathbf{A}_{1,-1}\mathbf{q}_{m-1,n+1} \\
+ \mathbf{A}_{-1,1}\mathbf{q}_{m+1,n-1} = 0, \; m \geq 1, n \geq 2, \\
(\mathbf{A}_{0,0} + (\alpha_1 + \alpha_2)\mathbf{M})\mathbf{q}_{m,n} + \mathbf{B}_{0,1}\mathbf{q}_{m,n-1} + \mathbf{B}_{1,1}\mathbf{q}_{m-1,n-1} \\
+ \mathbf{B}_{-1,-1}\mathbf{q}_{m+1,n+1} = 0, \; m \geq 1, n \leq -2, \\
(\mathbf{A}_{0,0} + (\alpha_1 + \alpha_2)\mathbf{M})\mathbf{q}_{m,0} + \mathbf{A}_{0,-1}\mathbf{q}_{m,1} + \mathbf{A}_{1,-1}\mathbf{q}_{m-1,1} \\
+ \mathbf{B}_{0,1}\mathbf{q}_{m,-1} + \mathbf{B}_{1,1}\mathbf{q}_{m-1,-1} = 0, \; m \geq 1, \\
(\mathbf{A}_{0,0} + (\alpha_1 + \alpha_2)\mathbf{M})\mathbf{q}_{m,1} + \mathbf{A}_{0,-1}\mathbf{q}_{m,2} + \mathbf{A}_{-1,1}\mathbf{q}_{m+1,0} \\
+ \mathbf{A}_{1,-1}\mathbf{q}_{m-1,2} + \mathbf{A}_{0,1}\mathbf{q}_{m,0} = 0, \; m \geq 1, \qquad (2) \\
(\mathbf{A}_{0,0} + (\alpha_1 + \alpha_2)\mathbf{M})\mathbf{q}_{m,-1} + \mathbf{B}_{0,1}\mathbf{q}_{m,-2} + \mathbf{B}_{-1,-1}\mathbf{q}_{m+1,0} \\
+ \mathbf{B}_{1,1}\mathbf{q}_{m-1,-2} + \mathbf{B}_{0,-1}\mathbf{q}_{m,0} = 0, \; m \geq 1, \\
(\mathbf{A}_{0,0} + \alpha_2\mathbf{M})\mathbf{q}_{0,n} + \mathbf{A}_{0,-1}\mathbf{q}_{0,n+1} + \mathbf{A}_{-1,1}\mathbf{q}_{1,n-1} = 0, \; n \geq 2, \\
(\mathbf{A}_{0,0} + \alpha_1\mathbf{M})\mathbf{q}_{0,n} + \mathbf{B}_{0,1}\mathbf{q}_{0,n-1} + \mathbf{B}_{-1,-1}\mathbf{q}_{1,n+1} = 0, \; n \leq -2, \\
\mathbf{A}_{0,0}\mathbf{q}_{0,0} + \mathbf{A}_{0,-1}\mathbf{q}_{0,1} + \mathbf{B}_{0,1}\mathbf{q}_{0,-1} = 0, \\
(\mathbf{A}_{0,0} + \alpha_2\mathbf{M})\mathbf{q}_{0,1} + \mathbf{A}_{0,-1}\mathbf{q}_{0,2} + \mathbf{A}_{-1,1}\mathbf{q}_{1,0} + \mathbf{A}_{0,1}\mathbf{q}_{0,0} = 0, \\
(\mathbf{A}_{0,0} + \alpha_1\mathbf{M})\mathbf{q}_{0,-1} + \mathbf{B}_{0,1}\mathbf{q}_{0,-2} + \mathbf{B}_{-1,-1}\mathbf{q}_{1,0} + \mathbf{B}_{0,-1}\mathbf{q}_{0,0} = 0.
\end{aligned}
$$

where

$$
\mathbf{A}_{1,-1} = \begin{pmatrix} 0 & 0 \\ 0 & \lambda \end{pmatrix}, \; \mathbf{A}_{0,-1} = \mathbf{B}_{-1,-1} = \begin{pmatrix} 0 & 0 \\ \alpha_2 & 0 \end{pmatrix}, \; \mathbf{A}_{0,0} = \begin{pmatrix} -\lambda & \mu \\ \lambda & -(\lambda + \mu) \end{pmatrix},
$$
$$
\mathbf{M} = \begin{pmatrix} 1 & 0 \\ 0 & 0 \end{pmatrix}, \; \mathbf{A}_{-1,1} = \mathbf{B}_{0,1} = \begin{pmatrix} 0 & 0 \\ \alpha_1 & 0 \end{pmatrix}, \; \mathbf{A}_{0,1} = (1-q)\mathbf{A}_{1,-1}, \; \mathbf{B}_{0,-1} = q\mathbf{A}_{1,-1}
$$

2.1 Preliminary Results

In the following we provide necessary conditions for the system to be stable.

Proposition 1. Let $p_{.,0}(0) = \sum_{i=0}^{\infty} p_{i,0}(0)$, $p_{0,.}(0) = \sum_{j=0}^{\infty} p_{0,j}(0)$. Then,

$$
P(C = 1) = \frac{\lambda}{\mu} \text{ and } \frac{\alpha_1 p_{0,.}(0) + \alpha_2 p_{.,0}(0)}{\alpha_1 + \alpha_2} = 1 - \frac{\lambda(\lambda + \alpha_1 + \alpha_2)}{\mu(\alpha_1 + \alpha_2)} \qquad (3)
$$

Proof. For each $i = 0, 1, 2, \ldots$ we consider the cut between the states $\{Q_1 = i, C = 1\}$ and $\{Q_1 = i+1, C = 0\}$. This yields

$$
\lambda \mathbb{P}(J = 1, Q_1 = i, C = 1) = \alpha_1 p_{i+1,.}(0).
$$

Summing for all $i = 0, 1, \ldots$ results in

$$
\lambda \mathbb{P}(J = 1, C = 1) = \alpha[\mathbb{P}(C = 0) - p_{0,.}(0)], \qquad (4)
$$

and similarly,

$$
\lambda \mathbb{P}(J = 2, C = 1) = \alpha[\mathbb{P}(C = 0) - p_{.,0}(0)]. \qquad (5)
$$

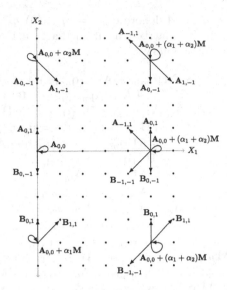

Fig. 1. Transition rate diagram of the transformed process.

Summing (4), (5) yields

$$\lambda \mathbb{P}(C = 1) = (\alpha_1 + \alpha_2)\mathbb{P}(C = 0) - [\alpha_1 p_{0,.}(0) + \alpha_2 p_{0,.}(0)]. \tag{6}$$

Summing the first in (1) for all $i, j \geq 0$ yields

$$(\lambda + \alpha_1 + \alpha_2)\mathbb{P}(C = 0) - \mu\mathbb{P}(C = 1) = \alpha_1 p_{0,.}(0) + \alpha_2 p_{0,.}(0). \tag{7}$$

Using (7), (6) and having in mind that $\mathbb{P}(C = 1) + \mathbb{P}(C = 0) = 1$ we derive $\mathbb{P}(C = 1) = \lambda/\mu$. Substituting back in (6) we finally derive

$$\frac{\alpha_1 p_{0,.}(0) + \alpha_2 p_{.,0}(0)}{\alpha_1 + \alpha_2} = 1 - \frac{\lambda(\lambda + \alpha_1 + \alpha_2)}{\mu(\alpha_1 + \alpha_2)} \geq 0.$$

It can be easily seen that if $\rho := \frac{\lambda(\lambda + \alpha_1 + \alpha_2)}{\mu(\alpha_1 + \alpha_2)} = 1$, then the system is not stable, i.e., $p_{i,j}(0) = p_{i,j}(1) = 0$, $i, j = 0, 1, \ldots$, and further details are omitted.

Assume hereon that $\rho < 1$. In the following sections we will also show that this condition is also sufficient for the system to stable. We now turn our attention to show that the equilibrium probabilities of the transformed process can be written as an infinite series of product forms.

2.2 Dimensionality Reduction

The equilibrium Eq. (2) have a similar structure as Eqs. (1–10) in [3], although in matrix form due to the modulation. Our aim is to exploit the structure of the balance equations, and proceed with a dimensionality reduction, which allows for applying the CM to a transformed two-dimensional random walk constructed by the original one. Such an operation reduces to the half the number of the equilibrium equations that we have to solve through the CM. More precisely:

1. Express the equilibrium probabilities for the idle states in terms of the equilibrium probabilities for the busy states.
2. Substitute the expressions derived in step 1, to the equilibrium equations that refer to the busy states. The resulting equilibrium equations are of the same form as those in [3]. In particular, they describe a standard (i.e., non-retrial) JSQ model of two queues with *appropriate* arrival and service rates.
3. Apply the CM to obtain the invariant measure of the transformed two-dimensional random walk.
4. Use the expressions derived in step 1 and 3 to obtain the equilibrium probabilities of the original random walk.

Simple computations on the balance equations leads to the following relation that relate the idle and the busy states for $n \in \mathbb{Z}$,

$$q_{m,n}(0) = \begin{cases} \frac{\mu}{\lambda + \alpha_1 + \alpha_2} q_{m,n}(1), & m > 0, \\ \frac{\mu}{\lambda + \alpha_1 1_{\{n \geq 1\}} + \alpha_2 1_{\{n \leq -1\}}} q_{0,n}(1), & m = 0, \end{cases} \tag{8}$$

Next, we substitute (8) in the rest of equilibrium equations that refer to the busy states. For convenience, set $p_{m,n} := q_{m,n}(1)$, and let $\rho := \frac{\lambda(\lambda + \alpha_1 + \alpha_2)}{\mu(\alpha_1 + \alpha_2)}$, $\rho_i := \frac{\lambda(\lambda + \alpha_i)}{\mu \alpha_i}$, $i = 1, 2$. Then, after the substitution, the equilibrium equations for the busy states are as follows:

$$p_{m,n}(\rho + 1) = \rho p_{m-1,n+1} + \frac{\alpha_1}{\alpha_1 + \alpha_2} p_{m+1,n-1}$$
$$+ \frac{\alpha_2}{\alpha_1 + \alpha_2} p_{m,n+1}, \ m > 0, n > 1, \tag{9}$$

$$p_{m,1}(\rho + 1) = \rho q p_{m,0} + \rho p_{m-1,2} + \frac{\alpha_1}{\alpha_1 + \alpha_2} p_{m+1,0}$$
$$+ \frac{\alpha_2}{\alpha_1 + \alpha_2} p_{m,2}, \ m > 0, n = 1, \tag{10}$$

$$p_{0,n}(\rho_2 + 1) = p_{0,n+1} + \frac{\alpha_1}{\alpha_1 + \alpha_2} \frac{\rho_2}{\rho} p_{1,n-1}, \ n > 1, \tag{11}$$

$$p_{0,1}(\rho_2 + 1) = \rho_2 q p_{0,0} + p_{0,2} + \frac{\alpha_1}{\alpha_1 + \alpha_2} \frac{\rho_2}{\rho} p_{1,0}, \tag{12}$$

$$p_{m,0}(\rho + 1) = \rho(p_{m-1,1} + p_{m-1,-1}) + \frac{\alpha_1}{\alpha_1 + \alpha_2} p_{m+1,-1}$$

$$+ \frac{\alpha_2}{\alpha_1 + \alpha_2} p_{m,1}, \; m > 0, \tag{13}$$

$$p_{0,0} = \frac{1}{\rho_1} p_{0,-1} + \frac{1}{\rho_2} p_{1,0}, \tag{14}$$

$$p_{m,n}(\rho + 1) = \rho p_{m-1,n+1} + \frac{\alpha_1}{\alpha_1 + \alpha_2} p_{m,n-1}$$

$$+ \frac{\alpha_2}{\alpha_1 + \alpha_2} p_{m+1,n+1}, \; m > 0, n < -1, \tag{15}$$

$$p_{m,-1}(\rho + 1) = \rho(1 - q)p_{m,0} + \rho p_{m-1,-2} + \frac{\alpha_1}{\alpha_1 + \alpha_2} p_{m,-2}$$

$$+ \frac{\alpha_2}{\alpha_1 + \alpha_2} p_{m+1,0}, \; m > 0, n = -1, \tag{16}$$

$$p_{0,n}(\rho_1 + 1) = p_{0,n-1} + \frac{\alpha_2}{\alpha_1 + \alpha_2} \frac{\rho_1}{\rho} p_{1,n+1}, \; n < -1, \tag{17}$$

$$p_{0,-1}(\rho_1 + 1) = \rho_1(1 - q)p_{0,0} + p_{0,-2} + \frac{\alpha_2}{\alpha_1 + \alpha_2} \frac{\rho_1}{\rho} p_{1,0}. \tag{18}$$

Note that Eqs. (9)–(18) has the same form as Eqs. (1–10) in [3], a fact that allows for applying the CM and derive a formal solution (i.e., meaning that for the moment we do not pay attention to its convergence) to the equilibrium Eqs. (9)–(18). Then, using the derived formal solution, and (8), we can obtain the stationary distribution of the original system.

3   The Compensation Method

CM attempts to solve the balance equations by a linear combination of product-form terms. First, it characterizes a sufficiently rich basis of product-form solutions satisfying the balance equations in the interior of the state space. Subsequently this basis is used to construct a linear combination that also satisfies the equations for the boundary states. Note that the basis contains uncountably many elements. The procedure to select the appropriate elements is based on a compensation argument: after introducing the first term, countably many terms may subsequently be added so as to alternatingly compensate for the error on one of the two boundaries.

CM starts with the solution describing the asymptotic behaviour of $p_{m,n}$ as $m \to \infty$. In Theorem 4.1, [9] we shown (for a more general model with additional dedicated arrival streams) that $p_{m,n} := q_{m,n}(1) \sim \gamma_0^m x_n(\gamma_0)$, as $m \to \infty$, for $\gamma_0 := \rho^2$, where ρ equals the decay rate of the corresponding single orbit system with retrial rate equal to $\alpha_1 + \alpha_2$. The form of the asymptotic results in [9] helps us to assume that $p_{m,n} = \gamma^m \delta^n$ satisfies (9), and $p_{m,n} =$

$\gamma^m \delta^{-n}$ (15), respectively, i.e., the equilibrium equations at the interior of the transformed state space. The next lemma characterizes a continuum of product-forms satisfying the inner equations.

Lemma 1. *i) The product $\gamma^m \delta^n$ is a solution of (9) iff*

$$\gamma\delta(\rho + 1) = \rho\delta^2 + \frac{\alpha_1}{\alpha_1+\alpha_2}\gamma^2 + \frac{\alpha_2}{\alpha_1+\alpha_2}\gamma\delta^2. \tag{19}$$

i) The product $\gamma^m \delta^{-n}$ is a solution of (15) iff

$$\gamma\delta(\rho + 1) = \rho\delta^2 + \frac{\alpha_2}{\alpha_1+\alpha_2}\gamma^2 + \frac{\alpha_1}{\alpha_1+\alpha_2}\gamma\delta^2. \tag{20}$$

Proof. The proof is direct by substituting $p_{m,n} = \gamma^m \delta^n$ in (9), and $p_{m,n} = \gamma^m \delta^{-n}$ in (15).

For fixed γ, (19) is solved by $X_\pm(\gamma) = \gamma\dfrac{\rho+1\pm\sqrt{(\rho+1)^2 - \frac{4\alpha_1(\rho+\frac{\alpha_2\gamma}{\alpha_1+\alpha_2})}{\alpha_1+\alpha_2}}}{2(\rho+\frac{\alpha_1\gamma}{\alpha_1+\alpha_2})}$. Let also by $Y_\pm(\gamma)$ the roots of (19) for fixed δ. Similarly $x_\pm(\gamma)$, $y_\pm(\delta)$ are the roots of (20) for fixed γ and δ, respectively.

Lemma 1 characterizes basic solutions satisfying (9), (15). The next lemma specifies the initial solution satisfying (9), (10), (13), (15), (16).

Lemma 2. *(Initial solution) For $\gamma_0 = \rho^2$, let $\delta_1 := X_-(\rho^2) = \frac{\alpha_1\rho^2}{\alpha_1+\alpha_2(1+\rho)}$, $\delta_2 := x_-(\rho^2) = \frac{\alpha_2\rho^2}{\alpha_2+\alpha_1(1+\rho)}$, such that $|\delta_1|, |\delta_2| \in (0, \rho^2)$. Then, the solution*

$$z_{m,n} = \begin{cases} d_1\gamma_0^m\delta_1^n, & m \geq 0, n \geq 1, \\ \gamma_0^m, & m \geq 0, n = 0, \\ d_2\gamma_0^m\delta_2^{-n}, & m \geq 0, n \leq -1, \end{cases} \tag{21}$$

satisfies (9), (10), (13), (15), (16), iff $d_1 = \frac{(\alpha_1+\alpha_2)\rho q + \alpha_1\gamma}{\alpha_1\gamma_0}$, $d_2 = \frac{(\alpha_1+\alpha_2)\rho(1-q)+\alpha_2\gamma_0}{\alpha_2\gamma}$.

The initial solution (21) does not satisfy the positive and negative vertical boundary equations (11), (17). To compensate for the error produced by $d_1\gamma_0^m\delta_1^n$, we seek for c_1, γ, δ such that $d_1\gamma_0^m\delta_1^n + d_1c_1\gamma^m\delta_1^n$ satisfies (11). We need to take $\delta = \delta_1$, $\gamma = \gamma_1 := Y_-(\delta_1)$. Insert $d_1\gamma_0^m\delta_1^n + d_1c_1\gamma_1^m\delta_1^n$ in (11), we obtain

$$c_1 = -\frac{(1+\rho_2)\delta_1 - \delta_1^2 - \frac{\alpha_1}{\alpha_1+\alpha_2}\frac{\rho_2}{\rho}\gamma_0}{(1+\rho_2)\delta_1 - \delta_1^2 - \frac{\alpha_1}{\alpha_1+\alpha_2}\frac{\rho_2}{\rho}\gamma_1}. \tag{22}$$

Similarly, we can compensate for the error produced in the negative vertical boundary by $d_2\gamma_0^m\delta_2^{-n}$, i.e., by adding a term $d_2c_2\gamma_2^m\delta_2^n$ with $\gamma_2 := y_-(\delta_2)$, and a similar expression as in (22) is derived. In general, the vertical compensation step is summarized in the following lemma.

Lemma 3. *(Vertical compensation (VC)) i) Let $z_{m,n} = Y_+^m(\delta)\delta^n + cY_-^m(\delta)\delta^n$, $m \geq 0$, $n > 0$. Then, $z_{m,n}$ satisfies (9) and (11) if c satisfies*

$$c = -\frac{(1+\rho_2)\delta - \delta^2 - \frac{\alpha_1}{\alpha_1+\alpha_2}\frac{\rho_2}{\rho}Y_-(\delta)}{(1+\rho_2)\delta - \delta^2 - \frac{\alpha_1}{\alpha_1+\alpha_2}\frac{\rho_2}{\rho}Y_+(\delta)}.$$

ii) Let $z_{m,n} = y_+^m(\delta)\delta^{-n} + cy_-^m(\delta)\delta^{-n}$, $m \geq 0$, $n < 0$. *Then,* $z_{m,n}$ *satisfies* (15) *and* (17) *if* c *satisfies*

$$c = -\frac{(1+\rho_1)\delta - \delta^2 - \frac{\alpha_2}{\alpha_1+\alpha_2}\frac{\rho_1}{\rho}y_-(\delta)}{(1+\rho_1)\delta - \delta^2 - \frac{\alpha_2}{\alpha_1+\alpha_2}\frac{\rho_1}{\rho}y_+(\delta)}.$$

Proof. The proof is similar to the one in [3, Lemma 2] and further details are omitted.

The updated solution after the VC step, does not satisfy the horizontal boundary Eqs. (10), (13), (16), so we need to compensate for the error produced by the VC step. This is done separately for each of the terms used to compensate the error in the vertical boundary, i.e., for $d_1c_1\gamma_1^m\delta_1^n$, $d_2c_2\gamma_2^m\delta_2^{-n}$. Specifically, for the term $d_1c_1\gamma_1^m\delta_1^n$, we seek for d_3, d_4, f_1, δ_3, δ_4 such that

$$\begin{cases} d_1c_1\gamma_1^m\delta_1^n + d_3c_1\gamma_1^m\delta_3^n, & m \geq 0, n > 0, \\ d_4c_1\gamma_1^m\delta_4^{-n}, & m \geq 0, n < 0, \\ c_1f_1\gamma_1^m, & m \geq 0, n = 0, \end{cases}$$

with $\delta_3 := X_-(\gamma_1)$, $\delta_4 := x_-(\gamma_1)$, such that $\delta_1 > \gamma_1 > \delta_3 > 0$, and the constants d_3, d_4, f_1 are derived by substituting in (10), (13), (16). The formal compensation step on the horizontal boundary is outlined in the following lemma.

Lemma 4. *(Horizontal compensation (HC)) i) Let*

$$z_{m,n} = \begin{cases} k_1\gamma^m X_+(\gamma)^n + k_2\gamma^m X_-(\gamma)^n, & m \geq 0, n > 0, \\ k_3\gamma^m x_-(\gamma)^{-n}, & m \geq 0, n < 0, \\ k_4\gamma^m, & m \geq 0. \end{cases}$$

Then, $z_{m,n}$ *satisfies* (9), (15), (10), (13), (16) *if*

$$k_2 = -k_1\frac{\frac{\alpha_1\gamma+q\rho(\alpha_1+\alpha_2)}{X_-(\gamma)} + \frac{\alpha_2\gamma+(1-q)\rho(\alpha_1+\alpha_2)}{x_+(\gamma)} - (\alpha_1+\alpha_2)(1+\rho)}{\frac{\alpha_1\gamma+q\rho(\alpha_1+\alpha_2)}{X_+(\gamma)} + \frac{\alpha_2\gamma+(1-q)\rho(\alpha_1+\alpha_2)}{x_+(\gamma)} - (\alpha_1+\alpha_2)(1+\rho)},$$

$$k_3 = -k_1\frac{\alpha_1(\alpha_2\gamma+(1-q)\rho(\alpha_1+\alpha_2))(\frac{1}{X_-(\gamma)} - \frac{1}{X_+(\gamma)})}{\alpha_2[\frac{\alpha_1\gamma+q\rho(\alpha_1+\alpha_2)}{X_+(\gamma)} + \frac{\alpha_2\gamma+(1-q)\rho(\alpha_1+\alpha_2)}{x_+(\gamma)} - (\alpha_1+\alpha_2)(1+\rho)]},$$

$$k_4 = k_3\frac{\alpha_2\gamma}{\rho(1-q)(\alpha_1+\alpha_2)+\alpha_2\gamma} = (k_1+k_2)\frac{\alpha_1\gamma}{\rho q(\alpha_1+\alpha_2)+\alpha_1\gamma}.$$

ii) Let

$$z_{m,n} = \begin{cases} k_1\gamma^m x_+(\gamma)^{-n} + k_2\gamma^m x_-(\gamma)^n, & m \geq 0, n < 0, \\ k_3\gamma^m X_-(\gamma)^n, & m \geq 0, n > 0, \\ k_4\gamma^m, & m \geq 0. \end{cases}$$

Then, $z_{m,n}$ *satisfies* (9), (15), (10), (13), (16) *if*

$$k_2 = -k_1\frac{\frac{\alpha_1\gamma+q\rho(\alpha_1+\alpha_2)}{X_+(\gamma)} + \frac{\alpha_2\gamma+(1-q)\rho(\alpha_1+\alpha_2)}{x_-(\gamma)} - (\alpha_1+\alpha_2)(1+\rho)}{\frac{\alpha_1\gamma+q\rho(\alpha_1+\alpha_2)}{X_+(\gamma)} + \frac{\alpha_2\gamma+(1-q)\rho(\alpha_1+\alpha_2)}{x_+(\gamma)} - (\alpha_1+\alpha_2)(1+\rho)},$$

$$k_3 = -k_1\frac{\alpha_2(\alpha_1\gamma+q\rho(\alpha_1+\alpha_2))(\frac{1}{x_-(\gamma)} - \frac{1}{x_+(\gamma)})}{\alpha_1[\frac{\alpha_1\gamma+q\rho(\alpha_1+\alpha_2)}{X_+(\gamma)} + \frac{\alpha_2\gamma+(1-q)\rho(\alpha_1+\alpha_2)}{x_+(\gamma)} - (\alpha_1+\alpha_2)(1+\rho)]},$$

$$k_4 = (k_1+k_2)\frac{\alpha_2\gamma}{\rho(1-q)(\alpha_1+\alpha_2)+\alpha_2\gamma} = k_3\frac{\alpha_1\gamma}{\rho q(\alpha_1+\alpha_2)+\alpha_1\gamma}.$$

Proof. The proof is similar to the one in [3, Lemma 3] and further details are omitted.

The CM leads to an expressions for the $q_{m,n}(1)$ (which is equal to the equilibrium probability for the busy states of the model at hand), written as an infinite sum of terms in the upper and lower quadrant. These γs and δs are represented by a binary tree as given in [3, Fig. 2, p. 14]. The γs and δs are numbered from the root and from left to right. We use the same notation as in [3]: $\delta_{l(i)}$ = the left descendant of γ, $\delta_{r(i)}$ = the right descendant of γ, $\gamma_{p(i)}$ = the γ-parent of δ_i. Let $L = \{l(i), i = 0, 1, \dots\}$, $R = \{r(i), i = 0, 1, \dots\}$, with $l(i) = 2i + 1$, $r(i) = 2i + 2$, $p(i) = \lfloor \frac{i-1}{2} \rfloor$, $i = 0, 1, \dots$. Starting from $\gamma_0 = \rho^2$, $\rho = \frac{\lambda(\lambda + \alpha_1 + \alpha_2)}{\mu(\alpha_1 + \alpha_2)}$. For $i \geq 0$ the left descendant $\delta_{l(i)}$ of γ_i is defined as the smaller root of Eq. (19) with $\gamma = \gamma_i$; and the right descendant $\delta_{r(i)}$ of γ_i is defined as the smaller root of Eq. (20) with $\gamma = \gamma_i$. The descendant $\gamma_{l(i)}$ of $\delta_l(i)$ is defined as the smaller root of (19) with $\delta = \delta_l(i)$, and descendant $\gamma_{r(i)}$ of $\delta_r(i)$ is defined as the smaller root of (20) with $\delta = \delta_r(i)$ (Note also that $0 < \gamma < 1$). Using induction, we show that $\delta_{l(i)} = X_-(\gamma_i)$, $\delta_{r(i)} = x_-(\gamma_i)$, $\gamma_l(i) = Y_-(\delta_{l(i)})$, $\gamma_{r(i)} = y_-(\delta_{r(i)})$, and $\gamma_i > \delta_{l(i)} > \gamma_{l(i)} > 0$, $\gamma_i > \delta_{r(i)} > \gamma_{r(i)} > 0$, so that $\{\gamma_i\}$, $\{\delta_i\}$ form a decreasing positive tree. Then, define the infinite sums

$$z_{m,n} = \sum_{i \in L} d_i (c_{p(i)} \gamma_{p(i)}^m + c_i \gamma_i^m) \delta_i^n, \ m \geq 0, n > 0, \tag{23}$$

$$z_{m,n} = \sum_{i \in R} d_i (c_{p(i)} \gamma_{p(i)}^m + c_i \gamma_i^m) \delta_i^{-n}, \ m \geq 0, n < 0. \tag{24}$$

By linearity the sum $p_{m,n}$ satisfies the conditions (9), (15), and we have to define coefficients d_i, c_i to satisfy also the boundaries (10), (11), (13), (16), (17). The coefficients c_i are such that $(c_{p(i)} \gamma_{p(i)}^m + c_i \gamma_i^m) \delta_i^n$ satisfies (10) for all $i \in L$ and such that $(c_{p(i)} \gamma_{p(i)}^m + c_i \gamma_i^m) \delta_i^{-n}$ satisfies (16) for all $i \in R$; see Lemma 3. So c_i can be obtained by $c_{p(i)}$ with initial condition $c_0 = 1$. We now rewrite (23), (24) as

$$z_{m,n}$$
$$= \begin{cases} d_1 \gamma_0^m \delta_1^n + \sum_{i \in L} c_i \gamma_i^m (d_i \delta_i^n + d_{l(i)} \delta_{l(i)}^n) + \sum_{i \in R} c_i d_{l(i)} \gamma_i^m \delta_{l(i)}^n), & m \geq 0, n > 0, \\ d_2 \gamma_0^m \delta_2^{-n} + \sum_{i \in R} c_i \gamma_i^m (d_i \delta_i^{-n} + d_{r(i)} \delta_{r(i)}^{-n}) + \sum_{i \in L} c_i d_{r(i)} \gamma_i^m \delta_{r(i)}^{-n}), & m \geq 0, n < 0, \end{cases}$$
$$\tag{25}$$

and define

$$z_{m,0} = \gamma_0^m + \sum_{i \in L} c_i f_i \gamma_i^m + \sum_{i \in R} c_i f_i \gamma_i^m, \ m \geq 0. \tag{26}$$

The coefficients d_i and f_i are such that for $i \in L$ the terms $\gamma_i^m(d_i \delta_i^n + d_{l(i)} \delta_{l(i)}^n)$, $d_{r(i)} \gamma_i^m \delta_{r(i)}^{-n}$, $f_i \gamma_i^m$, satisfies the horizontal boundary equations (i.e., by using Lemma 4), while for $i \in R$, the same conditions are satisfied by $\gamma_i^m d_{l(i)} \delta_{l(i)}^n$, $\gamma_i^m(d_i \delta_i^{-n} + d_{r(i)} \delta_{r(i)}^{-n})$, and $f_i \gamma_i^m$, starting with $d_i, f_0 = 1$ as in Lemma 2. Application of Lemma 4 yields that the coefficients $d_{l(i)}$, $d_{r(i)}$ can be expressed in terms of d_i (e.g., see [3, pp. 16–17]).

We may conclude that (25) satisfies the equilibrium Eqs. (9)–(11), (13), (15)–(17), except (12), (14), (18). Substituting (23) in (12) and make use of how we derive c_i through Lemma 3, we can show that (25) satisfies (12). Similarly, we can show that (25) is a formal solution to all equilibrium Eqs. (9)(18).

The next step is to formally prove that the series as formulated in (23), (24), (26), are absolutely convergent. However, these series may diverge for small values of m, n. Using similar arguments as in [3] we can show the following theorem:

Theorem 1. *There is an integer N such that:*

1. *the series (23) converges absolutely for all $m \geq 0$, $n \geq 0$ with $m + n > N$,*
2. *the series (24) converges absolutely for all $m \geq 0$, $n \leq 0$ with $m - n > N$,*
3. *the series (26) converges absolutely for all $m \geq N$,*
4. $\sum_{m \geq 0,\, m+|n|>N} |z_{m,n}| < \infty$.

The proof of Theorem 1 needs the proof of a series of results. First, we need to show that γ_i, δ_i decrease exponentially fast. So we need the following lemma:

Lemma 5. *For all $\gamma \in (0, \rho^2]$,*

1. *the ration $X_+(\gamma)/\gamma$ is decreasing and $X_-(\gamma)/\gamma$ is increasing.*
2. $X_+(\gamma) > \gamma > X_-(\gamma) > 0$.

The same properties hold also for $Y_\pm(\delta)$, $x_\pm(\gamma)$ and $y_\pm(\delta)$.

Proof. We only focus on $X_\pm(\gamma)$. Since $0 < \gamma \leq \gamma_0 = \rho^2$ the discriminant of (19) for fixed γ is strictly positive since

$$(\rho+1)^2 - \frac{4\alpha_1(\rho + \frac{\alpha_2\gamma}{\alpha_1+\alpha_2})}{\alpha_1+\alpha_2} \geq (\rho+1)^2 - \frac{4\alpha_1(\rho + \frac{\alpha_2\rho^2}{\alpha_1+\alpha_2})}{\alpha_1+\alpha_2} = (\frac{\rho}{\alpha_1+\alpha_2})^2(\alpha_1 + \alpha_2 + (\alpha_2 - \alpha_1)\rho)^2 > 0,$$

since $\alpha_1 < \alpha_2$. Thus, $X_+(\gamma)$, $X_-(\gamma)$ are distinct positive zeros and $X_+(\gamma)/\gamma$ is decreasing. Moreover,

$$\frac{X_-(\gamma)}{\gamma} = \frac{\alpha_1}{\rho(\alpha_1+\alpha_2)} \frac{\gamma}{X_+(\gamma)} = \frac{2\alpha_1}{(\alpha_1+\alpha_2)(1+\rho)+\sqrt{((\alpha_1+\alpha_2)(1+\rho))^2 - 4\alpha_1(\rho(\alpha_1+\alpha_2)+\alpha_2\gamma)}},$$

which is increasing in γ. Since $\gamma \leq \gamma_0$,

$$\frac{X_+(\gamma)}{\gamma} \geq \frac{X_+(\gamma_0)}{\gamma_0} = \frac{1}{\rho} > 1, \quad \frac{X_-(\gamma)}{\gamma} \geq \frac{X_-(\gamma_0)}{\gamma_0} = \frac{\alpha_1}{\alpha_1+\alpha_2(1+\rho)} < 1.$$

An immediate corollary, which can be proved by induction states that

Corollary 1. *For all $i = 0, 1, \ldots$, $\gamma_0 \geq \gamma_i > \delta_{l(i)} > \gamma_{l(i)} > 0$, $\gamma_0 \geq \gamma_i > \delta_{r(i)} > \gamma_{r(i)} > 0$, where*

$$\delta_{l(i)} \leq \frac{\alpha_1}{\alpha_1+\alpha_2(1+\rho)}\gamma_i, \quad \gamma_{l(i)} \leq \frac{2\rho(\alpha_1+\alpha_2)\delta_{l(i)}}{(\rho+1)(\alpha_1+\alpha_2)-\alpha_2\delta_1+\sqrt{((\rho+1)(\alpha_1+\alpha_2)-\alpha_2\delta_1)^2-4\alpha_1(\alpha_1+\alpha_2)\rho}},$$

$$\delta_{r(i)} \leq \frac{\alpha_2}{\alpha_1+\alpha_2(1+\rho)}\gamma_i, \quad \gamma_{r(i)} \leq \frac{2\rho(\alpha_1+\alpha_2)\delta_{r(i)}}{(\rho+1)(\alpha_1+\alpha_2)-\alpha_1\tilde{\delta}_1+\sqrt{((\rho+1)(\alpha_1+\alpha_2)-\alpha_1\tilde{\delta}_1)^2-4\alpha_1(\alpha_2+\alpha_2)\rho}},$$

for $\delta_1 := X_-(\gamma_0)$, $\tilde{\delta}_1 := x_-(\gamma_0)$.

Proof. Based on Lemma 5, $0 < \delta_{l(i)} = X_-(\gamma_i) \le \frac{X_-(\gamma_0)}{\gamma_0}\gamma_i = \frac{\alpha_1}{\alpha_1+\alpha_2(1+\rho)}\gamma_i$. Moreover, $0 < \delta_{l(i)} = X_-(\gamma_i) \le X_-(\gamma_0) = \delta_1$, and thus, $\gamma_{l(i)} = Y_-(\delta_{l(i)}) \le \frac{Y_-(\delta_1)}{\delta_1}\delta_{l(i)}$, which leads after some algebra in the above expression. Similarly we can handle the other assertion; see also [3, p. 20].

Then, the asymptotic behaviour of γ_i, δ_i is stated in the next lemma.

Lemma 6. *If the depth of γ_i in the parameter tree tends to infinity, i.e., $\gamma_i \to 0$ as $i \to \infty$, then*

$$\frac{\delta_{l(i)}}{\gamma_i} \to \frac{1}{A_2}, \quad \frac{\delta_{r(i)}}{\gamma_i} \to \frac{1}{a_2}$$

and if $\delta_{l(i)} \to 0$, $\delta_{r(i)} \to 0$, then,

$$\frac{\gamma_{l(i)}}{\delta_{l(i)}} \to A_1, \quad \frac{\gamma_{r(i)}}{\delta_{r(i)}} \to a_1,$$

where

$$A_1 = \frac{(\alpha_1+\alpha_2)(\rho+1)-\sqrt{((\alpha_1+\alpha_2)(\rho+1))^2-4\alpha_1\rho(\alpha_1+\alpha_2)}}{2\alpha_1},$$
$$a_1 = \frac{(\alpha_1+\alpha_2)(\rho+1)-\sqrt{((\alpha_1+\alpha_2)(\rho+1))^2-4\alpha_2\rho(\alpha_1+\alpha_2)}}{2\alpha_2},$$
$$A_2 = \frac{(\alpha_1+\alpha_2)(\rho+1)+\sqrt{((\alpha_1+\alpha_2)(\rho+1))^2-4\alpha_1\rho(\alpha_1+\alpha_2)}}{2\alpha_1},$$
$$a_2 = \frac{(\alpha_1+\alpha_2)(\rho+1)+\sqrt{((\alpha_1+\alpha_2)(\rho+1))^2-4\alpha_2\rho(\alpha_1+\alpha_2)}}{2\alpha_2}.$$

We further need to study the asymptotic behaviour of the coefficients c_i, d_i, following the lines in [3, pp. 21–24]. Then, these results ensure the proof of Theorem 1. The next theorem summarizes the main result.

Theorem 2. *For all m, n, such that $m \ge 0$, $m + |n| > N$, and for $m = N$, $n = 0$,*

$$q_{m,n}(1) = C^{-1}z_{m,n},$$

$$q_{m,n}(0) = C^{-1} \times \begin{cases} \frac{\mu}{\lambda+\alpha_1+\alpha_2}z_{m,n}, & m > 0, \\ \frac{\mu}{\lambda+\alpha_1 1_{\{n\ge1\}}+\alpha_2 1_{\{n\le-1\}}}z_{0,n}, & m = 0, \end{cases} \quad (27)$$

where $z_{m,n}$ as given in (25), (26) and C^{-1} a normalization constant. The value of constant N depends on the system parameters. In the symmetric case, i.e., $\alpha_1 = \alpha_2$, $N = 0$. In case $N > 0$, the equilibrium equations for $m + |n| \le N$ have to be solved numerically; see [3, Sect. 18].

4 Discussion on the Case of a Priority Line of a Finite Capacity

We briefly describe how we can handle the case where the main service station can handle at most $K > 1$ jobs, i.e., there is a finite priority line of capacity $K - 1$ in front of the service station. In such a scenario, arriving jobs are routed to the orbits if upon arrival they find the priority line fully occupied. Orbiting jobs can access the server only if upon a retrial they find the server idle, i.e., we do not allow orbiting jobs to access the priority line.

The matrix form of the equilibrium equations is as those in (2), where now the matrices are of order $(K+1) \times (K+1)$. We are still able to consider the dimensionality reduction, by expressing all the equilibrium probabilities $q_{m,n}(k)$, $k = 0, 1, \ldots, K-1$, in terms of $q_{m,n}(K)$. However, upon doing this operation, we will see that the resulting equations, i.e., the equations that result after the dimensionality reduction and are expresses in terms of $q_{m,n}(K)$, are more general than those in (9)–(18). In particular, the resulting two-dimensional random walk in the half plane has now fatter boundaries, and transitions to non-neighbour states, although the required assumptions to apply the compensation method are satisfied; to our best knowledge, the most related available literature refers to [2,17] that dealt with large jumps (i.e., to non-neighbour states) but only in the positive quadrant. In case $K > 1$, the transformed equations after the dimensionality reduction contain transitions to non-neighbour states both in the positive and in the negative quadrant of the half plane. For example, for $K = 3$, tedious computations yield

$$q_{m,n}(w) = s_{3-w}q_{m,n}(3) - s_{2-w}\left[q_{m-1,n+1}(3)1_{\{n\geq 1\}} + q_{m-1,n-1}(3)1_{\{n\leq -1\}}+\right.$$
$$+qq_{m,0}(3)1_{\{n=-1\}} + (1-q)q_{m,0}(3)1_{\{n=1\}}$$
$$\left. +(q_{m-1,1}(3) + q_{m-1,-1}(3))1_{\{n=0\}}\right], \, m > 0, n \neq 0, w = 1, 2,$$
$$q_{0,n}(w) = s_{3-w}q_{0,n}(3), n \neq 0, w = 1, 2,$$
$$q_{m,n}(0) = \frac{\mu}{\lambda + \alpha_1 1_{\{n<0\}} + \alpha_2 1_{\{n>0\}}} q_{m,n}(1), \, m \geq 0, n \in \mathbb{Z}.$$

where

$$s_{3-w} = \frac{\sum_{m=0}^{3-w} \lambda^{3-w-m}\mu^m}{\lambda^{3-w}}, \, w = 1, 2, 3.$$

After the dimensionality reduction, the resulting inner equilibrium equations in the positive and negative quadrant, respectively, reads for $p_{m,n} := q_{m,n}(3)$:

$$p_{m,n}[s_2(\rho + 1) - \frac{s_1(\lambda + \alpha_2)}{\alpha_1 + \alpha_2}] + p_{m-1,n+2}\frac{\alpha_2 s_1}{\alpha_1 + \alpha_2} = p_{m-1,n+1}[s_1(\rho + 1) - \frac{\lambda + \alpha_1 + \alpha_2}{\alpha_1 + \alpha_2}]$$
$$+p_{m+1,n-1}\frac{s_2\alpha_1}{\alpha_1 + \alpha_2} + p_{m,n+1}\frac{s_2\alpha_2}{\alpha_1 + \alpha_2}, \, m > 0, n > 2,$$
$$p_{m,n}[s_2(\rho + 1) - \frac{s_1(\lambda + \alpha_1)}{\alpha_1 + \alpha_2}] + p_{m-1,n-2}\frac{\alpha_1 s_1}{\alpha_1 + \alpha_2} = p_{m-1,n-1}[s_1(\rho + 1) - \frac{\lambda + \alpha_1 + \alpha_2}{\alpha_1 + \alpha_2}]$$
$$+p_{m,n-1}\frac{s_2\alpha_1}{\alpha_1 + \alpha_2} + p_{m+1,n+1}\frac{s_2\alpha_2}{\alpha_1 + \alpha_2}, \, m > 0, n < -2,$$

It can be easily seen from the above that for any state (m, n), $m > 0$, $n > 2$ (resp. $n < -2$) (of the transformed process) we can have transitions to $(m+1, n-2)$, $(m+1, n-1)$, $(m-1, n+1)$, $(m, n-1)$ (resp. to $(m+1, n+2)$, $(m+1, n+1)$, $(m-1, n-1)$, $(m, n+1)$).

Our intuition indicates that following similar arguments as in [2,17] we are able to apply the CM in the half plane. At that point, a crucial point is the choice of the initial candidate solution for the inner equilibrium equations, i.e., the initial γ_0, and δ_0. Note that by substituting the product $\gamma^m \delta^n$ in the above equations yields a cubic equation with respect to δ and a quadratic with respect to γ. Thus, it is first important to study the asymptotic behaviour of $q_{m,n}(K)$ as $m \to \infty$, and investigate whether it is of geometric form.

5   Conclusion and Future Work

In this work, by using a Markovian queueing network with retrials under the JSQ policy, we investigated the stationary behaviour of a certain non-homogeneous Markov modulated two-dimensional random walk. By exploiting its special structure, its invariant measure is obtained by applying the CM to a standard, i.e., non-modulated random walk in the half plane with a complicated vertical boundary behaviour. In particular, the resulting two-dimensional random walk describes the JSQ problem in two standard (i.e., non-retrial) queues with appropriate arrival/service rates. With such an operation, we reduce to the half the number of equilibrium equations to be solved through the CM.

The analysis we follow seems to be fully applicable for even more general cases, including: multiserver service station, Erlang (or PH) arrival streams, several stations that can accommodate a finite number of customers, as well as to incorporate the possibility of the bi-level JSQ policy, i.e., the possibility of retransmitting from orbit queues to the service node with the fewest number of jobs. The only limitation (due to the use of CM) relies on the number of orbit queues, which is restricted to two. Even with the above setting, we can ensure a dimensionality reduction, which allows to obtain the invariant measure through the CM by solving fewer (based on the model at hand) equilibrium equations.

References

1. Adan, I.J.B.F., Kapodistria, S., van Leeuwaarden, J.S.H.: Erlang arrivals joining the shorter queue. Queueing Syst. **74**(2–3), 273–302 (2013)
2. Adan, I.J.B.F., Wessels, J.: Shortest expected delay routing for Erlang servers. Queueing Syst. **23**(1–4), 77–105 (1996)
3. Adan, I.J.B.F., Wessels, J., Zijm, W.H.M.: Analysis of the asymmetric shortest queue problem. Queueing Syst. **8**(1), 1–58 (1991)
4. Adan, I.J.B.F., Wessels, J., Zijm, W.H.: Analysis of the symmetric shortest queue problem. Stoch. Model. **6**(1), 691–713 (1990)
5. Adan, I.J.B.F., Wessels, J., Zijm, W.: A compensation approach for two-dimentional Markov processes. Adv. Appl. Probab. **25**(4), 783–817 (1993)
6. Boxma, O.J., van Houtum, G.J.: The compensation approach applied to a 2 × 2 switch. Probab. Eng. Inf. Sci. **7**(4), 471–493 (1993)
7. Cohen, J., Boxma, O.: Boundary Value Problems in Queueing Systems Analysis. North Holland Publishing Company, Amsterdam, Netherlands (1983)
8. Dimitriou, I.: Analysis of the symmetric join the shortest orbit queue. Oper. Res. Lett. **49**(1), 23–29 (2021)
9. Dimitriou, I.: The generalized join the shortest orbit queue system: stability, exact tail asymptotics and stationary approximations. Probab. Eng. Inf. Sci. **37**(1), 154–191 (2023). https://doi.org/10.1017/S0269964821000528
10. Fayolle, G., Iasnogorodski, R., Malyshev, V.: Random walks in the quarter-plane: algebraic methods, boundary value problems, applications to queueing systems and analytic combinatorics. Springer, Cham (2017). https://doi.org/10.1007/978-3-319-50930-3
11. Haight, F.A.: Two queues in parallel. Biometrika **45**(3/4), 401–410 (1958)

12. Kingman, J.F.C.: Two similar queues in parallel. Ann. Math. Statist. **32**(4), 1314–1323 (1961)
13. Laneman, J.N., Tse, D.N., Wornell, G.W.: Cooperative diversity in wireless networks: efficient protocols and outage behavior. IEEE Trans. Inf. Theory **50**(12), 3062–3080 (2004)
14. Papadimitriou, G., Pappas, N., Traganitis, A., Angelakis, V.: Network-level performance evaluation of a two-relay cooperative random access wireless system. Comput. Netw. **88**, 187–201 (2015)
15. Pappas, N., Kountouris, M., Ephremides, A., Traganitis, A.: Relay-assisted multiple access with full-duplex multi-packet reception. IEEE Trans. Wireless Commun. **14**(7), 3544–3558 (2015)
16. Rong, B., Ephremides, A.: Cooperation above the physical layer: the case of a simple network. In: 2009 IEEE International Symposium on Information Theory, pp. 1789–1793. IEEE (2009)
17. Saxena, M., Dimitriou, I., Kapodistria, S.: Analysis of the shortest relay queue policy in a cooperative random access network with collisions. Queueing Syst. **94**(1–2), 39–75 (2020)
18. Selen, J., Adan, I.J.B.F., Kapodistria, S., van Leeuwaarden, J.: Steady-state analysis of shortest expected delay routing. Queueing Syst. **84**, 309–354 (2016)

Performance Analysis

Understanding Slowdown in Large-Scale Heterogeneous Systems

William Turchetta and Kristen Gardner$^{(\boxtimes)}$

Amherst College, Amherst, MA 01002, USA
kgardner@amherst.edu

Abstract. Modern computer systems are both large-scale, consisting of hundreds or thousands of servers, and heterogeneous, meaning that not all servers have the same speed. In such systems, slowdown—the ratio of a job's response time to its size—is an important performance metric that has not yet received significant attention. We propose a new definition of slowdown that is well-suited to large-scale, heterogeneous systems. We analyze mean slowdown and mean response time under the Probabilistic SITA family of dispatching policies, and use our analysis to present a numerical study of the tradeoff between these two performance metrics.

Keywords: Dispatching · Heterogeneity · Slowdown

1 Introduction

Today's computer systems typically consist of hundreds or thousands of servers that are *heterogeneous* in the sense that not all servers have the same speed. Deciding how to dispatch jobs to servers is a question of critical importance in achieving good performance in such systems; policies designed for homogeneous systems often perform poorly in the presence of heterogeneity [1]. Here "performance" typically refers to the size of the stability region or to mean response time; most of the work on large-scale heterogeneous systems focuses on the design, analysis, and evaluation of dispatching policies with respect to these metrics [1,6].

In this paper we consider an alternative performance metric: mean *slowdown*, where the slowdown of a job captures the ratio between the job's response time and its size. Slowdown is a well-studied metric in single-server systems; the Shortest-Processing-Time-Product (SPTP, also referred to as RS) scheduling policy is known to minimize mean slowdown [5,7], while Processor Sharing (PS) and Preemptive Last-Come First-Served (PLCFS) have the desirable property that a job's expected slowdown is independent of its size [3]. However, there is relatively little work studying slowdown in heterogeneous systems, and this work tends to focus on systems with only two or three servers [5].

We propose a new definition of slowdown for large-scale heterogeneous systems. We introduce a generalization of the Size Interval Task Assignment (SITA)

© ICST Institute for Computer Sciences, Social Informatics and Telecommunications Engineering 2023
Published by Springer Nature Switzerland AG 2023. All Rights Reserved
E. Hyytiä and V. Kavitha (Eds.): VALUETOOLS 2022, LNICST 482, pp. 197–206, 2023.
https://doi.org/10.1007/978-3-031-31234-2_12

policy [4], which we call Probabilistic SITA (PSITA). We analyze the mean
system slowdown and mean response time under PSITA and use our analysis
to identify optimal parameterizations of PSITA. Finally, using our analytical
results, we gain insight about the structure of optimal PSITA policies and the
relationship between mean response time and mean slowdown.

2   Model and Preliminaries

We consider a system with k servers that are heterogeneous in that different
servers may have different speeds. We assume that there are s server speed
classes and let $\mathcal{S} \equiv \{1, \ldots, s\}$ denote the set of all server classes. We denote the
number of servers in class i as k_i and the fraction of servers in class i as $q_i = k_i/k$,
$i \in \mathcal{S}$. Class-i servers have speed μ_i, where $\mu_1 > \cdots > \mu_s$; all servers operate
under the Processor Sharing (PS) scheduling discipline. We assume that each
job has a size X drawn from a general distribution. Following [2], the time that
a job with size X spends in service on a server with speed μ_i is X/μ_i. Arrivals to
the system follow a Poisson process with rate λk. Without loss of generality, we
assume that the total capacity of the system is k, i.e., we require $\sum_{i=1}^{s} q_i \mu_i = 1$.
To ensure stability, we assume that $\lambda < 1$.

Our primary metric of interest is the mean system *slowdown*. In a homogeneous system, i.e., one in which all servers have the same speed, the slowdown of
a job with size x is $S(x) \equiv \frac{T(x)}{x}$, where $T(x)$ is the job's response time. Notably,
this definition of slowdown implies that $S(x) \geq 1$, and hence captures the extent
to which the job is "slowed down" by the presence of other jobs, relative to the
response time it would experience running in isolation. Extending this definition
to heterogeneous systems presents a challenge: how should one account for the
differences in server speeds? One approach, used in [5], defines the slowdown
of a job with size x running on a class-i server (i.e., a server with speed μ_i)
as $S(x) \equiv \frac{T(x)}{x/\sum_j \mu_j}$. That is, the slowdown is normalized relative to the overall
capacity of the system. The disadvantage of this approach is that, as the number
of servers in the system grows, slowdowns can become extremely large, making
it difficult to draw meaningful comparisons between different system configurations.

To overcome this disadvantage, we propose a new definition of slowdown in
heterogeneous systems.

Definition 1. *The **slowdown** of a job with size x running on a class-i server
is $S_i(x) \equiv \frac{T_i(x)}{x}$.*

At first glance, this definition looks identical to the definition of slowdown in
a single-server (or homogeneous) system. However, we note that the term x in the
denominator does *not* include the server's speed: this is the job's "inherent size,"
and not the time it spends in service. Hence, using this definition of slowdown, a
job that runs in isolation on a class-i server will experience slowdown $1/\mu_i$, and in
general a job's slowdown is scaled by a factor of $1/\mu_i$ relative to its slowdown on

a speed-1 server (i.e., when a job's service time is equal to its size). For example, in an $M/G/1/PS$ system in which the server has speed 1, the mean slowdown is $\mathbb{E}[S] = \mathbb{E}[S|X] = \frac{1}{1-\rho_i}$ [3]. Using our heterogeneity-based definition, the mean slowdown at a class-i server under PS is $\mathbb{E}[S] = \frac{1}{1-\rho_i} \cdot \frac{1}{\mu_i}$, where in both cases ρ_i denotes the fraction of time that a class-i server is busy.

There are several key advantages to our definition of slowdown. First, our definition is easily interpretable: if a job experiences a slowdown less than 1, we know that the job ran on a fast server and did not compete with many other jobs. Meanwhile, if a job experiences a slowdown greater than 1, we know that it ran on a slow server or on a heavily-loaded server. This clean interpretation is in contrast to the definition used in [5], under which a job that runs in isolation on a fast server may nonetheless experience a very high slowdown. Second, our definition does not explicitly depend on the total system capacity, meaning that, unlike in [5], adding servers to the system will not artificially inflate slowdown values. Finally, our definition facilitates comparisons between the slowdowns obtained under different system configurations, given a fixed total system capacity.

With the goal of achieving low mean slowdown in mind, we propose a new dispatching policy called Probabilistic SITA (PSITA) that generalizes the SITA [4] policy. SITA is typically defined for *homogeneous* systems (i.e., systems in which all servers have the same speed). Under SITA, jobs are divided into k bins based on their sizes; recall that k is the number of servers in the system. One server is allocated to each bin; when a job arrives, it is dispatched to the server corresponding to its bin. In this way, small jobs are isolated from big jobs, thereby protecting the small jobs from experiencing high response times and high slowdowns.

The PSITA policy generalizes SITA by (i) allowing the number of bins to differ from the number of servers, and (ii) making dispatching decisions probabilistically, rather than deterministically. In particular, under PSITA, jobs are divided into b bins based on their sizes. When a job from bin j arrives, the job is dispatched to one of the server classes, where this class is chosen *probabilistically*. These two extensions render PSITA appropriate for use in heterogeneous systems.

Definition 2. *Let $0 \equiv x_1 \le x_2 \le \cdots \le x_b < x_{b+1} \equiv \infty$. A job is in bin j if it has size x such that $x_j \le x < x_{j+1}$, $j \in \{1, \ldots, b\} \equiv \mathcal{B}$. Under the **Probabilistic SITA (PSITA)** dispatching policy, when a job from bin j arrives it is sent to some class-i server with probability $p_{j,i}$, for all $i \in \mathcal{S}$. The specific server is chosen uniformly at random among all class-i servers.*

3   Analysis

In this section we derive mean slowdown, $\mathbb{E}[S]$, and mean response time, $\mathbb{E}[T]$, under PSITA dispatching and PS scheduling for fixed values of x_j, $j \in \mathcal{B}$, and $p_{j,i}$, $j \in \mathcal{B}$, $i \in \mathcal{S}$.

We begin by observing that

$$\mathbb{E}[S] = \sum_{i=1}^{s} p_i \mathbb{E}[S_i]$$

$$\mathbb{E}[T] = \sum_{i=1}^{s} p_i \mathbb{E}[T_i],$$

where $\mathbb{E}[S_i]$ and $\mathbb{E}[T_i]$ are respectively the mean slowdown and the mean response time on a class-i server, and p_i is the probability that an arbitrary job is dispatched to a class-i server. Note that the per-class mean slowdowns are weighted by the probability that an arbitrary *job* runs on a class-i server, not the probability that a *server* is of class i.

To find p_i, we will condition on the job's size, X; recall that, under PSITA, jobs in size bin j are dispatched to a class-i server with probability $p_{j,i}$. We find:

$$p_i = \sum_{j=1}^{b} p_{j,i} \mathbb{P}(X \in [x_j, x_{j+1})). \tag{1}$$

The PSITA dispatching policy amounts to Poisson splitting of the jobs within each bin, hence each class-i server behaves like an $M/G_i/1$. The total arrival rate to class-i servers is $\lambda k p_i$; because we dispatch uniformly within a server class, the arrival rate to an individual class-i server is

$$\lambda_i = \frac{\lambda k p_i}{k_i} = \frac{\lambda p_i}{q_i}. \tag{2}$$

The service time at a class-i server is distributed as $Y_i \sim X_i/\mu_i$. Here X_i denotes the size distribution of jobs that are dispatched to class-i servers. In an $M/G_i/1/\mathrm{PS}$ with arrival rate λ_i and service times Y_i, the mean slowdown and mean response time are given by:

$$\mathbb{E}[S_i] = \frac{1}{(1-\rho_i)} \frac{1}{\mu_i}$$

$$\mathbb{E}[T_i] = \frac{\lambda_i \mathbb{E}[Y_i^2]}{2(1-\rho_i)} = \frac{\lambda_i \mathbb{E}[X_i^2]}{2(1-\rho_i)} \frac{1}{\mu_i^2}.$$

We now proceed to find ρ_i, $\mathbb{E}[X_i]$, and $\mathbb{E}[X_i^2]$. The load at each class-i server is

$$\rho_i = \lambda_i \mathbb{E}[Y_i] = \lambda_i \frac{\mathbb{E}[X_i]}{\mu_i}. \tag{3}$$

We find the expected job size on a class-i server by conditioning on the job size bin:

$$\mathbb{E}[X_i] = \sum_{j=1}^{b} \frac{p_{j,i} \mathbb{P}(X \in [x_j, x_{j+1}))}{p_i} \mathbb{E}[X | X \in [x_j, x_{j+1})], \tag{4}$$

where the term $\frac{p_{j,i}\mathbb{P}(X\in[x_j,x_{j+1}))}{p_i}$ gives the fraction of jobs at class-i servers that are from bin j. Similarly, we have:

$$\mathbb{E}[X_i^2] = \sum_{j=1}^{b} \frac{p_{j,i}\mathbb{P}(X \in [x_j, x_{j+1}))}{p_i}\mathbb{E}[X^2|X \in [x_j, x_{j+1})]. \qquad (5)$$

At this point we have derived all of the components necessary to obtain the following results.

Proposition 1. *The mean slowdown and mean response time under PSITA dispatching and PS scheduling are:*

$$\mathbb{E}[S] = \sum_{i=1}^{s} p_i \frac{1}{(1-\rho_i)} \frac{1}{\mu_i}$$

$$\mathbb{E}[T] = \sum_{i=1}^{s} p_i \frac{\lambda_i \mathbb{E}[X_i^2]}{2(1-\rho_i)} \frac{1}{\mu_i^2}$$

where p_i, λ_i, ρ_i, $\mathbb{E}[X_i]$, and $\mathbb{E}[X_i^2]$ are given in (1)–(5).

Using our closed-form expressions for $\mathbb{E}[S]$ and $\mathbb{E}[T]$ given in Proposition 1, we can now find the PSITA policy that minimizes each metric by jointly optimizing over x_j, $j \in \mathcal{B}$, and $p_{j,i}$, $j \in \mathcal{B}$, $i \in \mathcal{S}$. Our optimization problem for mean slowdown is:

$$\min_{\substack{p_{j,i},j\in\mathcal{B},i\in\mathcal{S} \\ x_j,j\in\mathcal{B}}} \sum_{i=1}^{s} p_i \frac{1}{(1-\rho_i)} \frac{1}{\mu_i}$$

$$\text{s.t.} \quad p_i = \sum_{j=1}^{b} p_{j,i}\mathbb{P}(X \in [x_j, x_{j+1})) \qquad \forall i \in \mathcal{S}$$

$$\rho_i = \frac{\lambda p_i \mathbb{E}[X_i]}{q_i \mu_i} \qquad \forall i \in \mathcal{S}$$

$$\mathbb{E}[X_i] = \sum_{j=1}^{b} \frac{p_{j,i}\mathbb{P}(X \in [x_j, x_{j+1}))}{p_i} \cdot \mathbb{E}[X|X \in [x_j, x_{j+1})] \qquad \forall i \in \mathcal{S}$$

$$\sum_{i=1}^{s} p_{j,i} = 1 \qquad \forall j \in \mathcal{B}$$

$$\sum_{i=1}^{s} p_i = 1$$

$$0 \le p_{j,i}, p_i \le 1 \qquad \forall j \in \mathcal{B}, i \in \mathcal{S}$$

$$0 \le \rho_i < 1 \qquad \forall i \in \mathcal{S}$$

The optimization problem for mean response time is similar. While we opt to take $b = |\mathcal{B}|$ (the number of job size bins) as fixed, note that one could also leave b as a parameter of the optimization problem.

4   Results and Discussion

In this section, we present a brief numerical study of systems with $s = 2$ server speeds and $b = 2$ job size bins; we assume that $X \sim \text{Exp}(1)$. We let $r \equiv \frac{\mu_1}{\mu_2}$ denote the speed ratio between fast and slow servers.

Both the objective function and the constraints of the optimization problem given in Sect. 3 are non-convex in multiple dimensions, hence standard optimization algorithms are not guaranteed to yield globally optimal solutions. We thus carry out our optimization using a grid search, considering all $4\,080\,501$ combinations of $x_2 \in \{0, 0.04, \dots, 3.96, 4\}$ and $p_{1,1}, p_{2,1} \in \{0, 0.005, \dots, 0.995, 1\}$. We then select the parameters $(x_2^*, p_{1,1}^*, p_{2,1}^*)$ that yield the lowest mean slowdown and refer to this as the optimal solution for the given system settings.

Table 1. Optimal policy parameters and corresponding performance metrics when $q_1 = q_2 = 0.5$ and $r = 2$.

λ	$p_{2,1}^*$	$p_{1,1}^*$	x_2^*	$\mathbb{E}[S]$	ρ_1	ρ_2
0.1	0	1	3.96	0.88	0.14	0.03
0.2	0	1	2.76	1.02	0.23	0.14
0.3	0	1	2.4	1.18	0.31	0.28
0.4	0	1	2.28	1.38	0.4	0.4
0.5	0	1	2.2	1.65	0.48	0.53
0.6	0	1	2.2	2.05	0.58	0.64
0.7	0	1	2.2	2.72	0.68	0.74
0.8	0	1	2.24	4.06	0.79	0.83
0.9	0.01	1	2.24	8.07	0.89	0.92

4.1   Structure of Optimal PSITA Policies

In this section, we study the structure of PSITA policies that minimize mean slowdown. Table 1 shows the optimal policy parameters ($p_{1,1}^*$, $p_{2,1}^*$, and x_2^*) and corresponding performance metrics ($\mathbb{E}[S]$, ρ_1, and ρ_2) in a system in which $q_1 = q_2 = 0.5$, $r = 2$, and λ varies. (While Table 1 shows results only for one specific pair of q_1 and r values, we observed similar results for other parameter settings.) Interestingly, the optimal PSITA policies are in fact nearly always SITA policies. That is, the optimal policy nearly always has $p_{1,1}^* = 1$ and $p_{2,1}^* = 0$, meaning that all small jobs are dispatched to fast servers and all large jobs are dispatched to slow servers. This indicates that the primary factor that leads to low slowdown is the isolation of small jobs. Indeed, at all but the highest values of λ, the only policy parameter that changes with λ is the size cutoff above which jobs are considered large: as λ increases the optimal size cutoff decreases. This is because at higher values of λ, isolating the very smallest jobs requires us to offload more moderately-sized jobs to the slow servers. When λ is very high, the optimal policies change structurally in two ways. First, the optimal cutoff increases slightly. Second, the optimal PSITA policy is no longer a SITA policy. Together, these structural changes ensure that the slow servers remain stable. This highlights the additional flexibility that PSITA offers over SITA: under SITA, it would only be possible to maintain stability at the slow servers by increasing the size cutoff between small and large jobs.

4.2   Tradeoff Between $\mathbb{E}[S]$ and $\mathbb{E}[T]$

We now turn to the relationship between mean slowdown and mean response time. Figure 1 shows $\mathbb{E}[T]$ as a function of $\mathbb{E}[S]$ in a system where $q_1 = q_2 = 0.5$, $r = 2$, and $\lambda = 0.5$. Each point represents a different parameterization of the PSITA policy; we show all parameterizations considered in the grid search, giving a total of 4 080 501 points. In general, there is a roughly linear relationship between mean response time and mean slowdown. Both metrics depend strongly on the per-class loads, so a policy parameterization that leads to a high load at one or both server classes likely yields poor performance for both metrics.

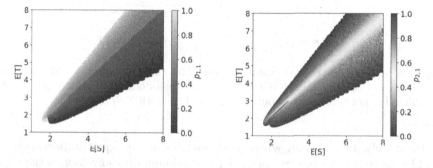

Fig. 1. Mean response time vs. mean slowdown for $\lambda = 0.5$, $q_1 = q_2 = 0.5$, $\mu_1 = \frac{4}{3}$, and $\mu_2 = \frac{2}{3}$, for all values of $x_2 \in \{0, 0.04, \ldots, 3.96, 4\}$ and $p_{1,1}, p_{2,1} \in \{0, 0.005, \ldots, 0.995, 1\}$. Colors represent the value of $p_{1,1}$ (left) and $p_{2,1}$ (right).

Despite the correlation between $\mathbb{E}[S]$ and $\mathbb{E}[T]$, it is clear that the optimal policies for slowdown are not necessarily optimal for mean response time. Two distinct regions emerge in Fig. 1: a "cone" with slightly lower $\mathbb{E}[S]$ (shown by yellow points in the left subfigure and by red points in the right subfigure) consisting of policies that send most of the small jobs to fast servers and most of the big jobs to slow servers, and a "cone" with slightly higher $\mathbb{E}[S]$ (shown by blue points in both subfigures) consisting of policies that do the opposite. Broadly, policies in the former cone obtain similar mean response times to their counterparts in the latter cone, but lower mean slowdowns. This pattern emphasizes the importance not only of isolating the small jobs, but of isolating the small jobs *on fast servers* in order to achieve low mean slowdown.

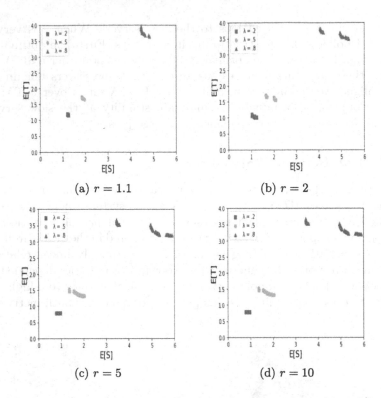

Fig. 2. Mean response time vs. mean slowdown for three values of λ and four values of r, where $q_1 = q_2 = 0.5$. Each point represents a non-dominated policy, i.e., a policy for which it is not possible to simultaneously reduce both $\mathbb{E}[S]$ and $\mathbb{E}[T]$.

Ultimately, in a system where both metrics are of equal importance, one would want to select a policy along the Pareto-dominating envelope of the region shown in Fig. 1. Figure 2 shows the tradeoff between $\mathbb{E}[S]$ and $\mathbb{E}[T]$ for these dominating policies, for three values of λ and four values of r. That is, each point represents a policy for which it is not possible to simultaneously reduce both $\mathbb{E}[S]$ and $\mathbb{E}[T]$. When λ is low, the Pareto-optimal policies are tightly clustered: the policies that are optimal with respect to $\mathbb{E}[T]$ are also nearly optimal with respect to $\mathbb{E}[S]$, and vice versa. As λ increases the tradeoff between $\mathbb{E}[S]$ and $\mathbb{E}[T]$ becomes more pronounced: there emerges a set of distinct Pareto-optimal policies. All of these policies behave similarly in the sense that all operate by isolating small jobs. However, the policies differ in *where* they isolate the small jobs. As previously observed, slowdown-optimal policies send small jobs to fast servers and large jobs to slow servers; meanwhile, the policies that minimize mean response time tend to do the opposite. While different policies are optimal for each metric, we note that $\mathbb{E}[T]$ is significantly less sensitive than $\mathbb{E}[S]$ to the choice of (Pareto-optimal) policy.

5   Conclusion

Our work represents an important first step towards understanding slowdown in large-scale, heterogeneous systems. Our key contribution is our definition of slowdown, which is interpretable, scalable, and allows for meaningful comparisons between system configurations. We analyze mean slowdown and mean response time under the PSITA dispatching policy and PS scheduling, and present a numerical study of the tradeoff between these two performance metrics. Our results indicate that, while mean slowdown and mean response time are generally correlated, minimizing one metric does not necessarily result in minimizing the other. In particular, slowdown is far more sensitive than response time to the particular choice of policy parameters, suggesting that when both metrics are of equal importance, it may be more valuable to select a policy aimed at minimizing slowdown.

While our numerical study considers only systems with two server speeds and exponentially distributed job sizes, and we allow our PSITA policies to include only two job size bins, we expect that the insights learned from this study are likely to translate to more general settings. In particular, we anticipate that isolating small jobs at fast servers will remain the most important factor in achieving low mean slowdown. Furthermore, preliminary results suggest that there are diminishing marginal returns when increasing the number of jobs size bins beyond two.

In this paper we focus on identifying optimal dispatching policies within the PSITA family; however these policies likely are not optimal more generally. For example, policies that yield lower mean response times, such as JSQ-d, JIQ, and the policies studied in [1], will likely also yield lower mean slowdowns; analyzing slowdown under such policies represents an important direction for future work.

References

1. Abdul Jaleel, J., Doroudi, S., Gardner, K., Wickeham, A.: A general power-of-d dispatching framework for heterogeneous systems. Queueing Syst. **102**, 431–480 (2022)
2. Gardner, K., Harchol-Balter, M., Scheller-Wolf, A., Van Houdt, B.: A better model for job redundancy: decoupling server slowdown and job size. IEEE/ACM Trans. Netw. **25**(6), 3353–3367 (2017)
3. Harchol-Balter, M.: Performance Modeling and Design of Computer Systems: Queueing Theory in Action. Cambridge University Press, Cambridge (2013)
4. Harchol-Balter, M., Crovella, M.E., Murta, C.D.: On choosing a task assignment policy for a distributed server system. J. Parallel Distrib. Comput. **59**(2), 204–228 (1999)
5. Hyytiä, E., Aalto, S., Penttinen, A.: Minimizing slowdown in heterogeneous size-aware dispatching systems. ACM SIGMETRICS Perform. Eval. Rev. **40**(1), 29–40 (2012)

6. Stolyar, A.L.: Pull-based load distribution in large-scale heterogeneous service systems. Queueing Syst. **80**(4), 341–361 (2015). https://doi.org/10.1007/s11134-015-9448-8

7. Yang, S., De Veciana, G.: Size-based adaptive bandwidth allocation: optimizing the average QoS for elastic flows. In: Proceedings. Twenty-First Annual Joint Conference of the IEEE Computer and Communications Societies, vol. 2, pp. 657–666. IEEE (2002)

Multi-Model Federated Learning
with Provable Guarantees

Neelkamal Bhuyan[1]([✉]), Sharayu Moharir[1], and Gauri Joshi[2]

[1] Indian Institute of Technology Bombay, Mumbai, India
neelkamalbhuyan@gmail.com
[2] Carnegie Mellon University, Pittsburgh, PA, USA

Abstract. Federated Learning (FL) is a variant of distributed learning where edge devices collaborate to learn a model without sharing their data with the central server or each other. We refer to the process of training multiple independent models simultaneously in a federated setting using a common pool of clients as multi-model FL. In this work, we propose two variants of the popular FedAvg algorithm for multi-model FL, with provable convergence guarantees. We further show that for the same amount of computation, multi-model FL can have better performance than training each model separately. We supplement our theoretical results with experiments in strongly convex, convex, and non-convex settings.

Keywords: Federated Learning · Distributed Learning · Optimization

1 Introduction

Federated Learning (FL) is a form of distributed learning where training is done by edge devices (also called clients) using their local data without sharing their data with the central coordinator (also known as server) or other devices. The only information shared between the clients and the server is the update to the global model after local client training. This helps in preserving the privacy of the local client dataset. Additionally, training on the edge devices does not require datasets to be communicated from the clients to the server, lowering communication costs. The single model federated learning problem has been widely studied from various perspectives including optimizing the frequency of communication between the clients and the server [17], designing client selection algorithms in the setting where only a subset of devices train the model in each iteration [9], and measuring the effect of partial device participation on the convergence rate [12].

Closest to this work, in [2], the possibility of using federated learning to train multiple models simultaneously using the same set of edge devices has been explored. We refer to this as multi-model FL. In the setting considered in

This work is generously supported by NSF CNS #2112471.

[2], each device can only train one model at a time. The algorithmic challenge is to determine which model each client will train in any given round. Simulations illustrate that multiple models can indeed be trained simultaneously without a sharp drop in accuracy by splitting the clients into subsets in each round and use one subset to train each of the models. One key limitation of [2] is the lack of analytical performance guarantees for the proposed algorithms. In this work, we address this limitation of [2] by proposing algorithms for multi-model FL with provable performance guarantees.

1.1 Our Contributions

In this work, we focus on the task of training M models simultaneously using a shared set of clients. We propose two variants of the Fed-Avg algorithm [15] for the multi-model setting, with provable convergence guarantees. The first variant called Multi-FedAvg-Random (MFA-Rand) partitions clients into M groups in each round and matches the M groups to the M models in a uniformly randomized fashion. Under the second variant called Multi-FedAvg-Round Robin (MFA-RR), time is divided into frames such that each frame consists of M rounds. At the beginning of each frame, clients are partitioned into M groups uniformly at random. Each group then trains the M models in the M rounds in the frame in a round-robin manner.

The error, for a candidate multi-model federated learning algorithm $\mathcal{P}$, for each model is defined as the distance between each model's global weight at round t and its optimizer. Our analytical results show that when the objective function is strongly convex and smooth, for MFA-Rand, an upper bound on the error decays as $\mathcal{O}(1/\sqrt{T})$, and for MFA-RR, the error decays as $\mathcal{O}(1/T)$. The latter result holds when local stochastic gradient descent at the clients transitions to full gradient descent over time. This allows MFA-RR to be considerably faster than FedCluster [5], an algorithm similar to MFA-RR. Further, we study the performance gain in multi-model FL over single-model training under MFA-Rand. We show via theoretical analysis that training multiple models simultaneously can be more efficient than training them sequentially, i.e., training only one model at a time on the same set of clients. Via synthetic simulations we show that MFA-RR typically outperforms MFA-Rand. Intuitively this is because under MFA-RR, each client trains each model in every frame, while this is not necessary in the MFA-Rand. Our data-driven experiments prove that training multiple models simultaneously is advantageous over training them sequentially.

1.2 Related Work

The federated learning framework and the FedAvg algorithm was first introduced in [15]. Convergence of FedAvg has been studies extensively under convexity assumption [12] and non-convex setting [13].

Personalised FL is an area where multiple local models are trained instead of a global model. The purpose of having multiple models [7] is to have the local models reflect the specific characteristics of their data. Although there are multiple models, the underlying objective is same. This differentiates personalised FL from our setting, which involves multiple *unrelated* models.

Clustered Federated Learning proposed in [16] involved performing FedAvg and bi-partitioning client set in turn until convergence is reached. FedCluster proposed in [5] is similar to the second algorithm we propose in this work. In [5], convergence has been guaranteed in a non-convex setting. However, the advantages of a convex loss function or the effect of data sample size has not been explored in this work. Further, the clusters, here, are fixed throughout the learning process.

Training multiple models in a federated setting has been explored in [10] also. However, the setting and the model training methodology are different from ours [2]. In [10], client distribution among models has been approached as an optimization problem and a heuristic algorithm has been proposed. However, neither an optimal algorithm is provided nor any convergence guarantees.

2   Setting

We consider the setting where M models are trained simultaneously in a federated fashion. The server has global version of each of the M models and the clients have local datasets (possibly heterogeneous) for every model. The total number of clients available for training is denoted by N. We consider full device participation with the set of clients divided equally among the M models in each round. In every round, each client is assigned *exactly one model* to train. Each client receives the current global weights of the model it was assigned and performs E iterations of stochastic gradient descent locally at a fixed learning rate of η_t (which can change across rounds indexed by t) using the local dataset. It then sends the local update to its model, back to the server. The server then takes an average of the received weight updates and uses it to get the global model for the next round. Algorithm 1 details the training process of multi-model FL

Table 1. Common variables used in algorithms

Variable Name	Description
n	round number
M	Number of Models
$\mathcal{S}_T$	Set of all clients
N	Total number of clients $= |\mathcal{S}_T|$
$\mathcal{P}$	Client selection algorithm
trainModel$[c]$	Model assigned to client c
globalModel$[m]$	Global weights of model m
localModel$[m, c]$	Weights of mth model of client c

Algorithm 1. Pseudo-code for M-model training at server

    Input: $\mathcal{S}_T$, algorithm $\mathcal{P}$
    Initialize: globalModel, localModel
1: globalModel$[m] \leftarrow \mathbf{0} \ \forall \ m \in \{1, 2, .., M\}$
2: Initialise parameters relevant to algorithm $\mathcal{P}$ in round 0
3: **repeat**
4:      localModel$[m, c] \leftarrow \mathbf{0} \ \forall \ c \in \mathcal{S}_T, m \in \{1, 2, .., M\}$
5:      Update parameters relevant to algorithm $\mathcal{P}$
6:      trainModel $\leftarrow$ call function for $\mathcal{P}$ $\triangleright$ MFA_Rand(t) or MFA_RR(t)
7:      **for** $c \in \mathcal{S}_T$ **do**
8:         $m \leftarrow$ trainModel$[c]$
9:         localModel$[m, c] \leftarrow$ globalModel$[m]$
10:       localUpdate[m,c] $\leftarrow$ update for localModel$[m, c]$ after E iterations of gradient descent
11:    **end for**
12:    **for** $m \in \{1, 2, .., M\}$ **do**
13:      globalUpdate[m] $\leftarrow$ weighted average of localUpdate[m,c]
14:      globalModel$[m] \leftarrow$ globalModel$[m]$ - globalUpdate[m]
15:    **end for**
16: **until** $n =$ max iterations

---

with any client selection algorithm $\mathcal{P}$. Table 1 lists out the variables used in the training process and their purpose.

The global loss function of the mth model is denoted by $F^{(m)}(\mathbf{w})$, the local loss function of the mth model for the kth client is denoted by $F_k^{(m)}(\mathbf{w})$. For simplicity, we assume that, for every model, each client has same number of data samples, $\mathcal{N}$. We therefore have the following global objective function for m^{th} model,

$$F^{(m)}(\mathbf{w}) = \frac{1}{N} \sum_{k=1}^{N} F_k^{(m)}(\mathbf{w}). \tag{1}$$

Additionally, $\Gamma^{(m)} = \min(F^{(m)}) - \frac{1}{N} \sum_{k=1}^{N} \min(F_k^{(m)}) \geq 0$.

We make some standard assumptions on the local loss function, also used in [6,12]. These are,

Assumption 1. *All $F_k^{(m)}$ are L-smooth.*

Assumption 2. *All $F_k^{(m)}$ are μ-strongly convex.*

Assumption 3. *Stochastic gradients are bounded:* $\mathbb{E}||\nabla F_k^{(m)}(\mathbf{w}, \xi)||^2 \leq (G^{(m)})^2$.

Assumption 4. *For each client k, $F_k^{(m)}(\boldsymbol{w}) = \frac{1}{N} \sum_{y=1}^{\mathcal{N}} f_{k,y}^{(m)}(\boldsymbol{w})$, where $f_{k,y}^{(m)}$ is the loss function of the yth data point of the kth client's m^{th} model. Then for*

each $f_{k,y}^{(m)}$,

$$||\nabla f_{k,y}^{(m)}(\boldsymbol{w})||^2 \le \beta_1^{(m)} + \beta_2^{(m)}||\nabla F_k^{(m)}(\boldsymbol{w})||^2,$$

for some constants $\beta_1^{(m)} \ge 0$ and $\beta_2^{(m)} \ge 1$.

The last assumption is standard in the stochastic optimization literature [1,8].

2.1 Performance Metric

The error for a candidate multi-model federated learning algorithm $\mathcal{P}$'s is the distance between the mth model's global weight at round t, denoted by $\overline{\mathbf{w}}_{\mathcal{P},t}^{(m)}$ and the minimizer of $F^{(m)}$, denoted by $\mathbf{w}_*^{(m)}$. Formally,

$$\Delta_{\mathcal{P}}^{(m)}(t) = \mathbb{E}||\overline{\mathbf{w}}_{\mathcal{P},t}^{(m)} - \mathbf{w}_*^{(m)}||. \tag{2}$$

3 Algorithms

We consider two variants of the Multi-FedAvg algorithm proposed in [2]. For convenience we assume that N is an integral multiple of M.

3.1 Multi-FedAvg-Random (MFA-Rand)

The first variant partitions the set of clients $\mathcal{S}_T$ into M equal sized subsets $\{\mathcal{S}_1^t, \mathcal{S}_2^t, ..., \mathcal{S}_M^t\}$ in every round t. The subsets are created uniformly at random independent of all past and future choices. The M subsets are then matched to the M models with the matching chosen uniformly at random.

Algorithm 2 details the sub-process of MFA-Rand invoked when client-model assignment step (step 6) runs in Algorithm 1. An example involving 3 models over 6 rounds has been worked out in Table 2.

Table 2. MFA-Rand over 6 rounds for 3 models.

Round	Model 1	Model 2	Model 3
1	$\mathcal{S}_1^1$	$\mathcal{S}_2^1$	$\mathcal{S}_3^1$
2	$\mathcal{S}_1^2$	$\mathcal{S}_2^2$	$\mathcal{S}_3^2$
3	$\mathcal{S}_1^3$	$\mathcal{S}_2^3$	$\mathcal{S}_3^3$
4	$\mathcal{S}_1^4$	$\mathcal{S}_2^4$	$\mathcal{S}_3^4$
5	$\mathcal{S}_1^5$	$\mathcal{S}_2^5$	$\mathcal{S}_3^5$
6	$\mathcal{S}_1^6$	$\mathcal{S}_2^6$	$\mathcal{S}_3^6$

Algorithm 2. Pseudo-code for MFA-Rand

1: **procedure** . MFA_RAND(t)
2:     $\{\mathcal{S}_1^t, \mathcal{S}_2^t, ..., \mathcal{S}_M^t\}$ ←Partition $\mathcal{S}_T$ randomly into M disjoint subsets
3:     **for** $\mathcal{S} \in \{\mathcal{S}_1^t, \mathcal{S}_2^t, ..., \mathcal{S}_M^t\}$ **do**
4:         **if** $\mathcal{S} = \mathcal{S}_j^t$ **then**
5:             trainModel$[c] \leftarrow j \ \forall \ c \in \mathcal{S}$
6:         **end if**
7:     **end for**
8:     **return:** trainModel
9: **end procedure**

3.2 Multi-FedAvg-Round Robin (MFA-RR)

The second variant partitions the set of clients into M equal sized subsets once every M rounds. The subsets are created uniformly at random independent of all past and future choices. We refer to the block of M rounds during which the partitions remains unchanged as a frame. Within each frame, each of the M subsets is mapped to each model exactly once in a round-robin manner. Specifically, let the subsets created at the beginning of frame l be denoted by $\mathcal{S}_j^{(l)}$ for $1 \leq j \leq M$. Then, in the uth round in frame l for $1 \leq u \leq M$, $\mathcal{S}_j^{(l)}$ is matched to model $((j + u - 2) \mod M) + 1$. Algorithm 3 details the sub-process of MFA-RR invoked when client-model assignment step (step 6) runs in Algorithm 1. An example involving 3 models over 6 rounds has been worked out in Table 3.

Table 3. MFA-RR over 6 rounds (2 frames) for 3 models.

Round	Model 1	Model 2	Model 3
1	$\mathcal{S}_1^1$	$\mathcal{S}_2^1$	$\mathcal{S}_3^1$
2	$\mathcal{S}_3^1$	$\mathcal{S}_1^1$	$\mathcal{S}_2^1$
3	$\mathcal{S}_2^1$	$\mathcal{S}_3^1$	$\mathcal{S}_1^1$
4	$\mathcal{S}_1^2$	$\mathcal{S}_2^2$	$\mathcal{S}_3^2$
5	$\mathcal{S}_3^2$	$\mathcal{S}_1^2$	$\mathcal{S}_2^2$
6	$\mathcal{S}_2^2$	$\mathcal{S}_3^2$	$\mathcal{S}_1^2$

Remark 1. An important difference between the two algorithms is that under MFA-RR, each client-model pair is used exactly once in each frame consisting of M rounds, whereas under MFA-Rand, a specific client-model pair is not matched in M consecutive time-slots with probability $\left(1 - \frac{1}{M}\right)^M$.

Algorithm 3. Pseudo-code for MFA-RR
```
 1: procedure MFA_RR(t)
 2:     if t mod M = 1 then
 3:         l = t−1/M + 1
 4:         {S₁ˡ, S₂ˡ, ..., S_Mˡ} ← Partition S_T randomly into M disjoint subsets
 5:     end if
 6:     for S ∈ {S₁ˡ, S₂ˡ, ..., S_Mˡ} do
 7:         if S = S_jˡ then
 8:             trainModel[c] ← ((j + t − 2) mod M) + 1 ∀ c ∈ S
 9:         end if
10:     end for
11:     return: trainModel
12: end procedure
```

4   Convergence of MFA-Rand and MFA-RR

In this section, we present our analytical results for MFA-Rand and MFA-RR. We have not included the proofs due to space constraints. The proofs of the theorems can be found in the extended version [3].

Theorem 1. *or MFA-Rand, under Assumptions 1, 2, 3, 4 and with* $\eta_t = \frac{\beta}{t+\gamma}$, *where* $\beta > \frac{1}{\mu}$ *and* $\gamma > 4L\beta - 1$, *we have*

$$\Delta_{MFA\text{-}Rand}^{(m)}(t) \le \frac{\sqrt{\nu}}{\sqrt{t+\gamma}} M \ge 1 \text{ and } E \ge 1,$$

where ν *and related constants are given in Table 4*

Table 4. Values of ν, B, C and $(\sigma_k^{(m)})^2$ as used in Theorem 1

Constant	Value
ν	$\max\left\{ \frac{\beta^2(B+C)}{\beta\mu-1}, \mathbb{E}\lVert \overline{\mathbf{w}}_{MFA\text{-}Rand,1}^{(m)} - \mathbf{w}_*^{(m)} \rVert^2 (1+\gamma) \right\}$
B	$6L\Gamma^{(m)} + (1/N^2)\sum_{k=1}^{N}(\sigma_k^{(m)})^2 + 8(E-1)^2(G^{(m)})^2$
C	$\left(\frac{M-1}{N-1}\right) E^2 (G^{(m)})^2$
$(\sigma_k^{(m)})^2$	$4(\beta_1 + \beta_2(G^{(m)})^2)$

The result follows from the convergence of FedAvg with partial device participation in [12]. Note that B and C influence the lower bound on number of iterations, $T_{\text{MFA-Rand}}(\epsilon)$, required to reach a certain accuracy. Increasing the number of models, M, increases C which increases $T_{\text{MFA-Rand}}(\epsilon)$.

Theorem 2. *Consider MFA-RR, under Assumptions 1, 2, 3, 4 and $\eta_t = \frac{\beta}{1+\lfloor \frac{t}{M} \rfloor + \gamma}$, where $\beta > \frac{1}{\mu}$ and $\gamma > \beta L - 1$. Further, $\mathcal{N}_s(t)$ is the sample size for SGD iterations at clients in round t. If*

$$\frac{\mathcal{N} - \mathcal{N}_s(t)}{\mathcal{N}} \le \eta_t \left(\frac{V}{2E\sqrt{\beta_1 + \beta_2 G^2}} \right)$$

for some $V \ge 0$, $\beta_1 = \max_m \beta_1^{(m)}$ and $\beta_2 = \max_m \beta_2^{(m)}$, then,

$$\Delta_{MFA\text{-}RR}^{(m)}(t) \le \frac{\phi}{\frac{t}{M} + \gamma} \forall\, M \ge 1 \text{ and } E \ge 1,$$

where $\phi = \frac{\beta E G^{(m)}(M-1)}{M} + \max\left\{ \frac{\beta^2 (Y+Z+V)}{\beta\mu - 1}, (1+\gamma)\Delta_{MFA\text{-}RR}^{(m)}(1) \right\}$,
$Y = \frac{LG^{(m)}E^2(M-1)}{2M}$ *and* $Z = LG^{(m)}E(E-1)$.

Here, we require that the SGD iterations at clients have data sample converging sub-linearly to the full dataset. For convergence, the only requirement is $\frac{\mathcal{N} - \mathcal{N}_s(t)}{\mathcal{N}}$ to be proportional to the above defined η_t.

We observe that Y, Z and V influence the lower bound on number of iterations, $T_{\text{MFA-RR}}(\epsilon)$, required to reach a certain accuracy. Increasing the number of models, M, increases Y which increases $T_{\text{MFA-RR}}(\epsilon)$.

A special case of Theorem 2 is when we employ full gradient descent instead of SGD at clients. Naturally, in this case, $V = 0$.

Corollary 1. *For MFA-RR with full gradient descent at the clients, under Assumptions 1, 2, 3, 4 and $\eta_t = \frac{\beta}{1+\lfloor \frac{t}{M} \rfloor + \gamma}$,*

$$\Delta_{MFA\text{-}RR}^{(m)}(t) \le \frac{\phi'}{\frac{t}{M} + \gamma} \forall\, M \ge 1 \text{ and } E \ge 1,$$

where $\phi' = \frac{\beta E G^{(m)}(M-1)}{M} + \max\left\{ \frac{\beta^2 (Y+Z)}{\beta\mu - 1}, (1+\gamma)\Delta_{MFA\text{-}RR}^{(m)}(1) \right\}$,
$Y = \frac{LG^{(m)}E^2(M-1)}{2M}$ *and* $Z = LG^{(m)}E(E-1)$.

Remark 2. MFA-RR, when viewed from perspective of one of the M models, is very similar to FedCluster. However, there are some key differences between the analytical results.

First, FedCluster assumes that SGD at client has fixed bounded variance for any sample size (along with Assumption 3). This is different from Assumption 4 of ours. When Assumption 4 is coupled with Assumption 3, we get sample size dependent bound on the variance. A smaller variance is naturally expected for a larger data sample. Therefore, our assumption is less restrictive.

Second, the effect of increasing sample size (or full sample) has not been studied in [5]. We also see the effect of strong convexity on the speed of convergence. The convergence result from [5] is as follows, $\frac{1}{T}\sum_{j=0}^{T-1} \mathbb{E}\|\nabla F(\overline{\mathbf{w}}_{jM})\|^2 \le$

$\mathcal{O}\left(\frac{1}{\sqrt{T}}\right)$. If we apply the strong convexity assumption to this result and use that $\mu||x - x_*|| \leq ||\nabla F(x)||$, we get $\frac{\mu^2}{T}\sum_{j=0}^{T-1}\mathbb{E}||\overline{\mathbf{w}}_{jM} - \mathbf{w}_*||^2 \leq \mathcal{O}\left(\frac{1}{\sqrt{T}}\right)$. Applying Cauchy-Schwartz inequality on the LHS we get, $\left(\frac{1}{T}\sum_{j=0}^{T-1}\mathbb{E}||\overline{\mathbf{w}}_{jM} - \mathbf{w}_*||\right)^2 \leq \frac{1}{T}\sum_{j=0}^{T-1}\mathbb{E}||\overline{\mathbf{w}}_{jM} - \mathbf{w}_*||^2$. Finally, we have $\frac{1}{T}\sum_{j=0}^{T-1}\mathbb{E}||\overline{\mathbf{w}}_{jM} - \mathbf{w}_*|| \leq \mathcal{O}\left(\frac{1}{T^{1/4}}\right)$, for any sampling strategy. With an increasing sample size (or full sample size), we can obtain $\mathcal{O}(1/T)$ convergence. This is a significant improvement over the convergence result of FedCluster.

5   Advantage of Multi-Model FL over Single Model FL

We quantify the advantage of Multi-Model FL over single model FL by defining the gain of a candidate multi-model Federated Learning algorithm $\mathcal{P}$ over FedAvg [15], which trains only one model at a time.

Let $T_1(\epsilon)$ be the number of rounds needed by one of the M models using FedAvg to reach an accuracy level (distance of model's current weight from its optimizer) of ϵ. We assume that all M models are of similar complexity. This means we expect that each model reaches the required accuracy in roughly the same number of rounds. Therefore, cumulative number of rounds needed to ensure all M models reach an accuracy level of ϵ using FedAvg is $MT_1(\epsilon)$. Further, let the number of rounds needed to reach an accuracy level of ϵ for all M models under $\mathcal{P}$ be denoted by $T_{\mathcal{P}}(M, \epsilon)$. We define the gain of algorithm $\mathcal{P}$ for a given ϵ as

$$g_{\mathcal{P}}(M, \epsilon) = \frac{MT_1(\epsilon)}{T_{\mathcal{P}}(M, \epsilon)}. \tag{3}$$

Note that FedAvg and $\mathcal{P}$ use the same number of clients in each round, thus the comparison is fair. Further, we use the bounds in Theorem 1 and Theorem 2 as proxies for calculating $T_{\mathcal{P}}(M, \epsilon)$ for MFA-Rand and MFA-RR respectively.

Theorem 3. *When $\epsilon < \min_{m}\Delta_{MFA\text{-}Rand}^{(m)}(1)$ and $M \leq \frac{N}{2}$, the following holds for the gain of M-model MFA-Rand over running FedAvg M times*

$$g_{MFA\text{-}Rand}(M, \epsilon) > 1 \,\forall\, M > 1$$

$$\frac{d}{dM}g_{MFA\text{-}Rand}(M, \epsilon) > 0 \,\forall\, M \geq 1$$

for all $E \geq 2$ and for $E = 1$ when $N > 1 + \max_{m}\left\{\frac{6L\Gamma^{(m)}}{(G^{(m)})^2}\right\}$.

We get that gain increases with M upto $M = N/2$, after which we have the $M = N$ case. At $M = N$, each model is trained by only one client, which is too low, especially when N is large.

For $E = 1$, Theorem 3 puts a lower bound on N. However, the $E = 1$ case is rarely used in practice. One of the main advantages of FL is the lower communication cost due to local training. This benefit is not utilised when $E = 1$.

6 Simulations in Strongly Convex Setting

6.1 Simulation Framework

We take inspiration from the framework presented in [12] where a quadratic loss function, which is strongly convex, is minimized in a federated setting. We employ MFA-Rand and MFA-RR algorithms and compare their performance in this strongly convex setting. In addition to that, we also measure the gain of MFA-Rand and MFA-RR over sequentially running FedAvg in this strongly convex setting.

The global loss function is

$$F(w) = \frac{1}{2N}\left(\mathbf{w}^T\mathbf{A}\mathbf{w} - 2\mathbf{b}^T\mathbf{w}\right) + \frac{\mu}{2}||\mathbf{w}||^2, \tag{4}$$

where $N > 1$, $\mathbf{A} \in \mathbf{R}^{(Np+1)\times(Np+1)}$, $\mathbf{w} \in \mathbf{R}^{(Np+1)}$ and $\mu > 0$.

We define local loss function of the kth client as

$$F_k(\mathbf{w}) = \frac{1}{2}\left(\mathbf{w}^T\mathbf{A}_k\mathbf{w} - 2\mathbf{b}_k^T\mathbf{w}\right) + \frac{\mu}{2}||\mathbf{w}||^2, \tag{5}$$

which satisfies our problem statement $F = \frac{1}{N}\sum_{k=1}^{N} F_k$. The structure of $\mathbf{A}_k$ is such that the loss function of each client is a function of only a subset of the weights in the weight vector $\mathbf{w}$. Moreover, this subset of weights is disjoint across clients. This introduces heterogeneity across clients. A detailed explanation of the framework can be found in the full version [3], which we skip due to space constraints.

Remark 3. We simulate the minimization of a single global loss function while talking about multi-model learning. The reason behind this is that we are doing these simulations from the perspective of one of the M models. Therefore, M-model MFA-Rand boils down to sampling N/M clients independently every round while M-model MFA-RR remains the same (going over subsets $\{\mathcal{S}_1^l, \mathcal{S}_2^l, .., \mathcal{S}_M^l\}$ in frame l). Further, the gain simulations, here, assume that all M models are of the same complexity.

6.2 Comparison of MFA-Rand and MFA-RR

We consider the scenario where $N = 24$, $p = 4$ and $\mu = 2 \times 10^{-4}$. We take $E = 5$, meaning 5 local SGD iterations at clients. We track the log distance of the current global loss from the global loss minimum, that is

$$gap(t) = \log_{10}(F(w) - F(w_*)) \tag{6}$$

for 1000 rounds. We consider both constant $(\eta_t = 0.1)$ and decaying learning rate $\left(\eta_t = \frac{30}{100+t}\right)$ for $M = 2$ and $M = 12$. The constant η_t cases have similar trend as that of decaying learning rate. Due to space constraints, we present

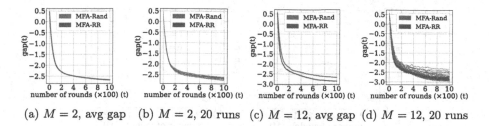

(a) $M = 2$, avg gap   (b) $M = 2$, 20 runs   (c) $M = 12$, avg gap   (d) $M = 12$, 20 runs

Fig. 1. MFA-Rand vs MFA-RR

only the cases of decaying η_t. The results of constant η_t can be found in the full version [3].

We perform 20 sample runs for MFA-Rand and MFA-RR each and compare both algorithms in terms of sample runs and their mean.

In Fig. 1a, we see that the mean performance for MFA-Rand and MFA-RR is similar. However, Fig. 1b reveals that the randomness involved in MFA-Rand is considerably higher than that in MFA-RR, showing the latter to be more reliable.

It is evident from Fig. 1c that MFA-RR, on an average, performs better than MFA-Rand when M is high. Again, Fig. 1d shows that MFA-Rand has considerably higher variance than MFA-RR.

Remark 4. In this set of simulations, each client performs full gradient descent. While the analytical upper bounds on errors suggest an order-wise difference in the performance of MFA-RR and MFA-Rand, we do not observe that significant a difference between the performance of the two algorithms. This is likely because our analysis of MFA-RR exploits the fact that each client performs full gradient descent, while the analysis of MFA-Rand adapted from [12] does not.

6.3   Gain Vs M

We test with $N = 24$ clients for $M \leq 12$ for $E = 1, 5$ and 10. Gain vs M plots in Fig. 2 show that gain increases with M for both MFA-Rand and MFA-RR.

7   Gain Results on Synthetic and Real Federated Datasets

We use Synthetic(1,1) [11] and CelebA [4,14] datasets for these experiments. The learning task in Synthetic(1,1) is multi-class logistic regression classification of feature vectors. Synthetic(1,1)-A involves 60 dimensional feature vectors classified into 5 classes while Synthetic(1,1)-B involves 30 dimensional feature vectors classified into 10 classes. CelebA dataset involves binary classification of face images based on a certain facial attribute, (for example, blond hair, smiling, etc.) using convolutional neural networks (CNNs). The dataset has many options for the facial attribute.

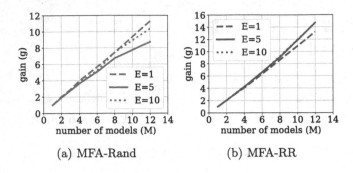

(a) MFA-Rand   (b) MFA-RR

Fig. 2. Gain vs M in strongly convex setting

The multi-model FL framework for training multiple unrelated models simultaneously was first introduced in our previous work [2]. We use the same framework for these experiments. We first find the gain vs M trend for Synthetic(1,1)-A, Synthetic(1,1)-B and CelebA. Then, we simulate a real-world scenarios where each of the M models is a different learning task.

7.1   Gain Vs M

Here, instead of giving M different tasks as the M models, we have all M models as the same underlying task. The framework, however, treats the M models as independent of each other. This ensures that the M models are of equal complexity.

We plot gain vs M for two kinds of scenarios. First, when all clients are being used in a round. Theorem 3 assumes this scenario. We call it full device participation as all clients are being used. Second, when only a sample, of the set of entire clients, is selected to be used in the round (and then distributed among the models). We call this partial device participation as a client has a non-zero probability of being idle during a round.

Full Device Participation: For both Synthetic(1,1)-A and Synthetic(1,1)-B, we have $N = 100$ clients and $T_1 = 70$. For CelebA, we have 96 clients and $T_1 = 75$.

For full device participation, we observe from Fig. 3 that gain increases with M for both Synthetic(1,1) and CelebA datasets with the trend being sub-linear in nature.

Partial Device Participation: For both Synthetic(1,1)-A and Synthetic(1,1)-B, we have $N = 200$ clients (out of which 32 are sampled every round) and $T_1 = 200$. For CelebA, we have 96 clients (out of which 24 are sampled every round) and $T_1 = 75$.

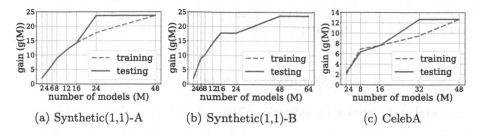

(a) Synthetic(1,1)-A   (b) Synthetic(1,1)-B   (c) CelebA

Fig. 3. Gain vs M for full device participation

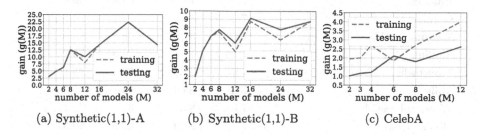

(a) Synthetic(1,1)-A   (b) Synthetic(1,1)-B   (c) CelebA

Fig. 4. Gain vs M for partial device participation

When there is partial device participation, for both datasets, we observe in Fig. 4 that gain increases with M for the most part while decreasing at some instances. We note that the gain is always more than 1.

Remark 5. It is important to note that the learning task in CelebA dataset invloves CNNs, rendering it a non-convex nature. This, however, does not severely impact the gain, as we still observe it to always increase with M for full device participation.

Remark 6. Although, Theorem 3 assumes full device participation, we see the benefit of multi-model FL when there is partial device participation. For all three datasets, gain is significant and always greater than 1.

7.2 Real-world Scenarios

We perform two types of real world examples, one involving models that are similar in some aspect and the other involving completely different models. In these experiments, T_1 denotes the number of rounds for which single model FedAvg was been run for each model. Further, T_M denotes the number of rounds of multi-model FL, after which each model an accuracy that is at least what was achieved with T_1 rounds of single model FedAvg.

Similar Models: First one tests Theorem 3 where each of the $M(=9)$ models is a binary image classification based on a unique facial attribute, using CelebA dataset. Table 5 shows the results of our experiment. Based on the values of T_1 and T_M from Table 5, we have the following for training and testing cases.

- Gain in training $= 9 \times 50/117 = \mathbf{3.846}$
- Gain in testing $= 9 \times 50/126 = \mathbf{3.571}$.

Table 5. MFA-RR training 9 different CNN models

Facial attribute for classification	Train Accuracy		Test Accuracy	
	$T_1 = 50$	$T_M = 117$	$T_1 = 50$	$T_M = 126$
Eyeglasses	74.7	84.6	69.1	71.9
Baldness	74.0	74.5	66.8	69.4
Goatee	74.3	83.5	64.7	68.7
Wearing Necklace	73.3	80.3	66.2	72.6
Smiling	72.0	78.7	76.0	79.7
Moustache	74.1	82.1	65.4	72.1
Male	77.1	85.0	58.7	63.5
Wearing Lipstick	75.4	83.8	65.9	72.7
Double Chin	75.3	83.9	63.9	69.3

Heterogeneous Models: In the second one, we do a mixed model experiment where one model is logistic regression (Synthetic(1,1) with 60 dimensional vectors into 5 classes) and the other model is CNN (binary classification of face images based on presence of eyeglasses). Based on T_1 and T_M from Table 6, we get the following values of gain for training and testing cases,

- Gain in training $= 2 \times 100/100 = \mathbf{2.0}$
- Gain in testing $= 2 \times 100/142 = \mathbf{1.41}$.

Table 6. MFA-RR training logistic regression and CNN simultaneously

Model Type	Train Accuracy		Test Accuracy	
	$T_1 = 100$	$T_M = 100$	$T_1 = 100$	$T_M = 142$
Logistic Regression	51.9	52.4	52.8	55.6
Convolutional NN	86.7	87.2	75.8	77.5

8   Conclusions

In this work, we focus on the problem of using Federated Learning to train multiple independent models simultaneously using a shared pool of clients. We propose two variants of the widely studied FedAvg algorithm, in the multi-model setting, called MFA-Rand and MFA-RR, and show their convergence. In case of MFA-RR, we show that an increasing data sample size (for client side SGD iterations), helps improve the speed of convergence greatly $\left(\mathcal{O}\left(\frac{1}{T}\right)\right.$ instead of $\left.\mathcal{O}\left(\frac{1}{T^{1/4}}\right)\right)$. Further, we propose a performance metric to access the advantage of multi-model FL over single model FL. We characterize conditions under which running MFA-Rand for M models simultaneously is advantageous over running single model FedAvg for each model sequentially. We perform experiments in strongly convex and convex settings to corroborate our analytical results. By running experiments in a non-convex setting, we see the benefits of multi-model FL in deep learning. We also run experiments that are out of the scope of the proposed setting, namely, the partial device participation experiments and the real world scenarios. Here also we see an advantage in training multiple models simultaneously.

References

1. Bertsekas, D.P., Tsitsiklis, J.N.: Neuro-dynamic programming: an overview. In: Proceedings of the 1995 34th IEEE Conference on Decision and Control, vol. 1, pp. 560–564. IEEE (1995)
2. Bhuyan, N., Moharir, S.: Multi-model federated learning. In: 2022 14th International Conference on COMmunication Systems & NETworkS (COMSNETS), pp. 779–783. IEEE (2022)
3. Bhuyan, N., Moharir, S., Joshi, G.: Multi-model federated learning with provable guarantees (2022). https://doi.org/10.48550/ARXIV.2207.04330, https://arxiv.org/abs/2207.04330
4. Caldas, S., et al.: Leaf: a benchmark for federated settings. arXiv preprint arXiv:1812.01097 (2018)
5. Chen, C., Chen, Z., Zhou, Y., Kailkhura, B.: FedCluster: boosting the convergence of federated learning via cluster-cycling. In: 2020 IEEE International Conference on Big Data (Big Data), pp. 5017–5026 (2020). https://doi.org/10.1109/BigData50022.2020.9377960
6. Cho, Y.J., Wang, J., Joshi, G.: Client selection in federated learning: convergence analysis and power-of-choice selection strategies. arXiv preprint arXiv:2010.01243 (2020)
7. Eichner, H., Koren, T., McMahan, B., Srebro, N., Talwar, K.: Semi-cyclic stochastic gradient descent. In: International Conference on Machine Learning, pp. 1764–1773. PMLR (2019)
8. Friedlander, M.P., Schmidt, M.: Hybrid deterministic-stochastic methods for data fitting. SIAM J. Sci. Comput. **34**(3), A1380–A1405 (2012)
9. Kairouz, P., et al.: Advances and open problems in federated learning. Found. Trends® Mach. Learn. **14**(1–2), 1–210 (2021)
10. Li, C., Li, C., Zhao, Y., Zhang, B., Li, C.: An efficient multi-model training algorithm for federated learning. In: 2021 IEEE Global Communications Conference (GLOBECOM), pp. 1–6 (2021). https://doi.org/10.1109/GLOBECOM46510.2021.9685230
11. Li, T., Sanjabi, M., Beirami, A., Smith, V.: Fair resource allocation in federated learning. arXiv preprint arXiv:1905.10497 (2019)

12. Li, X., Huang, K., Yang, W., Wang, S., Zhang, Z.: On the convergence of FedAvg on Non-IID data. arXiv preprint arXiv:1907.02189 (2019)
13. Li, X., Yang, W., Wang, S., Zhang, Z.: Communication efficient decentralized training with multiple local updates. arXiv preprint arXiv:1910.09126 5 (2019)
14. Liu, Z., Luo, P., Wang, X., Tang, X.: Deep learning face attributes in the wild. In: Proceedings of the IEEE International Conference on Computer Vision, pp. 3730–3738 (2015)
15. McMahan, B., Moore, E., Ramage, D., Hampson, S., y Arcas, B.A.: Communication-efficient learning of deep networks from decentralized data. In: Artificial Intelligence and Statistics, pp. 1273–1282. PMLR (2017)
16. Sattler, F., Müller, K.R., Samek, W.: Clustered federated learning: model-agnostic distributed multitask optimization under privacy constraints. IEEE Trans. Neural Netw. Learn. Syst. 32(8), 3710–3722 (2020)
17. Wang, J., Joshi, G.: Adaptive communication strategies to achieve the best error-runtime trade-off in local-update SGD. In: Talwalkar, A., Smith, V., Zaharia, M. (eds.) Proceedings of Machine Learning and Systems, vol. 1, pp. 212–229 (2019). https://proceedings.mlsys.org/paper/2019/file/c8ffe9a587b126f152ed3d89a146b445-Paper.pdf

A Large Deviations Model for Latency Outage for URLLC

Salah Eddine Elayoubi[1]([✉]), Nathalie Naddeh[2,3], Tijani Chahed[2],
and Sana Ben Jemaa[3]

[1] Université Paris Saclay, CentraleSupelec, L2S, CNRS, Gif-Sur-Yvette, France
salaheddine.elayoubi@centralesupelec.fr
[2] Institut Polytechnique de Paris, Telecom SudParis, Palaiseau, France
{nathalie.naddeh,tijani.chahed}@telecom-sudparis.eu
[3] Orange Labs, Chatillon, France
sana.benjemaa@orange.com

Abstract. In this paper, we develop an analytical model for radio resource dimensioning for latency-critical services in 5G networks. URLLC (Ultra-Reliable Low Latency Communications) service is introduced in the 5G networks to respond to the requirements of critical applications such as self driving cars, industry 4.0, etc. Its stringent requirements in terms of latency and reliability are challenging to meet and are usually tackled by resource over-dimensioning. In this paper, we develop large deviation bounds for the outage probability i.e., the probability that the packet delay exceeds a given target. Our numerical applications show that the bounds are sufficiently tight for mastering over-dimensioning. We then develop a resource dimensioning framework based on the developed bounds and apply it to a large scale system level simulator. Our simulation results show that the developed model, when coupled with field-based radio condition distributions, allows achieving the reliability targets with acceptable cost in terms of resource consumption.

Keywords: URLLC · large deviation bounds · latency · reliability · 5G Networks · dimensioning

1 Introduction

1.1 Context

Ultra-Reliable Low Latency Communications (URLLC) was introduced in the 3GPP 5G-NR (Third Generation Partnership Project Fifth Generation New-Radio) standardization [1,2] to tackle critical services such as autonomous driving, mission critical applications, smart grid, etc. Depending on the use case, the Quality of Service (QoS) requirements vary, such as $1ms$ and $99,999\%$ delay and reliability constraints [5]. Several features were introduced in the 3GPP standardization to help reach URLLC low latency and high reliability constraints.

© ICST Institute for Computer Sciences, Social Informatics and Telecommunications Engineering 2023
Published by Springer Nature Switzerland AG 2023. All Rights Reserved
E. Hyytiä and V. Kavitha (Eds.): VALUETOOLS 2022, LNICST 482, pp. 223–239, 2023.
https://doi.org/10.1007/978-3-031-31234-2_14

For instance, on the Medium Access Control (MAC) layer, short Transmission Time Interval (TTI) or a mini slot is applied which allows scheduling over 2, 4 or 7 Orthogonal Frequency Division Multiplexing (OFDM) symbols. These techniques enable latency reduction on the radio level [19], ensuring that the radio latency (i.e., the time between the packet generation and its decoding by the base station) is below 0.5 ms. However, the underlying assumption is that resources are always available and latency is only due to the packet alignment, scheduling grant reception, over-the-air transmission and packet decoding. When resources are scarce or traffic load is high, an additional component occurs is the queuing delay, i.e. the delay before a resource is available for the packet to be scheduled. This queuing delay has to be added to the other delay components and taken into consideration in the overall radio latency. When URLLC packets are in competition with large enhanced Mobile Broadband (eMBB) packets, the problem of queuing is solved by the feature of preemptive scheduling, where URLLC packets are served immediately upon arrival by preempting part of eMBB resources, provided that the resources are available and ready to serve URLLC packets, with the adequate numerology [16,17]. When URLLC packets are in competition with other URLLC packets, preemption is not possible and over-reservation of resources may be needed. When traffic is periodic, semi-persistent scheduling (SPS) is proposed and resources are pre-reserved for each of the users [11,15]. For sporadic traffic, SPS is highly inefficient and mastering the queuing delay for URLLC is still an open problem.

In this paper, we develop a mathematical model for computing the outage probability (i.e. the probability that the packet delay is larger than a target). Our model is based on the large deviations theory [21], and consists in finding an upper bound of the outage probability. We develop several bounds, suitable for the URLLC sporadic traffic model and show the tighter bounds in two cases: a very stringent delay budget where the radio procedures do not give room for further queuing delays, and a less stringent case where several slots are available for queuing within the delay budget. Our numerical results show that the derived models can be used for resource dimensioning and do not lead to an excessive over-dimensioning.

1.2 Related Works

A large number of papers in the literature deal with the mechanisms that allow reaching low latency on the radio interface, when multiplexing URLLC with eMBB. Authors in [10,18] examine the impact of changing the TTI length dynamically on serving the URLLC packets while meeting the deadline, while guarantying eMBB performance. Other works discuss the semi-persistent scheduling approach [15]. [11] computed the amount of resources to be reserved for URLLC users, knowing a deterministic traffic pattern and a target reliability. Preemptive scheduling has been analyzed in several studies. Authors in [17] present a new scheduling algorithm where URLLC traffic is dynamically multiplexed through puncturing the enhanced Mobile Broad-Band (eMBB) traffic, with added recovery mechanism for punctured eMBB packets. In [16], the authors propose a joint optimization framework for URLLC and eMBB with preemptive scheduling in order to achieve better URLLC performance while limiting the impact on eMBB throughput. Also the authors in [3] propose a deep reinforcement learning approach for preemptive scheduling.

Priority scheduling has also been the subject of a large pan of the literature. In [8], the authors proposed a priority-based resource reservation mechanism aiming to reduce URLLC delay and packet loss, while limiting the impact on eMBB. The authors in [13] proposed a multiplexing method for eMBB and URLLC with service isolation, formulated as an Adaptive Modulation and Coding (AMC) optimization problem.

In the above-discussed body of works, the objective was to achieve flexibility for serving URLLC in the presence of lower priority eMBB services, always with the assumption of a sufficiently large amount of resources in the cell. However, in some industrial situations, URLLC traffic load may be large and the (local) network operators have to provision sufficient resources while avoiding over-dimensioning, and preemption between URLLC users is not possible. In this context, many works proposed grant-free contention-based channel access for URLLC in the uplink. Authors in [20] proposed to send these replicas in a contention-based manner on different frequency resources on consecutive time slots, while in [9] the authors considered a more flexible scheme where replicas can be sent on any of the available time-frequency resources. These schemes focused on the uplink, as the centralized orthogonal resource allocation in the downlink is supposed to avoid collisions between packets. However, in high traffic regimes, the problem of resource dimensioning is still open and it is the focus of the current paper. There have been attempts for using classical queuing theory methods for dimensioning the system, but they needed to make strong hypotheses on the traffic and system. For instance, [7] proposed an M/M/1 model that is based on the assumption of Poisson arrivals of packets and an exponential model for the variation of packet sizes due to different radio conditions. In [14], the authors make use of M/M/m/K queue to model the system reliability for a worst case scenario where users are assumed to be at the cell edge. [12] relaxed the Exponential assumption for the service rate and adopted an M/G/1 model with vacations, but with two restrictive assumptions. First, the "General" service model is due to different packet sizes and not different radio conditions, and second, packets are supposed to be served by one server in continuous time, while the 5G NR system can multiplex packets in the spectrum dimension (several servers) and is time-slotted.

With regards to these limitations and the difficulty to find realistic and tractable queuing models for URLLC, we adopt a large deviations approach that is suitable to analyze the tail of the system, corresponding to the URLLC outage region. We make use of two types of simulations for validating the model. First, we compare the model to numerical simulations of the discrete-time Markov process describing the system evolution. And next, we implement the dimensioning framework based on the analytical model in a large scale system level simulator, and observe the URLLC performance in a realistic setting.

1.3   Paper Organization

The remainder of the paper is organized as follows: In Sect. 2, we describe the outage model based on the large deviations theory. Section 3 compares the model with respect to numerical resolution based on a realistic radio distribution. Section 4 applies the proposed dimensioning framework to a large scale system level simulator and quantifies the resulting resource reservation gap. Section 5 concludes the paper.

2   Outage Model

2.1   System and Traffic Model

For developing the analytical model, we consider a 5G cell with U URLLC users and with a 5G-NR like frame, where time/frequency resources are organized into Resource Blocks (RB) and (mini-)slots. The slot is of size T ms and there are R reserved RBs of the total bandwidth, dedicated for URLLC traffic. We consider a sporadic traffic model, i.e. a user is active (generates a packet) during a slot with probability q.

There are I different Modulation and Coding Scheme (MCS), numbered 0 to I, and a packet belongs to a user whose MCS is i with probability p_i. We assume that the MCS distribution in the cell is known. e.g. from field measurements. If a user uses MCS i, each of its packets consumes r_i RBs[1]. Without loss of generality, we suppose that the MCSs are sorted following increasing spectral efficiency, i.e. $r_0 > ... > r_I$.

2.2   Outage Bounds for a Tight Delay Budget (No Waiting)

Let $X_u(t)$ be the number of requested RBs by user $u \in 1, 2, ..., U$ during slot t. $X_u(t)$ are i.i.d. random variable that take the following values:

$$X_u(t) = \begin{cases} 0, & \text{with prob. } 1 - q \\ r_i & \text{with prob. } qp_i \end{cases} \tag{1}$$

The total number of resources requested by packets generated in a given slot is then given by:

$$\bar{R}(t) = \sum_{u=1}^{U} X_u(t) \tag{2}$$

---

[1] If the spectral efficiency of MCS i is equal to e_i (bit/s/Hz), a packet is of size P bit, and one RB spans over b Hz, the amount of consumed RBs is computed by:

$$r_i = \lceil \frac{P}{e_i bT} \rceil,$$

where $\lceil x \rceil$ is the smaller integer larger than x.

The outage occurs when the number of needed resources exceeds the amount of reserved resources. The objective is to ensure that the outage probability is below a small positive value ϵ:

$$Pr(\sum_{u=1}^{U} X_u > R) \leq \epsilon \tag{3}$$

Problem (3) can be solved using Large deviation techniques for which several bounds exist. We start by computing the mean and standard deviation of X_u and $\bar{R}$. For X_u, the mean value is:

$$\mu_0 = E[X_u] = q \sum_{i=1}^{I} p_i r_i \tag{4}$$

and the variance is:

$$\sigma_0^2 = E[X_u^2] - \mu_0^2 = q \sum_{i=1}^{I} p_i r_i^2 - q^2 (\sum_{i=1}^{I} p_i r_i)^2 \tag{5}$$

As for the total consumption of RBs, its mean and variance are $\mu = U\mu_0$ and $\sigma^2 = U\sigma_0^2$, respectively.

Define $x_u = X_u - \mu_0$. The outage constraint (3) can be rewritten as:

$$Pr(\sum_{u=1}^{U} x_u > R - \mu) \leq \epsilon \tag{6}$$

Define now $s = \frac{R-\mu}{\sigma}$, the constraint can be rewritten as:

$$Pr(\sum_{u=1}^{U} x_u > s\sigma) \leq \epsilon \tag{7}$$

Bienaymé-Chebychev Bound. The well-known Bienaymé-Chebychev bound [21] can be applied. Taking the bound as equal to ϵ, we have:

$$Pr(\sum_{u=1}^{U} x_u > s\sigma) \leq \frac{1}{s^2}, \tag{8}$$

leading to the required reservation:

$$R_1 = \mu + \frac{\sigma}{\sqrt{\epsilon}} \tag{9}$$

Bernstein Bound. The Bienaymé-Chebychev bound is known to be weak for a sum of random variables. x_i's have the advantage of being independent and bounded, we can apply more tight bounds. Let M be the upper bound of x_i:

$$M = r_0 - q \sum_{i=1}^{I} r_j p_j \tag{10}$$

Bernstein [6] proved that the sum of bounded independent random variables is bounded by:

$$Pr(\sum_{u=1}^{U} x_u > s\sigma) \leq \exp\left[-\frac{s^2}{2 + \frac{2}{3}\frac{M}{\sigma}s} \right] \tag{11}$$

Substituting the bound by the target, this leads to the reservation:

$$R_2 = \mu - \frac{M \ln \epsilon}{3} + \frac{\sigma}{2} \sqrt{\frac{4M^2 (\ln \epsilon)^2}{9\sigma^2} - 8 \ln \epsilon} \tag{12}$$

Bennet Bounds. Bennet [4] proposed two enhancements on Bernstein's bound, as follows.

First, the bound can be computed as:

$$Pr(\sum_{u=1}^{U} x_u > s\sigma) \leq \exp\left[-\frac{s^2}{1 + \frac{1}{3}\frac{M}{\sigma}s + \sqrt{1 + \frac{2}{3}\frac{M}{\sigma}s}} \right] \tag{13}$$

Leading to the reservation of resources:

$$R_3 = \sigma s_3 + \mu \tag{14}$$

with s_3 solution of the following equation:

$$\frac{s^2}{\ln \epsilon} + 1 + \frac{1}{3}\frac{M}{\sigma}s + \sqrt{1 + \frac{2}{3}\frac{M}{\sigma}s} = 0 \tag{15}$$

Bennet [4] also proposed another bound as follows:

$$Pr(\sum_{u=1}^{U} x_u > s\sigma) \leq e^{\frac{s\sigma}{M}} \left(1 + s\frac{M}{\sigma}\right)^{-(\frac{s\sigma}{M} + \frac{\sigma^2}{M^2})} \tag{16}$$

Leading to the reservation of resources:

$$R_4 = \sigma s_4 + \mu \tag{17}$$

with s_4 solution of the following equation:

$$e^{\frac{s\sigma}{M}} \left(1 + s\frac{M}{\sigma}\right)^{-(\frac{s\sigma}{M} + \frac{\sigma^2}{M^2})} = \epsilon \tag{18}$$

2.3   Model with Waiting

We consider now the case with a looser constraint, i.e. where a packet can stay for $\delta > 1$ slots in the system before its delay budget expires (e.g. 7 slots for a target delay of 1 ms and a slot length of 0.144 ms). We consider the same traffic model as in the previous section.

Outage Probability Formulation. In a given slot, numbered 0, knowing that there are R reserved RBs, the "overflow" of resources, i.e. the amount of RB's that will be needed in the future to serve the backlogged traffic is equal to:

$$B_{(0)} = \left(\sum_{u=1}^{U} X_{(0),u} + B_{(-1)} - R \right)^{+} \tag{19}$$

where $X_{(0),u}$ is the amount of resources required for serving the packet of user u generated at slot 0. $B_{(-1)}$ is the amount of overflow traffic from the previous slot (denoted by slot -1), and $(x)^{+} = \max(x, 0)$. Recursively, for a previous slot $-j$, the overflow is computed by:

$$B_{(-j)} = \left(\sum_{u=1}^{U} X_{(-j),u} + B_{(-j-1)} - R \right)^{+} \tag{20}$$

with $X_{(-j),u}$ the amount of resources required for serving the packet of user u generated at slot $-j$.

The outage probability is computed by the probability that the new packet has to wait for more than δ slots:

$$Pr(B_{(0)} > \delta R) \leq \epsilon \tag{21}$$

Approximate Outage Probability. We consider a system with memory of m slots, i.e. the probability that there are packets waiting from more than m slots is negligible. In this case, we neglect the term $B_{(-m-1)}$ in the overflow. Summing up to the previous m slots, and replacing $\left(\sum_{u=1}^{U} X_{(-j),u} + B_{(-j-1)} - R \right)^{+}$ by $\sum_{u=1}^{U} X_{(-j),u} + B_{(-j-1)} - R$, the outage constraint becomes:

$$Pr(\sum_{j=1}^{m} \sum_{u=1}^{U} X_{(-j),u} > (\delta + m + 1)R) \leq \epsilon \tag{22}$$

This approximation is twofold. First, by neglecting the overflow from slots that are older than m, we suppose that the system is not in overload for a large time. This assumption is reasonable for the URLLC regime. We will see in the numerical applications that a memory of 10 slots gives a good approximation. Second, by removing the $(.)^{+}$ operator from the overflow of Eq. 20, we allow the overflow to be negative as if the whole mR resources were used to serve the traffic arriving within the previous m slots. We shall test the validity of this approximation in numerical applications.

The delay constraint (22) can then be rewritten as:

$$Pr(\sum_{j=1}^{m}\sum_{u=1}^{U}X_{-(j),u} > (\delta + m + 1)R) \leq \epsilon \tag{23}$$

This constraint compares the sum of $U(m+1)$ independent variables with a threshold; it can be rewritten as:

$$Pr(\sum_{j=1}^{m}\sum_{u=1}^{U}x_{-(j),u} > \hat{\sigma}s) \leq \epsilon \tag{24}$$

with $\hat{\sigma} = \sqrt{U(m+1)}\sigma_0$ and

$$s = \frac{(\delta + m + 1)R - (m + 1)U\mu_0}{\hat{\sigma}}, \tag{25}$$

$x_{-(j),u} = X_{-(j),u} - \mu_0$ are centered independent random variables bounded by M computed as in Eq. (10).

We can apply the same bounds of Eqs. (8), (11), (13) and (16) on the system.

3   Numerical Applications

We now compare the analytical bounds with numerical simulations. We developed a simple simulator for the cell scheduler that operates as follows:

- Inputs: the simulator takes as input the traffic profile (number of users, average number of packets per second per user) and the radio conditions. For a realistic setting, we consider a typical MCS distribution issued from a system level simulator, as discussed later. The MCS distribution is illustrated in Fig. 1.
- Traffic generation: the time is divided into slots of size $T = 0.144$ ms and there are R reserved RBs for URLLC. In each slot, each user generates a packet following a Bernoulli law with parameter q, and if a packet is generated, it chooses at random an MCS following the input distribution. Packets are all of equal size (96 bits).
- Scheduler: Packets are served following a First-Come-First-Serve (FCFS) discipline. When a packet is generated, it is put at the end of the queue. A time slot is filled with the packets at the head of queue until all of the R RBs are occupied or the queue is empty. When a packet cannot be scheduled on 1 slot as the remaining resources are not sufficient, it can be scheduled on two consecutive slots.
- Output: For each of the packets, it is counted as an outage if the delay between its generation and its service exceeds a threshold.

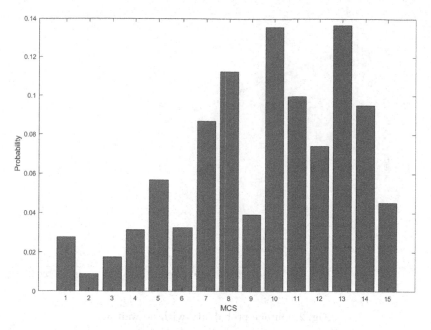

Fig. 1. MCS distribution.

3.1 Model with No Waiting

We start by the case of a very stringent delay budget, where there is no room for waiting. We illustrate in Fig. 2 the outage probability obtained by simulation, and using the bounds of Eqs. (8), (11), (13) and (16). The parameters taken for this simulation are: $U = 20$, $q = 0.072$. First, all the bounds give an outage probability that is larger than the simulation. Second, it can be observed that the second bound of Bennet (Eq. (16)) gives the closest bound to the simulation as it is adapted to a sum of independent variables. Third, the simulation stops for an outage rate that is below 10^{-7} as the outage event becomes too rare to be simulated.

Based on these results, we investigate the amount of over-dimensioning required when using the analytical bounds, compared with the simulation. For a target outage probability of 10^{-5}, the required reservation is of $R = 85$ RBs, based on simulations, while the Bennet bound (16) required 115 RBs. The Chebychev bound is so loose that the reservation requirement exceeds 500 RBs.

3.2 Model with Queuing Delay

We now move to a more common use case where there is room for multiple slots for queuing within the delay budget. Here we take the threshold on the waiting delay equal to 1 ms. Note that the threshold depends on the service requirements

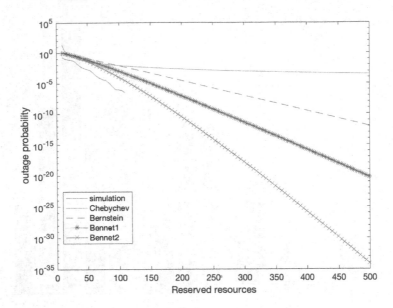

Fig. 2. Outage probability with no waiting.

and the radio settings, and the waiting delay threshold has to be computed as the difference between the service delay budget and the other non compressible delays (alignment, propagation, decoding, back-haul etc.).

We consider the same MCS distribution as previously. We first start by studying the impact of the approximation of finite memory m on the bound, considering the most tight bound of Bennet (16). We can observe in Fig. 3 that the amount of required reservation increases with m, and stabilizes starting from $m > 9$. We consider in the following $m = 10$.

We compare in Fig. 4 the analytical bounds with simulation results. We see that the difference between the Bennet2 bound achieves the closest bound to the simulation and that the gap is reduced compared to the no-waiting case.

In order to compare with queuing models used in the state of the art, we implement the M/M/c/K model proposed in [14], where arrivals are Poisson, service is approximated as exponential, c is the number of servers, and K is the maximum number of packets the system can hold. K is computed in [14] as the number of packets upon arrival that discourages a packet from being queued as it corresponds to an outage ($K = c\delta$ in our case for a fair comparison). However, the number of servers is not known as it is computed as the number of packets that can be served in parallel, while this number depends, for a fixed R, on the MCS. [14] considered the worst case, i.e. when all users are at the cell edge and computed c as the ratio between R and the number of resources occupied by a packet generated at cell edge (MCS 1). As this is too pessimistic, we consider

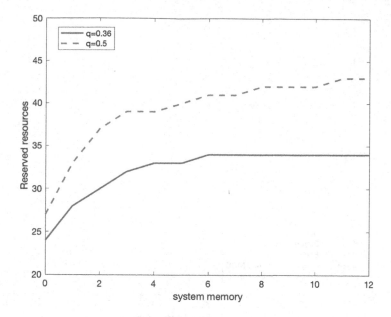

Fig. 3. Required resource reservation for a target reliability (1 ms budget).

the MCS used by the worst 10% of users (90% percentile), that corresponds to MCS 5. Figure 4 shows that the bound is too loose (very large outage). One can try to consider the average resource consumption instead of the worst case or the percentile ($c = \lceil \frac{R}{\sum_{i=1}^{I} r_i} \rceil$), but Fig. 4 shows that this method cannot be used for URLLC resource provisioning, as it sometimes largely underestimates the outage (the step-like behaviour comes from the necessity top have an integer number of servers in the M/M/c/K model).

The model can also be used for resource dimensioning, i.e. for computing the resource reservation for ensuring the target performance. Figure 5 compares the amount of reserved resources for the analytical bound (16) with the numerical simulations and shows that the bound is very tight.

4   Resource Dimensioning Framework

Having validated our analytical model based on simple numerical simulations, we now propose a resource dimensioning framework and test it on a large system level simulator.

4.1   Architecture

Figure 6 illustrates the architecture for implementing the proposed scheme. We propose that the resource allocation module for the URLLC slice be implemented within the Network Slice Subnet Management Function (NSSMF). Within the

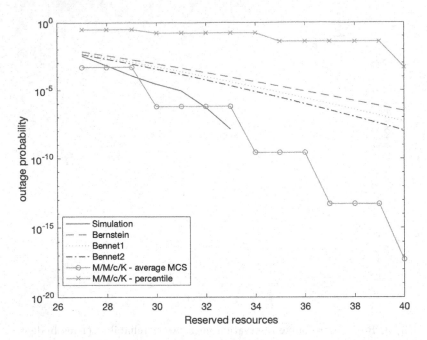

Fig. 4. Outage probability for the delayed case ($U = 20$, $q = 0.36$).

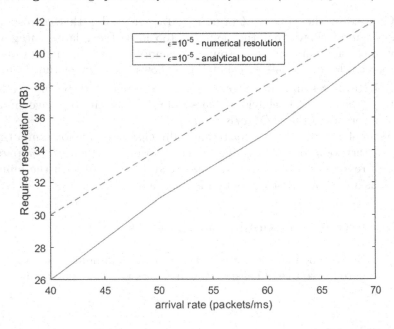

Fig. 5. Required resource reservation for a target reliability (1 ms budget).

NSSMF, two modules allow the dynamic management of the slices. First, an MCS distribution module allows building a per-gNodeB MCS distribution. Second, we use this distribution as input for the resource dimensioning module that takes as input the traffic (number of URLLC users, number of packets/user/s) and computes the needed amount of resources to be reserved for the URLLC slice in each of the gNodeBs, using the analytical model (Eq. (16)). The system applies the new configuration, dynamically changing depending on the NSSMF updates (traffic and radio conditions change).

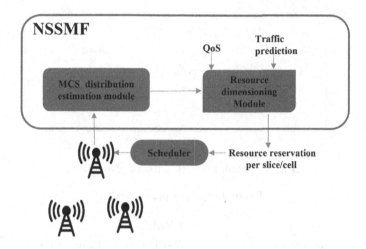

Fig. 6. Proposed architecture for the dimensioning framework.

4.2   System Level Simulation Results

Figure 7 illustrates the network created by the simulator, showing the positions of the gNodeBs and some URLLC UEs.

We perform three types of simulations. The simulation and configuration parameters are presented in Table 1.

In the first simulation, for each traffic intensity, we perform a series of simulations, changing the amount of reserved resources in each cell until reaching the target of 10^{-5} outage. This gives the system simulation resource reservation, which is not applicable in practice as it requires a large number of trials on the up and running network. Second, we apply our dimensioning framework where we extract the radio conditions distribution from the cells, and then apply the proposed analytical model to obtain the required reservation. Finally we simulate the M/M/c/K model with 90% percentile MCS. The second set of simulations is based on this analytical reservation (Eq. (16)) to verify that the outage is far below the target. Figure 8 compares the reservation obtained by extensive simulations with the analytical model and the M/M/c/K model [14] with a cell edge MCS (worst 10% of users). We first observe that the M/M/c/K model leads to

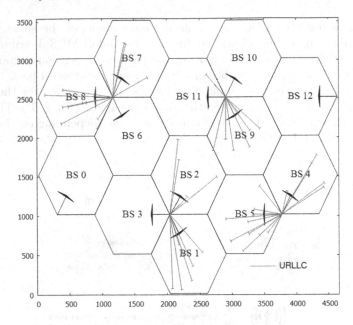

Fig. 7. Urban network with 13 gNodeBs.

Table 1. System parameters.

Parameters	URLLC
Environment	3GPP Urban Macro (UMa)
Number of gNodeBs	13
Bandwidth	20 Mhz
Sub-Carrier-Spacing (SCS)	15 Khz
Number of RBs	106
TTI size (ms)	0.143
Traffic model	Bernoulli
Packet size	96 bits
Speed	Static

a very large over-dimensioning. As of our proposed bound, we observe an average over-dimensioning ratio of 15% compared to the system simulator, which is acceptable for guaranteeing URLLC reliability, knowing that the bound is computed based only on the knowledge of the average traffic intensity and radio conditions.

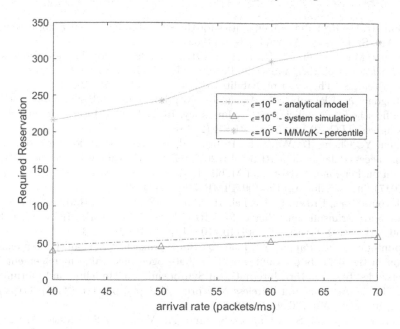

Fig. 8. System simulations versus analytical model.

5   Conclusion

In this paper, we developed a performance evaluation framework for URLLC traffic in 5G networks based on large deviation bounds. We consider the queuing delay and derive the outage probability bound, i.e. the probability that the delay exceeds a given target. We first compared the analytical model with a numerical simulation of the scheduler and showed that the proposed bound is tight. We then proposed a framework for resource dimensioning, that combines the analytical model with measurements of radio conditions issued from the network. We tested the proposed framework on a large scale system level simulator and showed that the URLLC targets are achieved with an acceptable over-dimensioning cost and a low management overhead.

References

1. 3GPP, TS 23.501: System Architecture for the 5G System (2017). Version 15.0.0 Release 15
2. 3GPP, TR 38.912: 5G; Study on New Radio (NR) access technology (2018). Version 15.0.0 Release 15
3. Alsenwi, M., Tran, N., Bennis, M., Pandey, S., Bairagi, A., Hong, C.S.: Intelligent resource slicing for eMBB and URLLC coexistence in 5G and beyond: a deep reinforcement learning based approach. IEEE Trans. Wirel. Commun. **PP**, 1 (2021). https://doi.org/10.1109/TWC.2021.3060514

4. Bennett, G.: Probability inequalities for the sum of independent random variables. J. Am. Stat. Assoc. **57**(297), 33–45 (1962)
5. Bennis, M., Debbah, M., Poor, H.V.: Ultra reliable and low-latency wireless communication: tail, risk, and scale. Proc. IEEE **106**(10), 1834–1853 (2018)
6. Bernšteın, S.: Theory of probability. Moscow. MR0169758 (1927)
7. Chagdali, A., Elayoubi, S.E., Masucci, A.M., Simonian, A.: Performance of URLLC traffic scheduling policies with redundancy. In: 2020 32nd International Teletraffic Congress (ITC 32), pp. 55–63. IEEE (2020)
8. Chen, Y., Cheng, L., Wang, L.: Prioritized resource reservation for reducing random access delay in 5G URLLC. In: 2017 IEEE 28th Annual International Symposium on Personal, Indoor, and Mobile Radio Communications (PIMRC), pp. 1–5 (2017). https://doi.org/10.1109/PIMRC.2017.8292695
9. Elayoubi, S.E., Brown, P., Deghel, M., Galindo-Serrano, A.: Radio resource allocation and retransmission schemes for URLLC over 5G networks. IEEE JSAC **37**(4), 896–904 (2019). https://doi.org/10.1109/JSAC.2019.2898783
10. Fountoulakis, E., Pappas, N., Liao, Q., Suryaprakash, V., Yuan, D.: An examination of the benefits of scalable TTI for heterogeneous traffic management in 5G networks. In: 2017 15th International Symposium on Modeling and Optimization in Mobile, Ad Hoc, and Wireless Networks (WiOpt), pp. 1–6 (2017). https://doi.org/10.23919/WIOPT.2017.7959871
11. Han, Y., Elayoubi, S.E., Galindo-Serrano, A., Varma, V.S., Messai, M.: Periodic radio resource allocation to meet latency and reliability requirements in 5G networks. In: 2018 IEEE 87th Vehicular Technology Conference (VTC Spring), pp. 1–6. IEEE (2018)
12. Jang, H., Kim, J., Yoo, W., Chung, J.M.: URLLC mode optimal resource allocation to support HARQ in 5G wireless networks. IEEE Access **8**, 126797–126804 (2020)
13. Korrai, P., Lagunas, E., Sharma, S.K., Chatzinotas, S., Bandi, A., Ottersten, B.: A RAN resource slicing mechanism for multiplexing of eMBB and URLLC services in OFDMA based 5G wireless networks. IEEE Access **8**, 45674–45688 (2020). https://doi.org/10.1109/ACCESS.2020.2977773
14. Li, C.P., Jiang, J., Chen, W., Ji, T., Smee, J.: 5G ultra-reliable and low-latency systems design. In: 2017 European Conference on Networks and Communications (EuCNC), pp. 1–5 (2017). https://doi.org/10.1109/EuCNC.2017.7980747
15. Li, Z., Uusitalo, M.A., Shariatmadari, H., Singh, B.: 5G URLLC: design challenges and system concepts. In: 2018 15th International Symposium on Wireless Communication Systems (ISWCS), pp. 1–6. IEEE (2018)
16. Morcos, M., Mhedhbi, M., Galindo-Serrano, A., Eddine Elayoubi, S.: Optimal resource preemption for aperiodic URLLC traffic in 5G networks. In: 2020 IEEE 31st Annual International Symposium on Personal, Indoor and Mobile Radio Communications, pp. 1–6 (2020). https://doi.org/10.1109/PIMRC48278.2020.9217111
17. Pedersen, K.I., Pocovi, G., Steiner, J., Khosravirad, S.R.: Punctured scheduling for critical low latency data on a shared channel with mobile broadband. In: 2017 IEEE 86th Vehicular Technology Conference (VTC-Fall), pp. 1–6 (2017). https://doi.org/10.1109/VTCFall.2017.8287951
18. Pedersen, K.I., Berardinelli, G., Frederiksen, F., Mogensen, P., Szufarska, A.: A flexible 5G frame structure design for frequency-division duplex cases. IEEE Commun. Mag. **54**(3), 53–59 (2016). https://doi.org/10.1109/MCOM.2016.7432148
19. Sachs, J., Wikstrom, G., Dudda, T., Baldemair, R., Kittichokechai, K.: 5G radio network design for ultra-reliable low-latency communication. IEEE Netw. **32**(2), 24–31 (2018). https://doi.org/10.1109/MNET.2018.1700232

20. Singh, B., Tirkkonen, O., Li, Z., Uusitalo, M.A.: Contention-based access for ultra-reliable low latency uplink transmissions. IEEE Wirel. Commun. Lett. **7**(2), 182–185 (2018)
21. Stroock, D.W.: An Introduction to the Theory of Large Deviations. Springer, Heidelberg (2012)

Networking and Distributed Computing

Some Basic Properties of Length Rate Quotient

Yuming Jiang[✉]

NTNU, Norwegian University of Science and Technology, Trondheim, Norway
yuming.jiang@ntnu.no

Abstract. Length Rate Quotient (LRQ) is the first algorithm of interleaved shaping – a novel concept proposed to provide per-flow shaping for a flow aggregate without per-flow queuing. This concept has been adopted by Time-Sensitive Networking (TSN) and Deterministic Networking (DetNet). In this paper, we investigate basic properties of LRQ interleaved shapers. One is the so-called "shaping-for-free" property, which is, when an LRQ interleaved shaper is appended to a FIFO system, it does not increase the worst-case delay of the system. The other basic properties include conformance, output characterization, a sufficient and necessary condition for bounded delay, Guaranteed Rate characterization, and delay and backlog bounds for LRQ interleaved shapers as stand-alone elements. The derived properties of LRQ shed new insights on understanding interleaved shaping, which may be further exploited to achieve bounded delay in TSN/DetNet networks.

Keywords: Interleaved Shaping · Length Rate Quotient (LRQ) · Time Sensitive Networking (TSN) · Deterministic Networking (DetNet) · Asynchronous Traffic Shaping · Interleaved Shaper · Interleaved Regulator

1 Introduction

Interleaved shaping is a novel concept for traffic shaping, originally proposed in [1]. Conceptually, its idea is to perform per-flow traffic shaping within a flow aggregate using only one FIFO queue. An appealing property of interleaved shaping is the so-called "shaping-for-free" property: When an interleaved shaper is appended to a FIFO system and shapes flows to their initial traffic constraints, it does not increase the worst-case delay of the system. Based on this property, an approach to achieve bounded worst-case end-to-end (e2e) delay in the network is investigated in [1]. The approach includes a specific way to allocate shaping and scheduling queues in switches and re-shaping flows to their initial traffic constraints using the corresponding interleaved shaping algorithms.

The concept of interleaved shaping, together with the approach of allocating queues and reshaping traffic [1], has been adopted and extended by IEEE Time-Sensitive Networking (TSN) [2] and IETF Deterministic Networking (DetNet)

© ICST Institute for Computer Sciences, Social Informatics and Telecommunications Engineering 2023
Published by Springer Nature Switzerland AG 2023. All Rights Reserved
E. Hyytiä and V. Kavitha (Eds.): VALUETOOLS 2022, LNICST 482, pp. 243–258, 2023.
https://doi.org/10.1007/978-3-031-31234-2_15

[3] to deliver bounded e2e latency. The concept is called Asynchronous Traffic Shaping (ATS) in the former [4] while Interleaved Regulation in the latter [5].

In [1], two algorithms for interleaved shaping are introduced, which are Length Rate Quotient (LRQ) and Token Bucket Emulation (TBE). While LRQ is for traffic constraints where the gap between consecutive packets satisfies a length rate quotient condition, TBE is for the well-known token bucket (TB) or leaky bucket (TB) traffic constraints. In [6], more types of traffic constraints are investigated under a unified traffic constraint concept called "Pi-regularity" and the resultant interleaved shapers are called Interleaved Regulators (IRs). The "shaping-for-free" property is also proved for IRs in [6].

Surprisingly, other than the "shaping-for-free" property, few other properties of interleaved shapers have been reported. To bridge the gap, this paper is intended. Specifically, we focus on *LRQ, the first interleaved shaping algorithm*. In addition to "shaping-for-free", a set of basic properties, not previously investigated, are proved in this paper, which include conformance, output characterization, a sufficient and necessary condition to ensure the existence of bounded delay, Guaranteed Rate [7,8] service characterization, and delay and backlog bounds for LRQ interleaved shapers as standalone elements.

The rest is organized as follows. In the next section, the LRQ interleaved shaping algorithm and its modeling are first introduced, followed by some other preliminaries. They include traffic and server models used in the investigation. In Sect. 3, various basic properties of LRQ are proved. Concluding remarks are given in Sect. 4

2   The LRQ Algorithm and Preliminaries

2.1   The LRQ Interleaved Shaping Algorithm

The LRQ Algorithm Length Rate Quotient (LRQ) is the first algorithm of interleaved shaping [1]. Consider an LRQ shaper, whose FIFO queue is shared by an aggregate of flows. The LRQ shaper performs per-flow *interleaved shaping* on the aggregate, according to the algorithm shown in Algorithm 1 [1].

The LRQ algorithm shown in Algorithm 1 takes the original form in [1]. As is clear from Algorithm 1, there is only one FIFO queue q where per-flow shaping is conducted. In Algorithm 1, q denotes the queue of the shaper, where packets join in the order of their arrival times. After reaching the head of the queue, the head packet p is checked for its eligibility of output from the queue, which depends on the flow f that it belongs to. Time stamp E^f stores the eligible time of flow f for its next packet. At the output time d of packet p, the time stamp E^f is updated to equal the present/output time $d(= t_{now})$ plus the quotient (l/r^f), where l is the length of p. In this way, the next packet of flow f after this packet p is at least delayed until the time t_{now} reaches E^f.

A Model for LRQ. To model the LRQ algorithm, let j denote the packet number of p in Algorithm 1, i.e., p is the j-th packet of the aggregate flow g

---

Algorithm 1 Pseudo code of the LRQ algorithm

Initialization: $\forall f : [f].eligibility\_time = 0$
Shaping:
1: **while** (true) {
2:     **wait until** $q.size > 0$;
3:     $p := q.head(); l := p.length; f := p.flow\_index$;
4:     $E^f := [f].eligibility\_time$;
5:
6:     **wait until** $t^{now} \geq E^f$; **output** p;
7:
8:     $E^f := t^{now} + \frac{l}{r^f}$;
9:     $[f].eligibility\_time := E^f$;
10: }

---

coming out of the queue q in Line 3. In addition, let a^j and d^j denote the arrival time and output/departure time of the packet. Furthermore, let $f_{(j)}$ denote the flow where the packet is from, $i_{(j)}$ its packet number in this flow $f_{(j)}$, and $E^{f,i}$ the eligibility time of packet $p^{f,i}$, i.e., the i-th packet of flow f.

Line 6 tells that under the condition implied by Line 2, LRQ outputs the packet immediately when the present time t_{now} reaches the eligibility time of the packet $E^{f_{(j)}, i_{(j)}}$. In other words, the output time equals the eligibility time, i.e., $d^j = E^{f_{(j)}, i_{(j)}}$. The condition of Line 2 is that the packet must have already arrived, i.e. $d^j \geq a^j$. In addition, the loop, particularly the two highlighted lines, Lines 2 and 6 imply the FIFO order is preserved when outputting packets, or in other words, $d^j \geq d^{j-1}$. Combining these, we have

$$d^j = \max\{a^j, d^{j-1}, E^{f_{(j)}, i_{(j)}}\} \tag{1}$$

with *the initialization condition* $E^{f,1} = 0$ for $\forall f$, and $d^0 = 0$ since the queue is initially empty, where the eligibility time function E^f is updated according to Lines 8 and 9 as:

$$E^{f_{(j)}, i_{(j)}+1} = d^j + l^j / r^{f_{(j)}}. \tag{2}$$

Remark on Model Difference. The concept of interleaved shaping has been extended to consider other shaping constraints, such as token-bucket constraint [1,4] and "Pi-regularity" constraint [6], and has been adopted by IEEE TSN [4] and IETF DetNet [3]. In these standards as well as in the modeling work [6], the interleaved shaping algorithms directly take (1) as the form, where the eligibility time function (2) is adapted according to the targeted shaping constraint. Specifically, the corresponding time functions of d and E are respectively called *GroupEligibilityTime* and individual flow' *schedulerEligibilityTime* in the IEEE Standard 802.1Qcr [4].

In the modeling work [6], the introduced Π^f function is indeed the function E^f (2) here. For interleaved LRQ, the Pi-function has the following expression:

$$\Pi_{LRQ}^{f,i}(r^f) = d^{f,i-1} + l^{f,i-1}/r^f \quad \text{for} \quad i \geq 2$$
$$\Pi_{LRQ}^{f,1}(r^f) = -\infty \qquad \qquad \text{for} \quad i = 1 \tag{3}$$

As a highlight, the initial condition for the Π^f function is different from that for E^f. While it is $E^{f,1} = 0$ in the initial LRQ algorithm [1] and the model (1) above, it is $\Pi_{LRQ}^{f,1} = -\infty$ in [6]. Also in [6], this initial condition is discussed to be necessary for its proposed "Pi-regularity" traffic constraint model.

2.2   Flow and Server Models

Notation. Consider a FIFO system. Let $\mathcal{F}$ denote the set of flows. For each flow f, let $p^{f,i}$ denote the i-th packet in the sequence, where $i \in \mathcal{N}^+ \equiv \{1, 2, \dots\}$, and $l^{f,max}$ its maximum packet length. For every packet $p^{f,i}$, we denote by $a^{f,i}$ its arrival time to the system, $d^{f,i}$ its departure time from the system, and $l^{f,i}$ its length. The maximum packet length of the system is denoted by l^{max}. In addition, define $A^f(t) \equiv \sum_i \{l^{f,i} | a^{f,i} < t\}$, i.e., the cumulative amount of traffic from flow f which has arrived up to time t, $A^f(s,t) \equiv A^f(t) - A^f(s)$, and $A^f(0) = 0$. For the departure process of the flow from the system, $D^f(t)$ is similarly defined. Sometimes, reference time functions are used to characterize how the flow f is treated by the system. Specifically, we use E^f and F^f to respectively refer to the times when the packets have reached the head of the queue and become eligible for receiving service, and the times when packets are expected to depart. They define reference eligible time $E^{f,i}$ and expected finish time $F^{f,i}$ for each packet $p^{f,i}$ of the flow f. When the concern is on a single flow, the upper script ^{f} may be removed for representation simplicity.

Flow Models. For flows, two specific traffic models are considered. One is the g-regularity model [9], also known as the *max-plus arrival curve* model [10,11]:

Definition 1. *A flow is said to be g-regular for some non-negative non-decreasing function $g(\cdot)$ iff for all $i \geq j \geq 0$, there holds $a^i \geq a^j + g(L(i) - L(j))$ or equivalently, $\forall i \geq 0$,*

$$a^i \geq \sup_{0 \leq k \leq i} \{a^k + g(L(i) - L(k))\} \equiv a \overline{\otimes} g^{(i)} \tag{4}$$

where $L(i) \equiv \sum_{k=0}^{i-1} l^k$ with $g(0) = 0$ and $L(0) = 0$, and $\overline{\otimes}$ is called the max-plus convolution operator.

In the case $g(x) = \frac{x}{r}$ with a constant rate r, which is equivalent to $a^{i+1} \geq a^i + \frac{l^i}{r}$, $\forall i \geq 1$, we also say the flow is $LRQ(r)$-**constrained**.

Another traffic model that will be used is the *(min-plus) arrival curve* model.

Definition 2. *A flow is said to have a (min-plus) arrival curve α, which is a non-negative non-decreasing function, iff the traffic of the flow is constrained by [12], $\forall s, t \geq 0$, $A(s, s+t) \leq \alpha(t)$ or equivalently, $\forall t \geq 0$,*

$$A(t) \leq \inf_{0 \leq s \leq t} \{A(s) + \alpha(t-s)\} \equiv A \otimes \alpha(t) \tag{5}$$

where define $\alpha(0) = 0$ and $\otimes$ is the min-plus convolution operator.

A special type of arrival curve has the form: $\alpha(t) = \rho \cdot t + \sigma$. In this case, we will also say that the flow is leaky-bucket or token-bucket (σ, ρ)-**constrained**. The (σ, ρ) model was first introduced by Cruz in his seminal work [13]. It can be verified that if a flow is $LRQ(r)$-constrained, it is also (σ, ρ)-constrained with $\sigma = l^{max}$ and $\rho = r$, i.e., having a (min-plus) arrival curve $\alpha(t) = rt + l^{max}$.

As shown by the two definitions, while the g-regularity or max-plus arrival curve model characterizes a flow based on the arrival time a^i, the (min-plus) arrival curve model does so based on the cumulative traffic amount function $A(t)$. In the literature, e.g., [9,11], the relationship between the min-plus and max-plus arrival curves has been investigated. Particularly, it has been shown [11] that they can be converted to and are dual of each other.

Server Models. For server modeling, define two reference time functions $E(\cdot)$ and $F(\cdot)$ iteratively as: $\forall i \geq 1$

$$E^i(r) = \max\{a^i, E^{i-1} + \frac{l^{i-1}}{r}\} \tag{6}$$

$$F^i(r) = \max\{a^i, F^{i-1}\} + \frac{l^i}{r} \tag{7}$$

with $E^0 = 0$, $F^0 = 0$, and $l^0 = 0$ where r denotes the reference service rate. Later E will also be referred to as the eligibility time or *virtual start time (VST)* function, and F the *virtual finish time (VFT)* function. The following relationship between functions E and F can be easily verified, e.g., see [14]: $\forall i \geq 1$,

$$F^i = E^i + \frac{l^i}{r^f} \tag{8}$$

Definition 3. *A system is said to be a Guaranteed Rate (GR) server with guaranteed rate r and error term e to a flow, written as $GR(r, e)$, iff it guarantees that for any packet p^i of the flow, its departure time satisfies [7,8]:*

$$d^i \leq F^i(r) + e \tag{9}$$

or equivalently

$$d^i \leq a \overline{\otimes} g^{(i)} + \frac{l^i}{r} \tag{10}$$

with $g^{(x)} = \frac{x}{r} + e$, where $\overline{\otimes}$ is the max-plus convolution operator.

It has been shown that a wide range of scheduling algorithms, including priority, weighted fair queueing and its various variations, round robin and its variations, hierarchical fair queueing, Earliest Due Date (EDD) and rate-controlled scheduling disciplines (RCSDs), can be modeled using GR [7,8]. For this reason and to simplify the representation, instead of presenting results for schedulers implementing specific scheduling algorithms, we use the GR model to represent them. A summary of the corresponding GR parameters of various scheduling algorithms can be found, e.g., in [14].

Considering the relationship (8), a server model may similarly be defined based on E, which is called the Start-Time (ST) server model, written as $ST(r, \tau)$, iff for any packet p^i of the flow, the system guarantees its departure time [14]:

$$d^i \leq E^i(r) + \tau \tag{11}$$

or equivalently

$$d^i \leq a \overline{\otimes} g^{(i)} \tag{12}$$

with $g(x) = \frac{x}{r} + \tau$ and $\tau = e + l^{max}/r$.

As indicated by the max-plus convolution operator used in (10) and (12), these models are server models for the max-plus branch of network calculus [9]. In the min-plus branch of network calculus, the *(min-plus) service curve* model is well-known. The latency-rate type (min-plus) service curve is defined as follows.

Definition 4. *A system is said to offer to a flow a latency-rate service curve* $\beta(t) = r(t - \tau)^+$ *iff for all* $t \geq 0$ *[12],*

$$D(t) \geq A \otimes \beta(t) \tag{13}$$

where $(x)^+ \equiv \max\{x, 0\}$.

In [12,14], the relationship between the GR model, the ST model, the latency-rate server model and the (min-plus) latency-rate service curve has been investigated. Particularly, it is shown [14] that the latency-rate server model is equivalent to the start-time (ST) server model. With the relation (8), it can be verified that if a system is a $GR(r, e)$ server to a flow, it is also a $ST(r, e + \frac{l^{max}}{r})$ server and provides a latency-rate service curve β to the flow [12,14]:

$$\beta(t) = r[t - (e + \frac{l^{max}}{r})]^+ \tag{14}$$

Conversely, if the system is an $ST(r, \tau)$ or latency-rate server with the same parameters to the flow, it is also a $GR(r, \tau - \frac{l^{min}}{r})$ to the flow [14].

Delay and Backlog Bounds. With the flow and server models introduced above, the following delay and backlog bounds can be found or proved from literature results, e.g., [8,12].

Proposition 1. *Consider a flow served by a system. The flow has an arrival curve α, and the system is a $GR(r, e)$ server to the flow. If $\lim_{t \to \infty} \frac{\alpha(t)}{t} \leq r$, the delay of any packet i, i.e., $d^i - a^i$, is upper-bounded by, $\forall i \geq 1$,*

$$d^i - a^i \leq \frac{\sup_{t \geq 0}[\alpha(t) - rt]}{r} + e$$

and the backlog of the system at any time, i.e., $D(t) - A(t)$, is upper-bounded by, $\forall t \geq 0$,

$$D(t) - A(t) \leq \sup_{t \geq 0}[\alpha(t) - r(t - e - \frac{l^{max}}{r})^+]$$

As a special case, the flow is (σ, ρ)-constrained, i.e. $\alpha(t) = \rho t + \sigma$. If $\rho \leq r$, the bounds in Proposition 1 can be written more explicitly as, $\forall i \geq 1$,

$$d^i - a^i \leq \frac{\sigma}{r} + e \tag{15}$$

for delay and $\forall t \geq 0$,

$$D(t) - A(t) \leq \sigma + \rho \cdot (e + \frac{l^{max}}{r}) \tag{16}$$

for backlog.

In the TSN/DetNet literature, the delay and backlog bounds are derived commonly based on the assumption that the flow has a (min-plus) arrival curve and the server has a latency-rate (min-plus) service curve [15], except in the initial interleaved shaping paper [1] that adopts a timing analysis technique directly on the reference time functions similar to our analysis in this paper. It has also been noticed that the delay bounds from the service curve analysis are more pessimistic than from the timing based analysis [15]. This difference is also seen here as discussed in the following.

Specifically, service curve-based analysis can result in a delay bound that is $\frac{l^{max}}{r}$ larger than the bound from GR-based analysis shown in Proposition 1. The difference is due to the extra term $\frac{l^{max}}{r}$ in the service curve characterization as shown in (14). By exploiting an advanced property of network calculus (NC), which is "the last packetizer can be ignored for delay computation" (see e.g. [12]), the packetizer delay can be deducted from the service curve based delay bound. However, considering that the delay bound must hold for all packets, only $\frac{l^{min}}{r}$ may thus be extracted. Consequently, the "improved" service curve based delay bound becomes:

$$\frac{\sigma}{r} + e + \frac{l^{max}}{r} - \frac{l^{min}}{r}.$$

Then its difference from GR-based analysis can be reduced to

$$\frac{l^{max}}{r} - \frac{l^{min}}{r}.$$

As a remark, the discussion on the delay bound difference is only based on the server models themselves. When delay bound analysis is conducted on a specific scheduling discipline, the GR-based analysis may benefit additionally, e.g., an example of this can be found in [16].

3   Basic Properties of Interleaved LRQ Shapers

3.1   The "Shaping-for-Free" Property

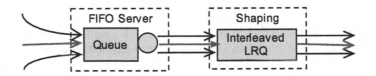

Fig. 1. The shaping-for-free property setup

As introduced in Sect. 2, functions (1) and (2) capture the essence of the LRQ algorithm. In addition, by adapting (2), interleaved shaping of flows with other traffic constraints can be implemented, for which, a systematic investigation has been conducted in [6]. Applying (2) to (1), we can rewrite and obtain the following model for LRQ: $\forall j \geq 1$,

$$d^j = \max\{a^j, d^{j-1}, d^{f(j),i(j)-1} + \frac{l^{f(j),i(j)-1}}{r^{f(j)}}\} \tag{17}$$

with **the initial condition:** $d^{f,0} = 0$ and $l^{f,0} = 0$ **for** $\forall f$, **which is equivalent to the initial condition** $E^{f,0} = 0$ for (1), since the three involved parameters d, l and r in (2) are non-negative in nature and r is non-zero.

In the literature, "shaping-for-free" is a well known property of per-flow shapers. Specifically, if a shaper is greedy and the initial traffic constraint of the flow is used as the shaping curve, the worst-case delay of the flow in a system composed of the shaper and a server is not increased in comparison with a system of the server only, in spite of the order of the shaper and the server in the combined system [9,12].

Figure 1 illustrates a typical setup when studying the shaping-for-free property, where interleaved shaping is performed after the FIFO system. In Theorem 1, we extend the study and prove that interleaved shaping does not affect the worst-case delay no matter if interleaved shaping is introduced before or after the FIFO system.

Theorem 1. *Consider a set of flows* $\mathcal{F}$, *where every flow* $f(\in \mathcal{F})$ *is* $LRQ(r^f)$-*regulated, i.e.,* $a^{f,i} \geq a^{f,i-1} + \frac{l^{f,i-1}}{r^f}$. *These flows pass through a system composed of a FIFO server and an interleaved LRQ shaper with rate* r^f *for* f, $\forall f \in \mathcal{F}$. *No matter about the order of the server and the shaper, a delay upper bound for the FIFO server is also a delay upper bound for the composite system.*

Proof. The property has two parts: (I) the LRQ shaper is before the FIFO server; (II) the FIFO server is followed by the LRQ shaper as illustrated in Fig. 1.

For part (I), the proof needs Lemma 1 and Lemma 2, which are introduced in Sect. 3.2. Specifically, with the former, the regulator introduces no delay. With the latter, the output from the regulator, i.e., the input to the server, is regulated with the same traffic constraint and hence the same delay bound remains.

For part (II), the proof is as follows. Let $\hat{a}$ denote the departure from the server and hence the arrival to the regulator. Suppose Δ is a delay bound for all packets through the FIFO server, i.e., $\hat{a}^j \leq a^j + \Delta$ for $\forall j \geq 1$. We prove by strong induction that for the composite system shown in Fig. 1, Δ is also a delay bound, i.e. $d^j - a^j \leq \Delta$ for $\forall j \geq 1$, where a^j and d^j respectively denote the arrival and departure times of the j-th packet through the composite system.

For the base step, consider both the 1st and the 2nd packets. By definition and the initial condition $d^{f,0} = 0$ and $l^{f,0} = 0$ for $\forall f$ as discussed above, for the 1st packet, it is obtained immediately $d^1 = \hat{a}^1 \leq a^1 + \Delta$. For the 2nd packet, by the LRQ model (17), $d^2 = \max\{\hat{a}^2, d^1, d^{f(2),i(2)-1} + \frac{l^{f(2),i(2)-1}}{r^{f(2)}}\} \leq \max\{a^2 + \Delta, a^1 + \Delta, d^{f(2),i(2)-1} + \frac{l^{f(2),i(2)-1}}{r^{f(2)}}\}$. There are two cases. (i) The 2nd packet is from a different flow, which is the first packet of that flow. In this case, $d^{f(2),i(2)-1} + \frac{l^{f(2),i(2)-1}}{r^{f(2)}} = 0$ by definition, and hence $d^2 \leq a^2 + \Delta$ since $a^2 \geq a^1$. (ii) The 2nd packet is from the same flow. Then, $d^2 \leq \max\{a^2 + \Delta, a^1 + \Delta, d^1 + \frac{l^{f(2),i(2)-1}}{r^{f(2)}}\} \leq \max\{a^2 + \Delta, a^1 + \Delta, a^1 + \Delta + \frac{l^{f(2),i(2)-1}}{r^{f(2)}}\} = \max\{a^2, a^1 + \frac{l^{f(2),i(2)-1}}{r^{f(2)}}\} + \Delta \leq a^2 + \Delta$. This completes the base step.

For the induction, assume the theorem holds for all packets till $j-1$ with $j > 2$, which implies (i) $d^{j-1} \leq a^{j-1} + \Delta$. The induction assumption also implies (ii) $d^{f(j),i(j)-1} \leq a^{f(j),i(j)-1} + \Delta$. Applying these to (17), together with $\hat{a}^j \leq a^j + \Delta$, gives:

$$d^j = \max\{\hat{a}^j, d^{j-1}, d^{f(j),i(j)-1} + \frac{l^{f(j),i(j)-1}}{r^{f(j)}}\}$$

$$\leq \max\{a^j + \Delta, a^{j-1} + \Delta, a^{f(j),i(j)-1} + \Delta + \frac{l^{f(j),i(j)-1}}{r^{f(j)}}\}$$

$$= \max\{a^j, a^{f(j),i(j)-1} + \frac{l^{f(j),i(j)-1}}{r^{f(j)}}\} + \Delta$$

$$= a^j + \Delta$$

where the last step is due to the *LRQ* traffic constraint. Note that in the induction step, we have implicitly assumed that packet j is not the first packet of flow $f(j)$ to apply (ii). In the case that j is the first packet, by definition and the initial condition, we also have $d^j = \max\{\hat{a}^j, d^{j-1}, 0\} \leq \max\{a^j + \Delta, a^{j-1} + \Delta\} \leq a^j + \Delta$, where we have applied the induction assumption (i). This completes the proof. □

Remark 1. Under interleaved shaping, the shaping-for-free property, corresponding to Part II of Theorem 1, is first investigated in [1], but only implicitly. In

[6], a generalized treatment is provided, where the property is proved for a wide range of traffic constraints, including both Chang's g-regularity and (min-plus) arrival curve constraints. However, it is worth highlighting that **the investigation in** [6] **requires a necessary initialization condition** (3), which is different from that used by LRQ, Algorithm 1. Theorem 1 has bridged the gap.

Remark 2. The shaping-for-free property investigated in [1] and [6] assumes that the interleaved shaper is immediately placed after the FIFO server as illustrated by Fig. 1, Theorem 1 extends this and additionally proves that placing the shaper before the FIFO server does not increase worst-case delay either.

3.2   Basic Properties of a Standalone LRQ Interleaved Shaper

In this subsection, a number of basic properties of a standalone LRQ interleaved shaper, which have not been previously reported, are proved.

Lemma 1. *(Conformance) Consider an interleaved LRQ shaper with a set of input flows $\mathcal{F}$, where for every flow $f \in \mathcal{F}$, rate r^f is applied. If at the input, every flow $f \in \mathcal{F}$ is $LRQ(r^f)$-regulated, then the shaper introduces no delay, i.e., for every packet p^j, there holds $d^j = a^j$.*

Proof. The proof is similar to that for the second part of Theorem 1. We prove by (strong) induction. For the base case, consider the 1st packet and the 2nd packet. By definition and the initial condition, it is obtained immediately $d^1 = a^1$. For the 2nd packet, $d^2 = \max\{a^2, d^1, d^{f_{(2)}, i_{(2)}-1} + \frac{l^{f_{(2)}, i_{(2)}-1}}{r^{f_{(2)}}}\} = \max\{a^2, a^1, d^{f_{(2)}, i_{(2)}-1} + \frac{l^{f_{(2)}, i_{(2)}-1}}{r^{f_{(2)}}}\} = \max\{a^2, d^{f_{(2)}, i_{(2)}-1} + \frac{l^{f_{(2)}, i_{(2)}-1}}{r^{f_{(2)}}}\}$. There are two cases. (i) The 2nd packet is from a different flow. In this case, $d^{f_{(2)}, i_{(2)}-1} + \frac{l^{f_{(2)}, i_{(2)}-1}}{r^{f_{(2)}}} = 0$ by definition, and hence $d^2 = a^2$. (ii) The 2nd packet is from the same flow. Then, $d^2 = \max\{a^2, d^1 + \frac{l^{f_{(2)}, i_{(2)}-1}}{r^{f_{(2)}}}\} = \max\{a^2, a^1 + \frac{l^{f_{(2)}, i_{(2)}-1}}{r^{f_{(2)}}}\} = a^2$. This proves the base case.

For the induction, assume the theorem holds for all packets till $j-1$, which implies $d^{j-1} = a^{j-1}$ and $d^{f_{(j)}, i_{(j)}-1} = a^{f_{(j)}, i_{(j)}-1}$. Applying these to (17) gives:

$$d^j = \max\{a^j, d^{j-1}, d^{f_{(j)}, i_{(j)}-1} + \frac{l^{f_{(j)}, i_{(j)}-1}}{r^{f_{(j)}}}\}$$

$$= \max\{a^j, a^{j-1}, a^{f_{(j)}, i_{(j)}-1} + \frac{l^{f_{(j)}, i_{(j)}-1}}{r^{f_{(j)}}}\}$$

$$= \max\{a^j, a^{f_{(j)}, i_{(j)}-1} + \frac{l^{f_{(j)}, i_{(j)}-1}}{r^{f_{(j)}}}\}$$

$$= a^j$$

which completes the proof. $\square$

An implication of Lemma 1 is that at any time, there is at most one packet in the LRQ system from each flow. This information may be used for conformance check. For instance, from each flow, at most one packet is allowed and additional non-conformant packets are dropped. This way can prevent delaying other flows' packets if one flow is non-conformant to its $LRQ(r^f)$-constraint.

Lemma 2. *(Output Characterization) Consider an interleaved LRQ shaper with a set of flows $\mathcal{F}$, where for every flow $f \in \mathcal{F}$, rate r^f is applied. Regardless of the traffic constraint for each flow at the input, the output of the flow f is constrained by $LRQ(r^f)$, i.e., $\forall i \geq 1$,*

$$d^{f,i} \geq d^{f,i-1} + \frac{l^{f,i-1}}{r^f}.$$

Proof. The output characterization result follows from (17), since the right hand side of (17) is not smaller than $d^{f,i-1} + \frac{l^{f,i-1}}{r^f}$ for any packet $p^{f,i}$ of the flow f. $\square$

Having proved Lemma 1 and Lemma 2, we now focus on the worst-case delay. Unfortunately, its analysis is notoriously challenging. In the rest of this section, we approach it step by step. First, the following result provides a sufficient and necessary condition for an LRQ interleaved shaper to have bounded delay.

Lemma 3. *(Sufficient and Necessary Condition) For an LRQ interleaved shaper with rates $\{r^f\}$ for its flow set $\mathcal{F}$, the delay for any packet is upper-bounded, if and only if there exists a non-negative constant $\Delta(< \infty)$ such that, $\forall j \geq 1$,*

$$d^{f(j),i(j)-1} + \frac{l^{f(j),i(j)-1}}{r^{f(j)}} - a^j \leq \Delta \tag{18}$$

and if the condition is satisfied, Δ is also an upper-bound on the delay.

Proof. For proving (18) is a necessary condition, let's first assume the condition does not hold and then prove the conclusion does not hold consequently. Specifically, the assumption is that for some j, $d^{f(j),i(j)-1} + \frac{l^{f(j),i(j)-1}}{r^{f(j)}} - a^j$ is not bounded. Since by definition $d^j \geq d^{f(j),i(j)-1} + \frac{l^{f(j),i(j)-1}}{r^{f(j)}}$ and hence $d^j - a^j \geq d^{f(j),i(j)-1} + \frac{l^{f(j),i(j)-1}}{r^{f(j)}} - a^j$, so for this j, $d^j - a^j$ is not bounded. This completes the necessary condition part.

For the sufficient condition part, we prove by induction that if (18) holds for $\forall j \geq 1$, we also have $d^j - a^j \leq \Delta$ for $\forall i \geq 1$, and hence it is a delay upper-bound. For the base case, $j = 1$. By definition, we have $d^1 = a^1$, and hence $d^1 - a^1 = 0 \leq \Delta$. For the induction case, let's assume Δ is an upper bound for $j-1, (\forall j > 1)$ and then prove it is also an upper bound for j. With the definition of d^j, we have for its delay:

$$d^j - a^j = \max\{a^j, d^{j-1}, d^{f(j),i(j)-1} + \frac{l^{f(j),i(j)-1}}{r^{f(j)}}\} - a^j$$

$$= \max\{0, d^{j-1} - a^j, d^{f(j),i(j)-1} + \frac{l^{f(j),i(j)-1}}{r^{f(j)}} - a^j\}$$

$$\leq \max\{0, d^{j-1} - a^{j-1}, \Delta\} \leq \max\{0, \Delta, \Delta\} = \Delta$$

which completes the proof. $\square$

Note that, in Lemma 3, the condition does not assume how each flow is regulated at the input. If the flow is $LRQ(r^f)$-regulated at the input, applying this traffic condition together with $d^{f_{(j)},i_{(j)}-1} = a^{f_{(j)},i_{(j)}-1}$ from Lemma 1 gives $d^{f_{(j)},i_{(j)}-1} + \frac{l^{f_{(j)},i_{(j)}-1}}{r^{f_{(j)}}} - a^j \leq 0$. In other words, the sufficient and necessary condition is satisfied with $\Delta = 0$. This also confirms Lemma 1 .

When the flow is not $LRQ(r^f)$-regulated, the condition constant Δ is not as easily found. Additional approaches are needed to help find delay bounds. For this, in Lemma 4, we relate the departure time with a generalized version of the virtual start time and virtual finish time functions defined in (6) and (7). Specifically, their generalized counterparts are: $\forall j \geq 1$,

$$\tilde{E}^j = \max\{a^j, \tilde{E}^{j-1} + \frac{l^{j-1}}{r^{(j-1)}}\} \tag{19}$$

$$\tilde{F}^j = \max\{a^j, \tilde{F}^{j-1}\} + \frac{l^j}{r^{(j)}} \tag{20}$$

with $\tilde{E}^0 = \tilde{E}^0 = l^0 = 0$ and $r^0 = \infty$, where, for ease of expression, we use $r^{(j)}$ to denote the rate of the flow that packet j belongs to, i.e., $r^{(j)} \equiv r^{f_{(j)}}$.

The difference between (19) and (6), and the difference between (20) and (7), are that while the rate in the function for each packet is the same in the latter, it may differ from packet to packet in the former. These generalized virtual start time and virtual finish time functions (19) and (20) are similarly defined in the generalized Guaranteed Rate server model [8].

Lemma 4. *(GR Characterization) Consider an interleaved LRQ shaper with a set of input flows $\mathcal{F}$, where for every flow $f \in \mathcal{F}$, rate r^f is applied. The departure time of any packet p^j is bounded by: for $\forall j \geq 1$*

$$d^j \leq \tilde{E}^j = \tilde{F}^j - \frac{l^j}{r^{(j)}} \tag{21}$$

where $\tilde{E}^j$ and $\tilde{F}^j$ are defined in (19) and (20) respectively.

Proof. The definitions of $\tilde{E}^j$ and $\tilde{E}^j$ imply the following relationship between them: $\forall j \geq 1$,

$$\tilde{F}^j = \tilde{E}^j + \frac{l^j}{r^{(j)}} \tag{22}$$

which can be verified with induction. For the base step, it holds because $\tilde{F}^1 = a^1 + \frac{l^1}{r^{(1)}}$ and $\tilde{E}^1 = a^1$. For the induction step, under the induction assumption $\tilde{F}^{j-1} = \tilde{E}^{j-1} + \frac{l^{j-1}}{r^{(j-1)}}$, it also holds.

With the fact $\tilde{E}^{j-1} \leq \tilde{E}^{j-1} + \frac{l^{j-1}}{r^{(j-1)}}$, $\tilde{E}^j$ can also be written as:

$$\tilde{E}^j = max\{a^j, \tilde{E}^{j-1}, \tilde{E}^{j-1} + \frac{l^{j-1}}{r^{(j-1)}}\}$$

Compare $\tilde{E}^j$ and d^j that is copied below

$$d^j = \max\{a^j, d^{j-1}, d^{f_{(j)},i_{(j)}-1} + \frac{l^{f_{(j)},i_{(j)}-1}}{r^{f_{(j)}}}\}$$

We prove (21) by induction. For the base case $j = 1$, since $d^1 = a^1$, $\tilde{E}^j = a^1$ and the initial condition, (21) holds, i.e., $d^1 \leq \tilde{E}^1$. For the induction step, we suppose (21) holds for all packets $1, \ldots, j - 1$, and consider packet j. There are two cases. (i) Packet p^{j-1} and packet p^j belong to the same flow. In this case, $\frac{l^{j-1}}{r^{(j-1)}} = \frac{l^{f(j),i(j)-1}}{r^{f(j)}}$ and hence $d^j \leq \tilde{E}^j$ under the induction assumption. (ii) Packet p^{j-1} belongs to a different flow. In this case, since packet p^{j-1} is the immediate previous packet of p^j, due to FIFO, packet $p^{f(j),i(j)-1}$ must be an earlier packet than p^{j-1}, implying $d^{f(j),i(j)-1} \leq d^{j-1}$. Let $j^*(< j - 1)$ denote the packet number of $p^{f(j),i(j)-1}$ in the aggregate. For $\tilde{E}^{j-1}$, by applying the definition of $\tilde{E}$ iteratively, we have

$$\tilde{E}^{j-1} = \max\{a^{j-1}, a^{j-2} + \frac{l^{j-2}}{r^{(j-2)}}, \ldots,$$

$$\tilde{E}^{f(j),i(j)-1} + \frac{l^{f(j),i(j)-1}}{r^{f(j)}} + \sum_{k=j^*+1}^{j-2} \frac{l^k}{r^{(k)}}\}$$

$$\geq d^{f(j),i(j)-1} + \frac{l^{f(j),i(j)-1}}{r^{f(j)}}$$

where for the last step, the induction assumption $d^{f(j),i(j)-1} \leq \tilde{E}^{f(j),i(j)-1}$ has also been applied. With the above and the induction assumption $d^{j-1} \leq \tilde{E}^{j-1}$, the three terms in $\tilde{E}^j$ are all not smaller than the corresponding ones in d^j. Hence $d^j \leq \tilde{E}^j$ also holds for the second case. Combining both cases, the induction step is proved, i.e. (21) holds for j. □

With Lemma 4, the following corollary is immediately from the definition of the generalized GR server model, the corresponding delay bound analysis [8] and Proposition 1.

Corollary 1. *The LRG regulator is (i) a generalized GR server with guaranteed rate $r = \min r^f$ and error term $e = -\min \frac{l^{f,min}}{r^f}$ and (ii) provides a service curve $\alpha(t) = \min_f r^f t$. (iii) If every flow is (σ^f, ρ^f)-constrained and $\sum_f \rho^f \leq r$, then the delay of any packet p^j is bounded by, $\forall j \geq 1$,*

$$d^j - a^j \leq \frac{\sum_f \sigma^f}{\min_f r^f} - \min_f \frac{l^{f,min}}{r^f} \tag{23}$$

and (iv) the backlog of the system at any time t is bounded by: $\forall t \geq 0$,

$$D(t) - A(t) \leq \sum_f \sigma^f + l^{max} \tag{24}$$

While it is encouraging to have the delay bound (23) for LRQ interleaved shapers as the first step, the condition $\sum_f \rho^f \leq \min_f r^f$ and the term $\min_f r^f$ in (23) make the bound conservative. We improve in the follow result.

Theorem 2. *Consider an interleaved LRQ shaper with rates $\{r^f\}$ for its flow set $\mathcal{F}$. If every flow $f(\in \mathcal{F})$ is (σ^f, ρ^f)-constrained, and $\sum_f \frac{\rho^f}{r^f} \leq 1$, the delay of any packet p^j is bounded by, $\forall j \geq 1$,*

$$d^j - a^j \leq \sum_f \frac{\sigma^f}{r^f} - \frac{l^{f,j}}{r^f} \tag{25}$$

which implies the following delay bound for all packets:

$$\sup_{j \geq 1}[d^j - a^j] \leq \sum_f \frac{\sigma^f}{r^f} - \min_f \frac{l^{f,min}}{r^f}$$

Proof. For any packet p^j, there exists a packet p^{j_0} whose arrival starts the "virtual busy" period that packet p^j is in, where for all packets that arrive in $[a^{j_0}, \tilde{F}^j]$ there holds $a^k \leq \tilde{F}^{k-1}, \forall k = j_0 + 1, \ldots, j$. Alternatively, the start of the period is by the latest packet with $a^{j_0} > \tilde{F}^{j_0 - 1}$.

Consider a virtual reference FIFO system which has the same input sequence a^j and its output is $\tilde{F}^j$. Then this period is a busy period in the virtual reference system. Note that such a "virtual busy" period always exists, since in one extreme case, p^{j_0} is the first packet for which $a^1 > \tilde{F}^0 = 0$ always holds, and in another extreme case, the period is started by the packet p^j itself and in this case, $j_0 = j$.

Applying $a^k \leq \tilde{F}^{k-1}$ to the definition of $\tilde{F}^j$ gives:

$$\tilde{F}^j = t^0 + \sum_{k=j_0}^{j} \frac{l^k}{r^{(k)}} = t^0 + \sum_{m=1}^{N} \frac{W_m(t^0, \tilde{F}^j)}{r^m} \tag{26}$$

where $W_m(t^0, d^j) = \sum_{k=j_0}^{j} l^k I_{p^k \in f}$ denotes the total amount of service (in accumulated packet lengths) from flow f, served in $[t^0, \tilde{F}^j]$, where the indicator function $I_{p^k \in f}$ has the value 1 when the condition $\{p^k \in f\}$, i.e. packet p^k is from flow f, is true.

Because of FIFO and that the virtual system is empty at t^0_-, $W_m(t^0, d^{g,j})$ is hence limited by the amount of traffic that arrives in $[t^0, a^{f_n,i}]$: $W_m(t^0, \tilde{F}^j) \leq A_m(t^0, a^{g,j})$.

We then have,

$$\tilde{F}^j \leq t^0 + \sum_f \frac{A^f(t^0, a^j)}{r^m} \tag{27}$$

Under the condition that $\sum_f \frac{\rho^f}{r^f} \leq 1$, we obtain:

$$\tilde{F}^j - a^j \leq \sum_f \frac{A^f(t^0, a^j)}{r^f} + t_0 - a^j \leq \sum_f \frac{\rho^f(a^j - t^0) + \sigma^f}{r^f} - (a^j - t_0) \leq \sum_f \frac{\sigma^f}{r^f}$$

with which, the delay bound is obtained together with Lemma 4, specifically (21). $\qquad\square$

4 Conclusion

Though being the first algorithm of interleaved shaping, the properties of LRQ were previously little studied. As a step towards filling the gap, a set of properties for LRQ have been derived in this paper. These properties include the shaping-for-free property that has been proved without altering the initialization condition introduced in the original LRQ algorithm. In addition, a set of basic properties of a standalone LRQ interleaved shaper, which were not previously investigated, have also been derived, which include conformance, output characterization, a sufficient and necessary condition for bounded delay, GR characterization, and delay and backlog bounds. These results provide new insights on understanding interleaved shaping, which may be further exploited to deliver bounded delays in TSN/DetNet networks [16].

References

1. Specht, J., Samii, S.: Urgency-based scheduler for time-sensitive switched ethernet networks. In: 28th Euromicro Conference on Real-Time Systems (2016)
2. IEEE. 802.1q - IEEE standard for local and metropolitan area networks - bridges and bridged networks. IEEE Standards (2018)
3. Finn, N., Thubert, P., Varga, B., Farkas, J.: Deterministic networking architecture. IETF RFC 8655, October 2019
4. IEEE. IEEE standard for local and metropolitan area networks-bridges and bridged networks - Amendment 34: Asynchronous traffic shaping. IEEE Std 802.1Qcr-2020, pp. 1–151 (2020)
5. Finn, N., Le Boudec, J.-Y., Mohammadpour, E., Zhang, J., Varga, B., Farkas, J.: Detnet bounded latency. IETF Internet Draft: draft-ietf-detnet-bounded-latency-05, April 2021
6. Le Boudec, J.-Y.: A theory of traffic regulators for deterministic networks with application to interleaved regulators. IEEE/ACM Trans. Netw. 26(6), 2721–2733 (2018)
7. Goyal, P., Lam, S.S., Vin, H.M.: Determining end-to-end delay bounds in heterogeneous networks. In: Proceedings of the Workshop on Network and Operating System Support for Digital Audio and Video (NOSSDAV 1995), pp. 287–298, April 1995
8. Goyal, P., Vin, H.M.: Generalized guaranteed rate scheduling algorithms: a framework. IEEE/ACM Trans. Netw. 5(4), 561–571 (1997)
9. Chang, C.-S.: Performance Guarantees in Communication Networks. Springer-Verlag, Heidelberg (2000). https://doi.org/10.1007/978-1-4471-0459-9
10. Xie, J., Jiang, Y.: Stochastic network calculus models under max-plus algebra. In: IEEE Global Telecommunications Conference (GLOBECOM), pp. 1–6 (2009)
11. Liebeherr, J.: Duality of the max-plus and min-plus network calculus. Found. Trends Netw. 11(3–4), 139–282 (2017)
12. Le Boudec, J.-Y., Thiran, P.: Network Calculus: A Theory of Deterministic Queueing Systems for the Internet. Springer-Verlag, Heidelberg (2001). https://doi.org/10.1007/3-540-45318-0
13. Cruz, R.L.: A calculus for network delay, part I and part II. IEEE Trans. Inf. Theory 37(1), 114–141 (1991)

14. Jiang, Y.: Relationship between guaranteed rate server and latency rate server. Comput. Netw. **43**(3), 307–315 (2003)
15. Zhao, L., Pop, P., Steinhorst, S.: Quantitative performance comparison of various traffic shapers in time-sensitive networking. CoRR, abs/2103.13424 (2021)
16. Jiang, Y.: Some properties of length rate quotient shapers. CoRR, abs/2107.05021 (2021)

Robustness of the Tangle 2.0 Consensus

Bing-Yang Lin[1(✉)], Daria Dziubałtowska[1], Piotr Macek[1], Andreas Penzkofer[1], and Sebastian Müller[1,2]

[1] IOTA Foundation, Berlin, Germany
{bingyang.lin,daria.dziubaltowska,piotr.macek,andreas.penzkofer,
sebastian.mueller}@iota.org
[2] Aix Marseille Université, CNRS, Centrale Marseille,
I2M - UMR 7373, 13453 Marseille, France
sebastian.muller@univ-amu.fr

Abstract. In this paper, we investigate the performance of the Tangle 2.0 consensus protocol in a Byzantine environment. We use an agent-based simulation model that incorporates the main features of the Tangle 2.0 consensus protocol. Our experimental results demonstrate that the Tangle 2.0 protocol is robust to the bait-and-switch attack up to the theoretical upper bound of the adversary's 33% voting weight. We further show that the common coin mechanism in Tangle 2.0 is necessary for robustness against powerful adversaries. Moreover, the experimental results confirm that the protocol can achieve around 1 s confirmation time in typical scenarios and that the confirmation times of non-conflicting transactions are not affected by the presence of conflicts.

Keywords: Simulation · Consensus protocol · Leaderless · Security · Fault-tolerance · Directed acyclic graph

1 Introduction

Since 2009 when Bitcoin [1] was first introduced, distributed ledger technologies (DLTs) have gained growing interest from academics, industries, and even governments [2]. In DLTs, ledger records have no need for central authority controls or maintenance, and the validity of each record relies on a decentralized consensus mechanism, or globally accepted truth between participants, also called nodes, in the network. In Bitcoin, a blockchain is adopted as the structure to store a ledger, Proof of Work (PoW) as the Sybil protection, and the longest chain rule as the consensus mechanism. Each block, which contains transactions, is linked in a linear growing chain. All nodes in the Bitcoin network are able to extend the chain by solving a numerical challenge that consumes a considerable amount of computation power. The node that solves the challenge first is elected as a "leader", can add the next block to the chain, and gain a reward. Although Bitcoin was revolutionary in enabling DLTs in the first place, the PoW

E. Hyytiä and V. Kavitha (Eds.): VALUETOOLS 2022, LNICST 482, pp. 259–276, 2023.
https://doi.org/10.1007/978-3-031-31234-2_16

mechanism is typically slow [3] and might demand an unsustainable energy consumption [4]. Also, the single chain structure of the Bitcoin ledger limits its throughput [5], and has a scalability problem [6].

As a consequence, instead of using a linear block chain to store the ledger, many non-linear ledger structures (e.g., SPECTRE [7], Byteball [8], Algorand [9], PHANTOM [10], Avalanche [11], Prism [12], AlephZero [13], Narwhal [14], and IOTA [15]) were proposed to improve the performance. The consensus mechanism in a Directed Acyclic Graph (DAG)-based system can be conceptually different from the one in a linear blockchain system, and the transaction throughput is potentially no longer limited. In [16], the scalability and efficiency of different DAG-based blockchain architectures were analyzed, based on their functional data structures. We also refer to [17] for an overview of the security and performance of several DAG-based blockchain systems.

1.1 Results and Contribution

A recent proposal for a DAG-based consensus protocol is the Tangle 2.0 protocol, [18]. Our paper builds on the theoretical foundations and mathematical models established in [18] and gives a first performance analysis of the protocol in a Byzantine environment. To this end, we provide an agent-based simulator, [19], that simulates the peer-to-peer layer, the leaderless block creations, and the consensus finding simultaneously. In contrast to previous DAG simulators, such as DAGSim [20], our simulator [19] allows to consider a Byzantine environment and incorporates the main features of the Tangle 2.0 consensus.

This work is the first paper that provides quantitative validations of the Tangle 2.0 consensus protocol. In addition, we show that confirmation time is in the order of a second. This good performance holds even in highly adverse environments, where attackers are effective up to their theoretical limits.

The Tangle 2.0 consensus protocol consists of two components: the asynchronous component, On Tangle Voting (OTV), and the synchronous part, Synchronised Random Reality Selection (SRRS). To explore the security of these components, an agent-based attack strategy, called Bait-and-Switch, is introduced in the simulations. In this kind of attack, adversaries can issue doublespends at arbitrary high frequency and aim to keep the honest nodes in an undecided state. The simulation results show that in the worst weight distribution case, where all the honest nodes have equal weight, the OTV protocol can still resist the Bait-and-Switch attack when the adversary node owns up to 20% of the total weight. In addition, we also show that the SRRS protocol can further resist the Bait-and-Switch attack, even when the adversary occupies up to 33% of the total weight, which is the theoretical upper bond.

1.2 Structure of the Paper

In Sect. 2.2, we introduce the fundamentals of the Tangle 2.0 protocol. In Sect. 3, we define the adversary model and describe the Bait-and-Switch strategy. In Sect. 4, we describe the components considered in our simulations and explain the setup in Sect. 5. The experimental results are given in Sect. 6, and a conclusion can be found in Sect. 7.

2   Fundamentals of the Protocol

We introduce several fundamental concepts relevant to the protocol in our context. First, we discuss the UTXO accounting model, before addressing the block DAG that, in combination with a suitable Sybil protection facilitates the voting schemes.

2.1   The UTXO Ledger and Conflicts

Tracking of funds and change of ownership between addresses is facilitated by employing the Unspent Transaction Output (UTXO) model, e.g., [1,21,22]. In this model, transactions specify the outputs of previous transactions as inputs and spend them by creating new outputs. In contrast to the account-based model, transactions can be verified without knowing the global state of the system but depend only on the status of the inputs. Moreover, it identifies conflicts as every output can only be spent once.

As consistency is the main requirement of a ledger, nodes eventually have to resolve this kind of double-spends. The Tangle 2.0 consensus protocol, [18], decides between the conflicting spending relying on an identity-based Sybil protection, Sect. 2.3, and a voting protocol introduced in more detail in Sects. 2.4 and 2.6.

2.2   The Tangle

One of the basic ideas of [23] was to abolish the role of the miners or validators, as a leader-based approach not only leads to a performance limitation but also makes fees necessary. Instead, a cooperative approach is followed, in which each new block validates at least two other previous blocks by referencing them. Each participant can thus add blocks simultaneously and asynchronously. The blocks together with the references then form a DAG, the so-called *Tangle*. The Tangle is both a record of the communication between nodes as well as facilitates a data structure for the voting schemes introduced in the next sections.

We call the referenced and approving blocks *parents* and *children*, respectively. The reference relationship is transitive in the sense that new nodes not only refer (or vote) for their direct parents but also indirectly for the entire ancestral line. We call all blocks, referenced directly or indirectly, the *past cone* of a given block. Similarly, all blocks that refer to the block directly or indirectly are called its *future cone*, see Fig. 1. The first block of the Tangle has no parents and is called *genesis*. Blocks that have not been yet approved are called *tips*. In [18] there exist different reference types that infer different past cones of a block. However, in this paper, we consider only the most fundamental reference type which represents approval for the block itself and its entire past cone of the Tangle.

Every block consists of several elements, of which the most relevant are: parent references, the signature of the issuer (the node that introduced the block into the Tangle), and a payload. In this paper, the payload is a transaction.

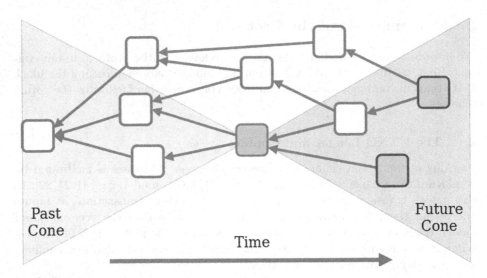

Fig. 1. The Tangle, the future, and the past cone of a block are highlighted with green and yellow triangles respectively. The orange blocks are tips. (Color figure online)

2.3 Sybil Protection

A system could be designed homogeneously or heterogeneously in respect to the impact different nodes can have. However, as the duplication of identities, a situation also described as *Sybil attack*, can be cheap in the DLT setting, a malicious actor could endanger a homogeneous system or even take it over by creating and controlling multiple entities [24]. To counter this each node has a score, called *weight*, which serves as a Sybil protection mechanism. Weights can be calculated in different ways, depending on the purpose. For example, it could be utilized in the context of (delegated) Proof-of-Stake systems. In the context of this paper, we employ it as voting power and access to the network's resources (share of the network throughput).

The total weight value within the network is the sum of the weights of all nodes. We note, that in a distributed network setting nodes can go offline and online at any time. Also, nodes may not be forced to issue blocks and use all of their bandwidth. However, in this work, we assume that the weights of the nodes are constant and that all nodes use their total share of the network throughput.

2.4 Approval Weight, Voting, and Confirmation

In this section, we define the concept of Approval Weight (AW). It is the core element of the consensus protocol. AW allows for measuring the endorsement of blocks and their corresponding transactions. The confirmation of a transaction is calculated by summing up the cumulative weight of all blocks' issuers in the future cone of the block that contains the transaction. It is in principle similar to the concept introduced in [23]. There, a weight of a block is corresponding to the amount of work put into creating a block and all blocks in its future cone. Instead, in this implementation block weight is equal to the issuer's weight and is counted at most once if a block is issued in the future cone. A block becomes confirmed whenever its accumulated weight reaches a certain threshold θ.

The On Tangle Voting (OTV), [18], allows voting on two conflicting transactions or double spends, A and B. A given node might receive transaction A and express its support for it (by issuing a block in the future cone of the block containing A) before receiving B. Once the node also receives B and its future cone, it compares each transaction's AW and votes for the transaction with the higher weights. In case the node changes its opinion in favor of B, the node's weight is revoked from the AW of transaction A, since for any pair of conflicts a node's weight is counted at most once.

Once a transaction is confirmed, i.e., its AW reaching θ, it will stay confirmed even if its AW falls below θ. Thus, the consensus protocol must be designed, such that the event of any two nodes confirming different transactions out of a set of mutually conflicting transactions occurs with negligible probability, or otherwise safety as discussed in the next section, is violated.

2.5 Liveness and Safety

Every consensus algorithm should ensure the following properties:

- **liveness**: all non-faulty nodes eventually take a decision,
- **safety**: all non-faulty nodes agree on the same values.

The satisfaction of the two properties depends on the underlying communication model. The most well-known communication models are synchronous, asynchronous, and partial synchronous, describing the network's synchronicity level.

The asynchronous model best reflects scenarios where an adversary can delay the transmission of blocks arbitrarily long. From the famous FLP impossibility result, [25], we know that reaching a (deterministic) agreement in an asynchronous setting is impossible. Therefore, there is a need for a so-called symmetry-breaking mechanism that uses a (shared) source of randomness to ensure liveness and safety.

It is crucial that the safety property always holds (at least with high probability). It is also essential that the progress of the protocol should happen eventually. The main goal of the performed simulations is to determine if it is possible to halt the termination of the voting mechanism and if the proposed symmetry or metastability breaking mechanism, described in the next section, ensures both the safety and liveness of the protocol can be guaranteed.

2.6 Synchronised Random Reality Selection

The concept of Synchronised Random Reality Selection (SRRS) was proposed in [18] and inspired by [26]. Because the OTV is an asynchronous protocol, a synchronization process on the communication level is lacking between nodes to overcome the deterministic FLP impossibility result. This synchronization of the nodes is done in the SRRS using a shared random number that is generated periodically. We denote D as the period (epoch) time. By the end of each epoch, every node in the network receives the newly generated random number. This "common coin" is used to *synchronize* the opinions of each node with the opinions of the other honest nodes. More details on the SRRS are described in Sect. 4.5.

3   The Adversary Model

We distinguish between two types of nodes: *honest* and *malicious*. Honest nodes follow the protocol, while malicious nodes are trying to actively disturb the protocol by not following protocol. We assume that the malicious nodes are controlled by an abstract entity that we call the *attacker*. We assume that the attackers are computationally limited and cannot break the signature schemes or the cryptographic hash functions involved.

In classic consensus protocols, the communication model already covers the adversary behaviors, as delaying blocks is essentially the only way an attacker can influence the system. This is no longer true for the Tangle 2.0 protocol and we focus in this paper on attacks on the voting layer. In these kinds of attacks, the attacker is in possession of some proportion of voting power, i.e. weight q, and uses this weight to manipulate the votes on the Tangle. We are interested in the problem of metastability, which aims to affect liveness and, in extreme cases, safety. The strategy of the attacker is then to keep the honest nodes in an undecided state.

3.1   Bait-and-Switch Attack

We implement several types of adversary strategies from [18] in the simulator [19]. However, we focus here on the Bait-and-Switch attack that seems to be the most effective strategy to attack liveness in the Tangle 2.0 protocol. Moreover, this attack is shown in theory to be effective even when the attacker has no control over the communication layer.

In contrast to typical balancing attacks, the Bait-and-Switch attack relies less on keeping the conflict weights symmetrical, but rather the attacker makes the honest nodes chase the ever-changing heaviest (measured in AW) transaction. The attack seems to be most effective in situations where the adversary has the largest weight among all nodes.

The attack starts with the adversary issuing a pair of conflicting transactions on which honest nodes start to vote. Then, before any of the two options accumulate more weight than the adversary has, the adversary issues another transaction conflicting with the previous ones, making it the heaviest transaction (measured in AW). The honest nodes will adapt their opinion to the newly issued conflict, but then the adversary issues another transaction conflicting with the previous ones and supports it with his weight. Thus, the new conflicting transaction becomes the heaviest in AW. This process can be repeated indefinitely unless a certain transaction accumulates more approval weight than the adversary has.

4   Simulation Components

To achieve efficient exploration of the Tangle 2.0 protocol, only the necessary components are implemented in the simulator, and some of them are simplified. In this section, we explain the simplifications of the simulator and the reasons for them.

4.1   Conflicts and Colours

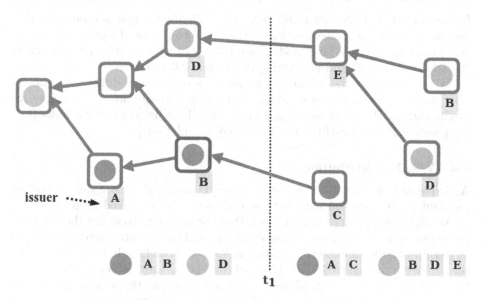

Fig. 2. Tracking of the supporters for AW calculation.

We encode conflicting transactions with different colors. For instance, Fig. 2 presents the Tangle with two conflicting transactions: the red and blue colors are introduced in a block by nodes A and D, respectively.

Considering the Tangle state until time t_1 separated by the dashed line, we can count the supporters for each branch by summing up the weights of block issuers in the future cone of the block that introduced each branch. Thus for $t < t_1$, red is supported by nodes A and B, and for blue by node D. After some time, the support changes. Notice that node B changed its opinion and attaches to the blue part of the Tangle, such that its previous vote for the red branch is canceled.

We want to note that two types of references are introduced in [18], i.e., block reference and transaction reference. Here we consider only the basic type of reference, which is a block reference. Thus, it is not allowed to reference blocks that belong to conflicting branches (i.e., they have different colors).

4.2   Communication Layer

The simulated environment reflects a situation in which network participants are connected in a peer-to-peer network, where each node has k neighbors. Nodes can gossip, receive blocks, request for missing blocks, and state their opinions whenever conflicts occur. In order to fully control the network topology, we produce a peer-to-peer network using a Watts-Strogatz network [27]. In order to mimic a real-world behavior, the simulator allows specifying the network delay and packet loss for each node's connection.

4.3 Agent-based Node Model

In the simulation, nodes act as different independent agents asynchronously. This means that different nodes can have different perceptions of the Tangle at any given moment of time. Thus, nodes have their own local Tangles for calculating the approval weights and performing the Tangle 2.0 protocol.

We assume that the number of nodes does not change during the simulation period, and all the honest nodes are actively participating in the consensus mechanism. With this assumption, all nodes can be considered active nodes (i.e., their weight is accounted for during the AW calculations).

4.4 Weight Distribution

As explained in Sect. 2.3 a scarce resource is assumed as a Sybil protection mechanism. We also consider that the node's weight is derived from or related to the underlying source token, which is the case in IOTA. To model the weight of the nodes in the network we use the Zipf empirical law, which is proven to govern an asymptotic distribution of weights near its upper tail [28]. In [29] it was shown that in the example of 100 IOTA's richest nodes, they follow approximately the Zipf law with $s = 0.9$. Moreover, the Zipf law has the advantage, i.e., by changing the parameter s, to model the network behavior for varying degrees of (de)centralization. For example, a homogeneous situation is modeled with $s = 0$, while for s above 1 a more centralized weight distribution can be investigated. Note that, in the simulator, nodes' weights are constant over time, and thus there is no concept of weight delegation or changes in the weight distribution caused by transactions and events happening in the network.

4.5 SRRS Implementation

If the conflict cannot be resolved until time D_{start}, then at the time of D_{start} and at the end of each epoch, every node will calculate a hash based on the opinion of the node and the random number x.

In our simulations, the random variable x is uniformly distributed on the interval [0.5, 0.66], where 0.66 is the value of the confirmation threshold θ. The hash is calculated as the SHA-256 of y, where $y = o + c * x$, and c is a predefined constant value. c is set to be 1000 in our experiments. Every node compares the AW of the different conflicting transactions with the random threshold x. If one of the conflicting transactions has more AW than x it will vote for this transaction. Otherwise, it will vote in the next D period for the transaction with the minimal hash described above. This process keeps running periodically until all honest nodes decide on the same transactions or the maximal simulation time of 60 s is reached.

Table 1. Default Experimental Settings

Symbol	Description	Value
N	Node count	100
s	Zipf parameter of weight distribution	0.9
θ	Confirmation threshold	66%
n_p	Parents count	8
BPS	Blocks per second (BPS)	100
l	Packet loss	0
γ	Watts-Strogatz rewiring probability	100%
k	Number of neighbors	8
q	Adversary weight	5%
d	Network delay	100 ms
t_{max}	Maximum simulation time	60 s

5 Simulation Setup

Table 1 lists the default experiment setup in our simulations. The node count is the number of nodes in the network. Each node has a weight, which influences its impact on the algorithm. The average block issuance rate of a node is assumed to be proportional to the weight. In addition, we assume the block issuance time interval of nodes follows a Poisson distribution [30]. The default confirmation threshold is set to be $\theta = 66\%$.

The parents' count (or the number of references) is set to be $n_p = 8$. These parents are chosen randomly (with replacement) among all visible tips. The throughput is measured as the total number of blocks per second (BPS) of all nodes combined; its default value is BPS $= 100s^{-1}$. The packet loss is set to be $l = 0$, i.e., no packets are lost. The minimum and maximum delays are the upper and lower latency bounds of packets between each pair of peers in the network, respectively. Both in the honest and adverse environments, the delay from an honest node or an adversary is set to be $d = 100$ ms, which is the packet delay transmitted from one node to its neighbors. The default Watts-Strogatz rewiring probability [27] is set to be $\gamma = 1$. In addition, the neighbor count is the number of neighbors of a node in the Watts-Strogatz topology, whose default value is 8. t_{max} denotes the maximum simulation time, and the default value is set to be $t_{max} = 60$ s. The simulation will be terminated automatically and regarded as a security failure if the conflicts cannot be resolved before the predefined t_{max}.

The adversary weight is set to be q, which is the percentage of the total weight controlled by the adversary node. Figure 3 shows weight distribution examples with $q = 33\%$, $N = 11$ for several values of s. In the figure, the index of the adversary node is 11, and nodes with indices 1 to 10 are honest nodes. As 33% of the total weight is occupied by the adversary, the remaining 67% of the total weight is distributed among the 10 honest nodes.

Based on the different settings of the above parameters, the robustness and efficiency of the Tangle 2.0 can be explored and simulated thoroughly.

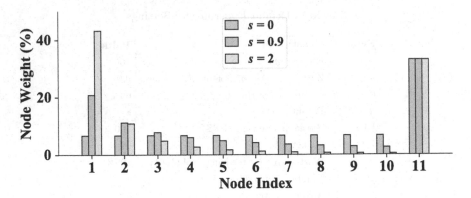

Fig. 3. Node weight distribution example with $q = 33\%$, $N = 11$. The node index of the adversary is 11.

6   Simulation Results

To demonstrate the robustness of the Tangle 2.0, we first explore the consensus time distributions of the OTV protocol under adversary environments. The consensus time is defined as the time period measured from the time that a double spend happens to the time that all the honest nodes decided on the same opinion, i.e., reach consensus. By measuring the consensus time, the safety and liveness of the protocol can be analyzed. Next, we analyze the confirmation time in expected scenarios (i.e., $N = 100$ and $s = 0.9$). The confirmation time is measured in the local Tangles of all honest nodes and is defined as the time period from the block issuance time to the time when its cumulative AW $> \theta$. By measuring the confirmation time distributions, the liveness of the protocol is analyzed. In the end, we show experimental results that non-conflicting blocks are immune to attacks from adversaries.

6.1   OTV Protocol Without SRRS

Figure 4 shows the experimental results of the OTV consensus time distributions under the Bait-and-Switch attack and without SRRS. Different adversary weights, ranging from 5% to 33%, and Zipf distributions, $s \in \{0, 0.9, 2\}$, are simulated. Each experimental setting is simulated 100 times. For each simulation run, the consensus time of the double spend is collected. As Fig. 4a shows, when $q \leq 20\%$, all of the 100 simulation runs can successfully resist the Bait-and-Switch attack, where all the conflicts can be resolved within 30s. When the adversary weight q is increased to $\geq 25\%$, liveness failures occur, i.e., conflicts are failed to be resolved within 60s.

With increased s, honest nodes are more likely to follow the opinions of the honest nodes with heavy weight, which makes the conflicts easier to be resolved. We can observe this in Fig. 4b, where the Zipf parameter is increased to $s = 0.9$. With the higher value of s no liveness failures occur for $q \leq 25\%$. Also, most of the runs can resist the Bait-and-Switch attack for $q = 30\%$.

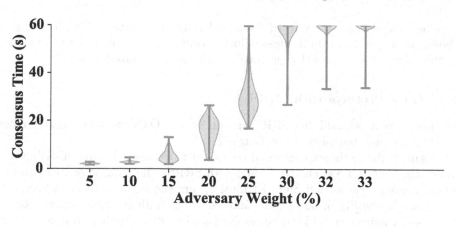

(a) $s = 0$

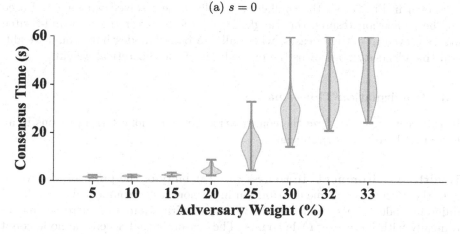

(b) $s = 0.9$

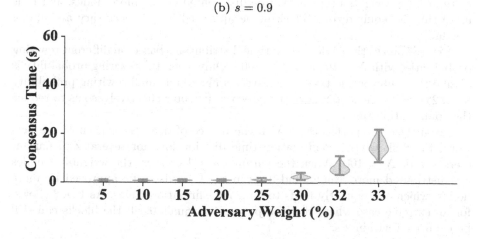

(c) $s = 2$

Fig. 4. OTV consensus time distributions under Bait-and-Switch attack, without SRRS ($N = 100$).

Figure 4c shows the results of $s = 2$ under the same attack. For all the cases shown, even $q = 33\%$, no liveness failures occur. This provides strong evidence of the robustness of the OTV protocol, in a more centralized setting.

6.2   OTV Protocol with SRRS

In this section, we add the SRRS on top of the OTV protocol, and further investigate the robustness of the Tangle 2.0.

Figure 5 shows the experimental results of the consensus time distributions under the Bait-and-Switch attack, and with SRRS. The parameter variations of the adversary weights and Zipf distributions are the same as those in Sect. 6.1. As shown in the Fig. 5, no security failures occur in all the simulations. For all the cases, conflicts are able to be resolved within 20 s. Furthermore, for $s = 2$, as shown in Fig. 5c, all the conflicts are able to be resolved within 7 s. Based on the simulation results, the Tangle 2.0 is able to resist the Bait-and-Switch attacks, even in extreme cases, where all the honest nodes have equal weight, and the adversary node owns the upper limit of the theoretical weight.

6.3   Confirmation Time Analysis

In this section, we analyze the confirmation times of honest transactions in an honest and adverse environment.

Healthy Environment To address the scalability of the protocol we investigate the confirmation time distribution in an honest environment, i.e. $q = 0$, for different node counts. As Fig. 6 shows, the confirmation time increases monotonically with increasing node counts. The reason is that when the node count increases, the weights of nodes will be distributed across more nodes, and thus more time is required for a block to be approved by the necessary amount of weights.

Figure 7 shows the confirmation time distributions based on different rewiring probabilities with $N = 100$ and $N = 1000$. Only when the rewiring probability is close 0 the confirmation time is relatively long, and a small rewiring probability (e.g., 2%) is sufficient to reduce the network diameter effectively, so as to reduce the confirmation time.

To analyze the performance with the degree of decentralization of the network, Fig. 8 shows the confirmation time distributions for several Zipf parameters s with $N = 100$. When the parameter s decreases, the weights of nodes are distributed more evenly, and a given block needs to be approved by more nodes, which consequently leads to longer confirmation times. As Fig. 8 shows, for an extreme case where the Zipf parameter equals 0, all the blocks can still be confirmed within 2 s.

Figure 9 shows the confirmation time distributions under different uniform random network delays. The confirmation time becomes longer monotonically with a longer network delay. Note that the delay for a modern network is around 100 ms, where ≤ 2 s confirmation time can be achieved in the protocol.

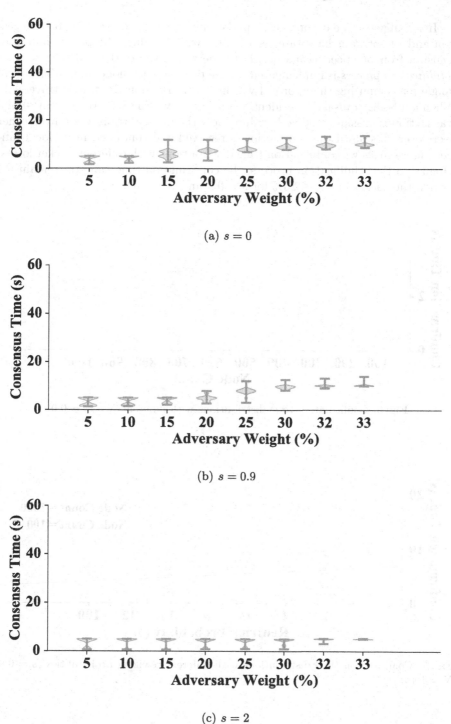

(a) $s = 0$

(b) $s = 0.9$

(c) $s = 2$

Fig. 5. OTV consensus time distributions under Bait-and-Switch attack, with SRRS ($N = 100$).

In a real network environment, a packet might get lost due to network congestion and/or software/hardware issues. This will introduce the packet failing to
transmit from one peer to another. In the network layer of the IOTA protocol, a
solidification process is implemented. In the process, each node maintains a local
tangle for computing the approval weights of transactions by tangle traversing.
When a missing transaction is identified in the traversing (i.e., the parent(s) of a
transaction is missing), the node will request the missing transaction from other
peers every 5 s, until the transaction is received and contained in its local tangle. Figure 10 shows confirmation time distributions with different packet losses.
Thanks to the solidification process, the confirmation time can still remain ≤ 2
s when the packet loss is $\leq 25\%$ for $s = 0.9$ and $N = 100$.

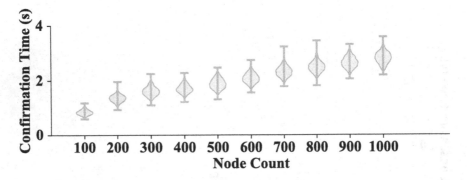

Fig. 6. Confirmation time distributions with different N's ($s = 0.9$).

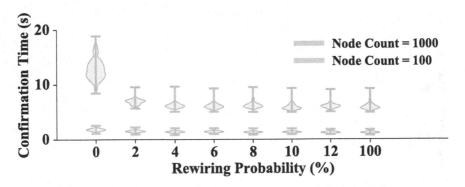

Fig. 7. Confirmation time distributions with different rewiring probabilities ($s = 0.9$,
$N = 100$).

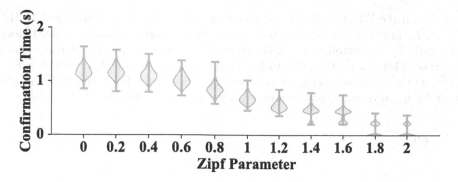

Fig. 8. Confirmation time distributions for different Zipf parameters s ($N = 100$).

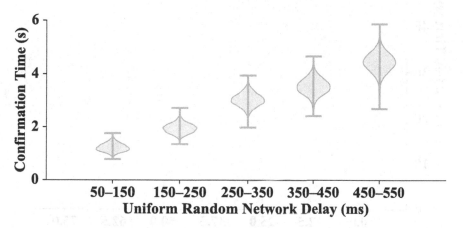

Fig. 9. Confirmation time distributions with different uniform random network delays ($N = 100$ and $s = 0.9$).

Adverse Environment Figure 11 shows the confirmation time distributions of non-conflicting transactions under the Bait-and-Switch attack, where the Zipf parameter and the node count are $s = 0.9$ and $N = 100$, respectively. As shown in the figure, most of the non-conflicting blocks can be confirmed within 1 to 2 s, which are not affected by the presence of conflicts. Note that there are a few outliers. These can be explained by non-conflicting transactions (i.e., the outliers) being orphaned because the voting powers of the honest nodes are split to vote for the different conflicting transactions before the conflict resolution. In the case of an orphanage, the issuers of the affected block reattaches the transaction in a new block after 5 s. This is possible, because the issuance of different blocks with the same transaction is not considered a double spend but rather, on the UTXO ledger level, is considered as the same transaction. In the IOTA 2.0 protocol, this liveness problem for honest transactions is resolved more elegantly by the introduction of the second type of reference, i.e., a transaction reference [18]. In addition, due to the fixed confirmation threshold, which is $\theta = 66\%$, as the adversary occupies more weight, non-conflicting transactions might wait for a longer time to accumulate their AW from different honest nodes.

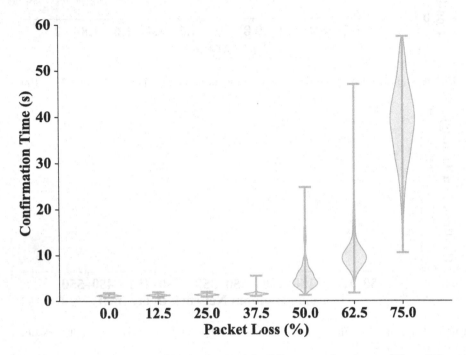

Fig. 10. Confirmation time distributions with different packet losses ($N = 100$ and $s = 0.9$).

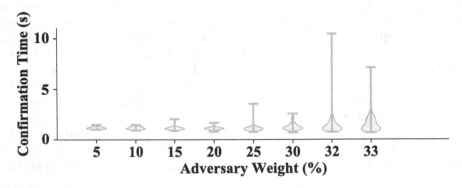

Fig. 11. Confirmation time distributions of non-conflicting transactions with $s = 0.9$ and $N = 100$.

7   Conclusion

In this paper, we gave a first performance analysis of the Tangle 2.0 protocol. The confirmation time distributions based on different environments and under attacks are analyzed. The experimental results show that the Tangle 2.0 can resist the Bait-and-Switch attack and achieve a short consensus time, even in extremely adverse environments. Moreover, in common scenarios, the protocol can achieve confirmation time in the order of seconds, and confirmation times of most non-conflicting transactions are not affected noticeably by the presence of conflicts.

Acknowledgment. The authors would like to thank the developer team of the GoShimmer software, to support this study with the prototype implementation of the Tangle 2.0 protocol.

References

1. Nakamoto, S.: Bitcoin: a peer-to-peer electronic cash system (2008)
2. Paulavičius, R., Grigaitis, S., Filatovas, E.: A systematic review and empirical analysis of blockchain simulators. IEEE Access **9**, 38 010–38 028 (2021)
3. Berger, C., Reiser, H.: Scaling byzantine consensus: a broad analysis, pp. 13–18, December 2018
4. Xiao, Y., Zhang, N., Lou, W., Hou, Y.T.: A survey of distributed consensus protocols for blockchain networks. IEEE Commun. Surv. Tutor. **22**(2), 1432–1465 (2020)
5. Hari, A., Kodialam, M., Lakshman, T.V.: ACCEL: accelerating the bitcoin blockchain for high-throughput, low-latency applications. In: IEEE INFOCOM 2019 - IEEE Conference on Computer Communications, 2019, pp. 2368–2376 (2019)
6. Zhou, Q., Huang, H., Zheng, Z., Bian, J.: Solutions to scalability of blockchain: a survey. IEEE Access **8**, 16 440–16 455 (2020)
7. Sompolinsky, Y., Lewenberg, Y., Zohar, A.: Spectre: a fast and scalable cryptocurrency protocol, Cryptology ePrint Archive, Report 2016/1159 (2016). https://ia.cr/2016/1159
8. Churyumov, A.: Byteball: a decentralized system for storage and transfer of value (2016). https://byteball.org/Byteball.pdf
9. Gilad, Y., Hemo, R., Micali, S., Vlachos, G., Zeldovich, N.: Algorand: scaling byzantine agreements for cryptocurrencies. In: Proceedings of the 26th Symposium on Operating Systems Principles, 2017, pp. 51–68 (2017)
10. Sompolinsky, Y., Wyborski, S., Zohar, A.: PHANTOM and GHOSTDAG: a scalable generalization of Nakamoto consensus, Cryptology ePrint Archive, Report 2018/104 (2018). https://ia.cr/2018/104
11. Rocket, T., Yin, M., Sekniqi, K., van Renesse, R., Sirer, E.G.: Scalable and probabilistic leaderless BFT consensus through metastability (2019)
12. Bagaria, V., Kannan, S., Tse, D., Fanti, G., Viswanath, P.: Prism: deconstructing the blockchain to approach physical limits. In: Proceedings of the 2019 ACM SIGSAC Conference on Computer and Communications Security, 2019, pp. 585–602 (2019)

13. Gągol, A., Leśniak, D., Straszak, D., Świętek, M.: Aleph: efficient atomic broadcast in asynchronous networks with byzantine nodes. In: Proceedings of the 1st ACM Conference on Advances in Financial Technologies, 2019, pp. 214–228 (2019)
14. Danezis, G., Kokoris-Kogias, L., Sonnino, A., Spiegelman, A.: Narwhal and Tusk: A DAG-Based Mempool and Efficient BFT Consensus, ser. EuroSys '22, pp. 34–50. Association for Computing Machinery, New York, NY, USA (2022). https://doi.org/10.1145/3492321.3519594
15. Popov, S., et al.: The Coordicide (2020)
16. Pervez, H., Muneeb, M., Irfan, M.U., Haq, I.U.: A comparative analysis of DAG-based blockchain architectures. In: 2018 12th International Conference on Open Source Systems and Technologies (ICOSST), 2018, pp. 27–34 (2018)
17. Dotan, M., Pignolet, Y. A., Schmid, S., Tochner, S., Zohar, A.: SOK: cryptocurrency networking context, state-of-the-art, challenges. In: Proceedings of the 15th International Conference on Availability, Reliability and Security, ser. ARES '20. Association for Computing Machinery, New York, NY, USA (2020)
18. Müller, S., Penzkofer, A., Polyanskii, N., Theis, J., Sanders, W., Moog, H.: Tangle 2.0 Leaderless Nakamoto Consensus on the Heaviest DAG (2022). https://arxiv.org/abs/2205.02177
19. IOTA Foundation. (2021) Tangle 2.0 simulator. https://github.com/iotaledger/multiverse-simulation
20. Zander, M., Waite, T., Harz, D.: DAGsim: simulation of DAG-based distributed ledger protocols. ACM SIGMETRICS Perform. Eval. Rev. **46**, 118–121 (2019)
21. Chakravarty, M.M.T., Chapman, J., MacKenzie, K., Melkonian, O., Peyton Jones, M., Wadler, P.: The extended UTXO model. In: Bernhard, M., et al. (eds.) FC 2020. LNCS, vol. 12063, pp. 525–539. Springer, Cham (2020). https://doi.org/10.1007/978-3-030-54455-3_37
22. Müller, S., Penzkofer, A., Polyanskii, N., Theis, J., Sanders, W., Moog, H.: Reality-based UTXO Ledger (2022). https://arxiv.org/abs/2205.01345
23. Popov, S.Y.: The tangle (2015)
24. Douceur, J.R.: The Sybil attack. In: Druschel, P., Kaashoek, F., Rowstron, A. (eds.) IPTPS 2002. LNCS, vol. 2429, pp. 251–260. Springer, Heidelberg (2002). https://doi.org/10.1007/3-540-45748-8_24
25. Fischer, M.J., Lynch, N.A., Paterson, M.S.: Impossibility of distributed consensus with one faulty process. J. ACM (JACM) **32**(2), 374–382 (1985)
26. Popov, S., Buchanan, W.J.: FPC-BI: fast probabilistic consensus within byzantine infrastructures. J. Parallel Distrib. Comput. **147**, 77–86 (2021)
27. Watts, D.J., Strogatz, S.H.: Collective dynamics of small-world networks. Nature **393**(6684), 440–442 (1998)
28. Powers, D.M.W.: Applications and explanations of Zipf's law, in New Methods in Language Processing and Computational Natural Language Learning (1998). https://aclanthology.org/W98-1218
29. Müller, S., Penzkofer, A., Kuśmierz, B., Camargo, D., Buchanan, W.J.: Fast probabilistic consensus with weighted votes. In: Proceedings of the Future Technologies Conference (FTC), vol. 2, no. 2021, pp. 360–378 (2020)
30. Penzkofer, A., Saa, O., Dziubałtowska, D.: Impact of delay classes on the data structure in IOTA. In: DPM/CBT@ESORICS, 2021 (2021)

Renting Edge Computing Resources for Service Hosting

Aadesh Madnaik$^{(\boxtimes)}$, Sharayu Moharir, and Nikhil Karamchandani

Indian Institute of Technology Bombay, Mumbai, India
aadesh.madnaik@iitb.ac.in, {sharayum,nikhilk}@ee.iitb.ac.in

Abstract. We consider the setting where a service is hosted on a third-party edge server deployed close to the users and a cloud server at a greater distance from the users. Due to the proximity of the edge servers to the users, requests can be served at the edge with low latency. However, as the computation resources at the edge are limited, some requests must be routed to the cloud for service and incur high latency. The system's overall performance depends on the rent cost incurred to use the edge server, the latency experienced by the users, and the cost incurred to change the amount of edge computation resources rented over time. The algorithmic challenge is to determine the amount of edge computation power to rent over time. We propose a deterministic online policy and characterize its performance for adversarial and stochastic i.i.d. request arrival processes. We also characterize a fundamental bound on the performance of any deterministic online policy. Further, we compare the performance of our policy with suitably modified versions of existing policies to conclude that our policy is robust to temporal changes in the intensity of request arrivals.

Keywords: Service hosting · edge computing · competitive ratio

1 Introduction

Software as a Service (SaaS) instances like search engines, online shopping platforms, navigation services, and Video-on-Demand services have recently gained popularity. Low latency in responding to user requests/queries is essential for most of these services. This necessitates the use of edge resources in a paradigm known as edge-computing [24], i.e., storage and computation power close to the resource-constrained users, to serve user queries. Due to limited computation resources at the edge, such services are often also deployed on cloud servers which can serve requests that cannot be served at the edge, albeit with more latency given the distance between the cloud servers and the users. Ultimately, introducing edge-computing platforms facilitates low network latency coupled with higher

This work is supported by a SERB grant on Leveraging Edge Resources for Service Hosting.

E. Hyytiä and V. Kavitha (Eds.): VALUETOOLS 2022, LNICST 482, pp. 277–291, 2023.
https://doi.org/10.1007/978-3-031-31234-2_17

computational capabilities. For instance, consider a scenario where a child goes missing in an urban setting [25]. While cameras are widely used for security, it is challenging to leverage the information as a whole because of privacy and data traffic issues. In the edge computing paradigm, a workaround would be to push a request to search for the child to a certain subset of devices, thereby making the process faster and more efficient than cloud computing. Several other avenues of edge computing exist in the forms of cloud offloading, AR/VR-based infotainment, autonomous robotics, Industry 4.0 and the Internet of Things (IoT). Several industry leaders offer services for edge resources, e.g., Amazon Web Services [3], Oracle Cloud Infrastructure [13] and IBM with 5G technology [12].

This work considers a system with cloud servers and third-party-owned edge servers. Edge resources, i.e., storage and computation power, can be rented via short-term contracts to host services. Storage resources are needed to store the code, databases, and libraries for the service and computation resources are required to compute responses to user queries. As edge servers are limited in computational capabilities, there is a cap on the number of concurrent requests that can be served at the edge [26]. The amount of edge computational resources rented for the service governs the number of user requests that can be served simultaneously at the edge. We focus on a service that is hosted both on the cloud and edge servers, and the amount of edge computational resources rented can be changed over time based on various factors, including the user request traffic and the cost of renting edge computation resources. Service providers provision for elasticity in the quantity of edge resources rented, and the clients can exploit this based on the number of request arrivals [18]. The total cost incurred by the system is modelled as the sum of the rent cost incurred to use edge resources, the cost incurred due to high latency in serving requests that have to be routed to the cloud, and the switching cost incurred every time the amount of edge computation resource rented is changed [30]. The algorithmic challenge in this work is to determine the amount of edge computation resources to rent over time in the setting where the request arrival sequence is revealed causally with the goal of minimizing the overall cost incurred.

1.1   Our Contributions

We propose a deterministic online policy called Better-Late-than-Never (BLTN) inspired by the RetroRenting policy proposed in [21] and analyze its performance for adversarial and, i.i.d. stochastic request arrival patterns. In addition to this, we also characterize fundamental limits on the performance of any deterministic online policy for adversarial arrivals in terms of competitive ratio against the optimal-offline policy. Further, we compare the performance of BLTN with a suitably modified version of the widely studied Follow the Perturbed Leader (FTPL) policy [5,19] via simulations. Our results show that while the performance of BLTN and FTPL is comparable for i.i.d. stochastic arrivals, for arrival processes with time-varying intensity, e.g., a Gilbert-Elliot-like model, BLTN significant outperforms FTPL. The key reason for this is that BLTN puts extra emphasis on recent arrival patterns of making decisions, while FTPL uses the entire request arrival history to make decisions. For all settings under consideration, the simulations demonstrate that BLTN differs little in performance from the optimal online policy despite not having information about the incoming request arrival process.

1.2 Related Work

There has been a sharp increase in mobile application latency and bandwidth requirements, particularly when coupled with time-critical domains such as autonomous robotics and the Internet of Things (IoT). These changes have ushered in the advent of the edge computing paradigm away from the conventional remote servers, as discussed in the surveys [1,15,23]. The surveys alongside several academic works elaborate on and model the dynamics of such systems. We briefly discuss some relevant literary works.

Representations of the problem considered in [6,26] model the decision making of which services to cache and which tasks to offload as a mixed-integer nonlinear optimization problem. In these cases, the problem is NP-hard. Similarly, [8] models the problem as a graph colouring problem and solves it using parallel Gibbs sampling. While these works try to solve a one-shot cost-minimization problem, in this work we consider the dynamic nature of decision-making based on the input request sequence.

Another model considered in [28] for service hosting focused on the joint optimization of service hosting decision and pricing is a two-stage interactive game between a base-station that provides pricing for edge servers and user equipment which decides whether to offload the task. In another game-theoretic setup, [14,29] delve into the economic aspects of edge caching involving interactions amongst different stakeholders. Some heuristic algorithms have been employed in the works [2,10]. Their approach for the problem is through resource constraint in the latency from the view-point of the edge-cloud infrastructure and not the application provider.

Stochastic models of the system have been considered in [9,17,27]. While [27] assumes that the underlying requests follow a Poisson process, [9,17] do not make any prior assumptions regarding the same. [9,17], through Contextual Combinatorial Multiarmed Bandits aim to use a learning-based approach to make decisions. [27] formulates the service migration problem as a Markov decision process (MDP) to design optimal service migration policies. These models do not provide any worst-case guarantees for the algorithm, simply average guarantees. In our work, we aim to provide both performance guarantees which are crucial to sensitive applications with large variations in the arrival patterns.

Closest to our work, [20–22] consider the setting where a service is always hosted at the cloud and consider the algorithmic task of determining when to host the service at the edge server as a function of the arrival process and various system parameters. The key difference between our work and [20–22] is that, in [20–22], once the service is hosted at the edge, the amount of edge computation resources available for use by the service is either fixed or effectively unlimited. Our model allows us to choose the level of computation resources to rent which is a feature available in popular third-party storage/computation resource providers like AWS and Microsoft Azure. Another critical difference between our model and the [20–22] is the fact that we consider the setting where a non-zero switch cost is incurred every time we change the level of computation resource rented. Contrary to this, in [20–22], switch cost is unidirectional, i.e., a switch cost is incurred only when a service is not hosted at the edge in a time-slot and has to be fetched from the cloud servers to host on the edge server. Due to this, the algorithms proposed in [20–22] and their performance analyses do not directly extend to our setting. Other works on the service hosting problem include [31]. At a high level, our work is related to the rich body of work on caching [4,5,7,19].

2   Setting

We study a system consisting of a cloud server and a third-party-owned edge server. We focus on the problem of efficiently using edge resources from the perspective of a specific service provider. This service is hosted both at the edge and on the cloud server. Each user query/request is routed either to the edge or the cloud and the answer to the query is computed at that server and communicated back to the user, thus necessitating computation power both at the edge and at the cloud servers. We consider a time-slotted setting where the amount of edge computation power rented by the service provider can be changed over time via short-term contracts.

Request Arrival Process: We consider adversarial and stochastic arrivals. Under the adversarial setting, we make no structural assumptions on the number of requests arriving over time. For our analytical results for stochastic arrivals, we consider the setting where arrivals are i.i.d. over time.

Assumption 1 *(i.i.d. stochastic arrivals). Let X_t be the number of requests arriving in time-slot t. Then, for all t, $\mathbb{P}(X_t = x) = p_x$ for $x = 0, 1, 2, \cdots$.*

In the Gilbert-Elliot-like Model, we make the following assumption:

Assumption 2 *(Gilbert-Elliot (GE) Model). Using [11] as a basis, we consider an arrival process governed by a two-state Markov chain, A_H and A_L. Transitions from state $A_H \rightarrow A_L$ and from state $A_L \rightarrow A_H$ occur with probabilities p_{HL} and p_{LH}. The state transition diagram has been described in Fig. 1. We refer to the two states as the high state and the low state. Under the GE model, if the Markov chain is in the high state, the requests arrive as Poisson(λ_H), and they are Poisson(λ_L) otherwise.*

Sequence of Events in Each Time-Slot: We first have request arrivals. These requests are served by the edge server subject to constraints due to limited computation power at the edge. The remaining requests, if any, are forwarded to the cloud server for service. The system then makes a decision on how much edge computation power to rent for the next time-slot.

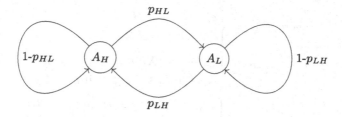

Fig. 1. Gilbert-Elliot Model as a Markov Chain

The algorithmic challenge is to determine how much edge computation power to rent over time. Let $\mathcal{P}$ be a candidate policy that determines the amount of computation power rented by the service provider over time.

2.1   Cost Model and Constraints

We build on the assumptions in [20–22]. Under policy $\mathcal{P}$, the service provider incurs three types of costs.

- *Rent cost* $(C_{R,t}^{\mathcal{P}})$: The service provider can choose one of two possible levels of edge computation power to rent in each time-slot, referred to as high (H) and low (L). The rent cost incurred per time-slot for levels H and L are denoted by c_H and $c_L(< c_H)$ respectively.
- *Service cost* $(C_{S,t}^{\mathcal{P}})$: This is the cost incurred due to the latency in service user requests. Given the proximity of the edge servers and the users, no service cost is incurred for requests served at the edge. A cost of one unit is levied on each request forwarded to the cloud server. The highest number of requests that can be served at the edge at edge computation power levels H and L are denoted by κ_H and $\kappa_L(< \kappa_H)$ respectively.
- *Switch cost* $(C_{W,t}^{\mathcal{P}})$: Switching from edge computation power level H to L and L to H results in a switch cost of W_{HL} and W_{LH} units respectively.

The number of requests that can be served by the edge server in a time-slot is limited to κ_H for state S_H and κ_L for state S_L in $\mathbb{Z}^+$, where $\mathbb{Z}^+$ is the set of all positive integers. Let $r_t \in \{H, L\}$ denote the edge computation power rented during time-slot t and X_t denote the number of request arrivals in time-slot t. It follows that

$$C_t^{\mathcal{P}} = C_{R,t}^{\mathcal{P}} + C_{S,t}^{\mathcal{P}} + C_{W,t}^{\mathcal{P}}, \tag{1}$$

$$\text{where, } C_{R,t}^{\mathcal{P}} = \begin{cases} c_H & \text{if } r_t = H \\ c_L & \text{if } r_t = L \end{cases}$$

$$C_{S,t}^{\mathcal{P}} = \begin{cases} X_t - \min\{X_t, \kappa_H\} & \text{if } r_t = H \\ X_t - \min\{X_t, \kappa_L\} & \text{if } r_t = L \end{cases}$$

$$C_{W,t}^{\mathcal{P}} = \begin{cases} W_{HL} & \text{if } r_{t-1} = H \text{ and } r_t = L \\ W_{LH} & \text{if } r_{t-1} = L \text{ and } r_t = H \\ 0 & \text{otherwise.} \end{cases}$$

Remark 1. We limit our discussion to the case where $\kappa_H - \kappa_L > c_H - c_L$. If $\kappa_H - \kappa_L \leq c_H - c_L$, the optimal policy is to always use computation level L.

2.2 Performance Metrics

We use the following metrics for adversarial and stochastic request arrivals.

For adversarial arrivals, we compare the performance of a policy $\mathcal{P}$ with the performance of the optimal offline policy (OPT-OFF) which knows the entire arrival sequence a priori. The performance of policy $\mathcal{P}$ is characterized by it competitive ratio $\rho^{\mathcal{P}}$ defined as

$$\rho^{\mathcal{P}} = \sup_{a \in \mathcal{A}} \frac{C^{\mathcal{P}}(a)}{C^{\text{OPT-OFF}}(a)}, \tag{2}$$

where $\mathcal{A}$ is the set of all possible finite request arrival sequences, and $C^{\mathcal{P}}(a)$ and $C^{\text{OPT-OFF}}(a)$ are the total costs of service for the request arrival sequence a under the policy $\mathcal{P}$ and the optimal offline policy respectively.

For i.i.d. stochastic arrivals, we compare the performances of a policy $\mathcal{P}$ with the optimal online policy (OPT-ON) which might know the statistics of the arrival process, but does not know the sample path. The performance metric $\sigma_T^{\mathcal{P}}$ is defined as the ratio of the expected cost incurred by policy $\mathcal{P}$ in T time-slots to that of the optimal online policy in the same time interval. Formally,

$$\sigma^{\mathcal{P}}(T) = \frac{\mathbb{E}\left[\sum_{t=1}^{T} C_t^{\mathcal{P}}\right]}{\mathbb{E}\left[\sum_{t=1}^{T} C_t^{\text{OPT-ON}}\right]}, \tag{3}$$

where $C_t^{\mathcal{P}}$ is as defined in (1).

Goal: The goal is to design online policies with provable performance guarantees for both adversarial and stochastic arrivals.

3   Policies

In our analysis, we focus the discussion towards *online* policies. At each time-slot, a singular decision must be made determining whether to switch states.

3.1 Better Late Than Never (BLTN)

The BLTN policy is inspired by the RetroRenting policy proposed in [21]. BLTN is a deterministic policy that uses recent arrival patterns to evaluate decisions by checking if it made the correct choice in hindsight. Let $t_{\text{switch}} < t$ be the most recent time when the state was changed from $H \to L$ or $L \to H$ under BLTN. The policy searches for a time-slot τ such that $t_{\text{switch}} < \tau < t$, and the total cost incurred is lower if the state is switched in time-slot $\tau - 1$ and switched back in time-slot t than the cost incurred if the state is not changed during time-slots $\tau - 1$ to t. If there exists such a time τ, BLTN switches the state in time-slot t.

Consider a scenario where the state in time slot t is S_H. Let $t_{\text{switch}} < t$ be the time when the server had last changed state to S_L under BLTN. Let H_i and L_i denote cost incurred in time slot i where H_i and L_i are evaluated for $r_i = r_{i-1} = H$ and L respectively. Analytically, the decision to switch to state S_L is made if the algorithm can find a time τ such that

$$W_{LH} + W_{HL} + \sum_{t_{\text{switch}} \leq i < \tau} H_i + \sum_{\tau \leq j \leq t} L_j < \sum_{t_{\text{switch}} \leq i \leq t} H_i$$

$$\text{which simplifies to } W_{LH} + W_{HL} < \sum_{i=\tau}^{t}(H_i - L_i). \tag{4}$$

A similar analytical condition can be made for the decision to switch from S_L to state S_H. The decision is made if the algorithm can find a time-slot τ such that

$$W_{LH} + W_{HL} < \sum_{i=\tau}^{t}(L_i - H_i). \tag{5}$$

A naive implementation of the algorithm has been constructed in the Appendix of [16].

While a naive implementation of the BLTN policy can have $\mathcal{O}(T)$ space and time complexity, using techniques proposed in [21], the time and computational complexity can be reduced to $\mathcal{O}(1)$ as shown through Algorithm 1.

3.2 Follow the Perturbed Leader (FTPL)

FTPL [5,19] is a randomized policy. In time-slot t, it compares suitably perturbed versions of the cost incurred from time 1 to t under two static decisions, i.e., state L from time 1 to t and state H from time 1 to t. The state of the system is then set to the one which has the lower perturbed cost.

The variation of the perturbation $\mathcal{N}(0, \sqrt{t})$ increases as $\sqrt{t}$, while the total difference in cost scaled linearly with time. This implies that the FTPL policy, over time, chooses to remain static in the state with the least cost.

Algorithm 1: Better Late than Never (BLTN)

---

1   Input: Sum of switch costs W units, maximum number of our service requests served by edge server (κ_H and κ_L), rent cost: c_H and c_L, number of requests: x_t, $\underline{x}_t^H = \min\{x_t, \kappa_H\}$, $\underline{x}_t^L = \min\{x_t, \kappa_L\}$, $t > 0$

2   Output: Service hosting strategy $r_{t+1} \in \{H, L\}$, $t > 0$

3   Initialize: Service hosting variable $r_1 = 0$, $\Delta(0) = 0$

4   **for** *each time-slot t* **do**

5       $\Delta(t-1) = \Delta(t)$

6   **if** $r_t = H$ **then**

7          $\Delta(t) = \max\left\{0, \Delta(t-1) + \underline{x}_t^L - \underline{x}_t^H + c_H - c_L\right\}$

8   **if** $\Delta(t) > W$ **then**

9             $t_{\text{switch}} = t$

10            $\Delta(t) = 0$

11   return $r_{t+1} = L$

12   **else**

13   return $r_{t+1} = H$

14   **end**

15   **else if** $r_t = L$ **then**

16          $\Delta(t) = \max\left\{0, \Delta(t-1) + \underline{x}_t^H - \underline{x}_t^L + c_L - c_H\right\}$

17   **if** $\Delta(t) > W$ **then**

18            $t_{\text{switch}} = t$

19            $\Delta(t) = 0$

20   return $r_{t+1} = H$

21   **else**

22   return $r_{t+1} = L$

23   **end**

24   **end**

25 **end**

Algorithm 2: Follow the Perturbed Leader (FTPL)

---

1   Input: Switch costs W_{HL} and W_{LH} units, maximum number of our service requests served by edge server (κ_H and κ_L), rent cost: c_H and c_L, number of requests: x_t, $\underline{x}_t^H = \min\{x_t, \kappa_H\}$, $\underline{x}_t^L = \min\{x_t, \kappa_L\}$, $t > 0$, Gaussian distribution with mean μ and variance σ: $\mathcal{N}(\mu, \sigma)$

2   Output: Service hosting strategy $r_{t+1} \in \{H, L\}$, $t > 0$

3   Initialize: Service hosting variable $r_1 = 0$, $\Delta(0) = 0$

4   **for** *each time-slot t* **do**

5       $\Delta(t-1) = \Delta(t)$

6       $\Delta(t) = \Delta(t-1) + \underline{x}_t^L - \underline{x}_t^H + c_H - c_L$

7   **if** $\Delta(t) + \gamma \mathcal{N}(0, \sqrt{t}) > 0$ **then**

8   return $r_{t+1} = L$

9   **else**

10   return $r_{t+1} = H$

11   **end**

12 **end**

3.3   An Illustration

We consider a sample sequence of arrivals. Let r_t be the state sequence with time index t. We consider the case where $W_{LH} = W_{HL} = 275, c_H = 600, c_L = 400, \kappa_H = 700, \kappa_L = 300$ and a request sequence

Number of requests:	900	900	900	900	900	900	200	200	200	200	200
Time-slot index:	1	2	3	4	5	6	7	8	9	10	11

Initially, we consider the edge server to be in state S_L. We observe that the optimal state to serve 900 incoming requests is S_H. While hosting under the BLTN policy, the first switch to state S_H occurs in the time-slot 3, thus $r_4 = H$ and $r_{1,2,3} = L$. The cost incurred in the case where the state is S_L till $t = 3$ is $\sum_{l=1}^{3}(x_l - \kappa_L)^+ + (3 - 1 + 1) \times c_L = 3000$, while the cost incurred in state S_H is $\sum_{l=1}^{3}(x_l - \kappa_H)^+ + (3 - 1 + 1) \times c_H = 2400$. The difference in the cost equates $600 > W = 550$, and that is the first time the condition 5 is satisfied. t_{switch} is updated to 3, and $r_4 = H$.

From time-slot 4 onward, BLTN hosts in state S_H up to time-slot 8. We set $\tau = 6 > t_{switch}$ and evaluate the condition 4. Setting $t = 8, \tau = 6$, we have $\sum_{l=6}^{8}((x_l - \kappa_H)^+ - (x_l - \kappa_L)^+) + (8 - 6 + 1) \times (c_H - c_L) = 600 \geq W = 550$. This is the first time-slot since 3 that the condition is satisfied, thus $r_8 = H, r_{9,...} = L$ till the next time BLTN decides to switch.

4   Main Results and Discussion

Our first theorem characterizes the performance of BLTN for adversarial arrivals by giving a worst-case guarantee on the performance of the BLTN policy against the optimal offline policy. We also characterize a lower bound performance of any deterministic online policy.

Theorem 1. Let $\Delta\kappa = \kappa_H - \kappa_L$, $\Delta c = c_H - c_L$, $W = W_{LH} + W_{HL}$. If $\Delta\kappa > \Delta c$ then,

(a) $\rho^{BLTN} \leq \left(1 + \dfrac{2W + \Delta\kappa}{W\left(1 + \frac{c_H}{\Delta\kappa - \Delta c} + \frac{c_L}{\Delta c}\right)}\right)$,

(b) $\rho^{\mathcal{P}} \geq \min\left\{\dfrac{\Delta\kappa + c_L}{c_H}, \dfrac{c_H}{c_L}, \dfrac{\Delta\kappa + c_L + c_H + W}{c_H + c_L + W}\right\}$, for any deterministic policy $\mathcal{P}$.

Theorem 1 provides a worst-case guarantee on the performance of the BLTN policy against the optimal offline policy. Unlike the BLTN policy, the optimal offline policy has complete information of the entire arrival sequence beforehand. We note that the competitive ratio of BLTN improves as the sum of switch costs ($W_{LH} + W_{HL}$) increases. Also, the competitive ratio of BLTN increases linearly with the difference of the caps on requests served at the edge, $\Delta\kappa$. Supplementing it, we have Theorem 1 (b) which shows that the competitive ratio of any deterministic online policy increases linearly with $\Delta\kappa$. While Theorem 1 (a) provides a worst-case guarantee for the BLTN policy, it must be noted that through subsequent simulations, the performance of BLTN is substantially closer to the optimal offline policy.

Next we summarize the performance of the BLTN policy for i.i.d. stochastic arrivals (Assumption 1, Sect. 2).

This lemma gives a bound on the expected difference between the costs incurred in a time-slot by the BLTN policy and the optimal online policy. We use the functions $f(\cdot), g(\cdot)$ which are defined in the Appendix of [16]. The functions $f(\cdot), g(\cdot)$ are formulated using Hoeffding's inequality to bound the probability of certain events. We use the functions $f(\cdot), g(\cdot)$ for the sake of compactness.

Lemma 1. Let $\Delta_t^P = \mathbb{E}[C_t^P - C_t^{OPT\text{-}ON}]$, $\mu_H = \mathbb{E}[\underline{X}_{t,H}]$, $\mu_L = \mathbb{E}[\underline{X}_{t,L}]$, $\Delta\mu = \mu_H - \mu_L$, $\Delta\kappa = \kappa_H - \kappa_L$, and $\Delta c = c_H - c_L$.

$$f(\Delta\kappa, \lambda, W, \Delta\mu, \Delta c) = (W + \Delta\mu - \Delta c) \times \left(2\left\lceil \frac{\lambda W}{\Delta\mu - \Delta c} \right\rceil \frac{\exp\left(-2\frac{(\Delta\mu - \Delta c)^2 \frac{W}{\Delta c}}{(\Delta\kappa)^2}\right)}{1 - \exp\left(-2\frac{(\Delta\mu - \Delta c)^2}{(\Delta\kappa)^2}\right)} \right.$$
$$\left. + \exp\left(-2\frac{(\lambda - 1)^2 W(\Delta\mu - \Delta c)}{\lambda(\Delta\kappa)^2}\right) \right), \quad and$$

$$g(\Delta\kappa, \lambda, W, \Delta\mu, \Delta c) = (\Delta c - \Delta\mu + W) \times \left(\exp\left(-2\frac{(\lambda - 1)^2(\Delta c - \Delta\mu)W}{\lambda(\Delta\kappa)^2}\right) \right.$$
$$\left. + 2\left\lceil \frac{\lambda W}{\Delta c - \Delta\mu} \right\rceil \frac{\exp\left(-2\frac{(\Delta c - \Delta\mu)^2 \frac{W}{\Delta\kappa - \Delta c}}{(\Delta\kappa)^2}\right)}{1 - \exp\left(-2\frac{(\Delta c - \Delta\mu)^2}{(\Delta\kappa)^2}\right)} \right).$$

Then, under Assumption 1,

– *Case $\Delta\mu > \Delta c$:*

$$\Delta_t^{BLTN}(\lambda) \leq \begin{cases} W + \Delta\mu - \Delta c, & t \leq \left\lceil \frac{\lambda W}{\Delta\mu - \Delta c} \right\rceil \\ f(\Delta\kappa, \lambda, W, \Delta\mu, \Delta c), & t > \left\lceil \frac{\lambda W}{\Delta\mu - \Delta c} \right\rceil \end{cases}.$$

– *Case $\Delta\mu < \Delta c$:*

$$\Delta_t^{BLTN}(\lambda) \leq \begin{cases} W + \Delta c - \Delta\mu, & t \leq \left\lceil \frac{\lambda W}{\Delta c - \Delta\mu} \right\rceil \\ g(\Delta\kappa, \lambda, W, \Delta\mu, \Delta c), & t > \left\lceil \frac{\lambda W}{\Delta c - \Delta\mu} \right\rceil \end{cases}.$$

We can conclude that for large enough t, the difference between the cost incurred by BLTN and the optimal online policy in time-slot t, decays exponentially with W and $|\Delta\mu - \Delta c|$.

Theorem 2 gives an upper bound on the ratio of the expected cost incurred under BLTN and the optimal online policy in a setting where request arrivals are stochastic. In the statement of this theorem, we used the functions f and g which are defined in Lemma 1.

Theorem 2. *Let $\nu = \mathbb{E}[X_t]$, $\mu_H = \mathbb{E}[\underline{X}_{t,H}]$, and $\mu_L = \mathbb{E}[\underline{X}_{t,L}]$. Let the rent cost per time-slot be c_H or c_L depending on the states S_H or S_L respectively. Define $\Delta\mu = \mu_H - \mu_L$, $\Delta\kappa = \kappa_H - \kappa_L$, $\Delta c = c_H - c_L$. Recall the definition of σ_T^P given in (3).*

– *Case $\Delta\mu > \Delta c$: For the function f defined in Lemma 1,*

$$\sigma^{BLTN}(T) \leq \min_{\lambda>1}\left(1 + \frac{\lceil\frac{\lambda W}{\Delta\mu-\Delta c}\rceil(W + \Delta\mu - \Delta c)}{T(\nu - \mu_H + c_H)} + \frac{\left(T - \lceil\frac{\lambda W}{\Delta\mu-\Delta c}\rceil\right)f(\Delta\kappa, \lambda, W, \Delta\mu, \Delta c)}{T(\nu - \mu_H + c_H)}\right),$$

– *Case $\Delta\mu < \Delta c$: For the function g defined in Lemma 1,*

$$\sigma^{BLTN}(T) \leq \min_{\lambda>1}\left(1 + \frac{\lceil\frac{\lambda W}{\Delta c-\Delta\mu}\rceil(W + \Delta c - \Delta\mu)}{T(\nu - \mu_L + c_L)} + \frac{\left(T - \lceil\frac{\lambda W}{\Delta c-\Delta\mu}\rceil\right)g(\Delta\kappa, \lambda, W, \Delta\mu, \Delta c)}{T(\nu - \mu_L + c_L)}\right).$$

We observe that the bounds in Lemma 1 worsen with an increase in $\Delta\kappa$. It must be noted that this is a bound obtained using Hoeffding's inequality which does not assume any specific i.i.d. process (Chernoff bound presents a stronger inequality here). For generic cases, the performance of BLTN does not worsen with an increase in $\Delta\kappa$ as shown via simulations in the next section.

For large values of T, the bound on the ratio of total expected costs reduces exponentially with the sum of switch costs W. The performance guarantees obtained for BLTN in this section show that BLTN performs well in both the general and the i.i.d. stochastic settings without making any assumptions on the request arrival process.

5 Simulations

Since our analytical results only provide bounds on the BLTN policy, we now compare the performance of BLTN, FTPL, and the optimal online policy which uses the knowledge of the statistics of the arrival process to make decisions via simulations. Recall that both BLTN and FTPL do not know the statistics of the arrival process.

Unless stated otherwise, the parameter values in the simulations are as follows: $c_L = 300$; $\Delta c = 300$; $k_L = 400$; $\Delta\kappa = 400$; $W_{HL} = W_{LH} = 300$. For the GE model, the transition probability from either state of the two-state Markov chain is 0.01. In Algorithm 2, we set $\gamma = 500$, through empirical observations of overall performance. All the simulations have been averaged over the same set of 50 random seeds over 10,000 time-slots. The captions highlight the arrival sequence model - Assumption 1 (i.i.d. Poisson) or Assumption 2 (GE).

In Fig. 2, we see that for i.i.d. Poisson arrivals, the performance of BLTN matches that of FTPL for most of the λ values considered except around $\lambda = 600$. At this value of λ, the expected cost incurred at levels L and H is very close and as a result, the switch cost incurred by FTPL is high, thus leading to poor performance. We note that for the GE model, BLTN outperforms FTPL for a large range of λ_H. The superior performance of BLTN is a consequence of the fact that unlike FTPL, BLTN puts added emphasis on recent arrival patterns when making decisions. The same trend follows in Figs. 3, 4, 5 and 6.

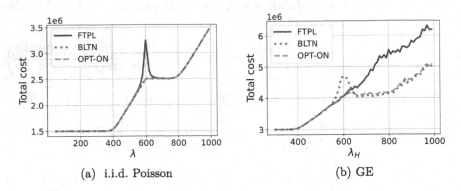

(a) i.i.d. Poisson   (b) GE

Fig. 2. Performance of various policies as a function of the request arrival rate. For the GE model, we fix $\lambda_L = 300$ and vary λ_H.

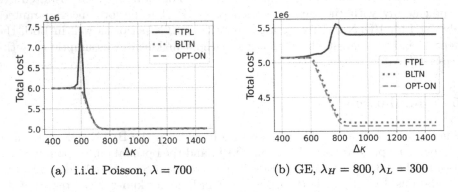

(a) i.i.d. Poisson, $\lambda = 700$ (b) GE, $\lambda_H = 800$, $\lambda_L = 300$

Fig. 3. Performance of various policies as a function of $\Delta\kappa$

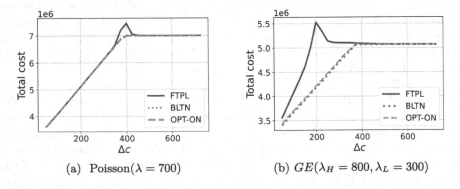

(a) Poisson($\lambda = 700$)   (b) $GE(\lambda_H = 800, \lambda_L = 300)$

Fig. 4. Performance of various policies as a function of difference in rent costs Δc

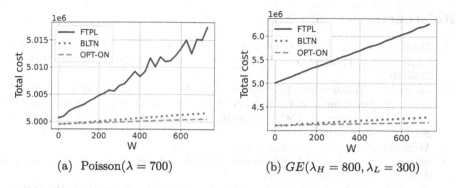

(a) Poisson($\lambda = 700$)
(b) $GE(\lambda_H = 800, \lambda_L = 300)$

Fig. 5. Performance of various policies as a function of switch costs, $W = W_{HL} = W_{LH}$

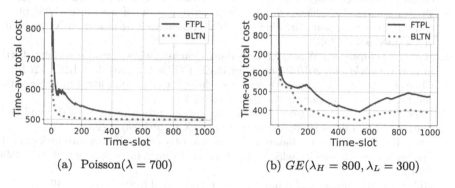

(a) Poisson($\lambda = 700$)
(b) $GE(\lambda_H = 800, \lambda_L = 300)$

Fig. 6. Time averaged total cost

Through Theorems 1 and 2, it is suggested that the bounds worsen as $\Delta\kappa$ increases. However, under Assumption 1, there is significant difference in performance only when $\Delta\kappa = \Delta c$, and under Assumption 2, there is significant difference whenever $\Delta\kappa > \Delta c$.

In arrival sequences characterized by Assumption 2, usually BLTN performs better owing to its ability to draw conclusions from history. FTPL fails to account for switching costs and so, is sub-optimal.

6 Conclusion

We consider the problem of renting edge computing resources for serving customer requests at the edge. We propose an online policy called Better-Late-Than-Never (BLTN) and provide performance guarantees for adversarial and stochastic request arrivals. Further, we compare the performance of BLTN with the widely studied FTPL policy. We conclude that BLTN outperforms FTPL for most settings considered, especially when the statistics of the arrival process are time-varying. The main reason for this is that BLTN makes decisions based on recent request arrival patterns while FTPL uses the entire request arrival history to make decisions.

References

1. Abbas, N., Zhang, Y., Taherkordi, A., Skeie, T.: Mobile edge computing: a survey. IEEE Internet Things J. **5**(1), 450–465 (2018). https://doi.org/10.1109/JIOT.2017. 2750180
2. Ascigil, O., Tasiopoulos, A.G., Phan, T.K., Sourlas, V., Psaras, I., Pavlou, G.: Resource provisioning and allocation in function-as-a-service edge-clouds. IEEE Trans. Serv. Comput. **15**(4), 2410–2424 (2022). https://doi.org/10.1109/TSC. 2021.3052139
3. AWS (2022). https://aws.amazon.com
4. Belady, L.A.: A study of replacement algorithms for a virtual-storage computer. IBM Syst. J. **5**(2), 78–101 (1966)
5. Bhattacharjee, R., Banerjee, S., Sinha, A.: Fundamental limits on the regret of online network-caching. Proc. ACM Meas. Anal. Comput. Syst. **4**(2), 1–31 (2020)
6. Bi, S., Huang, L., Zhang, Y.J.A.: Joint optimization of service caching placement and computation offloading in mobile edge computing system. arXiv preprint arXiv:1906.00711 (2019)
7. Borst, S., Gupta, V., Walid, A.: Distributed caching algorithms for content distribution networks. In: 2010 Proceedings IEEE INFOCOM, pp. 1–9. IEEE (2010)
8. Chen, L., Xu, J.: Collaborative service caching for edge computing in dense small cell networks. arXiv preprint arXiv:1709.08662 (2017)
9. Chen, L., Xu, J.: Budget-constrained edge service provisioning with demand estimation via bandit learning. arXiv preprint arXiv:1903.09080 (2019)
10. Choi, H., Yu, H., Lee, E.: Latency-classification-based deadline-aware task offloading algorithm in mobile edge computing environments. Appl. Sci. **9**(21), 4696 (2019)
11. Gilbert, E.N.: Capacity of a burst-noise channel. Bell Syst. Techn. J. **39**(5), 1253–1265 (1960). https://doi.org/10.1002/j.1538-7305.1960.tb03959.x
12. IBM (2022). https://www.ibm.com/cloud/edge-computing
13. Infrastructure, O.C. (2022). https://www.oracle.com/a/ocom/docs/cloud/edge-services-100.pdf
14. Jiang, C., Gao, L., Wang, T., Luo, J., Hou, F.: On economic viability of mobile edge caching. In: ICC 2020–2020 IEEE International Conference on Communications (ICC), pp. 1–6. IEEE (2020)
15. Luo, Q., Hu, S., Li, C., Li, G., Shi, W.: Resource scheduling in edge computing: a survey. IEEE Commun. Surv. Tutor. **23**(4), 2131–2165 (2021). https://doi.org/10. 1109/COMST.2021.3106401
16. Madnaik, A., Moharir, S., Karamchandani, N.: Renting edge computing resources for service hosting (2022). https://doi.org/10.48550/ARXIV.2207.14690, https:// arxiv.org/abs/2207.14690
17. Miao, Y., Hao, Y., Chen, M., Gharavi, H., Hwang, K.: Intelligent task caching in edge cloud via bandit learning. IEEE Trans. Netw. Sci. Eng. **8**(1), 625–637 (2020)
18. Mouradian, C., Naboulsi, D., Yangui, S., Glitho, R.H., Morrow, M.J., Polakos, P.A.: A comprehensive survey on fog computing: State-of-the-art and research challenges. IEEE Commun. Surv. Tutor. **20**(1), 416–464 (2017)
19. Mukhopadhyay, S., Sinha, A.: Online caching with optimal switching regret. In: 2021 IEEE International Symposium on Information Theory (ISIT), pp. 1546–1551. IEEE (2021)
20. Narayana, V.C.L., Agarwala, M., Karamchandani, N., Moharir, S.: Online partial service hosting at the edge. In: 2021 International Conference on Computer Communications and Networks (ICCCN), pp. 1–9. IEEE (2021)

21. Narayana, V.C.L., Moharir, S., Karamchandani, N.: On renting edge resources for service hosting. ACM Trans. Model. Perform. Eval. Comput. Syst. **6**(2), 1–30 (2021)
22. Prakash, R.S., Karamchandani, N., Kavitha, V., Moharir, S.: Partial service caching at the edge. In: 2020 18th International Symposium on Modeling and Optimization in Mobile, Ad Hoc, and Wireless Networks (WiOPT), pp. 1–8. IEEE (2020)
23. Puliafito, C., Mingozzi, E., Longo, F., Puliafito, A., Rana, O.: Fog computing for the internet of things: A survey. ACM Trans. Internet Technol. **19**(2), 18:1–18:41 (2019). https://doi.org/10.1145/3301443, http://doi.acm.org/10.1145/3301443
24. Satyanarayanan, M.: The emergence of edge computing. Computer **50**(1), 30–39 (2017)
25. Shi, W., Cao, J., Zhang, Q., Li, Y., Xu, L.: Edge computing: vision and challenges. IEEE Internet Things J. **3**(5), 637–646 (2016). https://doi.org/10.1109/JIOT.2016.2579198
26. Tran, T.X., Chan, K., Pompili, D.: COSTA: cost-aware service caching and task offloading assignment in mobile-edge computing. In: 2019 16th Annual IEEE International Conference on Sensing, Communication, and Networking (SECON), pp. 1–9. IEEE (2019)
27. Wang, S., Urgaonkar, R., Zafer, M., He, T., Chan, K., Leung, K.K.: Dynamic service migration in mobile edge computing based on Markov decision process. IEEE/ACM Trans. Netw. **27**(3), 1272–1288 (2019). https://doi.org/10.1109/TNET.2019.2916577
28. Yan, J., Bi, S., Duan, L., Zhang, Y.-J.A.: Pricing-driven service caching and task offloading in mobile edge computing. IEEE Trans. Wirel. Commun. **20**(7), 4495–4512 (2021). https://doi.org/10.1109/TWC.2021.3059692
29. Zeng, F., Chen, Y., Yao, L., et al.: A novel reputation incentive mechanism and game theory analysis for service caching in software-defined vehicle edge computing. Peer-to-Peer Netw. Appl. **14**, 467–481 (2021). https://doi.org/10.1007/s12083-020-00985-4
30. Zhang, M., Zheng, Z., Shroff, N.B.: An online algorithm for power-proportional data centers with switching cost. In: 2018 IEEE Conference on Decision and Control (CDC), pp. 6025–6032 (2018). https://doi.org/10.1109/CDC.2018.8619443
31. Zhao, T., Hou, I.H., Wang, S., Chan, K.: RED/LED: an asymptotically optimal and scalable online algorithm for service caching at the edge. IEEE J. Sel. Areas Commun. **36**(8), 1857–1870 (2018)

TAWNS – A Terrestrial Acoustic and Wireless Network Simulation Framework

Leonhard Brüggemann[1]([✉])(iD), Bertram Schütz[2](iD), and Nils Aschenbruck[1](iD)

[1] Institute of Computer Science, Osnabrück University, 49074 Osnabrück, Germany
{brueggemann,aschenbruck}@uni-osnabrueck.de
[2] Fraunhofer Institute for Communication, Information Processing and Ergonomics, 53177 Bonn, Germany
bertram.schuetz@fkie.fraunhofer.de

Abstract. Wireless Sensor Networks that address audio-related applications have been researched for over a decade. But reproducibility and customizability are a challenge when focusing on research questions in outdoor environments (e.g., localization of wildlife species). It usually involved the design of customized prototypes and time-consuming and often error-prone deployments to generate a ground truth. In this paper, we propose TAWNS, an Open Source model framework for Omnet++/INET which supports researchers conducting simulations on wireless *acoustic* sensor networks - either as the main focus of study or as a component. It inherits all the networking and wireless communication elements supported by the library INET and provides a novel, easy-to-use spatial audio simulator for 3-D sound environments. For the latter, we adapted and extended the library Scaper by adding a customized model for attenuating and delaying the acoustic signals. Our model parameters are derived from multiple measurements with different hardware. We share them in this paper, serving as a basis for other researchers. To give an impression of the hardware requirements, we also evaluate the system resources of our simulator.

Keywords: TAWNS · WASN · simulator · Omnet++ · INET · wireless acoustic sensor networks · spatial sound generation · bioacoustic research

1 Introduction

Wireless Acoustic Sensor Networks (WASN) in terrestrial environments are, among others, applied in the military context, surveillance, or bioacoustic applications (e.g., [15]). Such networks consist of multiple wireless communicating devices, each equipped with at least one microphone, a processing unit, and at least one communication interface. Such networks must meet various requirements due to their constrained resources and the vast amount of recorded data that must be processed and transferred, especially in outdoor environments when exposed to weather and various structures.

E. Hyytiä and V. Kavitha (Eds.): VALUETOOLS 2022, LNICST 482, pp. 292–306, 2023.
https://doi.org/10.1007/978-3-031-31234-2_18

We designed and deployed our low-cost, customized, wireless acoustic sensor network to acquire a ground truth for our localization idea. Although the localization of sound sources is a well-researched problem in the military context (e.g., [18]), it is far from being solved when it comes to locating wildlife, especially birds and similar. That is mainly the case because acoustic signals of, e.g., bird species are much more sophisticated and, thus, harder to distinguish, detect, or identify, aggravating the localization of wildlife significantly. When we wanted to compare our results to other datasets, it was quite difficult because no public available ground truth data exists. Instead, it is the current state of the art that research in WASN requires building custom-designed sensor nodes and performing some deployments to acquire a dataset that is used for evaluation (e.g., [16]). We see three major challenges with this current state of the art:

1. Comparability: The custom-designed prototype and the deployment site affect the performance of the system and the acquired data, so it becomes difficult to compare the results.

2. Reproducibility: The measured data is seldom publicly available and, thus, cannot be used by other researchers. Furthermore, it is impossible to reproduce other measurements because the deployments of different research groups extend throughout the world with different species and conditions at the deployment sites.

3. Costs and Time: The hardware used in the deployments might cost some hundred euros per device. That makes it pretty expensive if large deployments should be conducted.

Furthermore, conducting field measurements is quite time-consuming and error-prone due to their vulnerability to weather and high power consumption, which requires a periodic change of batteries. Of course, these challenges are already known and have been stated by [11,21]. They propose developing a framework for providing ground-truth datasets and various other features in demand for bioacoustic recognition and localization systems. In this paper, we do not aim to provide a whole bioacoustic framework but focus on the lack of ground-truth data. Instead of simply providing a platform that can be used to share measured datasets, we provide a simulator extension for Omnet++, which everyone can use to generate ground-truth data themselves. The contributions of this paper are the following:

- We will describe our simulator's design and system architecture as well as the requirements that guided its design.
- We share multiple sets of parameters based on our measurements for the sound simulation in outdoor environments that everyone can use.
- We share our results for two scenarios to give an impression on the simulator's hardware requirements when the simulation time and the number of entities increase.
- We publish our simulator as Open Source under this link[1].

The paper is structured as follows: Sect. 2 summarizes the related work on WASN simulation. Section 3 states a short requirements analysis that guided our design decisions. Then, Sect. 4 describes the system architecture and our

---

[1] https://sys.cs.uos.de/tawns/index.shtml.

Table 1. Survey of frameworks that support sound generation and fit to 3-D outdoor environments

Framework	Mixing Audios	Sound Attenuation	Sound Delay	3-D Environment	Application Context
Blender	✓	✓	–	✓	gaming
Panda 3D	✓	✓	–	✓	gaming
Audaspace	✓	✓	–	✓	audio engine gaming
OpenAl-Soft	✓	✓	–	✓	audio API gaming
FMOD	✓	✓	–	✓	audio API gaming
Pyroomacoustics	✓	✓	✓	✓	room acoustic
SoundScape Renderer	✓	✓	✓	–	real-time spatial audio reproduction
Scaper	✓	✓	✓	✓	sound synthesis and augmentatiosn

modifications and extension for WASN simulations. After that, we share our evaluation of the system requirements in Sect. 5. In Sect. 6, we summarize our contributions and identify the immediate steps in the ongoing development of our simulator.

2   Related Work

While simulators for wireless networks have been part of research for decades, there are only a few simulators for generating sounds. Both kinds of simulators abstract reality, make various assumptions, and have helped answer various research questions. However, a single simulation for one domain lacks features for the second domain. In the past, this had already been the case when, e.g., running traffic or vehicular network simulations, which resulted in the Omnet++ frameworks VEINS [25] and SUMO [20]. Now, it is a similar case for research on wireless acoustic sensor networks. To the best of our knowledge, no simulator similar to the here proposed framework has been implemented yet. We will survey related work of wireless network simulators and frameworks for spatial sound simulation in the following subsections.

2.1   Wireless Network Simulators

Various wireless network simulators have been part of the research community for years and are still constantly extended. For this paper, we focused on two state-of-the-art simulators supporting many networking and wireless communication elements. NS-3 [22] is a well-known Open Source framework and the successor of ns-2 [4], which was quite a popular simulator during the early 2000s. NS-3 targets primarily research and educational use, evolves around building a testbed environment, and is still used in research (e.g., [9]). Like NS-3, the popular Open Source simulator Omnet++ [5] also aims at a testbed environment. It does so by developing modules that interact together to build complex systems. The INET framework [3] for Omnet++ provides many elements of networking and wireless communication that are required for simulating network devices and various protocols.

Although both simulators provide many general features required when simulating wireless sensor networks, they do not include any audio-related entities or applications. For example, it is impossible to simulate an acoustic environment whose sounds are recorded by simulated network devices and then transmitted.

2.2 Generating Spatial Audio Mixtures

While there are many audio-related frameworks, APIs, or libraries, only a few target the generation of spatial audio mixtures with various sources, so-called soundscapes. Of those few, we are unaware of any framework that already supports the generation of spatial sound mixtures for 3-D *outdoor* environments. We looked closely at multiple frameworks and checked whether they might be adapted or extended to use cases concerning species identification or individual census or localization. For that, we set four mandatory criteria such as (1) mixing multiple sounds into new audio files, (2) applying a sound attenuation to the acoustic signals, (3) delaying the audio signal according to the distance between the receiver and sender, and (4) adapting to a 3-D environment. The latter implies that the frameworks should not require indoor obstacles such as walls or ceilings to calculate the propagation of acoustic signals. If those four features are supported, it is possible to extend such a library without fundamental modifications to its frameworks. We summarized our analysis in Table 1.

Computer games are prominent applications in which the replayed sounds generate an environmental feeling. Well known Open Source game engines are Blender [17], or Panda 3D [7] that use audio frameworks such as Audaspace [1], FMOD [2] or OpenAl-Soft [6]. Although they support the mixing and attenuating of audios, the audio signals are not delayed, probably because it is insignificant in computer games. However, it is a crucial feature for time-related evaluations in WASNs, e.g., for the localization of acoustic sound sources.

The Python library Pyroomacoustic [24] assists acoustic research in indoor environments. They provide many utilities that assist in many acoustic use cases. Sadly, the propagation of the acoustic signal requires an indoor environment consisting of walls and similar because the propagation of acoustic signals is based on ray-tracing. This library needs to be extended for outdoor scenarios.

The SoundScape Renderer [10] is a framework for real-time spatial audio rendering. It supports three sound rendering modules, but only one of its renderers supports attenuating and delaying acoustic signals according to the distance between the source and listener. That renderer does not only attenuate a signal according to the source-listener distance but also to their angle. In addition, SoundScape Renderer always requires 2-D environments and must be fundamentally extended to adapt to 3-D outdoor environments.

Scaper [23] is a library focusing on sound synthesis and augmentation. This framework always requires an audio library that has to be provided by the user. It distinguishes between background and foreground audios mixed according to customized parameters. The foreground audios are added according to a set distribution or might be added manually. It supports the configuration of various other parameters, including an attenuation parameter and a delay which can be set for each foreground audio.

In our opinion, most existing frameworks do not fit our stated criteria and are probably relatively complex to extend for simulating soundscapes in 3D outdoor environments. The Python library Scaper appears to be the best candidate for extending its functionality to generate spatial soundscapes.

3   Requirement Analysis

There are some specific challenges in designing a simulator for terrestrial wireless acoustic sensor networks, so an initial requirement analysis is conducted. Due to page limitations, we do not provide a complete, formal analysis here but state the key functionalities that guide the simulator's design.

Support of various Network Technologies: The simulator should support various network types and communication technologies that are relevant when deploying a WASN in reality.

Generation of spatial Soundscapes: Each sound source emits acoustic signals that propagate through the air and, thus, are delayed and attenuated by its environment. The mixture of multiple sounds is called soundscapes.

Simulation of Movement: The wireless nodes, as well as the sound sources, should be able to stay in one place or move in all directions.

Setup in 3-D Environment: As most research in terrestrial environments concerns 3-D environments, the simulator should support it as well.

Extendability and Customization: The simulator's entities should be extendable and customizable, e.g., it should be possible to customize the network and its devices or apply various kinds of sound sources. Thus, Open Source software is preferred.

4   System Architecture

The TAWNS works as a stand-alone framework and consists of three parts: (1) the wireless acoustic sensor network consisting of other network devices and the sound sources, (2) an audio library for acoustic data of the sound sources, and (3) our extension for the Python library Scaper to generate the spatial soundscapes. Although those three components exist separately, they are glued together in TAWNS by adding modules with new functionalities or developing modules that wrap up specific information. Figure 1 illustrates the three components.

(1) To support various elements of networking and wireless communication, the already stated simulators, NS-3 and Omnet++/INET, are appropriate candidates. Due to its modular design and excellent documentation, we finally decided to use Omnet++ combined with the framework INET. Furthermore, we think its design with the configuration files is more user-friendly, especially for non-computer scientists. Our network components of TAWNS are based on the INET library. Thus, they inherit its network stack and all its corresponding functionality. We extended some of INET's modules by audio-related functions, e.g., the

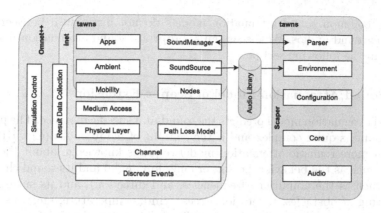

Fig. 1. Illustration of TAWNS' system architecture

network nodes can now be configured to have a customized number of micro-phones or transmit actual audio data instead of dummy traffic. We added new modules that hold the information required for generating the soundscapes, such as the module SoundSource, which handles all movement and acoustic emissions of a sound entity during a simulation or the module Ambient to set background acoustic. Both modules refer to the audio library that provides the acoustic files. Of special importance is the module SoundManager. It collects all information from the modules that are necessary for the generation of spatial soundscapes and initiates the audio generation for each sensor node. Our implementation is written mainly in C++, Omnet++'s configuration files, and Python. We delib-erately decided not to use any libraries that Omnet++/INET and Scaper do not already use to keep the number of dependencies at a minimum.

(2) The audio library contains all audios used in generating soundscapes and is already required by the library Scaper. It contains the back- and foreground audios. Preparing such a library allows extended customization of the sound environment in the simulation. Furthermore, there are various databases for sounds. For wildlife in general, there is the Tierstimmenarchiv Berlin[2], or if focusing on birds, there is the database at xeno-canto[3].

(3) While the wireless sensor network's core functionality could be inherited from existing work, generating spatial soundscapes for a simulated 3-D outdoor environment is more complicated. Scaper distinguishes between fore- and back-ground audios. Many parameters can be set during its configuration, including the parameters delay and signal-to-noise. Our new spatial soundscape extensions evolve around those two parameters by adapting them to the 3-D environment used in Omnet++. By calculating the distance between a sound source and the sensor node and assuming a particular speed of sound, it is straightforward to cal-culate the delay by dividing the distance by the speed of sound. However, fitting Scaper's signal-to-noise parameter (snr) to an existing sound model is tricky

---

[2] www.tierstimmenarchiv.de (accessed: 16.06.2022).
[3] www.xeno-canto.org (accessed: 16.06.2022).

because common sound attenuation models do not distinguish between back- and foreground audios. We discuss an appropriate sound attenuation model for Scaper in the following section.

4.1   Sound Attenuation Model of Scaper-Extension

A sound attenuation model predicts the sound at a specific distance. The physical background is quite complex and is the content of many books (e.g., [1]). Generally, a more realistic attenuation model requires knowledge about the sound source (such as the behavior, height, or emission angle) and its sound characteristics (such as the amplitude, frequencies, and direction), and its surroundings (consisting of obstacles, vegetation, trees, wind, temperature, etc.). Especially the sound characteristics become complicated for some kinds of wildlife such as birds, cicadas, or bats. For example, bird sounds can cover a wide range of frequencies that propagate differently, or birds might constantly change their location or direction, affecting, among others, the amplitude and propagation of their sound, resulting eventually in complex sound characteristics. Besides, there is the 3-D outdoor environment, where various sounds combine and interfere. Thus, applying more realistic sound models will not only result in much more detailed modeling, but will also not fit Scaper's approach of mixing back- and foreground audios.

We think the following simple model based on the inverse square law provides a sufficient abstraction for our use case:

$$L_{p_2} = L_{p_1} - 20 \cdot \log_{10} \left(\frac{R_2}{R_1} \right) \tag{1}$$

where L_{p_x} is the sound pressure level measured in decibel (dB_{SPL}) at location x and R_x is the distance to location x. Note that the model refers to the sound pressure level measured in dB and requires some information about the distances. Sadly, such a model will also not fit with Scaper's back- and foreground audio concept. Neither the dB_{SPL} values nor the distance information are (usually) available for wildlife recordings. The samples within the recorded audios are typically measured in dB relative to their bit-depth, which is referred to as dB_{FS} (dB relative to full-scale). Without detailed specifications on the recording system (e.g., microphone's sensitivity, applied gain, or digitizer's input clip voltage), it is not possible to convert the values from dB_{FS} to dB_{SPL}. But even then, it is seldom the case that the distance information on acoustic recordings is known.

We finally decided to design a model based on measurements we conducted in the past. Our model's idea is as follows: When we record audio, we basically convert the sound pressure and its changes at the microphone to an electronic signal that might be amplified and eventually digitized and saved on the device. So, we have an indirect relation to the sound pressure that, by theory, propagates according to the inverse square law. Therefore, we can assume a logarithmic model but due to many technical, environmental and biologic factors (e.g., birds

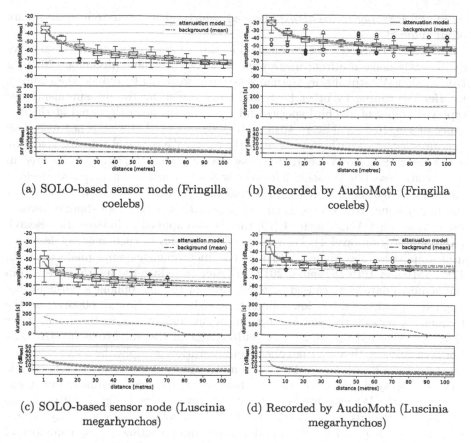

(a) SOLO-based sensor node (Fringilla coelebs)

(b) Recorded by AudioMoth (Fringilla coelebs)

(c) SOLO-based sensor node (Luscinia megarhynchos)

(d) Recorded by AudioMoth (Luscinia megarhynchos)

Fig. 2. Exemplary illustration of the sound attenuation for two species on two kinds of sensor nodes

are no acoustic point sources or the environment affects the acoustic propagation and recording systems), we do not know the parameters.

In the following, we assume a logarithmic attenuation of sounds, such as

$$A(x) = a \cdot \log_{10}(\max\{1, x + b\}) + c, \quad \text{where } a, b, c \in \mathbb{R} \qquad (2)$$

with A(x) referring to the attenuation relative to the background noise (= environment sounds), x referring to the distance between source and recorder, and a,b,c being constant parameters we will derive next. We will set an upper bound due to the high values that are returned by a logarithmic function for values below 1. Such a model is close to being adequate for extending Scaper. According to the specification of the signal-to-noise parameter, it is measured in dB_{LUFS}, which involves the perceived loudness of audio for the human ear [8]. In our understanding, using a human-perceived unit when modeling physical phenomena is not reasonable, even in a simple model like the one proposed here. Hence, we modified Scaper to use dB_{RMS} instead, which calculates to root mean square of an audio file.

In order to estimate the parameters in Eq. 2, experiments are necessary. We deliberately make use from measurements taken in winter (december 2019) in North Rhine-Westphalia in Germany because we want to reduce the acoustic interference caused by other birds and similar. During the measurements, we replayed audios of five bird species and recorded the acoustic signal at the distance of 1 m, 10 m, and every 10 m up to 100 m. Note that we did not record all distances simultaneously but one after the other. We recorded the bird voices by a Raspberry Pi Zero W-based recording device similar to [26], which is used in bioacoustic research. As some hardware was not available anymore, we decided on Rohde VideoMic[4], Sabrent USB soundcard[5], and set a fixed gain of 12dB for the microphone. We also recorded the data with a popular low-budget recording device called AudioMoth v1 [19] that is also applied in bioacoustic research (Audiomoth' gain level 4). We replayed four species in their more or less natural amplitudes according to [13,14]. The measurements were made on 16th, 17th, 18th and 19th December 2019. In order to reduce the interference within the acquired data, e.g., caused by wind, cars, or the microphone's self-noise, we applied a bandpass filter (lower bound: 2000Hz, upper bound: 8000Hz) on the frequencies outside the power spectrum of our replayed acoustic signal. After that, we extracted the bird voices and calculated the amplitude (in dB_{RMS}). For bird voices with more than one-second duration, we split the audio into one-second intervals with an overlap of 500 milliseconds. The main reason for this is that our replayed bird voice does not hold one amplitude constantly but might change rapidly. We visualized our results for two species in Fig. 2. Although the confidence intervals are relatively small, the boxplots do not constantly decline over the distance and show some deviation and sometimes a high number of outliers. We identify three primary reasons for that:

1. The bird songs on the audio are not always performed in the same amplitude and have different power spectrums, resulting in different attenuations.

2. The audio recordings lasted at least six minutes in which some acoustic interference was measured, e.g., a loud car on a distant street or similar. We excluded such intervals when the interference was dominant.

3. The used microphone has a relatively high sensitivity (e.g., for our custom-based device, it is -33.0dB re 1 V/Pascal) which means that the same sound pressure at the microphone can cause different audio samples.

It is important to note that the visualized sample sizes and audio durations of the boxplots vary over the distances because some features became less and less clear to identify during the manual extraction of signals. That was especially the case for the species Regulus regulus or Luscinia megarhynchos, in which no songs could be identified at a 70m distance or more.

We used the extracted data to fit 10000 attenuation models with different initial guesses of the start parameters and selected the model with the lowest

---

[4] www.rode.com/de/microphones/on-camera/videomicro (accessed: 18.06.2022).

[5] www.sabrent.com/products/au-mmsa (accessed: 18.06.2022).

Table 2. Derived parameters for Eq. 2 including standard deviation and rmse

Bird Species	db_A	SOLO-based recording device				AudioMoth			
		a	b	c	rmse	a	b	c	rmse
Turdus philomelos	100	-9.2 ± 0.3	1.4 ± 0.3	-23.5 ± 1.1	6.1	-7.1 ± 0.2	-0.2 ± 0.1	-14.9 ± 0.7	4.7
Fringilla coelebs	92	-10.8 ± 0.3	2.3 ± 0.3	-23.5 ± 1.2	4.7	-8.6 ± 0.3	0.9 ± 0.2	-14.8 ± 1.0	4.9
Luscinia megarhynchos	86	-7.3 ± 0.4	1.8 ± 0.6	-40.3 ± 1.8	8.4	-5.7 ± 0.3	-0.5 ± 0.1	-29.3 ± 1.1	7.2
Regulus regulus	75	-5.6 ± 0.2	-0.7 ± 0.0	-55.2 ± 0.7	4.8	-3.5 ± 0.2	-0.9 ± 0.0	-46.4 ± 0.7	4.2
Luscinia megarhynchos	74	-5.4 ± 0.4	-0.0 ± 0.3	-53.5 ± 1.3	6	-4.2 ± 0.3	-0.8 ± 0.1	-40.7 ± 0.9	5.4

rmse. The red lines in Fig. 2 refer to that best-fit model. The dashed line refers to the model's lower and upper bound when considering the estimated parameters' standard deviation. By computing the difference between the fitted model and the loudness of background (in Scaper referred to as the parameter ref_db), we can eventually calculate the attenuation model for each species and each recording device. We share our acoustic sensors' model parameters in Table 2 including their standard deviation and rmse. Note that the birds' amplitudes cover their typical ranges and might be used for other bird species. To derive a more precise model for other custom-designed acoustic sensor, we recommend to repeat above's procedure. With these parameters TAWNS can be configured now allowing for realistic performance calculations.

5   Simulation Performance

Running simulations can quickly become time-consuming, also requiring a lot of memory and disk space. In order to get an idea of the simulation time and system resources, we provide a performance evaluation of our simulator, address critical parameters, and identify bottlenecks that will be dealt with in the future.

We focus on two research scenarios: (1) In one scenario, we assume wireless acoustic sensor nodes and sound sources that do not move, e.g. to check primarily on localization methods. The sensor nodes transmit their acoustic data to a sink. In other words, during the simulation, the wireless sensor nodes and the sound sources do not move but stay in one place. (2) In the second scenario, both, sensor nodes and sound sources, will move according to traces previously generated by the random walk model of BonnMotion [12].

To compare the measurements, we have to fix some configuration parameters in order to assure comparability between the runs:

Constrained Area: We will assume a constrained area of a width and length of 1000 m, and a height of 100 m. No entity can leave the simulation.

Adhoc Network: We will assume an ad-hoc network with distance-sequenced vector routing.

Sensors: Each sensor is equipped with one microphone (sampling frequency: 44.1kHZ, bit-depth: 16 bit). They will record acoustic data continuously and, if possible, transfer it to the nearby base station. They are configured identically, except for their initial location.

Basestation: We assume a base station in the center of the constrained area that receives the acoustic data of all sensors.

Ambient: We provided an ambient sound with some wind rustling and little other interference.

Soundsource: During the simulation, we allow only one kind of sound source, a bird that emits the acoustic signal every time. We assume that each sound source will emit at most 300 times their sound during the simulation. All sound sources are configured identically, except for their starting location and mobility model.

Audio Data: The audio files are generated in WAVE format by Scaper and will be transferred as in the lossless audio codec FLAC.

Mobility: All generated mobility traces have the same fixed length during all runs.

Power Consumption: We neglect any power consumption constraints during the simulation.

Seed-based Evaluation: To make the simulation runs comparable with each other, a set of static seeds is used for the random number generator, thus, assuring identical placements of the sensors and sound sources.

All simulations run on an x86-64bit computer running the operating system Ubuntu 5.15 and being equipped with 64 CPUs (2xAMD EPYC 7452 32-Core Processor, 2,35 GHz), 251 Gbyts DIMM DDR4 (3200 MHz), and 500 GByte disk capacity. For each scenario, we will increase the number of wireless sensor nodes (1, 5, 10, 15, 20), the number of sound sources (1, 5, 10, 15, 20), and run different simulation times (450 s, 900 s, 1800 s, 3600 s). Each simulation is repeated ten times. During the measurements, we monitor the run-time, the residual set size (RSS), and the required disk capacity. In the following evaluation, we will focus on the worst-case measurements to identify the upper bound of system resources.

Before discussing our results, it is essential to note that multiple processes are spawned during a simulation. Their sequential and parallel execution as well as the invocation order affect the run-time, consumed memory, and required disk capacity. Some spawned processes belong to the Omnet++ framework and function as a wrapper, e.g., to run the compiled simulation file. They show little CPU usage and consume a constant amount of memory. While all 2000 measured simulation runs, they have never exceeded 30 MB. Thus, we decided to neglect them in the evaluation. When running a simulation with TAWNS, two kinds of processes require many system resources. The first process is of the TAWNS executable that initializes all modules required for the scenario, simulates the network and wireless communication part, and spawns subprocesses to generate the audios. Those (sub-)processes are the second kind and generate the acoustic data for each sensor node. To reduce the risk of memory overruns during

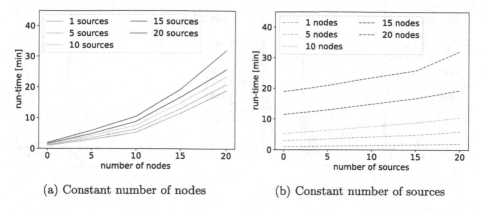

Fig. 3. Exemplary visualization of mean maximal run-times for a simulation time of 1800 s in scenario II

data generation, the (sub-)processes are spawned sequentially due to their high memory consumption.

5.1 Run-Time

Due to page limitations, we focus on the run-time for scenario II and a simulation time of 1800 s and 20 sources (see Fig. 3). The run-time increases by the number of nodes from about 2.0 min to about 5.9 min, then 10.5 min and 19.2 min until it reaches 32 min. Meanwhile, the increasing number of sources seems to have only little impact. While the run-time increases exponentially with the number of nodes, it grows more or less linearly with the number of sources. These trends are profound for low simulation times in both scenarios. For the sake of clarity, we did not visualize the relatively high standard deviation that proved to be caused by the different seeds. Our analysis has shown that the standard deviation stays below one minute when using the same seed multiple times. Note that the simulation time affects the run-time linearly.

5.2 Memory

We focus on the residual set size (RSS), the process's actual physical memory. In order to give a worst-case estimate, we focus on the mean over the maximal RSS measured for each run. For the sake of clarity we dropped the standard deviation that always stayed below 0.5 GB. In Fig. 4, we visualize the impact of the number of sources which is the dominant factor besides the simulation time. According to our data, the number of nodes does not affect the RSS significantly. When focusing on one simulation time, e.g., 3600 s in both scenarios, it becomes apparent that the RSS increases with the number of sources from about 17 GB to 67 GB, then 129 GB and 190 GB until it reaches about 250 GB. When the simulation time declines, so does the RSS. These observations can be made for

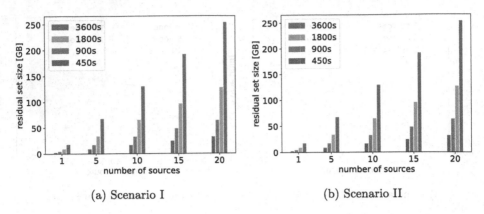

(a) Scenario I   (b) Scenario II

Fig. 4. Visualization of RSS for both scenarios when number of sound sources increases

both scenarios. We can summarize that memory consumption is proportional to the number of sources and simulation time. For a simulation time of 3600 s and 20 sources, it requires 250 GB of memory. Our analysis shows that the processes to generate the audio mixtures cause the high RSS. More specifically, it increases the moment when the Scaper library starts to generate the audio mixtures, so we think that this is an issue within the Scaper library. Still, we are unsatisfied with the high memory consumption and are currently working on a solution for the next version of TAWNS.

5.3 Disk Capacity

At least two kinds of information are stored on the disk permanently when running a simulation. For network and wireless communication, that is the network statistics, such as the routing tables and the wireless traffic. As such data depends on the scenario, we neglect that for our evaluation and focus on the mandatory disk capacity when generating the audio files. The audio mixtures are created using Scaper, whose audio mixtures are always stored in the wave format. The mixtures can be encoded by other audio codecs (supported by our simulator), but the audio generation itself requires storing the data in wave format first. With that in mind, we can calculate the upper bound that is met for the last simulated node by summarizing the consumed disk capacity for all previous audios (with the optional applied audio codec) and adding the consumed capacity of the current node. All interdependences mentioned above can be summarized in the following formula:

$$C = \sum_{j \in \{n_0, \dots, n_{i-1}\}} A_j(f_j \cdot b_j \cdot s_{n_i} + o_j) + f_{n_i} \cdot b_{n_i} \cdot s_{n_i} + o_{n_i} \qquad (3)$$

with n_i referring to the node i, A_j referring to the applied audio codec of node j, f_j referring to the sampling frequency of node j, b_j referring to the bit-depth of node j, s_j referring to the recording time of node j in seconds, and o_j referring to the header information of the WAVE format. As the sampling frequency and bit-depth are constants and the disk capacity saved by the applied audio codecs might also be regarded as a scaling factor, the required disk capacity scales with the number of simulated nodes and the recorded time. During our above-specified scenarios, which use FLAC audio codec, we measured a maximum disk capacity of at most 2,823.13 MB for 3600 s simulation time, which is about half when generating audios in WAVE format. It declines almost linear to the simulation time.

6 Conclusion

In this paper, we presented a solution for the challenge of comparing, reproducing, and conducting research in wireless acoustic sensor networks. Our simulator does not only provide the option to compare and reproduce research results in WASNs, but it also allows everyone to evaluate research questions without building and deploying expensive wireless acoustic sensor devices in the field. In order to achieve that, we used the Omnet++ simulator and combined and extended the libraries INET and Scaper. Our simulator can be equally used when focusing on network communication in WASN or generating acoustic sounds in a 3-D environment. As a starting pitch, we shared ten sets of model parameters derived from real measurements that can be used for generating sound mixtures. We also evaluated the performance of our simulator. For now, we recommend running the simulator on clusters (e.g., in a docker image), especially when performing long simulation runs or using many sound sources. In the future, there will always be some technical improvements continuously added to TAWNS, extending its features and making it easier to use. For example, we plan to support other sound simulation frameworks, such as Pyroomacoustic, to fit indoor acoustics better.

References

1. Audaspace. https://audaspace.github.io/. Accessed 18 Aug 2022
2. FMOD. https://www.fmod.com/. Accessed 18 Aug 2022
3. INET Framework. https://inet.omnetpp.org/. Accessed 18 Aug 2022
4. The Network Simulator - ns-2. https://www.isi.edu/nsnam/ns/. Accessed 18 Aug 2022
5. OMNeT++ Discrete Event Simulator. https://omnetpp.org/. Accessed 18 Aug 2022
6. OpenAL Soft. https://openal-soft.org/. Accessed 18 Aug 2022
7. Panda3D. https://www.panda3d.org/. Accessed 18 Aug 2022
8. Loudness normalisation and permitted maximum level of audio signals. EBU European Broadcasting Union (2020)
9. Abdel-Malek, M.A., Akkaya, K., Bhuyan, A., Ibrahim, A.S.: A proxy signature-based swarm drone authentication with leader selection in 5G networks. IEEE Access **10**, 57485–57498 (2022)

10. Ahrens, J., Geier, M., Spors, S.: The SoundScape renderer: a unified spatial audio reproduction framework for arbitrary rendering methods. In: 124th Convention of the Audio Engineering Society. Audio Engineering Society (2008)
11. Blumstein, D.T., et al.: Acoustic monitoring in terrestrial environments using microphone arrays: applications, technological considerations and prospectus. J. Appl. Ecol. **48**(3), 758–767 (2011)
12. Bothe, A., Aschenbruck, N.: BonnMotion 4 – taking mobility generation to the next level. In: 2020 IEEE 39th International Performance Computing and Communications Conference (IPCCC), pp. 1–8 (2020)
13. Brackenbury, J.H.: Power capabilities of the avian sound-producing system. J. Exp. Biol. **78**(1), 163–166 (1979)
14. Brumm, H.: Song amplitude and body size in birds. Behav. Ecol. Sociobiol. **63**(8), 1157 (2009)
15. Cobos, M., Antonacci, F., Alexandridis, A., Mouchtaris, A., Lee, B.: A survey of sound source localization methods in wireless acoustic sensor networks. Wirel. Commun. Mob. Comput. **2017** (2017)
16. Collier, T.C., Kirschel, A.N.G., Taylor, C.E.: Acoustic localization of antbirds in a Mexican rainforest using a wireless sensor network. J. Acoust. Soc. Am. **128**(1), 182–189 (2010)
17. Community, B.O.: Blender - a 3D modelling and rendering package (2018)
18. Damarla, T., Kaplan, L.M., Whipps, G.T.: Sniper localization using acoustic asynchronous sensors. IEEE Sens. J. **10**(9), 1469–1478 (2010)
19. Hill, A.P., Prince, P., Piña Covarrubias, E., Doncaster, C.P., Snaddon, J.L., Rogers, A.: AudioMoth: evaluation of a smart open acoustic device for monitoring biodiversity and the environment. Methods Ecol. Evol. **9**(5), 1199–1211 (2018)
20. Lopez, P.A., et al.: Microscopic traffic simulation using SUMO. In: 2018 21st International Conference on Intelligent Transportation Systems (ITSC), pp. 2575–2582 (2018)
21. Rhinehart, T.A., Chronister, L.M., Devlin, T., Kitzes, J.: Acoustic localization of terrestrial wildlife: current practices and future opportunities. Ecol. Evol. **10**(13), 6794–6818 (2020)
22. Riley, G.F., Henderson, T.R.: The ns-3 network simulator. In: Wehrle, K., Güneş, M., Gross, J. (eds.) Modeling and Tools for Network Simulation, pp. 15–34. Springer, Berlin, Heidelberg (2010). https://doi.org/10.1007/978-3-642-12331-3_2
23. Salamon, J., MacConnell, D., Cartwright, M., Li, P., Bello, J.P.: Scaper: a library for soundscape synthesis and augmentation. In: 2017 IEEE Workshop on Applications of Signal Processing to Audio and Acoustics (WASPAA), pp. 344–348 (2017)
24. Scheibler, R., Bezzam, E., Dokmanić, I.: Pyroomacoustics: a python package for audio room simulation and array processing algorithms. In: 2018 IEEE International Conference on Acoustics, Speech and Signal Processing (ICASSP), pp. 351–355 (2018)
25. Sommer, C., et al.: Veins: the open source vehicular network simulation framework. In: Virdis, A., Kirsche, M. (eds.) Recent Advances in Network Simulation. EICC, pp. 215–252. Springer, Cham (2019). https://doi.org/10.1007/978-3-030-12842-5_6
26. Whytock, R.C., Christie, J.: Solo: an open source, customizable and inexpensive audio recorder for bioacoustic research. Methods Ecol. Evol. **8**(3), 308–312 (2017)

Author Index

E. Hyytiä and V. Kavitha (Eds.): VALUETOOLS 2022, LNICST 482, pp. 307–308, 2023.
https://doi.org/10.1007/978-3-031-31234-2

Printed in the United States
by Baker & Taylor Publisher Services